Hoplites at War

Hoplites at War

*A Comprehensive Analysis
of Heavy Infantry Combat
in the Greek World, 750–100* BCE

PAUL M. BARDUNIAS *and*
FRED EUGENE RAY, JR.

Ash,

I hope you see yourself in these pages. I don't mean just a picture of you being squashed in othismos, but in all of the details that I have learned from you and other reenactors over the years.

See you in the phalanx,

McFarland & Company, Inc., Publishers
Jefferson, North Carolina

LIBRARY OF CONGRESS CATALOGUING-IN-PUBLICATION DATA

Names: Bardunias, Paul M., author. | Ray, Fred Eugene, 1949– author.
Title: Hoplites at war : a comprehensive analysis of heavy
infantry combat in the Greek world, 750–100 BCE /
Paul M. Bardunias and Fred Eugene Ray, Jr.
Description: Jefferson, North Carolina : McFarland & Company,
Inc., 2016 | Includes bibliographical references and index.
Identifiers: LCCN 2016034150 | ISBN 9781476666020
(softcover : acid free paper) ∞
Subjects: LCSH: Military art and science—Greece—History—
To 1500. | Greece—History, Military—To 146 B.C.
Classification: LCC U33 .B47 2016 | DDC 356/.1140938—dc23
LC record available at https://lccn.loc.gov/2016034150

BRITISH LIBRARY CATALOGUING DATA ARE AVAILABLE

ISBN (print) 978-1-4766-6602-0
ISBN (ebook) 978-1-4766-2636-9

© 2016 Paul Michael Bardunias and Fred Eugene Ray, Jr.
All rights reserved

*No part of this book may be reproduced or transmitted in any form
or by any means, electronic or mechanical, including photocopying
or recording, or by any information storage and retrieval system,
without permission in writing from the publisher.*

Front cover image of a statue from
Delphi, Greece © 2016 TPopova/iStock

Printed in the United States of America

*McFarland & Company, Inc., Publishers
Box 611, Jefferson, North Carolina 28640
www.mcfarlandpub.com*

For my father, Peter P. M. Bardunias,
who raised a boy on Spartan tales and George Greenberg,
the first engineer to understand the dome in the shield

Table of Contents

Preface   1
Introduction   3

I. The Tools

1. Weapons   5
2. Shields   24
3. Body Armor   36
4. Other Devices   48

II. The Men

5. Culture   61
6. Physicality   73
7. Psychology   87

III. The Phalanx

8. Hoplite Formations   105
9. The Phalanx in Action   122
10. Special Tactics   140
11. Phalanx Maneuvers   160
12. Use of Terrain   175

Conclusions   189
Chapter Notes   193
Bibliography   221
Index   229

Preface

This book presents a broad study of warfare in the ancient world, as fought by the heavily equipped Grecian spearmen known as hoplites—the arbiters of conflicts that framed the history of the western world. Though it has been some 2500 years since they dominated the battlefield, these iconic warriors continue to fascinate us today, sparking the imagination of a new generation through a wave of popular action films, graphic novels, documentaries and other mass media.

This popularity has been accompanied by the myth-making of a Hollywood version of history that fosters a distorted view of ancient realities, even among respected historians. Those better versed in the military field have struggled to address this; these efforts have, however, fallen short due to a tendency toward narrow, specialized studies, generally confined to publications not accessed by non-academic readers.

In this book, we make use of traditional sources, but combine these with cutting-edge (apt for a book on warfare!) science to break through an impasse of thought that has held back the study of Greek military affairs for decades. This study draws upon geology and related aspects of known battlefields, the physics of weapons design, and a modern understanding of how order emerges from chaos in crowds of humans to reconstruct ancient Greek warfare, with a focus on fighting methodology and the combat gear. We hope the result provides a comprehensive source on hoplite warfare that will advance key debates for modern scholars, while entertaining the general reader.

As practicing professionals in the physical sciences of behavioral biology and geology, we have both published books and articles based on our respective scientific disciplines and our mutual life-long interest in ancient Greek warfare. Our style here draws upon that experience, but is also informed by those ancient treatises on warfare and history known as Tactica. Writings by men like Aeneas Tacticus and Xenophon brought readers into the action through tales of combat and of the feats and foibles of famous generals. In the spirit of these works, each of the following chapters opens with a detailed account of a renowned battle told from the viewpoint of an ancient commander facing challenges related to the subject matter.

A famed expert on ancient Greek military history once said that "only an unusually arrogant scholar could claim to know exactly what kind of thing went on in a hoplite battle."[1] His words are not to be taken lightly, and we make no claim that what we present here is undisputed truth; rather, it is an assessment of what we firmly believe to be *most probable* based on all the evidence at hand. And in light of the sparseness and frequent ambiguity of our surviving ancient literary and archaeological sources, the process necessarily entails a good deal of speculation. However, we hope that by attempting to reconcile ancient data with the most apt historical analogs and the best modern experimental studies, that this vital guesswork is as informed as possible.

All ancient and modern literary sources are referenced in the endnotes section by chapter. Transliteration of the Greek alphabet has always been difficult. A common approach, the one taken here, is to use Romanized or Anglicized versions of Greek words wherever they are thought to be more familiar to readers of English. All dates cited are BCE unless otherwise specified. Maps, diagrams and other illustrations are embedded throughout near the relevant text.

We would like to thank all those colleagues who have shared information and assisted us over the years. These include fellow searchers after ancient knowledge like Paul McDonnell-Staff, Michael Park, Dan Powers, James Sulzen, Stefanos Skarmintzos, Patrick Waterson, Ruben Post, Barry Jacobsen, Josho Brouwers, and Jasper Oorthus, as well as Joan Huckaby, whose drafting skills have considerably enhanced some of the illustrations herein. We thank all those who don the panoply and show what hoplites were capable of, especially Giannis Kadoglou, Christian G. Cameron, Jeffrey Hildebrandt, Craig Sitch, Sean Manning, Didier Froesel, Emmanuel Fourre, Kevin Astic, Chris Verwijmeren, Ashley Holt, John Conyard, Alan Rowell, Anthony Haegeman, Johan Waroux, Giorgios Kafetzis, Kostas Dimitriadis, Marco Giordani, Sean Campana, all of the loyal Plataeans, and those who shared in the Marathon Archeon Dromena of 2015. These good folk are innocent of any factual errors or inaccuracies that might reside within the following pages—the authors alone are responsible for those—and must be credited with doing their level best to keep us on the path toward likely truth.

Introduction

Coming to prominence around 750 BCE, the Greek hoplite was for a period of some 400 years the premier fighting soldier of Western civilization. And he remained a valued element of that world's war-making for another quarter century or so thereafter. It was an unprecedented span of utility that gave him lasting fame. Indeed, even today in our age of computerized, high-tech weaponry, the venerable image of the bronze-helmeted soldier with distinctive shield and spear remains an exemplar of a true warrior.

Yet, much of what we know (or think we know) about these men runs the gamut from frustratingly vague to outright wrong. Very little hard data has survived over the better than two millennia since the last actual practitioner of hoplite warfare walked the earth. As a result, our view of it has been distorted by popular conceptions of the military cultures of intervening eras, as well as by romantic (and false) images in works of art. This has obscured the true nature of hoplite battle, subjecting its wider appreciation and even academic study to misconceptions, often passionately held. Still, like a cold case crime scene, enough clues linger that we can reasonably hope to reconstruct a vision of the hoplite that is much closer to his reality.

This begins with recognition that Greek hoplites were not the idealized figures portrayed in stone and bronze statuary and fanciful artworks of later centuries (including films of our own age), or as glorified in verse and prose from ancient to modern. They were human beings, subject to the same limitations of technology, dynamics of societal interaction in group efforts, and physical/psychological attributes that have influenced our species throughout history. We can thus learn a great deal about the realities of hoplite warfare by examining weapons, armor, and other items from archaeological sites or as depicted in contemporary artworks. Measuring and testing accurate reproductions of these tools of war allow us to discover how they most probably worked as independent devices. It can also demonstrate the most likely manner they were integrated into a comprehensive combat system.

Equally useful is an examination of the culture, physicality, and psychology of hoplites, providing vital insights into both the elective and inherent practical restrictions within which their military gear and formational tactics were confined. While the physical and mental aspects of hoplite warfare remained essentially constant (indeed, there is little difference on most of these points between the warriors of ancient Greece and the soldiers of today), this was not the case with hoplite culture. The hoplite was born when aristocrats and their retinues—who brought the arms and tactics of the Mediterranean world home to Greece through marauding and mercenary service—came into conflict with the amateur militias of their own and neighboring cities. Hoplite tactics that developed in this crucible of border skirmishes became a system of warfare that dominated the battlefields of their world. With time, the proven tactics of the hoplite would again be commercialized within Greece, with warriors-for-pay tending to fight in vastly wider and more total wars, driven not by issues of common community concern, but rather by the personal ambitions of imperial masters. Yet, even these professionals were not all that fundamentally different from their amateur forebears. In the basics of their armaments, combat methods, and, most of all, interaction with their ranked and filed companions, they closely resembled the classic Greek hoplite of yore.

The traditional study of warfare over the last few centuries looked to the great generals and treated their armies as anonymous masses that were moved like pieces on a game board; while John Keegan's *Face of Battle* has more recently turned a spotlight on the experience of the individual soldier, showing him to be much more than just a cog in the machinery of war. This book aims to bridge the gap between man and army by demonstrating how the combined interactions of individual warriors can lead to the emergence of seemingly complex group phenomena. The tools of the hoplites set limits on their perception and interactions with others, while their physicality and psychology governed how they came together for group action. As a result, these self-organized combat units had distinct "personalities" that were greater than the sum of their parts.

These truths span the ages and tie the ancient Greek hoplite to the soldiers of today. Tactics evolve as groups of warriors adapt to terrain and the challenge of new enemies. Yet the role of the individual is not lost in the crowd, but often magnified. Like the "butterfly effect" of modern proverb, the outcome of a battle may hinge on one well-timed strike, a call for men to rally, or the brilliance of a single tactician. Rather than the general's game piece or the footman's folly, an army is an entity with a head, hands, and heart. It is a beast borne of war—ugly in its brutality, yet, like any natural predator, magnificent in its functionality.

I. The Tools

1

Weapons

The term "hoplite" for the heavy infantryman of ancient Greece derives from the general word in Greek for military arms (*hopla*), to identify him in modern parlance as a "man-at-arms." Indeed, for a then unprecedented span of centuries, the hoplite was *the* man-at-arms across much of Europe—the very definition of what it meant to be a real soldier. His distinct array of gear or panoply (*panoplia*) featured a long, thrusting spear (*doru* or *dory*) with a brilliant design that struck a practical balance between reach and durability. It was this fearsome tool that shaped both the nature and science of Grecian combat. Of course, other weapons saw action on Greek battlefields. These most notably included a variety of swords and sabers, for use should a spear be shattered. Yet it was as a spearman that the Greek hoplite would win his lasting fame as an implacable warrior, capable of defeating the mightiest of foes, foreign or domestic.

Thermopylae—Day Three (480): Last Stand

Xerxes, Great King of the Achaemenid Persian Empire, launched the classical world's most extensive military operation in the year 480 BCE. This massive invasion of Europe saw the largest army ever assembled to that date marched around the north rim of the Aegean Basin. A marvel of logistics, the campaign was supplied by a huge fleet of ships that sailed alongside the advancing army, dispensing caches of war materials that sustained Xerxes' colossal formation as it moved along the coast toward Greece under his personal command. A well-trained soldier and experienced general in his prime,[1] the Persian ruler was heading an expedition in which his late sire, Darius I, had invested years of preparation. Its triumph would thus cement his father's legacy. Yet more to Xerxes' present needs, such success would also set his own reputation. This would result from his making a substantial conquest such as had come to be expected from the Empire's new rulers since the days of its very first, Cyrus the Great.[2]

Ancient sources appear to greatly exaggerate the size of Xerxes' army; modern writers project no more than about 200,000 combatants.[3] Still, this was a host of unprecedented size for its time. With high mobility best designed for action on the broad plains of its homeland, this army was nonetheless a flexible force quite capable of adapting to a wide range of settings. Therefore, while strongest in missile-armed troops (both afoot and mounted), it actually possessed fair "shock combat" (hand-to-hand) capacity as well.

I. The Tools

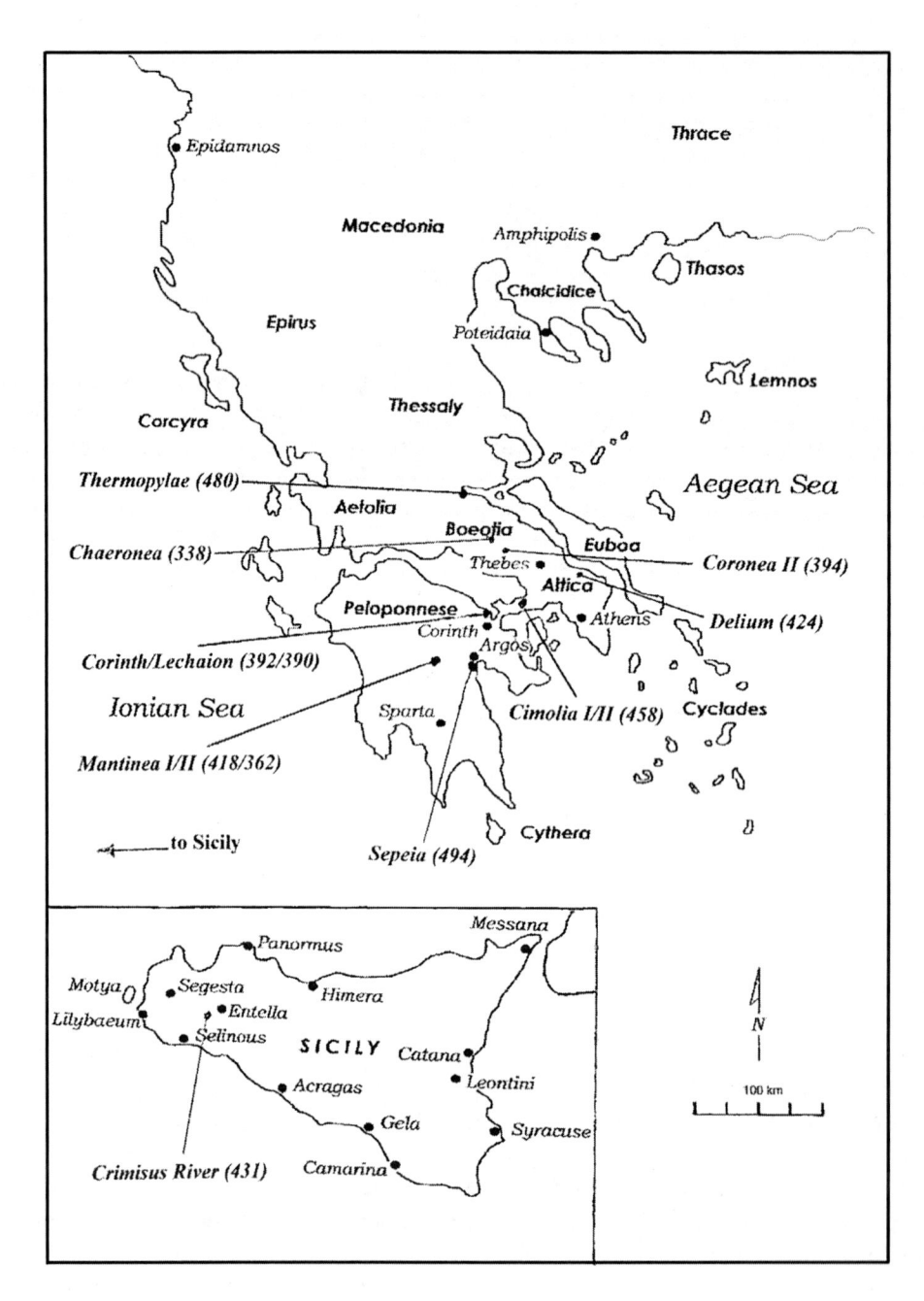

Ancient Greece and Sicily, showing the major cities and battlefields referenced in this book (Joan Huckaby).

And that would be a key against the king's pending opposition, which would come from heavily equipped Grecian hoplites (*hoplitai*)—spearmen who were pure shock fighters. The Persians had in fact handled such foes quite effectively in the past.[4] But Xerxes and his men were about to learn a painful lesson. Battling hoplites across open ground in Asia was not the same as taking them on in Greece, a land of rugged terrain where their unique fighting methods had been honed to a fine edge through many decades of combat.

Well aware of the slowly unfolding threat, the Greek polis (city-state) of Athens took the lead in devising a strategy to fend off Xerxes. This in part reflected that city's status as a prime mark for Persian wrath.[5] Yet it also recognized that the Athenians alone among the Greeks possessed a combination of previous exposures on the field of battle to Persia's way of war and military assets sufficiently versatile to allow for a creative approach to the land's defense.[6] Informed by past trials against large and mobile Asian armies,[7] the first step taken was to seek a "chokepoint" along the projected enemy line of advance; a restricted passage where a modest force of hoplites standing in close order might block a larger foe along a narrow front.

Initial consideration fell upon a position at the northern border of Thessaly. The mountains came all the way down to the sea there, which would briefly divert the Persians landward through a slender gap (Tempe Pass) between two high peaks. This seemed a promising chokepoint; however, it proved to have major flaws. One was that open ground to the north would allow Persian detachments to skirt around westward, access other passes, and then come across to cut off a blocking force at Tempe. The only possible counter was to post troops to hold all of those other western passages, a highly risky proposition in that failure at any one of these would doom the entire defense effort. But perhaps more troubling still was that Xerxes might choose the even simpler course of using his huge fleet to make an amphibious landing below Tempe. And open waters off the Thessalian coast gave no real chance for the smaller Greek naval force on hand to oppose such a move.[8] Therefore, though it meant yielding all northern Greece, it was decided to abandon Tempe.

Instead, a stronger position was found at Thermopylae. This was a narrow, nearly east-west trending passage that ran between steep, cliffs parallel to the shoreline and the sea at the foot of Thessaly. With tight entrances at either end, there was an optimum chokepoint at the center where the coastal path, in 480, pinched down to some 50m across (today the pass is considerably wider). And, unlike Tempe, this could not be easily turned from offshore, since its seaward flank rested upon a slim, defendable waterway running inside of the large island of Euboa. A coalition army under the Spartan king Leonidas therefore set up astride that central area at what was known as the Middle Gate.

Leonidas had quite a substantial force[9]; still, it was insignificant compared to the vast manpower he would have to face. And that reality joins with the strictly defensive posture taken at Thermopylae to highlight the true nature of the Greek strategy being pursued. The Spartan king did not have the task of directly defeating the martial juggernaut marching down on him—that was patently impossible. Rather, he was to delay it in support of a primary effort by coalition naval forces.

The northern entry into the Euboan Channel was at Artemisium where a slim opening ran between the mainland and the tip of Euboa. The Greeks had stationed their ships just within that passage toward confronting the enemy armada in a restricted area that precluded its full deployment. Able then to duel the Persians on equal terms, the Greek fleet might best their greater numbers a few at a time for an outright naval victory. Much more likely, it might be possible to stall them in more exposed waters outside the channel long enough for one of the seasonal storms notorious in that region to strike. That had potential to devastate enough of the less seaworthy Persian transports to cripple Xerxes' logistics train and bring a halt to his campaign. As such, Leonidas' hoplites and their mariner fellows were actually utilizing the same chokepoint concept with each being dependent on the other. Just as the fleet shielded Leonidas from offshore bypass, so his spearmen prevented Persian land forces from moving down to the inner channel's narrowest expanse, where they might well block the only safe escape route from Artemisium should the effort there fall short.[10]

Finding a Greek army at Thermopylae, Xerxes waited four days for his long column to catch up with him. He then launched a furious assault on the enemy position, mounting no less than three separate attacks. All of these failed as the Middle Gate's tight quarters denied a flanking role to cavalry and light infantry alike,[11] thus dictating close-order spear fights along narrow fronts that gave an overwhelming edge to hoplites who were masters of that kind of warfare. The last Persian foray ended as the sun sank to mark a final, embarrassing failure by the Great King's finest troops. These were elites of the picked division that supplied his own bodyguard with a constant string of recruits such that it and they had come to be known as "Immortals."

Desperate to somehow better match up against such shock-proficient foes, the Persians spent much of the next day assembling a composite force drawn from their best shield-bearing spearmen.[12] But going into action either in late afternoon or early that evening, these select warriors came no closer to clearing the pass, withdrawing badly battered at dark without having dislodged the stubborn hoplites. And just as all these efforts by Xerxes at Thermopylae were meeting with frustration, so his fleet had been kept in check by both opposing ships and violent weather at Artemisium and around Euboa's far side. In truth, the Greeks were doing no better than holding their own in all of this; nonetheless, their modest tactical upsets were keeping hope alive that a nation-saving stalemate might yet be gained. It was at this crucial juncture that a local man came forward to tip the scales in Persia's favor.

There was a rough track through the south-flanking highlands that circumvented the Middle Gate and came down to the coast beyond. Aware of this, Leonidas had posted 1,000 Phocian hoplites to block that route, known as the Anopaia Path. The Persians were themselves a mountain people and knew that such lesser trails were common around almost every highland pass; still, they had been unable to scout one out among the warren of faint goat tracks running up the slopes. Now, a Thessalian guide offered to show them the way. Setting out just about the time that the composite brigade was in retreat, the Immortals division marched behind their guide, hoping to hit the Greeks from behind. The Phocians were well placed to foil such a move, which must have had to pick its way slowly along the narrow rugged path, no more than two men abreast. However, they took fright upon being pummeled by a hail of missiles coming out of the gloom and pulled aside to seek safer ground. The Persians sped them off with a few more arrows and kept on moving. A runner brought this alarming news to Leonidas near dawn. With his position fatally compromised, the Spartan king sent the bulk of his army away lest the Immortals trap it. He also readied a sizeable rearguard to screen his fleeing men from pursuit by confronting the final Persian charge that was sure to come down the pass once it was light.

Probably in his 60s, Leonidas had, as far as we know, never held a significant combat command[13]; yet he was obviously well schooled in war despite any shortage of actual field experience. And he had put that knowledge to devastating use thus far, proving amazingly adept at exploiting the restricted space at the Middle Gate in conjunction with his hoplites' unmatched skills in shock battle to turn back one massive attack after another. Not only did he and his spearmen hold their ground as Greek strategy required, but they took much fewer casualties than they inflicted in doing so. This last was due to having heavier protective gear and longer reaching weapons than their foes plus singular fighting techniques ideally suited to that equipment.

All of the Persian assaults had featured troops of the type known as "sparabara" (shield-carriers). These formed the core divisions of Xerxes' host and took their name from the rectangular tower-shields (*spara*) of wicker that their bravest men in the front rank (or possibly the first couple of ranks on occasion) used edge-to-edge to form a wall at the prow of battle arrays. With those elites at the fore defending this shield-front over its top with spears of modest length (2m and counter-weighted on the butt-end), the rest of each file was comprised of archers. Their fire sought to wither opponents stalled in place against the shield-wall, bleeding them until they either broke in flight or were outflanked and taken in the rear by large bodies of horsemen operating off the sides of Persian formations. But at Thermopylae, there was simply no way that cavalry could get around the flanks of Greek spearmen fixed against the cliffs and seashore on either boundary. Standing in short files (four to twelve deep) with shield touching shield along each rank in the close array known as a phalanx, Leonidas and his men had advanced inside of spear-length against each assault. And by charging forward at a reasonably rapid pace, they suffered only brief exposure to barrages from the enemy after-ranks before getting within the opposing formation's protective shadow.

Gaining the Persian front, hoplite armor and large, round, metal-faced shields (*aspides*) had provided superior protection even as the Greeks' longer spears (2.5m or more, with spikes on the butt-end) made deeper and more harmful strikes.[14] Some special maneuvers by Leonidas' exceptionally well-drilled Spartans fatally disrupted Persian fronts at first[15]; however, most of the ensuing Greek success resulted from either the unequal duel of spears cutting past Persian shield-walls or hoplites setting shield-on-shield to push through them. It was the concave design of the aspis that enabled the latter tactic. Suspending it on his forearm, a man pressed into the back of his comrade ahead, who could still breathe with chest sheltered inside the hollow bowl of his own aspis. Hoplites thus brought pressure to bear from entire files,[16] shoving into foes, at best a couple of shields deep, who couldn't push back effectively due to the center-grip style of their cumbersome *spara*. Once Greek spearmen breached a shield-wall to get at Persian after-rankers, who lacked either shields or body armor, a great slaughter and rout soon followed. With Persian divisions necessarily arrayed by sub-units one behind the other across the pass' narrow expanse[17] and with Leonidas rotating in fresh troops during any pause in the action, these lethal scenarios of penetration by spear-thrust and/or shield-shove had played out again and again to Xerxes' considerable cost.

But the strategic situation was much different than previously, with the Persians being the ones seeking to draw out the action so their flanking force could come up from behind. Leonidas therefore chose to advance farther toward the west than

10 I. The Tools

he had previously. That would let him spread out his phalanx and engage a broader enemy front, thereby reducing the number of shield-walls that he would have to penetrate to gain the opposition's last ranks. It was there where he must have thought to find Xerxes, taking the field himself to claim personal glory from clearing the pass, which finally seemed a certainty. He would be at the very back under protection of his separate and most elite regiment of bodyguards and, should Leonidas and his men somehow reach that post, they just might be able to kill him and bring the invasion to a sudden and surprising end.[18] As it turned out, Xerxes was in fact just so situated at the rear that morning; however, getting through the ethnic Persian baivarabam of maybe 8,000

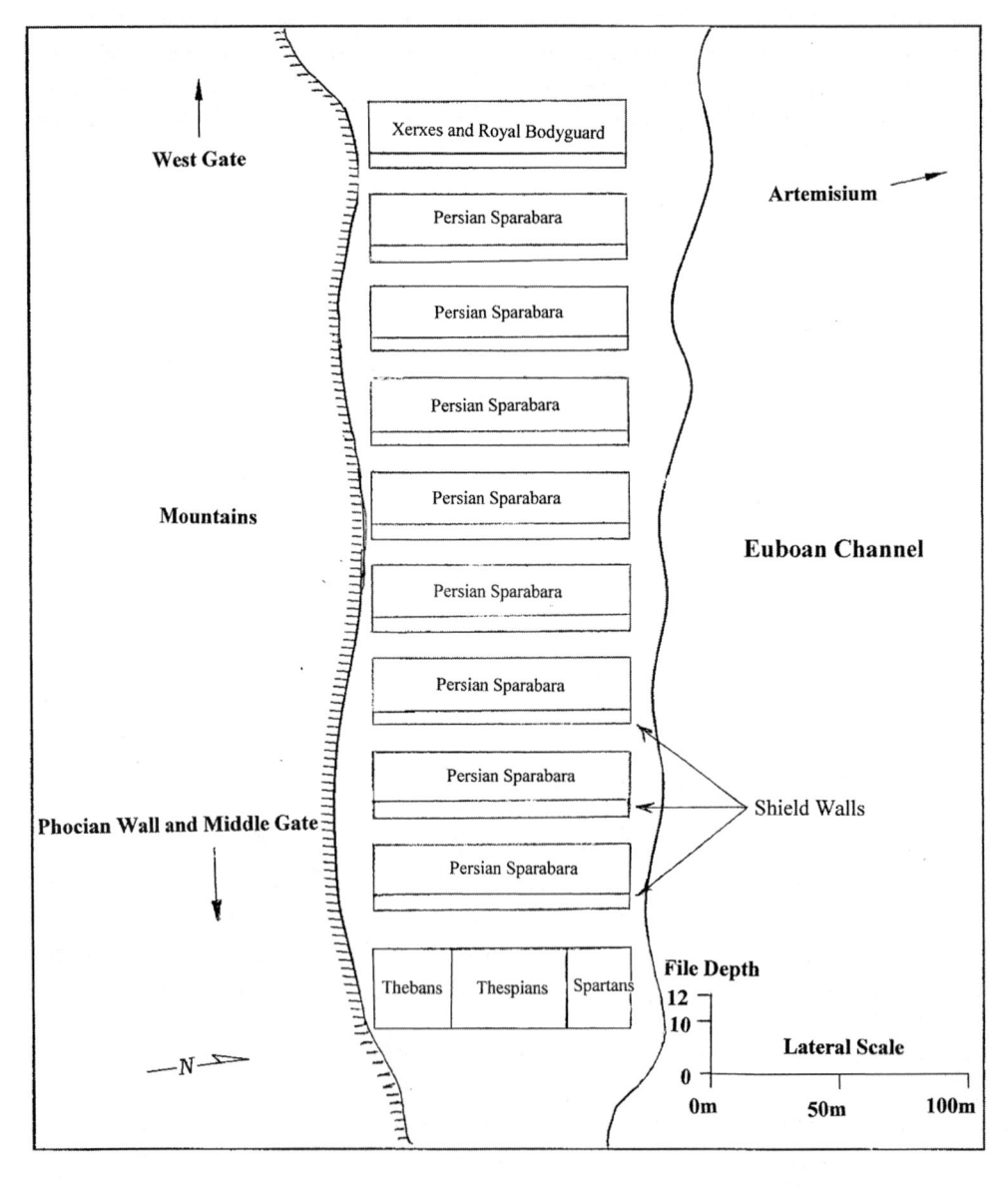

Battle of Thermopylae, Day Three—480 BC (Joan Huckaby).

sparabara that stood before him was to prove an unattainable goal for Leonidas and his band of badly outnumbered hoplites.[19]

As the Persians marched into bow range to set up their leading shield-wall, Leonidas charged his phalanx as fast as he could while still maintaining good order, across the free-fire zone that stretched between the opposed fronts. Moving up along the seashore on their right wing, the Spartan king and his elite Spartiates would have had the Thespians and then the Thebans ranging out leftward all the way to the south-bounding cliff face. It's unclear just how wide Thermopylae was farther forward where this advance took place; however, a phalanx of some 1,200 men could have spanned 100m at twelve shields deep. The 800 or so *spara*-carrying men on the other side (not counting the royal bodyguard) could have fronted only eight arrays with individual shield-walls over that same width. Twice that many deployments were possible across the 50m minimum cited at the Middle Gate—the Asians were indeed more vulnerable to a complete penetration than in any prior engagement.[20]

Coming up into missile-sheltering contact with the Persian front, the Greeks began lancing their long spears down over top of the opposing *spara* at the helmetless heads and exposed throats of the enemy front-fighters. Dealing out much more damage to their lightly protected Asian foes than their own heavy gear permitted in return, Leonidas' hoplites pierced the first shield-wall to kill and scatter its after-ranks; they then moved to do the same to the next line of *spara* standing behind. How many times this was repeated is unknown, surely several at least; and though a few Greeks went down here and there, Persians died in much greater numbers as their arrays were speared and shoved through time and again. But as the action continued to extend, heavily overused Greek weapons began to degrade; spears shattered, forcing men to continue the fight either with shaft stubs and attached butt-spikes or with swords, neither of those being any better than the offensive tools on the other side.[21] And as more hoplites including Leonidas then began to fall, the hard-driving Greek offensive finally ran out of steam. Having battled its way close enough to Xerxes to make him uncomfortable, it had taken a toll among nobles that must have stood near the royal post, slaying two half-brothers and two full brothers of the Great King. Word then arrived that the Immortals had finally made it down the Anopaia Path and were moving on the Middle Gate.

The surviving Spartans and Thespians withdrew, carrying the bodies of Leonidas and others with them. Bloodied and exhausted, Xerxes' men let them get away for the moment, but rallied to cut off what was left of the Theban contingent on the Greek left wing, forcing it to surrender. Meanwhile, the other hoplites had retreated just below the Middle Gate's narrowest point and beyond the partially restored ruins of an old Phocian defense wall that stood there. Perhaps numbering only a few hundred and aware that the Immortals were rapidly coming up against them, these men decided to make their final stand atop a low hill close to the pass' south-side cliffs. The Persians came against this isolated position, surrounded it all about, and killed the Greeks there to the last man under a sky-darkening barrage of arrows.[22]

Word of the Persian victory at Thermopylae quickly reached the Greek fleet at Artemisium, which made a hasty retreat down the Euboan Channel before the enemy could close it off. Falling back upon the Peloponnese, the defending coalition repositioned its army on the Isthmus of Corinth and collected its ships just below on the island of

Salamis. All to the north and east was effectively ceded to Xerxes and he rapidly seized both Boeotia and Attica, burning Athens to highlight the latter conquest. It was without doubt Greece's darkest hour. Yet just a few weeks later, the seemingly invincible Great King would suffer a devastating naval defeat in the waters off Salamis as a foretaste of what was to come. The following year, the Greeks reapplied the same unique weaponry and much the same tactics that had fallen ever so slightly short of success at Thermopylae. They not only busted the invasion for good but even went so far as to take the fight all the way onto Asian soil. So dominant would Greek arms prove that no future Persian monarch would dare to think about making another attempt on mainland Greece; indeed, adding hoplites or their like to Persia's own arsenal would become a high priority.

Thrown Spears

Hoplites were spearmen; they won land "by the spear," slaves were chattel "taken by the spear,"[23] and battle itself was a "storm of spears."[24] Archilochus, a 6th century hoplite from Paros, declared his success as a mercenary hinged on his skill with the spear: "In the spear is my kneaded bread, in the spear my Ismarian wine, when I drink I recline on the spear."[25] But what form did this spear take, and how was it employed in battle?

I would be a mistake to assume that the spear remained unchanged throughout the period of warriors identifiable as hoplites. The first commonly accepted depiction of hoplites in what can be interpreted as group combat occurs on the Proto-Corinthian olpe, commonly known as the Chigi vase, dating from approximately 640.[26] If the men depicted are contemporary hoplites, then early hoplites were armed with a pair of spears. Near the vase's handle, the artist has shown two pairs of spears standing upright with the large shield of a hoplite resting against them. There are two curious features of the spears as depicted. First, they are not the same length. One spear is shown to be something less than the height of a warrior, the other somewhat taller. The other feature shown is that both spears have a cord lashed to the haft that appears to be an ankyle or leather throwing thong, used to add velocity to a thrown javelin. The presence of the ankyle on the two weapons shown for these early hoplites led Snodgrass to opine: "it seems an inescapable conclusion that the early hoplite often, though not invariably, went into battle carrying two or more spears…one at least of these was probably thrown."[27]

The shorter spear may be identified as an akontion or javelin, meant to be thrown and generally too light for close-in combat. These spears possessed a narrow-bladed spearhead and a length that is generally less than the height of the hoplites depicted with them. The shafts of these spears are either untapered (unworked), or taper towards the rear so that the center of balance is moved forward. This is crucial, because if the center of gravity of a thrown spear is towards the rear, the rear will rotate forward in flight and the weapon will not reliably land point-first. If the center of gravity is towards the head of the spear, the point will tend to drop onto the intended target.

The second, longer spear we see on the Chigi olpe also appears to be untapered, and other images from this period show either untapered shafts or a rearward taper as with the javelins. A lack of taper alone does not indicate that a spear was meant to be thrown. The easiest way to make a spear is to affix a head to a pole with minimum shaping. But it does mean that the shape of the shaft does not preclude effective throwing. There were more than 20 varieties of spearheads available to the early hoplite, rendered in either bronze or iron. The spearheads of these longer spears are of the form (type J) that Snodgrass termed: "The long spear par excellence."[28] He described these as having a relatively long socket and narrow blade compared to the many spearhead types available in the early hoplite period, features which aid in its use when thrown.

The most telling feature in showing that the longer spear could be thrown is the presence of a throwing thong. Modern research has shown that even on a spear with the length and weight to be used for thrusting in close combat, the use of a thong can increase the range when thrown by over 50 percent, to an average distance of 24 meters.[29] When used with the akontion, the throwing thong was simply wrapped around the shaft with a hitch and was retained in the hand after the throw to be used with successive missiles. If we may find analogies to these early hoplite spears in the dual-use throwing/thrusting spears known as longche that were used by the troops that supplanted hoplites as line troops in the Hellenistic period, then the ankyle would have been firmly fixed to the shaft.

The manner in which the ankyle functioned bears some explanation. When accelerating any weapon, the amount of force applied is of course crucial, but just as important is the length of time that the accelerating force can be applied. This is probably most readily understood by the example of length of barrel in a firearm. Once a bullet leaves the gun barrel, the expanding gas that was accelerating it dissipates and the bullet begins to decelerate due to air resistance. For this reason, "muzzle velocity" is the measure of when the bullet is moving fastest. The longer the barrel, the more time the confined gas spends accelerating the bullet, and the more velocity imparted. The ankyle functions in a very different manner to produce the same result. The thin leather thongs, generally less than a meter in length, were wrapped around the shaft of the spear at a point just behind where it would have been gripped to throw. The thrower would insert his first two fingers into a loop in the thong and grip the shaft. As he released his grip on the shaft, his fingers pulled on the thong, which unwrapped as the spear moved forward, lengthening the period of acceleration. The thong also caused the shaft to spin, which—as with rifling in a gun barrel—enhanced stability in flight.

The throwing motion involves many major muscle groups, but over half of the accelerating force is derived from elasticity in joint structures in a manner similar to a torsion catapult. In fact, humans may have specifically evolved to throw objects, because our nearest ancestor, the chimpanzee, cannot perform this motion due to limitations in the shoulder carriage.[30] When launching a spear or javelin, it must be released at an angle of around 40° upwards so that it follows an arching trajectory to gain distance. This means that the thrower must release the shaft, thus ending acceleration, when the arm has moved through only a portion of its arc rotating around the shoulder. The ankyle remedies this. The spear is still released at an upward angle, but the two fingers in the thong's loop continue to pull the spear forward even after the shaft has left the hand. It is this extension of the time that the thrower spends in contact with the shaft and accelerating it that accounts for the additional velocity. As the shaft moves forward, the angle between thong and shaft becomes greater, imparting less and less acceleration and eventually slipping free of the thrower's fingers.

Hoplites with a pair of spears of different sizes are a common feature of vases throughout the 6th century. These have often been interpreted as anachronistic representations of older styles of warfare because the subjects portrayed are scenes from Homer, mythology, or folktales.[31] Others have suggested that two spears were the norm throughout the archaic period.[32]

Thrusting Spears

By the end of the archaic period, we see the use of spears (doru or dory) that have become specialized for thrusting and have lost their function as effective missiles. A red figure amphora in the Vatican collection attributed to the "Achilles painter" shows what is perhaps the best representation of a hoplite standing at ease and holding this spear type.[33] His spear has a small leaf-shaped blade, a long shaft that is at least half again as tall as the hoplite, and appears to taper towards the spearhead such that the shaft is narrower where the head is affixed than at the back end of the shaft. The most important feature of this spear is the robust metal spear-butt, called a sauroter or styrax. The form of the sauroter was highly variable, ranging from a simple metal cap to an elongated cone or pyramidal spike in bronze or iron. The primary role of the sauroter was to allow the spear to be stood upright when not held, but it could also serve as a weapon.[34] This butt-spike is an important feature because it renders the spear unfit for long accurate throws (see above). The amphora shows one further feature not often depicted by painters less dedicated to detail. The spear is fitted with a grip in the form of a sleeve of either textile or leather which appears to be stitched around the shaft. The placement of this grip indicates that the spear was held well towards the rear, roughly a quarter of the length up from its base. Holding the spear at this point would be very difficult if the center of balance was in the middle. A spear held at the center of balance requires only the strength required to support the mass of the spear to hold it level when striking. This is because the hand acts as a fulcrum, and the portion of the shaft ahead and behind the hand balance each other. As you attempt to move your grip back away from the center of balance, the longer part now benefits from leverage more than the shorter part. You must exert force to compensate and the more unbalanced the two portions are, the more effort you must produce. Thus, a grip near the rear quarter of the shafts length implies that the two portions of spear shaft are of equal mass when gripped at that point.

Chris Matthew has done an excellent job putting together the information on how this rear balancing was achieved.[35] He tabulated average dimensions for the type J spearhead and long bronze sauroters, the most common form. Comparing just the mass and socket dimensions we see that the spearhead and sauroter share an equal average inner diameter of around 18mm, though less common forms of sauroter could have wider sockets. The spearhead (153g) on average weighs about half as much as the sauroter (329g). If we ignore the mass of the spear shaft, and assume a roughly equal length for both, then we can work out what physicists call a "moment" for each end of the spear that represents the mass times the length of shaft from the hand. Using the average mass estimates for spearhead and sauroter, we can see that the spear would be balanced in the hoplite's grip if the front end were twice as long as the rear end.

The spear shaft could have been around 20mm thick, roughly the outer diameter of the sockets of spearhead and sauroter. If so, the socket would not simply fit over the shaft, but its base would lay flush to wood to avoid rupturing the socket as it is pushed back on the shaft. That would leave a spear balanced to about a third up from the base. Ash (*Fraxinus spp.*) or cornel (*Cornus mas*) wood were both suggested by ancient authors for spear making and are strong enough to withstand combat conditions at widths as narrow as 20mm.[36] It has been pointed out that spears made in the field might need to be thicker if made of poorer quality trees.[37] While many spears do appear very narrow on vase depictions, a spear this narrow is difficult to grip. As handle diameter becomes smaller, the way in which the skin of our fingers fold means that less of our flesh is actually in contact with the shaft. In addition, our fingers are working at a muscular disadvantage in that average hands appear to be optimized to hold cylinders of closer to 30–40mm diameter.[38] It may also be less comfortable to hold than one that swells to around 25mm at the grip. A long taper from the spearhead towards the rear of the spear to 25mm, followed by a more severe taper to 20mm down to the sauroter, would also serve to make the front portion of the shaft lighter and enable more of the shaft to project forward when at the balance point.

Kromayer and Veith derived a spear length of half again as long as a hoplite was tall from an examination of vase images.[39] Matthew cleverly used the published length of a spear excavated at Vergina, one of the few that has been excavated with the remnants of the shaft *in situ*, to estimate the length of a thrusting spear by simply substituting the long sauroter commonly seen, for the short version actually borne by this spear.[40] The result was a spear measuring 242cm, or almost 8ft in length. For a 253cm spear he estimated weight of 1332g (2.9lb) based on a 25mm tapered shaft similar to that of Kromayer and Veith. This is a big spear, but it is its shape and balance, not simply its weight, that precludes effective throwing (indeed, Murray et al. used a heavy 1200g spear in their ankyle assisted throwing tests).

When wielding a spear with one hand, the length between your grip and the point dictates the reach of the weapon, while the length of shaft extending behind you serves only to help balance the mass of the fore end. Although not always the case, in many situations maximizing reach is the prime force in spear development. It is axiomatic among hoplite re-enactors—who strive to build historically accurate panoply and test the manner in which weapons and armor were used—that a 12ft (366cm), untapered, mid-balanced spear is about the upper limit for one-handed use.[41] If this size is in fact a maximum for average sized humans, then the farthest reach would be around 6ft (183cm) plus the extension of the arm bearing the spear. The downside of a 12ft spear with 6ft of reach is the other 6ft has to balance the shaft back of the hand. For men fighting in open formations this is not a problem, and many cultures make use of very long levers behind the grip to balance the fore section. But a 6ft projection behind hoplites greatly limits their ability to fight in close formation without fouling each other. Moving the center of gravity of hoplite spears toward the rear was a solution to this problem. A spear of 8ft (244cm) balanced one third up from the base has a reach of 5ft 4in (162cm), while a balance point one quarter of the way from the base has the same

6ft (183cm) reach as a 12ft (366cm) center balanced shaft. You don't get something for nothing though: the rear-weighted spear has to be a bit heavier than the longer untapered spear because of the loss of leverage.

Making tapered spear shafts required a fair amount of work with a spoke shave (a hooked whittling knife), though given a young, straight tree—perhaps one specifically grown or coppiced for the purpose—the carver can follow the natural taper of the tree. Moreover, rear balancing required the use of a metal sauroter. If more weight was needed to move the balance point, there is evidence that metal balls were fitted around the socket of the sauroter.[42]

In the early 4th century the Athenian general Iphicrates created a new troop type that has been called a light hoplite or heavy peltast and might have been a proto-pikeman.[43] We are told by Diodorus that he changed the shield and "increased the length of the spears by half."[44] In light of the dimensions of the tapered spear above, it is possible that these new troops were simply cheap hoplites, with a shield of simple manufacture and a spear that did not require the labor needed to properly taper the shaft, nor the expense of a metallic sauroter. If we replace the 8ft tapered spear with one half again as large but untapered, we are left with an inexpensive 12ft spear/pike that retains the reach of the more specialized hoplite spear.

Use of Spears in Battle

The method of employing the spear has been the subject of much controversy. To date, no author has presented a portrayal of hoplite spear use that is "correct." In part this arises from the fact that the hoplite era was a long one and there were surely variations in use over time and in different situations. The notion that the hoplite spear was used like a lance, as densely formed opposing phalanxes crashed into each other, has dominated modern discussion to the point of it being labeled "orthodox."[45] After this initial collision, the spear would be restricted to stabbing forward from within a dense mass of men, presumably at targets beyond the man directly in front of you given the inability for such a long weapon to be employed at close range. Both Bardunias and Matthew have shown why this initial crash is unlikely to have been a common feature of hoplite warfare, albeit for different reasons (crowd versus hedge).[46] A number of authors, often called "heretics," have suggested as an alternative that hoplites fought in less dense formations.[47] Although the "orthodox" and "heretics" differ a great deal their proposed mechanics of hoplite combat, they concur on the posture of hoplites in battle.

The stance hoplites adopted in battle is important beyond spear fencing with other hoplites. It is also crucial in determining how close hoplites can stand beside each other (this is detailed in later chapters).[48] Both the orthodox and heretics advocate what is termed a side-on stance. This has been invoked by the orthodoxy as a means of allowing a hoplite to brace his shoulder behind his shield while fighting[49]; Van Wees (a standard bearer of the heretics) has offered that hoplites could shelter their whole body behind their shield if they stood sideways "like a fencer."[50] While this stance is a clever solution to the problems arising from each of the arguments, it only takes a few moments with

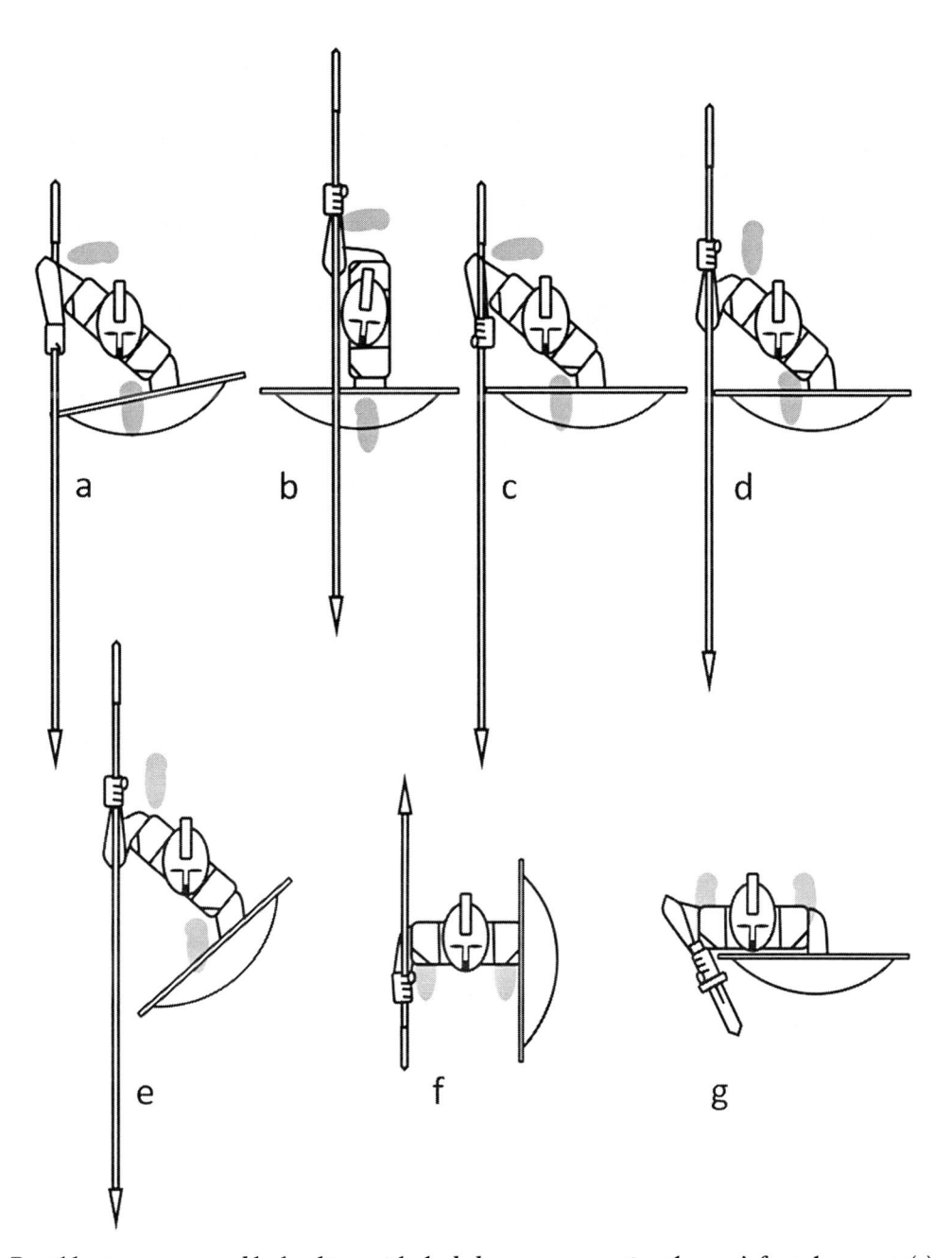

Possible stances assumed by hoplites, with shaded areas representing the man's foot placement: (a) couched underhand; (b) side-on; (c) high underhand; and (d) overhand; (e) represents the stance a hoplite assumed for single combat based on analogy with the teachings of renaissance arms masters; (f) is an "at ease" stance with the aspis resting on the shoulder; (g) is the posture assumed by front-rank fighters when in othismos and pushing while sword fighting.

an authentic spear and shield to show that this is not a viable stance for either single or group combat, though it would serve well for a hoplite involved in a missile duel.

The problem with this stance is that you cannot strike effectively from it. Fencers lead with their weapon, but a hoplite in this stance leads with his shield. In order to strike, the hoplite must not only rotate his right shoulder forward, but must also take a step to the right with his right foot. If you do not do this, you are relegated to ineffectively jabbing alongside your head with much reduced force and reach. A strike that properly rotates the torso to add force to the blow brings his body into what is called the "frontal" or "squared-to-fore" position. In a side-on stance, this transition is slow and clumsy, telegraphing any attack well ahead of the strike and leading to a slow recovery back into the side-on "ready" position. In a missile duel this is less of a problem because the hoplite was only expected to "strike" once, or at most twice as he threw his spears.

If we allow a hoplite to take that first step needed to strike from a side-on position, he would be in what is termed a "three quarter" or "oblique" stance. This is the stance advocated by Bardunias, Matthew, and other re-enactors who have used shield and spear in mock combat. Again, it should be remembered that this is a "ready" stance and not a "striking" stance. Even from this pose, the right shoulder must be brought forward or the strike will be weak and the range limited. Thus, when striking, all hoplites are in a frontal stance, probably with the toes both turned forward, and no scheme of inter-hoplite spacing that limits the hoplites ability to assume this pose is likely to be valid.

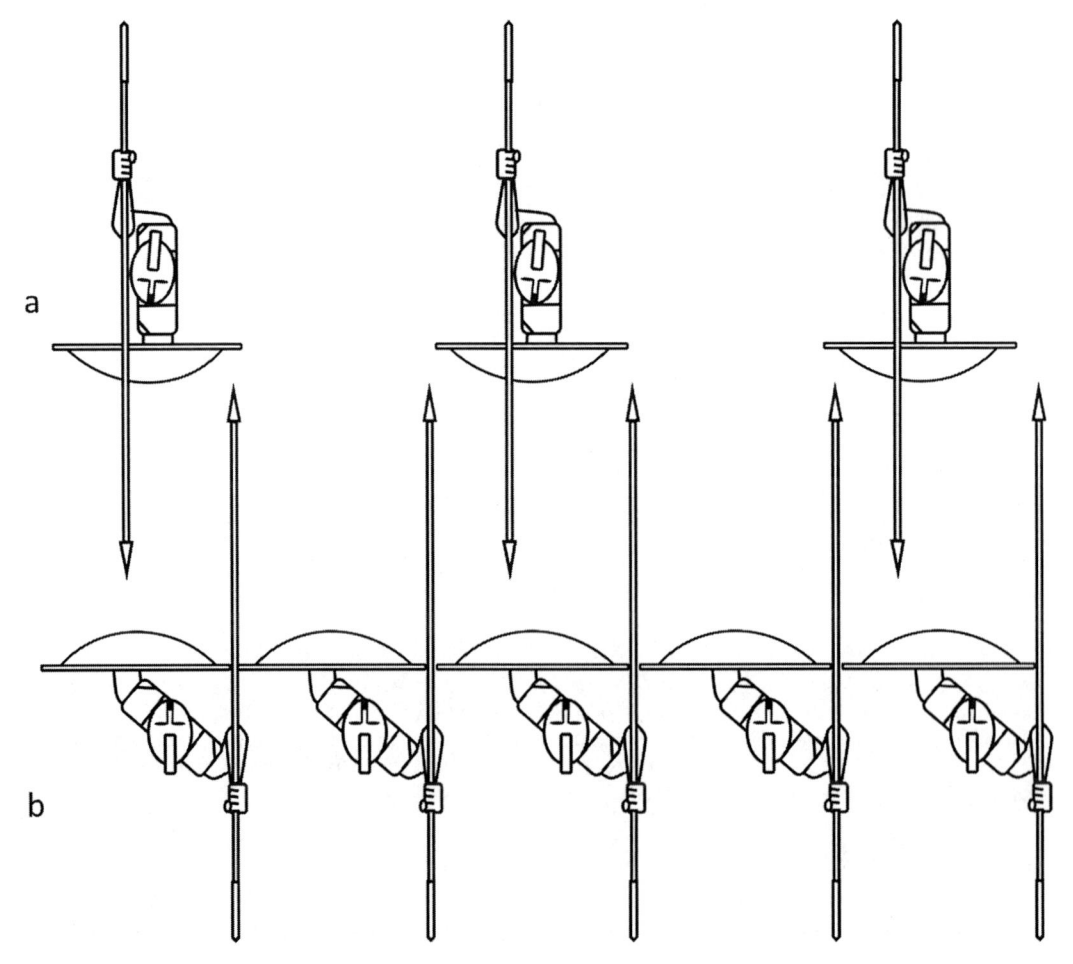

A comparison of men standing side-on at 2m frontage and men at three-quarter stance and 1m frontage.

Bardunias described a highly constrained frontal stance, where the feet are actually both in line beneath the shoulders and the hoplite is standing almost straight up.[51] This has been misunderstood as a spear-fencing stance, but he invoked this solely for use in the densest of hoplite crowds having no room for any other stance.

The biggest controversy among re-enactors is how the spear was held in the hand, and there are advocates for different grips and strikes. There are five basic types of strike with the hoplite spear. The underhand strike is done with the thumb pointing forward, fingers curling away from the head, putting the shaft beneath the hand. There are three ways to use this grip: low-underhand at waist level; couched or shoulder level underhand; and high-underhand above the shoulder. The other way to use the spear is to strike overhand. This involves the thumb pointing behind and the fingers curling towards the head. Two different versions of this have been described: an "ice pick" strike with the spear held high and the arm relatively stiff to produce a downward arcing trajectory for the spear, and a strike akin to the spear throwing motion described earlier without letting go with the hand.[52] Of these strikes, the low-underhand, cannot be used if shields are brought together or overlap because the spear will be trapped below the line of shields. We see this strike often on vases, and this may indicate an opened style of fighting or perhaps anachronistic dueling, but may also be intended to show the vicious and disordered fighting that occurs after one side of battle routs. The high-underhand strike and overhand strike are the most common methods used by re-enactors.

Studies examining the velocity and force produced by these various grips have been conducted, but there has been confusion in comparing the results due to differences in methodology. Gabriel and Metz tested the low-underhand and overhand strikes, recording velocities of 7.3m/s and 16.8m/s respectively.[53] Connolly et al. conducted laboratory tests for low-underhand, shoulder level or couched, and overhand strikes, recording 4.8m/s, 3.8m/s, and 6.7m/s respectively.[54] Although these two studies diverged greatly in recorded velocities, perhaps due to differing strength of subjects, they are consistent in showing that low-underhand and couched strikes produced substantially lower velocities than overhand strikes. In light of these findings, it is curious that Matthew recorded the opposite trend in testing underarm and over-arm strikes.[55] He tested a hoplite in full panoply conducting low underarm, couched, high underhand, and overhand strikes for 8.1m/s, 8.3ms, 6.5m/s, and 6.5m/s in that order. In contrast to the previous studies, where the velocity of underhand strikes was only ½ to ¾ that of an overhand strike, Matthew found overhand strikes to be only 75 percent as powerful as underhand. De-Groote has recently shown a far greater average penetration for overhand strikes.[56] How can these seemingly conflicting findings be reconciled?

Matthew discounted the overhand strike velocity of Gabriel and Metz as being a misreported throw rather than strike. In this he was correct, at least in spirit, because it is clear from his description that he was using a very different striking method than the other studies. In fact, Mathew's description of the downward arching trajectory of his overhand strike clearly identified it as the "ice pick," overhand method. This is far different than the more likely overhand strike that engaged all of the major muscle groups and a catapult-like joint flexion, as if throwing, but doing so without releasing the spear. The simple arm rotation of the "ice pick" strike, and to a lesser extent the high-underhand strike, is weak in comparison. Beyond the cocking back of the arm rather than rotating it up, the major difference is that the spear is not gripped tightly at the end of the strike, but allowed to rotate in the grip. A firm grip is maintained with the first two or three fingers and the thumb; however, the shaft rotates such that it maintains a flat to upward trajectory for the blow. Not only is this strike much more powerful than the couched underhand strike, it is exceptionally accurate. Re-enactors who employ this often practice by hitting a softball suspended by a cord.[57] Any athlete who was raised playing throwing sports, like baseball or American football, will find that such accuracy comes easily. The very real possibility that an opponent could throw the dory with the same motion as a strike plays havoc with a spear-fencers calculation of his opponent's reach. A common objection to this strike is that it is fatiguing to hold up the arm; however, it should be clear that the arm is not held up continually when this technique is done properly. The shaft can be rested on the shoulder by simply moving the hand forward of its usual grip point at the center of balance.

It has been argued that reach is diminished with an overhand strike, but this is true only in the static extension of the spear. If warding an enemy away with the length of the spear were the goal, then the ability to hold the spear extended horizontally for long periods of time would be an advantage. However, this is not needed in a clash of phalanxes because your foe cannot easily break free from his shield-line; therefore, as long as anyone in close proximity is striking, the space between lines will be maintained. Moreover, the type of prodding attacks against opponents' shields aimed at knocking them back to create an opening like those commonly created in Society for Creative Anachronism (SCA) style sport-combat is an artifact of the weapons in such events being purposefully dull for safety's sake. A properly sharpened dory that is simply dropped a few feet onto a poplar plank of the type used in shield making will stick deep enough that it requires a critical few seconds to pull it free and may even result in a bent point.

It has also been claimed that a benefit of the couched grip is that you can hold the shaft past the point of balance by supporting it with the forearm, rendering it point-heavy but gaining reach. Yet a hoplite can make use of a physics trick to do the same with an overhand grip. The length of the spear shaft extending in front of the hand applies a great deal of torque to the hand when trying to rotate the wrist to bring it level. If we recall the "moment" formula explained earlier, it is the mass times length of extension of the spear. In fact, it is a bit more complicated, because the force dragging the spear tip down is gravity. If you let your spear slope downwards to a 45° angle, then you reduce the horizontal extension of the spear, and all that matters is how far the spear extends parallel to the earth. The spear now feels substantially "lighter" due to the reduced torque. This sloped shaft is an excellent guard position to aid in parrying, for, like a rapier, the spear should parry at the equivalent to a *forte* (nearer the grip than point).

With a spear gripped nearer the sauroter—as on a back-weighted and tapered spear—and held at a downward angle, the overhand strike will never hit a man behind you. From the overhand grip, short, quick stabs can be made at targets of opportunity by rotating the wrist to bring the spear up to bear. For stronger thrusts, the hoplite must simply bring the hand up above head level as he cocks back to strike. Then the motion of the hand follows a "J-shaped" trajectory, with the hand moving forward as the sauroter comes down and the spear assumes a horizontal trajectory. Finally, it should be noted that a good many ancient artworks show hoplites making just such overhand/overhead blows.[58]

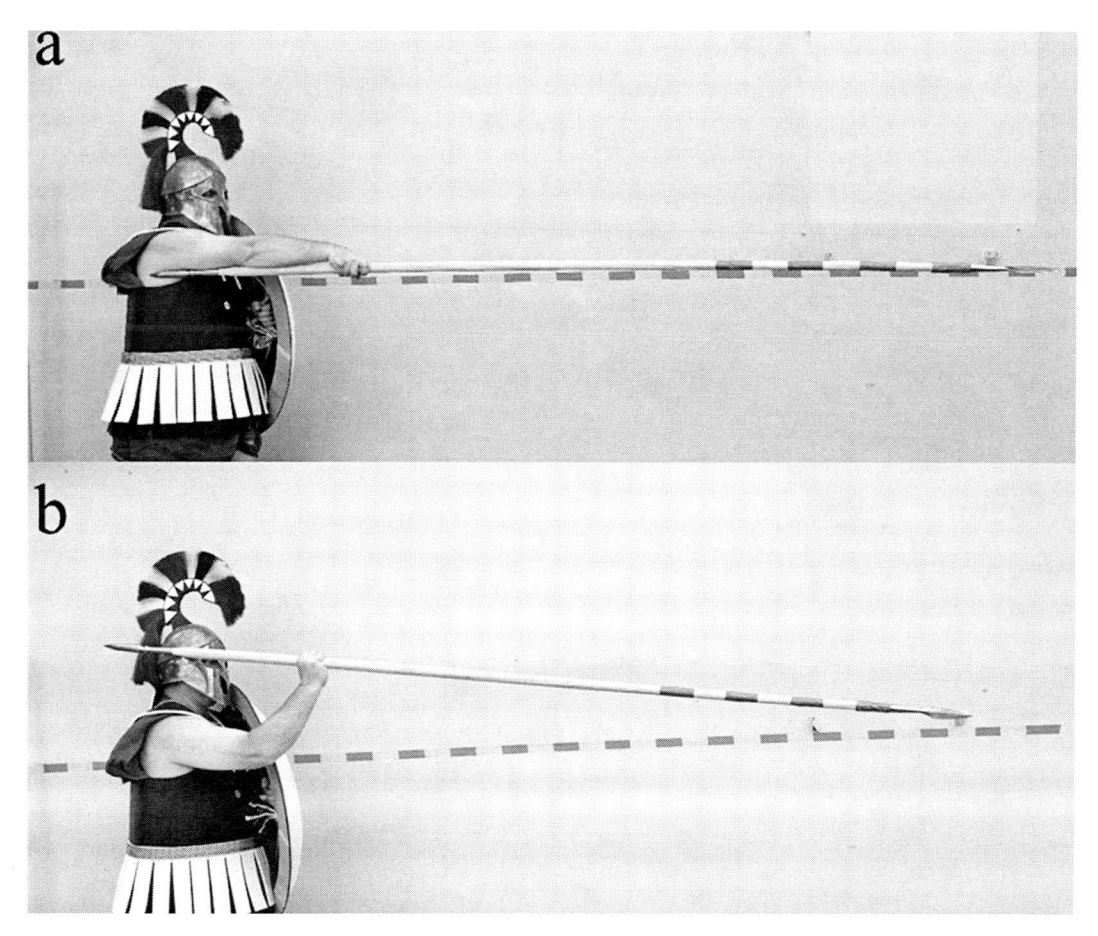

Comparison of maximum reach with (a) the couched underhand strike, and (b) the proper hoplite overhand strike. Note that the dory cannot be statically held at maximum extension in overhand, and the pinky finger is curled under only to support the shaft for the photograph. The arm and spear would extend on a flat horizontal plane at maximum reach, but even here the reach advantage is less than 20cm for underhand. Hash marks indicate 10cm.

Swords

The hoplite spear was a deadly weapon, with reach enough to allow multiple ranks of men to present spear points to their foes. But the reach made this spear useless if your enemy closed in to fight shield-to-shield because you cannot reach back far enough to accelerate the spear into a man at that distance. Instead, hoplites turned to their auxiliary weapon, the sword. Hoplite swords came in five broad categories, the popularity of each waxed and waned over time with fashion and emerging tactics.

The xiphos was a cut and thrust sword whose history goes back well before the hoplite era.[59] Meant for use in one hand, as all ancient Greek swords were, it possessed a straight blade of variable length, though seldom more than 60cm (2ft).[60] The blade was narrow at the base, swelling towards the tip and then tapering back to an effective point. It was often forged with a strong mid-rib running the length of the blade to provide stiffness.[61] The blade may have been of high quality "Chalcidian" Steel.[62] The

The "J" shaped curve that the hand follows in an overhand strike. With the arm cocked back (a), the sauroter is above the level of the head of the second rank men. As the spear is thrust forward, and the point is brought up towards horizontal, (b) the hand begins to come down, but the sauroter is still above the second ranker. Midway through the extension, (c), the sauroter is at its closest to the head of the man behind. By the time the sauroter is at the level of the head of the second rank man, the arm has moved forward so far that it is well clear of the second ranker (d).

hilt of the sword is usually shown with a cylindrical pommel that swells in the middle to aid in gripping and a robust cross guard. A variant of the xiphos has a similar hilt, but rather than a flattened diamond cross section, it was maximized for thrusting in the manner of a medieval tuck or estoc, having a thick diamond cross section near the hilt. This blade widens only slightly as it progresses towards the point, but the cross section flattens into an effective cutting blade.[63]

The kopis (chopper) or machaira seems to have been an import from Anatolia.[64] Its blade hooked forward and became wider towards the point. This rendered it point heavy, facilitating chopping or slashing with a feel in the hand in some ways similar to that of a hatchet. Although this sword was ideal for cutting, it could be used to thrust and is often shown with a strong point and false edge on the back of the blade near the tip. Another sword type that may have been a variant of the kopis was shaped like a machete, with a straight back and belly that swelled near the front of the blade. This sword was a dedicated chopper, and may have evolved from non-military cutting knives.

The last type of sword is attributed to Sparta. It was referred to as a dagger (enchiridion). Sekunda[65] points out that the first anecdote on record regarding the small size of Spartan swords probably took place around 387, when we see small swords on Theban stelae as well. This may indicate that sword's popularity originated in Sparta in the 5th century and then spread along with Spartan victories at the end of that century.

Use of Swords in Battle

The shape of each sword dictated in broad terms how it was employed, but we know little about the exact striking methods. Use of the sword to Xenophon was something that came naturally, without any specific training[66]; and perhaps this was to some extent true in the press of men where room to strike was limited (as we can perhaps see in contemporary iconography). One of the most common striking positions in art by the 5th century is the so-called the "Harmodios" blow. This is a strike made with the hand up above shoulder level, either downwards or laterally with a forehand or backhand strike. Interestingly, this strike is often shown used by unarmored men; and the manner in which this leaves the body open to retaliation has been noted.[67] This strike makes sense if we imagine the hoplite is normally using the sword in conjunction with a shield. The xiphos and kopis both swell towards the tip in a manner that favors chopping blows coming from the elbow and wrist, while the thrusting xiphos and Spartan enchiridion can be used in a stabbing strike that arches down from above in a manner seen on many vases.[68] Any of these swords would have been devastating in the close press of combat, raining down blows from above the line of shields; however, the enchiridion in particular was a vicious weapon for close-in fighting in its ability to strike at the unprotected throat of an opponent.

Other Weapons

Hoplites made use of other, specialized weapons in certain circumstances. Etruscan hoplites may have employed double-bitted battleaxes.[69] Men equipped as hoplites from Lycia are shown carrying *drepanon* (sickles) in place of swords. Greek hoplite marines made use of a sickle on the end of a pole or spear, the *dorudrepanon*, to cut the rigging of opposing ships.[70] Rhodian hoplites knew from their youth how to use the sling, and could be pressed into serving with that device.[71] And many hoplites would have known how to ride and could function as cavalry when horses were available; in which case, they might have employed javelins, the most common mounted weapon of their era. But all of these alternatives aside, the true prime weapon of the hoplite was really the man himself; and when his manufactured tools of war failed, he fought with his hands and even teeth.[72]

2

Shields

The hoplite's panoply underwent a good deal of change over the centuries as various new items were added and old ones discarded. Throughout the hoplite period, only the shield remained constant. In fact, we recognize hoplites by their large, round, hollow shields. The shield was no simple thing, having evolved on the basis of hard-won practical experience into an engineering marvel. A sophisticated construction of wood, linen, leather, and bronze, this device gave its bearer not only critical protection, but provided offensive support as well—all through a design perfectly matched to the unique needs of phalanx warfare. The hoplite's shield was so integral to his effectiveness in combat that keeping it in his possession was a vital key to victory or defeat, life or death.

Delium (424): Not Without a Struggle

Athens was riding high as the seventh year of the Peloponnesian War drew toward a close. Having survived the horrors of a deadly plague, it had abandoned a largely defensive stance to hit hard and often at the enemy's homelands. This more aggressive strategy used the polis' powerful fleet to mount discomfiting raids all along the Peloponnesian coast that had quickly delivered success on several battlefields. Worse yet for the Spartans, each of those victories had let the Athenians set up a fortified site nearby.[1] Called *epiteichismoi*, these outposts were sustainable from the sea and acted as forward bases for launching sudden strikes into the interior. They also provided safe havens for slaves and serfs fleeing the adjacent countryside with the ensuing loss of agricultural manpower adding to ravaged crops in delivering heavy economic blows across much of the Spartan coalition. Epiteichismoi were also great for propaganda. This questioned the Spartans' long cherished reputation for martial prowess in that they no longer seemed capable of defending either their allies or native soil.[2]

It was thus with the Athenians' fortunes in ascendance and their foes suffering all around the Peloponnese that they devised a new and daring campaign to spread similar pain to another quarter. A bold strike at Boeotia to the north could not only show the Thebans and others there that their alliance with Sparta was ill advised, but might even send local dissidents into rebellion across much of the region. This was to be accomplished by a simultaneous pair of attacks.[3] Demosthenes would come ashore at Siphae on the Corinthian Sea at the head of an army of Athenian marines and allied troops and advance in support of rebels pledging to put all of western Boeotia into his hands. On the same day, Hippocrates would invade far to the east with another host. He was to set up an epiteichismos at Delium, where a shrine of Apollo sat next to the Euboan Channel. The theory was that this two-front offensive would cause the Boeotians to disperse so widely as to preclude any effective counter.

Overly confident from their recent successes, Athens' planners seemed oblivious to the many risks inherent in what they were doing. Among these was a need for their two commanders to coordinate movements even though out of effective contact at considerable distance. And that went wrong first when a misunderstanding led to Demosthenes landing at Siphae well before his counterpart's diversion had begun. Demosthenes was also counting upon catching his foes by surprise as well as on strong support from insurgents not under his direct control. And both those aspects now conspired to increase his troubles. It seems that Sparta had warned his intended targets based on a Phocian informant close to the rebels; and as Boeotian troops then arrived in response, those plotters refused to take action. Seeing his operation fall completely apart, Demosthenes was left with no choice but to withdraw.

Hippocrates had in the meantime finally departed for Delium, unaware that his partner's effort had failed and the enemy forces sent to meet that threat were already back and available to oppose him. Reaching Delium on the second day with no resistance, he set up a fortified outpost there over the next three days. Staying behind with his cavalry to oversee the work's finishing touches, Hippocrates sent his infantry back toward home around dinnertime on day five. What he did not know was that the Boeotians had been gathering against him the entire time, with troops collecting nearby at Tanagra under Pagondas. That Theban general now had a powerful army in hand with 7,000 hoplites,[4] a contingent of 1,000 horsemen, and more than 10,000 in light foot; the last mostly attendants, but including 500 peltasts (perhaps Thracians) and likely javelineers trained to support horsemen (hamippoi) in strength equal to the cavalry.[5]

With plenty of time to scout them, Pagondas had excellent intelligence on his Athenian foes. This included that their hoplites were a match for his in number; however, the relative ability of Hippocrates' heavy infantry was open to question. It represented all of the spearmen to be found in the city at a time when a variety of commitments elsewhere had drained Athens of many regulars. The hoplites that had come with Hippocrates were therefore quite a mixed bag. They included not only older citizens well past their prime, but also resident aliens (metics) and other foreigners likely to be short on combat experience. With his spearmen thus probably superior in quality, it's likely that Pagondas decided to attack upon learning that the enemy's column was largely bereft of light-armed support as well. This was due to its horsemen still being at Delium, while most of the light footmen had kept on for Athens after leaving the hoplites behind to wait for their general at a spot just inside the Attic frontier.

Pagondas' men were at first reluctant to engage. After all, there was no need to risk their lives to chase off opponents that had already left Boeotian territory. But the aged commander[6] was able to rouse them to action by recalling how their nation's arms had triumphed over Athens in the past[7] and that the justification for fighting now was not simply to expel their foes, but rather to punish them for what they had just done and thereby discourage them from ever doing it again:

Remembering this, the old must equal their ancient exploits, and the young ... must endeavor not to disgrace their native valor ... we must march against the enemy and teach him that he must go and get what he wants by attacking someone who will not resist him, but that men whose glory it is to be always ready to give battle for the liberty of their own country ... will not let him go without a struggle.[8]

So inspired, the Boeotians marched out and closed on the place where Athens' heavy infantry held station; Pagondas taking good advantage of the lay of the land to hide his approach behind a long ridge[9] overlooking the enemy position from the southwest. This tall screen sheltered his troops as they deployed into battle formation. Their phalanx had the Theban levy on its right wing with 2,500 spearmen[10] standing at the exceptional depth of 25 shields with their first three ranks filled by picked men of an elite unit known as the "charioteers and footmen."[11] Hoplites from Haliartus, Coronea, and Copais held the center of the array, with Thespians, Tanagrans, and Orchomenians filling out the left wing; all of these contingents filed to suit themselves, but perhaps generally eight deep. The entire formation therefore covered a front something like 650–700m long with its cavalry and other light-armed taking post off each flank. With his contingents now in order, Pagondas led them up the slope until his forward rank reached the crest, holding there in sight of the Athenians below with its menacing line of spears and overlapping shields backlit by a sun now hanging low in the November sky.

Hippocrates had got warning that the Boeotians were coming after him and sent word ahead that his own hoplites should get ready for action. Leaving some 300 horsemen behind at Delium, he then rushed with the remainder (200–400) to join his heavy column. By the time he arrived, his phalanx had stretched its 7,000 or so spearmen across better than 850m at a depth of eight shields to face what was clearly a much shorter enemy line. It's likely that Hippocrates now misjudged the force opposing him; unable to see its true configuration behind the ridge, he would have assumed eight-man files and that he had about 25 percent more men than the enemy. Thus, when the Boeotians struck up their battle cry and began to move down at him, Hippocrates broke off exhorting his own troops and confidently sent them upslope on the quick at what he believed to be a smaller array. And no doubt standing far right with a poor view at best of the deep Theban files diagonally distant, it's unlikely that the Athenian commander ever did come to realize that error.

There were water-cut ravines at either end of the ridge that confined the ensuing engagement across a width of about 900m.[12] The longer Athenian phalanx filled most of this space with its few horsemen and foot-skirmishers covering what very little remained on either lateral extreme. Across the way, Pagondas had plenty of light-armed troops to plug the much wider gaps off his flanks; in fact, broad as these were, he actually lacked sufficient room for all of his cavalry and had to hold 200 riders (two squadrons) out of action at the rear. It seems clear that the Theban general had sacrificed the width of his formation in order to achieve great depth on its right, hoping that his crack Thebans could push through the much thinner opposing array there in short order once the initial spear-fighting closed into a shoving contest.

But that was not to be, since though his hoplites did begin to press with shields face-to-face and "got the better of the Athenians and shoved them further and further back," they did so only "gradually at first."[13] The combat thus became drawn out, which

2. Shields

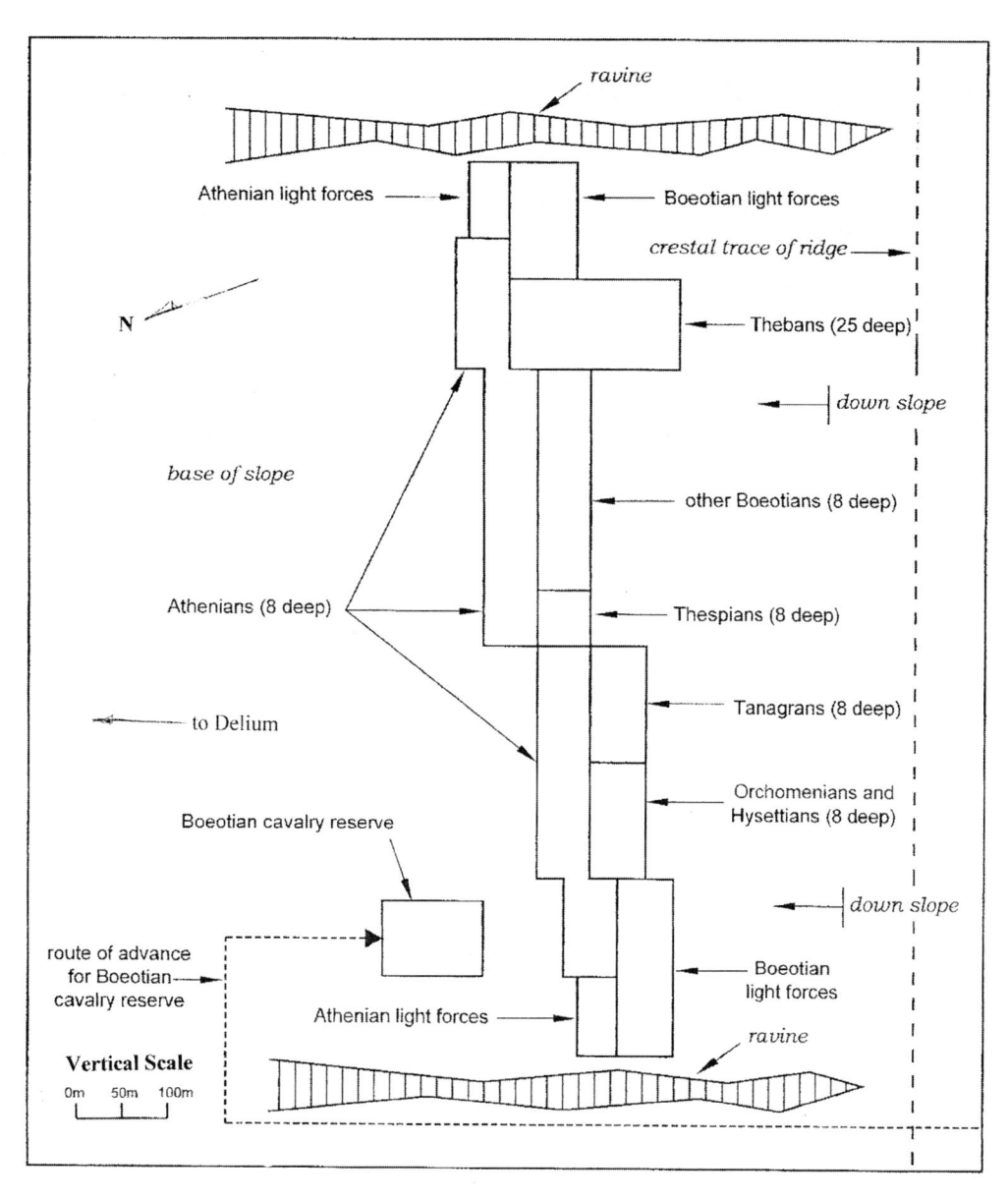

DELIUM (424 B.C.)

Battle of Delium—424 BC. (Joan Huckaby).

gave Hippocrates and his right wing the opportunity for their breadth of front to force back the Boeotian light-armed troops on that flank and wrap around it. The Orchomenian and Tanagran levies enveloped there fled for shelter in back of their still intact right wing. But the men from Thespis next in line held firm at heavy cost as the Athenians closed about and intermingled in such fury that they struck down not only Boeotians but some of their own men as well.[14]

But costly as their heroic resistance was to the Thespians,[15] it proved crucial in buying time for Pagondas to address the potentially fatal collapse of his under-extended left wing. Seeing the Orchomenians and Tanagrans fleeing behind him, the crafty old commander improvised brilliantly. He sent into action all of the horsemen that had been forced to stand idle at the rear due to the battlefield's narrow dimensions. These troopers rode "where they could not be seen, round the hill, and their sudden appearance [at Hippocrates' right-rear] struck a panic into the victorious wing of the Athenians, who thought that it was another army coming against them."[16]

Not only did the Athenians fall apart in fear and confusion, but the terrified sense of imminent defeat spread almost instantly to the other wing of Hippocrates' phalanx as well. There, his hoplites had put up dogged resistance against the Theban levy filed at three times their depth, engaging "with the utmost obstinacy, shield against shield."[17] These spearmen had to this point given ground only very grudgingly under the powerful pressure coming downhill from that great stack of foemen as they mashed ahead in concert within the hollows of their aspides. However, as the men on their right broke away in frantic flight, those on Athens' left were soon equally caught up in the panic. The rising disorder that followed let the Thebans finally push through, and within minutes the entire Athenian army was racing away in a headlong quest for safety. This saw what had been a coherent and nearly triumphant battle array shatter into three terrified mobs, one breaking back toward Delium and the others making separately for Attic territory (in the direction of the port of Oropus on the east and south toward Mount Parnes); all suffering an intense chase from the Boeotians, and their swift and numerous horsemen in particular.

Among those fleeing the battleground was the philosopher Socrates, who at 46 years of age was a veteran of several campaigns, and one of the many older men who had marched off under Hippocrates. His commander now lying among the dead left on the field by the flight of Athens' routed right wing, he retreated in the company of Laches, a friend and general who had been fighting at his side in the ranks. Their pursuers were likely to pass up dangerous looking opponents in favor of softer targets, such as those who had tossed away their shields and weapons to gain speed. So, keeping alert with aspides and weapons at the ready, Socrates and Laches withdrew slowly and encouraged their foes to look elsewhere for easier prey. Thus they escaped with reputations and lives intact[18]; yet many of their fellows were not so lucky. Nearly 1,000 Athenian hoplites died at Delium, along with a goodly number of attendants and camp followers caught up in the battle's aftermath.[19] At around 14 percent of the spearmen deployed, this counted as the most costly defeat in Athens' history at the time.[20] And things would have been worse still if the engagement had not begun so late on a short winter day that saw early darkness curtail pursuit. Losses on the other side were not as severe, but still ran high for a victorious phalanx at better than 7 percent (500 spearmen) as a reflection of how badly things had gone on the Boeotian left.

On the strategic plane, Athens' defeat at Delium marked a serious reversal of its previously soaring fortunes in the war; while in context of operations, it served to underscore the folly of attempting such complex schemes without having communications and intelligence assets to properly back them up. Yet it was at the tactical level where Delium taught some of its most fundamental lessons; and for the most part, these revolved around the Greek aspis. It was by shoving into those concave devices to create an overwhelming wave of othismos that the Thebans had finally expunged the last vestiges of Athenian resistance. Nor were hoplite shields any less vital either before or after that ultimate turning point. By holding onto their aspides when others dropped them in flight, the Thespians had been able to trade their blood for the time their Theban allies needed to rescue the engagement. And among the losers, most of those retaining their aspis (like Socrates) survived; even as many others threw away both shield and honor, and in many cases their life as well. Truly, if one can speak of some battles being won by the Dorian spear,[21] then Delium might with some justification be called a victory of the Argive shield.

Pre-Hoplite Shields

A Proto-Corinthian aryballos dating from the early 8th century shows men fighting with two styles of shield.[22] One is known as a dipylon, and is larger (taller than it is wide) and wasp-waisted. It is held by a single handle placed in the center of the constriction along the mid-line. The second shield is round, roughly 1m in diameter, and appears to be supported by a band in the center through which the forearm passed and a second grip near the edge held by the hand. Looking at the representation of these men fighting, there is no indication that either shield presents an advantage the other lacks. Yet, within a generation, the dipylon would be eclipsed by the round shield to begin the hoplite era.

Two similar shields were used among the Philippine Moros well into the 20th century. They made use of both a large round, double-grip shield, the taming, and an oddly shaped oblong shield that is vaguely hourglass shaped. We have good accounts of their use in combat.[23] A 1913 report from the R. F. Cummings Philippine expedition describes:

> The offensive weapons used by the Bagobo are spears, knives, and at times bows and arrows. For defense they carry shields, either round or oblong, and cover the body with so many strips of hemp cloth that a knife thrust is warded off. Turning his body sideways to the enemy, the warrior crouches behind his shield, keeping up a continuous capering, rushing forward or dancing backward, seeking for an opening but seldom coming to close quarters. Arrows and spears are glanced off with the shield. An attack is usually initiated by the throwing of spears, then, if the enemy is at a disadvantage or confused, the warriors rush in to close combat. For this purpose they rely entirely on their knives, and as fencers they are unexcelled.

This may be a close approximation of the type of small-scale combat that preceded the hoplite era, though Van Wees has suggested that it survived well into the hoplite era.[24]

The round shield appears in iconography in the middle of the 7th century, and archeological finds date from late in that century. The shield appears to have originated in the northeast Peloponnese, with early dedications of this shield type at Olympia coming primarily from Argos and Corinth. Many of the decorative elements point to styles prominent in Corinth, but Argives dedicated the lion's share of early shields to the temple and the earliest known shield maker named on a dedication was Aristodemos of Argos.[25] Perhaps this indicates construction in Argos with distribution through Corinth, one of Greece's busiest ports. The ancient Greeks themselves seem to have believed the shield originated in Argos, referring it as the "Argive shield" or aspis.

It was made in the form of a flattened dome some 10cm deep (averaging around 90cm in a range of 80cm to 120cm in diameter). This included a robust, offset rim of some 4–5cm. The Bomarzo shield in the Vatican's Museo Gregoriano Etrusco, which retains large portions of its wooden core, is typical of aspides for which we have core fragments.[26] The shield's core is only 5–6mm thick over much of the shield's face, thickening to 8mm in the center where the *porpax* (a cuff for the arm—see below) was affixed. Near the rim of the bowl, the shield curves back sharply to form side-walls of 10–14mm that taper towards the shield face. The rim, and often the whole face of the shield was covered in a single sheet of bronze 0.2–0.5mm thick. This shield has traditionally been thought of as exceptionally heavy (7–9kg), but Krentz has suggested a more likely 6.8kg or less[27]; and more recently, Mikko Sinkkonen has been making aspides built of wooden laths in multiple, alternating layers, that weigh less than 5.5kg.

Many of these features are found in shields of neighboring cultures outside of Greece. Warriors with large, round shields are commonly shown on Assyrian images. These may be made of wicker and covered with leather and metal. The aspis might have evolved from a wicker predecessor, because a consistent feature of the aspis was a mock-woven pattern embossed on the bronze rim known as "guilloche." Woven shields might seem weak, but wicker shields are used today by riot police and were common into modern times.[28] A transitional stage that might explain the survival of the guilloche rims may have been a shield with a wooden core surrounded by a woven section, something seen in Philippine shields.[29] In 8th century Urartu, a kingdom to the north of Assyria and locked in a battle for survival with it, shields have been recovered that show another feature of the aspis. These shields were 80–100cm and made completely of bronze. In profile they look very much like the aspis, with its turned-back side-wall section. There was a tradition of bronze shields of the type called "herzsprung" from the Balkans and brazen shields with strong central spikes from Cyprus. But these shields, as well as those from Assyrian and Urartu, were gripped by a single handle. The Urartian shields probably had a strap that went over the shoulder to help bear its weight based on their odd internal support structures. This included a central grip that was oriented vertically, but off-center towards the upper rim, flanked by what were probably loops for a strap.

The aspis had an uncommon double grip system. The left arm was slipped through a bronze cuff (*porpax*) placed either at the shield's center or just to the right of center. The porpax either accepted a wood and leather sleeve or was itself lined with leather and tapered to accept the forearm up to just below the elbow. A second grip (*antilabe*) near the rim of the shield was for the hand, and tension from this acted to hold the arm in the porpax. When properly fitted, the porpax acted like the cuff of a modern artificial limb, holding the arm snuggly so that the shield would not rotate around it.[30]

In shields from other cultures that have a double-grip system, the grips for forearm and hand usually flank the center of the shield and allows most of the shield to be brought up in front of its bearer. However, central location of the porpax allows only half the shield to cover a man's front, the other half jutting out to his left. This central placement of the porpax in the aspis is an advantage in holding the shield up on the bent forearm because it reduces the proportion of the shield's mass that is to the right of the elbow and must be pivoted up.[31] A double-grip limits the range through which a shield can be moved, making it difficult for a hoplite to defend against strikes below knee level. Because the shield cannot be lowered, a hoplite must dip his whole body.[32] Also, the aspis cannot be held as far away from the body as a shield gripped solely by the hand, which leaves a greater portion of the body vulnerable to incoming strikes and reduces the distance a strike must penetrate to wound.[33] And the limited range of motion of the arm makes it impossible to punch the shield into an opponent. Any shield-bash with the aspis would have to involve rotation of the whole torso and be far less effective than with a single-hand gripped shield. Van Wees describes hoplites pushing with the bottom rim of their aspides.[34] The bottom rim naturally tilts up when the arm is raised with a properly fitted porpax; however, there is very little strength behind this and any pressure on the bottom of the shield would push the rim into the hoplite's throat or face. A hoplite could prod with the shield if he held his arm straight towards his foe, but this position is taxing.

A domed or conical shield is not unique to the Greek world. A convex shape functions to transfer force away from the site of impact, while an offset rim reinforces the face of the shield so that it does not split when struck. Exceptionally convex shields, conical in profile, are common in many cultures because the profile ensures that an incoming strike will encounter a sloped shield-face. This has two benefits. When a strike encounters an angled surface, the surface resists. If the weapon is moving perpendicular to a flat plate, then the resistance is directly against the direction that the strike is coming in from and equal on all sides. But when an angled surface is struck, part of the resistance is pushing against the incoming attack at an angle. This can redirect the strike and lead to a ricochet. Even if a strike is not redirected, when a weapon encounters armor that is sloped, it has to effectively pass through a greater thickness of armor than with a perpendicular plate.[35] This might explain the convex Assyrian shields, for their cone shape is the optimal profile to maximize this effect. The Greek shield is less well made for this because the greatest slope is relegated to only a small area at the outer edge, while the broad face of the shield has but a shallow curve. Curvature also insures that chopping weapons will impact on a broad area rather than biting into the rim of a shield. The hemi-cylindrical examples of the classic Roman shield (scutum) may benefit from this, but in the aspis the robust rim would be more likely to intercept an incoming blow than the curved shoulder region.

A shallow dome tends to spread outward under pressure, and the wide, perpendicular rim acts to keep the face from splitting. As a result, an aspis under pressure tends to fail instead where the side-wall and face join. This odd profile has inspired the suggestion that the aspis' great weight required such a curve to allow a man to carry the shield on his shoulder. Leaving aside that the mass of the aspis has probably been overestimated, some rough calculations show that this explanation is unlikely. The aspis' weight did not likely motivate the curved outer portion because, even though only 3–4cm wide, the greater thickness and large diameter of the "ring" of wood that makes up this side-wall section itself accounts for fully 20–40 percent of the total mass of wood making up the shield-face! Schwartz relates that using an aspis by turning side-on and letting the shield hang from the shoulder is the "*only possible* way" of fighting with it.[36] Not only could a hoplite fight without hanging the aspis from his shoulder, it would be suicidal to fight behind a hanging shield. The posture suggested would render a hoplite unable to twist the torso to strike with any force and greatly limit reach. Moreover, a man would have to pull the aspis awkwardly into his body to allow the shield to hang, eliminating even the limited space the aspis provides against penetrating weapons. Some confusion may stem from the fact that ancient and modern replica aspides are often shown curving over or touching the shoulder, but this is far different from "hanging" in the sense of bearing the weight of the shield. Because the porpax is in the center of the aspis along its vertical axis, the weight above and below it is perfectly balanced. It does not naturally lean back against the shoulder as it would if it were gripped lower and the top portion were heavier than the bottom.

Instead, hoplites fought with the aspis supported by the arm and presented in line with the rest of the phalanx, his body at an oblique angle behind it. He would rapidly shift from this position to move up parallel to his aspis when striking with force. Some vases clearly show carrying straps, separate from the antilabe, so the notion that the rim was developed to bear its weight in place of a strap or telamon is unlikely. This is not to say that the aspis cannot be rested on the shoulder. This can be a fine "at ease" or marching posture, with the aspis on the left shoulder, facing edge-forward as you walk.

The shape of the aspis remained remarkably unchanged throughout the whole hoplite period. The latest study of existing aspis fragments dates them by changes in cosmetic style (guilloche pattern for example) and shows that there was no trend towards a different diameter or depth, though there was a tendency over time towards simpler decoration.[37] It is unclear what percentage of shields had full coverings of bronze sheet for the shield face, and in many aspides only a sheath around the rim is bronze.

Three main modes of construction can be determined from the surviving examples of aspides. The first method, used to build the wooden core of a shield found at Olympia, was similar to boat hull construction. Two crossing or converging ribs were laid down. Onto this form, planks were affixed until the proper profile was achieved. A second, much stronger method is suggested by the fragments of a shield now lost from Olynthus. Steaming or soaking was used to make wooden strips pliable, and then they were bent to produce a domed shape. This lamination technique is the method used on the later Roman scutum. This creates a very strong shield because, unlike a single plank of wood, there is no consistent natural grain to serve as a fault line when the wood is stressed. They would have built the shield-face from two or three layers of strips laid down in alternating, cross-hatched, layers. This would have either been built up within a round rim section or affixed to it after formed.

But the technique used to make the majority of shields that have survived was very different. Most of these have come from excavations of temples and tombs, with the best preserved from Etruscan and Macedonian burials. Shields found at these sites retain enough of their wooden cores to get a clear picture of their construction; and these were all manufactured in a similar manner. The wooden cores were made of either willow or poplar, both of which will "self-heal" when damaged as the natural springiness of the fibers will come back together when cut, often gripping the weapon between them.[38] Planks ranging in width from 4–7.3cm and the length of the shield were bent, perhaps by steaming or soaking, and then glued into a roughly shield-shaped bowl. If the planks were not of equal size, the thicker planks were in the center with the grain running horizontally in the final shield. Sometimes these planks would be a composite of two or more boards glued together with a stepped scarf-joint with their grain running in different directions.[39] The roughly shaped bowl would then be turned on a lathe. Parallel radial grooves can be seen on the outside of some shields that are most likely made by a chisel against a spinning shield. Once the bowl achieved the proper profile with an integral rim, thick side-walls, a thin face and a thickened section beneath where the porpax will be fastened, the joint between planks may be reinforced with either inset wooden dovetail brackets or a pair of opposing metal oval brackets nailed through adjacent boards.

The aspis was a composite construction. Once the core was finished, the shield maker added elements that account for much of the final shield's strength. The shield was coated with pitch or tar on the inside, and then a layer of thick fabric. This was then covered in one or more layers of goat or sheep skin. The outer surface was also coated with pitch over a layer (or layers) of fabric; however, tough, twinned linen was used instead of leather for the outer layers. The white powder found associated with this linen has been interpreted as a gesso, rendering the shield an analog for a primed artist's canvas. Obviously, this surface could be painted upon, but it is also possible that a blazon pattern was embroidered directly in the linen.[40] The rim was made stronger by applying strips of wood to the upper surface of its integral core in a manner that ensured the grain ran in opposite directions.

In place of this out-facing of linen, a 0.2–0.5mm thin sheet of bronze (cooper-tin alloy) or brass (copper-zinc alloy[41]) could have been applied either to the whole face of the shield or just the perpendicular rim section, with no evidence existing that leather was ever used for such facings.[42] Bronze this thin would provide abrasion resistance and present a stunning display when polished, and has been shown to protect against penetration.[43] However, it might have served a structural function. The bronze is shown tight-fitting (perhaps a sheet molded around the wooden core on a lathe) and such a taut covering, even one so thin, would act like modern metal packing strips, holding together structure beneath. This would be of most use at the rim and at the upper curve of the side-wall section where stress pushing outwards was greatest. Interestingly, while in the 5th century we see a reduction in the number of full bronze facings, there is also the appearance then of another support on the inside of the shield, near the transition to the side-wall. Here we see a hoop of iron that is 0.5–0.7mm thick and secured by many nails. This could be an internal truss to help keep the core from spilling or flattening outwards under pressure. On the inside of the finished aspis, there are a series of discs or rosettes (usually eight) with wide staples securing them to the inner surface of the shield. These hold rings, which in turn support an enigmatic cord that runs around the inner surface and forms the antilabe hand grip. Bardunias[44] has suggested that this cord may have had its origins as a cable truss to add additional support to the inner face of the shield, perhaps when the shield was still made of wicker. The Greeks used such cable trusses (upozwmata) to keep their ships from bending or "hogging" from pressure on the hull. Attached to these rings was a hand-grip for the shield. Surprisingly, we often see two such grips, one on each side. One hand-grip's use is obvious (holding the shield in combination with the porpax), but that of the second is speculative; perhaps it let one carry objects in the bowl of the shield.

The last major feature that defines the aspis is the porpax. This sleeve for the forearm has a metal strip extending above and below towards the perimeter of the shield. In an example from the Vatican, this appears to be mostly decorative; however, in other shields the edges of these strips are perforated to receive nails used to join together adjacent boards beneath. The flat surface of this strip is often beautifully embossed with heroic scenes. The porpax itself could be a simple cylinder of metal, sized and shaped to accept the forearm. This cylinder could be made stronger by including "ears" of metal in the form of a back-turned rim at each opened edge of the cuff. The porpax appears to have at times been lined with leather. Hoplites are often shown with a sash wrapped around their arm at the elbow, which may have aided in fitting the cuff of the porpax or prevented chaffing on the elbow. Other porpaxes were clearly made of multiple pieces and a thin metal strip in place of the broad cuff would have accepted a wooden or leather core on these variants.

In the early 5th century we see a curious addition to shields. About the time of the Persian wars we see a broad apron of textile or leather affixed to the bottom of the aspis. Hoplites are sometimes shown with sashes wrapped around their left arm that hang below the shield, and perhaps this was the origin of the custom. The apron is often shown hanging from an upraised shield. This position with the bottom of the shield tipped up may have been adopted in order to present a slanted shield face to incoming arrows.[45] Raising the shield like this would obviously expose one's lower body; thus, the apron may have been a stop-gap means of obscuring the legs as possible targets. Moreover, tests with twinned linen aprons show that layered aprons could "catch" arrows and absorb their energy when fired from a distance.[46]

More than just a defensive device, the aspis was also a piece of art. The face of the shield could be gleaming bronze or brilliant linen, painted with a wide range of heraldic blazons such as gorgons, eyes, or mythic animals. The aspides found in tombs in Macedonia had wood and ivory appliqué eyes (perhaps representing those of a gorgon whose stare could legendarily turn a man to stone) or other decorative features. Beautiful hammered bronze blazons that cover much of the face of the shield can be seen at the Museum in Olympia. Throughout the archaic period we see shields bearing what are probably family or clan emblems. In the 5th century, we see a rise in blazons that are associated with individual poleis. Early on this may have been heroic elements associated with the city, like the club of Heracles at Thebes, but by the 4th century many poleis had adopted the initial of their city's name. We know this was the case for cities like Sicyon and Messene, but the existence of this standardization for bigger states such as Sparta has been doubted. An obvious source for this trend towards city-shields is a polis that was producing shields for hoplites at state expense. When Sparta armed large numbers of helots to form neodamodeis, men who had no heraldic tradition of their own, it might have been natural that they marked the shield with the uniform insignia of Lacedaemon.

The shape of the aspis is unique enough to require explanation. That the aspis is thinner at its center than at the edges indicates that protection from penetration was not the only factor in its design. In fact, we read of a number of occasions when a hoplite's shield "turned traitor"[47] and allowed a weapon to pass through. In contrast, the turned-back side-walls that join the shield-face to the rim is thicker. Blyth noted that this section helps to keep the shield from buckling under asymmetrical stress much in the manner of a rimmed metal lid.[48] He described the shield as defeating the type of stress thought to be most important in the description of hoplite battles at the time he was writing, a hoplite attempting to push between two others. Bardunias has described a new model of hoplite combat that requires a means of protecting hoplites from asphyxiation.[49] A domed profile can support great weight without collapsing and may indicate a load-bearing function. The dome of the aspis is shallow and less efficient, so increased force on its flattened surface will put outward pressure on the rim. Trusses or supports that resist this outward force are needed to keep the shallow dome from popping inside out like an umbrella in the wind. In the aspis, this was accomplished by its thickened rim. The off-set design presents the maximum thickness of wood against the force attempting to push the rim outwards; and a bronze sheath or internal metal ring adds to this as the tensile strength of the metal resists stretching.

Critically, it is this depth of the thickened side-wall that allows a man to survive the press of crowded combat by protecting his torso from compression. To do so, the hoplite would have held the aspis directly in front of his body with the top right half of the shield resting on the hoplite's upper chest and the front of his left shoulder, the bottom on his left thigh. Replica aspides have been shown to be able to support almost half a ton of weight on the shield face without buckling.[50] The shield as a "life preserver" in the killing press of a crowd explains the constancy of this shape over time. The deep, flattened dome could not vary much and still retain its ability to resist compression. Thus, when the shield was found inadequate as protection from missiles, an apron of leather was hung from the round shield rather than remaking the shield into a weaker oval that would provide the same coverage.

The End of the Aspis

In the 4th century we begin to see the erosion of the supremacy of the aspis as the premier shield for heavy spearmen. The first challenge comes from the reforms of the Athenian general Iphicrates, who created a force of spearmen designed to face hoplites. He lengthened the spear and sword and adopted a new type of small oval shield (the "peltas summetrous") for his men. This foreshadowed the adoption of a long two-handed pike (*sarissa*) at Macedonia.[51] The need to handle the sarissa with both hands required adoption of a smaller, rimless pelta that was suspended on a strap around the shoulder. The last major state to have universally used the Argive aspis took up use of the Macedonian pelta when Cleomenes reformed the Spartan army in the late 3rd century.[52] This followed earlier erosion of widespread use of the Argive aspis in the wake of the Gallic invasion of Greece in the early 3rd century.[53] After this incursion, many cities had replaced their hoplites with a new troop type equipped with a large, door-like shield of oblong shape (*thureos*) similar to those of the Celts. This development can been seen as a sort of ultimate vengeance of the long obsolete dipylon shield in that these new thureos-carriers (*thureophoroi*) were in many ways a tactical throwback to the Proto-geometric warriors, who similarly bore the oblong dipylon with a pair of throwing spears.

3

Body Armor

The protective equipment worn by Greek fighting men underwent a good deal of development during the long history of hoplite warfare. This process saw archaic warriors heavily covered in bronze armor give way in classical times to men wearing less burdensome attire. This confined heavy and expensive metal to only a few parts of the panoply; specifically, a helmet, snap-on greaves for the lower legs, and a torso-covering "bell" cuirass. Entering the Hellenic era (c.500), hoplites would exchange those bronze cuirasses for ones of leather and stiffened linen. Not only much lighter and less costly, these were cleverly designed to be just as effective as the old metal device. All of this sort of gear was of considerable value in warding hoplites against the deadly weapons of their fellow spearmen; moreover, it gave them a great and famous edge when battling more lightly equipped barbarian foes.

Mycale (479): A Line in the Sand

The Achaemenid Persian Empire's invasion of Europe in 480 suffered a major setback in the defeat of its supporting armada off Salamis. This prompted withdrawal of all surviving naval forces to Asia. It also led to Persia's Great King, Xerxes, going home lest his absence on what now promised to be a long campaign encourage plots against the throne.[1] However, the Greek defenders still faced a potent threat going into 479. This came from Mardonios, who had replaced Xerxes in local command after receiving the office of satrap (governor) of Greece from that monarch.

No longer able to rely on ship-borne logistics, Mardonios retained a smaller army than the one that had first marched from Persia; yet it was a more effective force for the conflict at hand. That was because he had shed the many small and largely useless units of light foot in the original complement[2] while adding shock-fighting potential vital to opposing the enemy's heavy spearmen. That improved capability for close-in combat in part reflected experience-based upgrading of tactics for the sparabara at the heart of the Persian host. It also came from transfer ashore of a substantial body of Egyptian marines that carried spears and large wooden shields.[3] But perhaps most significant, the freshly minted satrap could now call upon numerous hoplites from poleis under his sway in northern and central Greece.

Pulling up into Boeotia, Mardonios established a huge camp near recently allied

Thebes. He not only enjoyed an adequate source of land-based supplies there, but the wide plain below gave free rein to his large cadre of Asian horsemen as well as riders from newly acquired Grecian subjects. He thus waited to receive Greek coalition forces; these had reluctantly taken the field under a dire threat from Athens that it would abandon the war unless they shed their defensive posture, recovered Attica, and then went on to expel the invaders entirely.

As this was playing out on the mainland, the Greek fleet sat idle to the east on Delos in the Cyclades Islands. Unable to affect the coming battle ashore, it suddenly got a chance to take aggressive action when a delegation arrived from the island polis of Samos just off the southern coast of Ionia. This mission alerted the admiral in charge, king Leotychides of Sparta, that the Persians had disbanded much of their navy. Cutting costs, they had dismissed their best flotilla from Phoenicia as well as the large (and now marine-less) one from Egypt. Left with only a modest collection of ships, many of them crewed by Ionian Greeks tired of foreign rule and emboldened by Salamis, the imperials were in poor shape to confront a surprise counter-invasion. Leotychides and his staff quickly saw that such a campaign could not only strike a hard tactical blow on the spot but also might yield important strategic benefits in Greece.

There was a definite danger that Mardonios would refuse to promptly engage in Boeotia, waiting instead for a chance to do so under the most favorable conditions possible for his own troops. Yet a delay of any great length in pursuit of that sort of cautious course might prove disastrous for the Greek coalition. The fact was that it was already showing signs of pending dissolution, moving now only under the very real fear of coming apart at the instigation of Athens, its most powerful member state. But should an attack in Ionia stoke an uprising there, Mardonios could well face imminent recall to resolve it. That prospect might rush him into battle in a manner more conducive to the Greeks' political cohesion and in a setting better suited to their tactical doctrines. He might even have to march away without a fight, under orders to deal at once with a crisis raging so much nearer the Persian homeland.

The fleet's leaders considered all of this and agreed upon an attack into Asia. Preparing rapidly, they set off with some 175 war galleys (triremes, fast hulls with three banks of oars). Most of these were of a fully decked design accommodating up to 40 hoplite passengers,[4] but 110 of them were the latest models from Athens. These last had only partial decking and carried but 14 marines (ten hoplite spearmen, called "epibatai" in this role, and four archers).[5] The expedition's embarked combatants thus likely totaled some 3,700 hoplites and 440 bowmen. There were also thousands of rowers aboard[6] that could provide additional light-armed support if needed. The Persians retreated when confronted by this armament, beaching to encamp on the south side of the east-west trending Mycale Peninsula that stretched just inboard of Samos.[7] Joined there by the garrison division (*baivarabam*) for the province (*satrapy*) containing Ionia, the Persian admirals, Artayntes and Ithamitres, reinforced their position by throwing up a stone and wood palisade fronted by stakes across its landward approaches. The Greeks sailed past this construction, calling on the Ionians within to defect as they went by; they then beached their ships unopposed well down the peninsula toward the east.

The path from the Greek landing site to the Persian camp lay along a restricted expanse between the sea and broken ground (a ravine and hills) to the north. How broad this ran in 479 is not on record; however, something like 250m seems reasonable.[8] Leotychides and his second-in-command, Xanthippos of Athens,[9] elected to split their troops for an advance that accommodated this layout. The Spartan took 1,700 spearmen and half the archers and circled through the hills, looking to come down on the prospective Persian left flank. Meanwhile, Xanthippos was to march down the shore with the remaining hoplites (2,000) and bowmen to offer combat and thereby entice the enemy from their ramparts.[10] With slightly more than half the available spearmen in his phalanx, the Athenian could array them eight shields deep astride the available space; and thusly deployed, he would then seek to fix the imperials in place until Leotychides was able to descend and complete his flanking maneuver.

The commanders of the imperial land force at Mycale, Tigranes and Mardontes, saw Xanthippos approaching. Noting the modesty of his array, they considered a sally. Those Ionians deemed least trustworthy had been sent away to pursue make-do duties elsewhere; still, a fair number of Greeks remained within camp. That meant keeping a force of native Persians inside to guard against treachery, which would reduce assets for an offensive. Total strength for the long-standing garrison unit on hand must have run well below its authorized count of 10,000 men. Indeed, it probably consisted of 6,000 or fewer sparabara, mostly young men meeting their national service obligation.[11] Yet even if most of two regiments (hazaraba) were held back to secure the camp,[12] there were still around 5,000 soldiers left for an attack. And that outnumbered the visible opposition by better than 2-to-1. Therefore, ignorant of the other hoplites in the hills, the Persian generals elected to rely upon what looked like much superior manpower and fight in the open rather than try to hold their hastily erected palisade.

Emerging through a gate in the camp's east-facing wall, Tigranes and Mardontes advanced their array far enough to bring its after-ranks into bow-range of the Greeks, with their shield-front spanning the flat from strand to interior rise. Tigranes was in charge with Mardontes as his second, and both were quite familiar with the capabilities of their hoplite foes across the way. The year before, Tigranes had led the division of Medes that made the first failed assault against Leonidas at Thermopylae[13]; and while Mardontes' lesser contingent in the host of Xerxes hadn't seen combat, he had no doubt then and later heard much of a disturbing nature about the enemy's spearmen from Tigranes and others who had. After-action discussions centering on how to counter those deadly warriors must have been rife between the officers on Xerxes' staff, with the more astute among them like Mardonios and Tigranes desperately looking for some way of using their sparabara to better advantage.

Such tactical brainstorming would inevitably have come to focus on the relative vulnerability of the multiple shield-walls serially employed in most of the actions in the pass. This contrasted with the much more even fight put up on the second day by a single, deep mass of shield-bearers composited from across the army. Those sparabara had held their ground and denied the enemy any opportunity to rotate fresh troops into the fight. They had still taken unequal damage due to their lesser protective gear and shorter weapons; yet they avoided the sort of heavy slaughter that came when hoplites broke into unshielded after-ranks. Though it failed operationally, the composite brigade had wrestled its Greek spearmen foes to an exhausted tactical stalemate, yielding the field only with the fall of night.

It would seem obvious from this that the deeper one could line up spara the better. Thus, when fighting within restricted space, it would be best to break with previous Persian practice and crowd all the normally file-leading shield-holders at the head of the formation. That would eliminate the single ranks of spara before each dathabam/file that had cost so many lives against Leonidas and company. The challenge before Tigranes now[14] was just how to put those ideas to work in the current situation; where he couldn't draw shield-carriers from other divisions and had to contend with a front that, while restricted, was not nearly so narrow as those at Thermopylae. With maybe a quarter kilometer to cover with some 5,000–6,000 sparabara, he would have to stand them two dathaba (20) deep. If he truly had but one shield per section of ten soldiers, then he could put only two or so at the head of each file; though it's possible that there were enough spara in camp to outfit a pair of men in each dathabam and create a front that was four shields in depth.[15] Either way, his formation was not as stout as that of the composite brigade. Hoping to remedy this weakness, Tigranes had his leading rank of shield-carriers scrape a shallow furrow across the beach and seat the flat base of their spara within, forming a line in the sand that would hopefully be somewhat harder for the opposing hoplites to push through. Having thus done all he could to get his command ready to fight, the Persian general gave the order for his archers to open fire.

On the other side of the field, Xanthippos and his phalanx had been waiting for their detached right wing to appear when shafts suddenly began to rain down by the tens of thousands.[16] It was a tremendous assault of the sort that must have blown away many a Persian foe in the past; but these heavily armored Greeks were something else entirely. Pressed into his large, metal-coated shield, with a thick bronze helm (*kranos*, often of a nose-guarded variety know as "Corinthian"), a protective corselet (*thorax*) with shoulder pieces (*epomides*) plus possibly kilt-like strips of material to ward the loins (*pteryges*), and brazen greaves (*knemides*) over the shins, a hoplite was almost impervious to arrows being directed at him from afar in this manner.[17] Yet, "almost" was not the same as "completely"; it seems there were always ways an arrow could find its way into some bit of inadvertently exposed flesh over the course of an intense and lengthy bombardment.[18] Leotychides' contingent seemed to be moving more slowly than expected up in the hills, and Xanthippos had no way to know how long he and his men would have to endure this cruel peppering until it showed up. Of particular concern for the Athenian general were the better than 200 archers present from his own polis and any oarsmen acting as auxiliaries, neither having the protection of hoplite equipment. Finally, after seeing a few of his men hit and hearing others suddenly crying out in pain, he could tolerate no more. Xanthippos signaled for a charge that would take his array up against the opposing formation; there, the enemy's own high profiled front would block both line of sight and easy access for missiles from the archers behind.

As the phalanx closed ground, sparabara in the leading ranks dropped their bows to grab spear and shield in anticipation of the looming shock fight.[19] Their hoplite foes then halted a step or two away and began thrusting powerfully over top of the proffered spara; long spears targeting Persian faces, throats, and chests to good effect. Lunging to ram down hard blows, the Greeks dealt out considerably greater harm than they took in return. This deadly differential in damage reflected not only the greater reach of the hoplites' weapons, but also the much better protection afforded by their body armor. For while the latter was effective enough in screening flights of arrows, it had actually been designed and perfected for just the sort of close-in combat now at hand.

Under such duress, it was only a brief matter of time before the Persian front began to waver; and eventually, the Greeks began to press aspis-on-spara, with their surge powerfully enhanced by pressure coming from files in the rear. Irresistibly, the hoplites "pushed their way through the wicker shields," penetrating deeply to break and put the shield-less rearward ranks to flight.[20] With hundreds of their fellows speared down from behind, the surviving Asians fled in so much haste and disorder through the still open gate in their eastern palisade wall that it could not be closed before the fast-pursuing Greeks ran inside as well. And just then, Leotychides and his right-wing force arrived at last to add their weight to the assault.

The Persians on guard within the camp joined with those of their fleeing comrades that managed to rally and put up a spirited resistance. But relatively few in number[21] and scattered in small parties, they had no real chance, and the action turned into a massacre that saw more of the Asians running than fighting. The men that fled sped through a gate in the camp's western wall; and those fainter hearts included both admirals, who survived to face charges of cowardice and incompetence. The reputations of Tigranes and Mardontes faired better as they got some respect for joining perhaps half their countrymen among the dead. Meanwhile, hoplite fatalities on the day probably came to no more than 100–150[22]; a ratio of 40 to 1 or better in the Greeks' favor that can in no small measure be attributed to their superior weapons and armor.[23]

Helmets

Men with large shields can protect most of the body, but the head will always remain vulnerable. Prior to the hoplite period, warriors all around the eastern Mediterranean were already wearing helmets of bronze that protected the head and to some extent the neck.[24] One feature of early Anatolian helmets that will be seen throughout the hoplite period is a high crest of horsehair. This crest could rise directly from the top of the helmet or be elevated on elaborate support structures. They could go from forehead to neck, or transverse across the helm from ear to ear. In the late 8th century we see a helmet type, the kegelhelm, consisting of a central conical helm with exaggerated cheek and neck pieces and often riveted brow reinforcement.[25] Around this same time, the Corinthian helmet, the quintessential hoplite helmet, emerged in primitive form.[26] Both of these helmets show the trend towards greater protection of the throat that characterized the early hoplite period. A major difference is that the Corinthian helm evolved over time to include greater protection for the face, with cheek pieces converging beneath the eyes until only a slit remained for mouth and nose. A nose-guard extended outward and downward, covering all but the mouth itself. The helmet was probably hammered out of a single sheet of bronze, but it has been suggested that it was in fact cast in the proper shape.[27] This helmet would dominate for more than two centuries, evolving with the needs of contemporary hoplites as conditions changed on the field of battle.

Corinthian helmets of the 7th century fit over the head like a pot. As time went on, that pot constricted inwards and was designed to fit rather snuggly over the face.

The importance of this has been shown by men wearing modern replicas into mock combat. If there is space between the cheeks and the lining of the helmet, then a struck blow projects the entire helmet back against the face, with the nose-guard then usually transferring the full force of the blow into the nose to greatly damaging effect.[28] By the late 6th century, the helmet had achieved its classical form and was a marvel of functionality fused with esthetics. The cheek pieces had elongated to better protect the throat, while the crown of the helmet swells away from the skull, presumably to provide ventilation to the top of the head and space to make it harder for crushing or penetrating blows to impact the skull. The nape of the neck flares outward, and in combination with the elongated cheek pieces allows the helmet to sit firmly on top of the head in a manner often seen on many vases of the period. The ability of hoplites to tilt the helmet back into this position would be an efficient way to ventilate the head; and if you watch modern American football players on the sidelines between plays, they will often do something similar with their helmets. The last major change of this style of helmet occurred at the end of the 6th century when we see holes being cut around the ears, presumably to enable the wearer to better hear commands. When you are inside of a Corinthian helmet, you can see very well save for a bit of peripheral visual field and a band just below your eyes that is blocked by the cheek pieces; however, though you can hear, localizing sound becomes very difficult. The ear holes remedy that. In some helmets with ear holes we also see a rounding of the cheek pieces. This type of helm is called "Chalcidian." In the 5th century, helmets became more open, with both Corinthian and Chalcidian varieties having hinged cheek pieces, while helmets known as "Attic" and "Cretan" had the nose guard reduced.

The basic form of the early kegelhelm did not disappear. A helmet type labeled "Illyrian" (though actually originating in the Peloponnese) was in continuous use alongside the Corinthian; and it followed the former's major developmental trends in gaining longer cheek pieces and ear holes. The face had always been open in this helm, being framed by cheek pieces sans nose-guard.

The most radical change in helmets occurred sometime in the mid 5th century. Two varieties emerge that appear to be metal renderings of civilian hats. The pilos was a simple conical cap that may have been worn beneath older helmet types as an "arming cap" to provide padding beneath the helm and ensure a snug fit. The Spartans appear to have started wearing just this cap in place of regular helmets, making them of felt or textile at first,[29] but then going to sturdier bronze. The steep-sided pilos protects the top of the head from downward strikes, but leaves the face completely open. Its simple shape may have allowed for ease of production in that it could be lathed over a pilos-shaped form much as per the process for making bronze aspis coverings.[30] Likewise, the Boeotian helm followed the lines of a civilian hat that was tied down on the head. It had a rounded peak and, unlike the pilos, a robust brim that descended to protect the cheeks to some degree. It was favored by Xenophon for cavalry.[31] About this same time, in Italy the push towards more open helmets resulted in an odd design. The Italo-Corinthian helmet was fashioned as if an old-style Corinthian were taken into battle in the pulled up position and, in its extreme form, had a miniature fake nose piece and eyes incised above the forehead.

Late in the hoplite period we see a return to prioritizing protection for the face and neck. Pilos helmets acquired additional neck and cheek pieces and styles known as Phrygian (with a forward tilted crown), Thracian (with a rounded peak), and konos (with an onion-shaped cap) became popular.[32] Throughout the whole hoplite period, crests of horse hair or feathers were a feature of many helms, and some late helmets displayed a wide range of metal adornments such as mock bull-horns, fins, or wings.

Armor

Hoplites of the Archaic period truly were "men of bronze."[33] The earliest example of the bronze armor for the chest and torso called a thorax and commonly known as a "bell cuirass," was found in Argos and dates from the last quarter of the 8th century.[34] These armors possessed raised or incised patterns that portray a fanciful outline of human musculature, with whorls over the pectoral region and lines in imitation of the muscles of the torso. They are undeniably beautiful and may have served to intimidate opponents by giving the wearer a dangerously fit appearance.[35] However, the raised portions with designs may have been functional as well, acting to stiffen the frame in the manner of corrugations in sheet metal and presenting an angled surface to weapons.[36] The bell cuirass often had a high cylindrical collar rising to protect the neck, but the metal was not extended over the shoulders in order to allow freedom to raise the arms. These cuirasses did not extend down as far as the hips, because to do so would make bending forward impossible. Instead, they flared outwards at the bottom in a manner that served to protect the lower torso from weapon strikes coming from above. Additional protection for the lower abdomen could be provided by a belly-plate (mitre) suspended from the front of the cuirass on bronze rings.[37] It is also possible that some hoplites wore a thick skirt or perizoma to help protect the abdomen.

The bronze thorax would over time become more anatomical in appearance, rivaling the best sculpture of the age for accuracy in portraying the musculature of the human torso (see photo). Normally, hoplites wore nothing beneath their armor save a simple garment (*chiton* or *exomis*). In order to protect the lower abdomen, many cuirasses were paired with a fringe of leather or textile (*pteryges*), which were often reinforced with metal plates or scales and arranged in two overlapping rows. The overlap ensured that no matter how the wearer moved, at least one row would be presented to an opponent's weapon.

During the 6th century, we see the emergence of a new type of corselet that was constructed of leather or textile in the manner of the pteryges. This armor consisted of a dual row of pteryges that extended upwards in a solid tube until it covered the upper chest and back. Usually a band was drawn across the upper chest at roughly the height of the pectoral muscles and another at the waist where the tube and pteryges met. Affixed to the back of the tube was a yoke-shaped pair of shoulder guards called epomides that were joined at the back by a section of material that flared up to protected the rear of the neck, and tied down forward onto the chest piece of the tube (see photo). These broad flaps protected the shoulder and upper chest from attack and provided a flat, padded surface to rest the aspis against when pushing.[38] The tube itself was fastened together on the left side with a thong that passed through holes in the material or around studs or rings. This placed the seam, a potential source of weakness, beneath the shield.[39] Properly fitted, the tube section should extend down to the top hip bones and be cinched (sometimes with a sash) until the weight falls upon the hips (see photo). The epomides can be fastened down to help support the weight, but the armor should not hang from the shoulders. The ability to fasten the epomides independently allows the wearer to tune the amount of weight distributed to each side depending on the range of motion needed in each arm.

This "tube and yoke" design supplanted the bronze thorax as the predominant hoplite armor in the 5th century.[40] It was probably cheaper to make than the bronze alternative and surely more versatile. Unlike the bronze thorax, a man could easily put this armor on and take it off by himself. Just as the Corinthian helmet had taken on a form allowing it to be worn at the top of the head for comfort, this armor could be quickly unfastened on the side, letting the left epomide hang solely from the right epomide to greatly increase air flow and comfort. Such a posture has been widely misinterpreted on vase imagery as showing a double-breasted corselet. But it is more likely that the artists were trying to stress that the hoplite was "at ease" with the left-side panel overlapping the front in a manner that it could not when fastened tight.

The form of the tube and yoke corselet is generally agreed on; however, the material composing it is one of the most contended points in the study of Greek armor. Armor is characteristically shown white on vases, though it may be colored in other media.[41] If the armor was not metallic, a pair of options exist for the base material: leather or linen. And within these two broad categories, the exact type of the material and its related construction technique are subject to hot debate.[42] In many cultures leather was a common material for covering shields, though, perhaps importantly, not the aspis, and hoplites appear to have had a form of heavy leather garment or armor available to them. Xenophon described an incident during the famed retreat of the 10,000 where the hoplites donated armor to men who would act as cavalry and so could not use a shield. They donated "spolades and thorakes."[43] We are told by authors of later centuries that the spolas was a thorax made of leather,[44] which can be very effective against all but the sharpest weapons.[45]

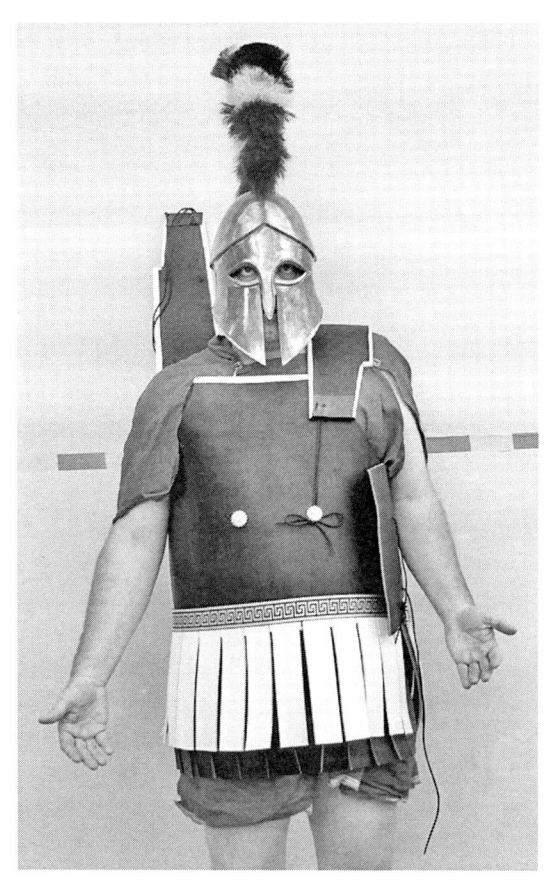

A hoplite wearing a tube and yoke armor unfastened in an at ease position. Note that the lateral panel appears to come in front of the front panel. This feature is exaggerated on vase figures to show a state of undress.

Common vegetable-tanned leather can be rendered hard by boiling it in water, oil or wax, but the result can be brittle. So if thicker armor is required, layers of leather can be laminated together since it will stick to itself via its own collagen; and casein, an alkaline solvent from milk, is commonly used for gluing as well. A tanned ox hide is usually not pale enough to warrant it being illustrated in white, though buff leather tanned in oil, alum-tawed leather, and rawhide might be pale enough for this. Alum-tawed leather, in particular, is vivid white and can be either very stiff like rawhide or creamy soft, depending on its processing; yet, like rawhide, it is unstable and vulnerable to moisture. Perhaps the most likely candidate is a combination of processes. Alum-tawed leather can be processed like buff or vegetable tanned leather and then treated again with alum in order to produce a stiff, white product with an appearance much like the famed Cordovan or Cordwain leathers of Medieval times.

The first reference to linen armor that is truly relevant to the tube and yoke corselet comes from the 7th century poet Alcaeus from Mytilene on Lesbos, who served with the Egyptians as a mercenary (his brother doing the same for the Babylonians). He described *"white corselets of new linen"* hanging on a wall with other armor and weapons.[46] Hoplite mercenaries serving abroad like Alcaeus and his sibling may have brought home new types of armor or ideas for making armor from different materials. Herodotus described the Assyrians as wearing linen *"thoraces,"* the Persians as making use of *"Egyptian thoraces,"* and noted that Amasis, King of Egypt, sent *"Thorakes lineoi"* to the temple of Athena at Lindos and Sparta.[47] Interestingly, there may be mentions of linen and leather armors together. Aeneas Tacticus wrote on smuggling military gear into a city that it included *"Thorakes lineoi, Stolidia, perikephalaia, hopla, knemides."*[48]

If linen armor for hoplites existed, how was it made? Since a single, simply woven layer of textile could not provide protection, Peter Connolly has suggested an ingenious solution by making stiff, flat linen panels out off multiple layers of fabric by gluing them together in 0.5 cm thick slabs. The resulting armor weighed 3.6 kg, which is less than a bronze cuirass of similar size.[49] Many have since followed his suggestion and constructed tube and yoke corselets of linen and glue. The product is stiff and hard, but is also vulnerable to moisture, sweat being the biggest threat. And once soggy, it becomes gummy and gains weight from the absorbed fluid; therefore, a waterproof layer of resin, lanolin, oil (olive or linseed), or beeswax is needed. Glued linen construction seems to have become the default for the tube and yoke.[50] This is troubling because there is no archeological data or pre-existing industry on which to base such manufacturing. Analogies must be drawn from far different applications, such as the lamination of wood or the production of masks for the theater,[51] though the method of applying the linen face to aspides perhaps begs more investigation as a parallel usage. In the end, the argument boils down to the fact they could have made glued linen given the technology of the day and it seems to provide adequate protection.

Of course, many layers of cloth can simply be stitched together, and if the rows of stitching are close, the result can be very stiff[52] and subject to notable difficulty in the sewing of many layers into a single patch.[53] Perhaps there is another solution. Linen presents a challenge to the weaver in forcing one thread over another if they are thick and a dense weave is desired; however, by simply doubling the warp threads per each weft line in a process called twinning, a denser weave is achieved without having to force the linen to bend around each individual warp thread. Bardunias has suggested such warp twinning as a means of rendering heavy cloth for the tube and yoke corselet[54]; and more recently, Gleba has proposed that warp-twinned linen greave found at Dura Europos may be a model for the tube and yoke as well.[55] She notes that twinning of many yarns would explain Pliny the Elder's comment that a thorax dedicated by Amasis had an exceptional thread-count of 360.[56] Certainly, a breastplate that Alexander acquired from the spoils taken at Issus and composed of "two-ply linens" could only have been made of so few layers if they were exceptionally robust.[57]

We acquired a sample of twinned linen artist's canvas[58] to test the ability of twinned linen to resist penetration. Test patches of one square foot were constructed of 4, 8, 12, 16, and 20 layers and secured to a tuff block archery target. These were shot with arrows from a 30lb recurve bow at a distance of 2m to minimize velocity lost to drag over distance. When field-points were used, even four layers caused the arrows to simply bounce off the target. Field-points are far less deadly than the arrowheads used by ancient archers; thus, not having easy access to period accurate arrowheads, we erred on the other extreme and used modern steel broadheads employed for hunting. These have a cutting tip and three razor-like blades. Three arrows were shot in each test, but in every case the result for all three was the same within each treatment. The results were as follows:

Layers of Linen	Tuff Block	Turkey Breast	Kaolin Treated with Tuff Block
4	Complete penetration	—	Complete penetration
8	Complete penetration	—	No penetration
12	Incomplete penetration	Compete penetration	
16	No penetration	Incomplete	
20	No penetration	No penetration	

Because these tests are a preliminary survey, we categorized the results qualitatively. A "Complete penetration" occurred when the arrow cut through the fabric and penetrated into the target beyond the arrowhead. An "incomplete penetration" occurred when the arrowhead cut through the fabric, but only the tip of the point passed through and the head remained caught in the fabric. The tip would have lacerated flesh, but this would probably have been considered a sufficient level of protection. We considered an event as "no penetration" if the arrow did not cut through the last layer of cloth. Using a type of arrowhead that Aldrete et al report was unstoppable in some of their testing (albeit at middling velocity), we were able to provide complete protection with multiple layers of linen. The more realistic backing of animal muscle may have required additional layers because it was a much stiffer backing that allowed less flexion of the linen panel. Aldrete et al. noted that unstitched layers benefitted from the ability to flex and absorb the arrows impact.[59]

Aelian uses an enigmatic term *argilos*, meaning "white clay," to describe an armor appropriate for light troops.[60] Some have translated this as a bright white tunic, while others have taken him to have meant "flashy"; however, it could well be that he literally white-colored clay. A type of fine white clay, known to as kaolin, was widely used by the ancient Greeks. It was a white pottery glaze, and a slip of kaolin formed the drawing surface on white oil jars (lekythoi), which became popular in early the 5th century. Theophrastus of Eresos, on Lesbos, in his late 4th century treatise *On Stones* described possible kaolins as Melian and Samian earths. They were commonly used in fulling and bleaching textiles.

We are benefited in our study of ancient armor that textile body armor has come back into fashion. A recent study showed that the ability of Kevlar armor to defeat spike and knife threats can be significantly increased if kaolin is intercalated into the weave. The clay stiffens through a process called "shear-thickening," wherein the clay-coated fibers are pliable if slowly pushed against, but resist sliding past each other at speed and when impacted at high velocity. This sees the clay particles form an atomic lattice that for the briefest moment is hard as ceramic.[61] Reinforcement with kaolin has an advantage over other techniques proposed to make textile tube and yoke corselets in that such clay was often a component of the bleaching process of linen garments. A clear evolution of the armor from incompletely rinsed white linen is thus easy to envision. The tube and yoke became popular at Athens not long before the appearance of white-ground pottery, perhaps reflecting an increase in imports of fine kaolin for a variety of tasks. The intercalation of kaolin clay unambiguously improved the ability of linen to resist the razor-tipped arrows. These results in no way prove that hoplites made use of the properties of non-Newtonian fluid physics to make their armor more resistant; all the same, they do suggest a provocative new course for our study. Our only source for the exact appearance of the tube and yoke comes from images on vases, so perhaps it is fitting that the culture that made this pottery famous spread its influence not by ranks of bronze, but rather by rows of clay.

Panels of the same dimensions of latigo tanned leather, 4 mm thick, affixed to the tuff block were also tested against razor broadhead arrows from a 30 lb bow at 2 m.[62] One layer was completely penetrated, two layers showed incomplete penetration, and three showed no penetration. For comparison, 8 layers of the linen tested above are roughly 4–5 mm thick. We are currently carrying on further experiments using an archer equipped with period-appropriate arrowheads and bows with draw weights up to 120 lbs.

Whatever the base material of the tube and yoke corselet, the ancient Greeks often found it necessary to augment its protection with a layer of bronze or iron scales. These come in a bewildering variety of sizes and patterns. Scale armor was very common in the Near East, where warriors are depicted covered in long coats of scales. While hoplites are shown in some images with the tube and yoke completely covered in a layer of overlapping scales, it is more common to find the scales restricted to particular areas. The areas that were deemed to require reinforcement are indicated by where scales persist as fewer are added to the armor. Images show a spectrum, from fully scaled, to scales reinforcing the whole tube below the level of the yoke's attachment in the back and the upper chest in front, to just on the right side of the armor.

Greaves

The round, double-gripped Argive shield was at a great disadvantage when it came to blocking strikes to the lower legs.[63] To address this vulnerability, early hoplites made use of bronze greaves (knemides). We can see on the Chigi olpe and others of the mid

7th century that early hoplite greaves covered the calf, but stopped just below the knee.[64] By the late 7th century, the greave achieved a form that would last with minor changes throughout the hoplite period. Bronze sheets long enough to cover from knee cap to ankle were hammered out in such a fashion that the metal took on the form of the calf.[65] Such greaves follow closely the decorative style of the bronze thorax, with spiraled ridges and incised patterns representing realistic musculature. These greaves were probably lined with leather cuffs to help avoid chaffing, but they relied on the natural springiness of the metal to hold them securely. By the end of the 5th century, we see greaves that are anatomically correct renditions of the knee and calf. Most of these new greaves lack perforations around the ankle, requiring the hoplite to wear a separate padded leather band around his ankle.

Many hoplites by the end of the 5th century appear to have switched from greaves to high booted sandals, often with leather protection on the instep (see photo). And Iphicrates, the 4th century Athenian general and son of a professional shoe-maker, is credited with originating a new boot type.[66]

Auxiliary Armor

After helmets, greaves and thorakes the most common piece of armor recovered from Archaic period sites is the ankle guard.[67] These were, as the name implies, bronze sheets hammered out to fit around the ankle from the rear as protection for the Achilles tendon and ankle joint. Foot guards were metal sheets that covered from instep to toes and were designed to mimic the appearance of the foot beneath. Often the toe section was hinged to allow freedom of movement.[68] Thigh guards (*parameridia*) are not uncommon on archaic vases. They are formed from hammered bronze in the same manner as greaves and again follow the general artistic trends seen in thorakes and greaves regarding anatomical features and realistic musculature. These fit over the thigh from the outside in, putting the opened gap between flanges down the mid-line of the inner thigh. They could extend down far enough to include the upper knee, or solely cover mid-thigh.[69]

Hoplites of the Archaic period are often shown with upper and lower arm guards.[70] These are again made like greaves and follow the same trends. On vases these can often be identified by the spiral patterns that vaguely follow the lines of the musculature of the arm below. The upper arm guards extend up from the elbow to the shoulder, often with a gorgon face or other pattern at the shoulder itself. Obviously, it would be more important to armor the right arm in this fashion as that limb was used to wield one's weapons and was thus most greatly exposed to harm.

4

Other Devices

Greek hoplites employed physical devices other than their personal weapons and armor in the course of many a phalanx battle. These instruments ranged from long-standing barrier walls to much more modest temporary constructions on prospective battle grounds. They even include our earliest examples of field artillery. And such devices, whether clever adaptations of existing features or purpose-built, could have significant impact on hoplite combat. This is well illustrated by an engagement that took place near the overland pathway into the Peloponnese at Corinth.

The Long Walls of Corinth (392): Heaps of Corpses

In 394, Sparta led its allies against a coalition of poleis headed by Athens and Thebes. Opening with grand battles (at Nemea River and Coronea II[1]), this struggle rapidly devolved into a grind of small actions around the coalition's base at Corinth (hence the conflict would be known as the "Corinthian War"). The Spartans and their allies ended up surrounding that site ("investing" it in military terms) to essentially put the city under siege. However, they soon found their prospects for success seriously hamstrung due to Corinth's ability to resupply by sea through its port at Lechaion. This harbor sat some 4km to the north on the Corinthian Gulf and was joined to the city proper by a corridor between two high defensive walls[2] that drew closer together toward town. Unable to breach those barriers to cut off the marine supply route and starve Corinth into submission, the besiegers found their efforts stalled going into 392. That's when Tyche smiled upon the Spartans and the city erupted into a vicious episode of civil strife. This was connected to a decision by the polis' leadership to join Argos in a single democratic state. Athens and Thebes had encouraged this unusual union as a way to dilute and thus preempt a popular movement within Corinth that included a majority among the wealthier classes, who were dismayed at the disproportionate damage they were suffering on the coalition's behalf. These men wanted to negotiate an immediate end to the war. Attacked and defeated by the ruling faction, many in this pro-peace movement lost their lives and even more fled into exile.[3] But a few remained within the city and retaliated by seeking to betray Corinth to Sparta. Approaching the local Spartan general, Praxitas, who was headquartered nearby at Sicyon, they arranged to let him in through a gate in the long corridor under cover of darkness so that he could capture Lechaion.

4. Other Devices

It seems that Praxitas had only a modest host on hand for the task. This likely consisted of just over 3,000 hoplites, with his own regiment (mora) of 1,000 Spartans,[4] perhaps 2,000 or so Sicyonians (two-thirds of that polis' probable manpower per the Spartan alliance norm), and 150 Corinthian exiles.[5] In support of these heavy-armed soldiers, he also had a few Spartan horsemen plus perhaps 500–1,000 peltasts. Praxitas faced his troops south toward Corinth once inside the gate and prepared to hold off any sally from that direction until reinforcements could arrive and help secure his position. Yet though he was able to anchor flankward against the substantial walls on either side, it was quite clear that he had far too few men to form a phalanx between those barriers at anything close to an adequate depth of file.[6]

Praxitas cannily met this challenge by having his men construct field-works ahead of their line of battle. These appear to have consisted of a shallow trench in front of a low barrier of some sort. The latter was most likely a heap of locally available debris plus dirt from the trenching that gave some cover to a portion of the lower bodies of men stationed behind it. These mounds would hopefully permit engagement of facing spearmen on a more equal basis, since, along with the ditch, it could inhibit othismos and thereby keep the enemy from fully exploiting what were very likely to be deeper files. This might theoretically let hoplites two-deep on each side fight with their spears while turning the opposition's following ranks into mere spectators. Praxitas stretched the works all the way between the long walls and placed his troops in back of them. His Spartans held the right wing, the Sicyonians stood across the middle, and the small band of Corinthian exiles abutted the eastern wall farthest left. He scattered his javelineers behind this thin but hardened line so that they could provide support by firing over the heads of their hoplite front-fighters.[7] Thus set, the Spartan commander and his men waited for friend or foe to show. As events unfolded, no one came either the rest of that night or the next day, and it was only after the second dawn that an opposing force finally emerged from Corinth.

The array that now bore down on the Spartans' static defense consisted of a trio of elements spread across a matching frontage. On the left and facing the Spartans themselves were some 2,000 hoplites from Corinth. To their right marched around 3,000 hoplites from the Corinthians' newly associated fellow citizens at Argos, who were targeting the Sicyonians in the center of the field. Finally, off the far right wing of the approaching phalanx, there came a contingent of mercenaries under Iphicrates of Athens. These last were possibly a mixed arms force, but much more likely entirely peltasts at least 800 strong.[8] They arrayed to confront the opposing left[9] where it extended beyond the flank of their hoplites likely standing four deep.[10]

The troops from the city charged up to the field-works to engage their foes in a vigorous spear-fight. All the hoplites behind the earthworks and the first two ranks of their attackers now traded steel in fierce overhand thrusts, most clanging against a bronzed aspis, but with an ever increasing few striking home into vulnerable arms, throats, and faces unavoidably exposed above a shield-rim. Amid the clamor of clashing metal, shouts of triumph, and cries of fear and pain, the field-works gave some aid to Praxitas' men. The ditch disturbed their enemy's footwork and the low, mounded wall made it hard for the deeper opposing files to effectively bring shield-pressure to bear. But these were really only supplemental benefits. It was still at best a matter of doratismos at even odds; a series of hoplite-on-hoplite bouts that were up for grabs to the better men there and then. And the Spartans reigned supreme in this. Those highly trained and deadly warriors from Lacedaemon out-dueled the Corinthians all across their front; killing, wounding, and, at last, sending them into panicked flight back toward the city as the Spartans threatened to come over their barrier and deal out damage more fearsome yet. And even as this developed on the western side of the battle, something similar was coming to pass at the opposite end of the field. Iphicrates and his peltasts on that front had been unable to hurt the well-protected hoplites standing in opposition. Tough enough targets for javelineers under any circumstance, the field-works on this occasion served to make the spearmen virtually invulnerable. Once those heavy infantrymen then made to come over their rampart for closer combat, the Athenian's mercenaries chose discretion over valor and fled.

But things had gone very differently in the middle of the field where the Argives had proven much more capable than their Sicyonian foes. The latter couldn't hold fast even with support from their barricade; and backing away to avoid the worst enemy spearthrusts coming over its top, they let the men from Argos have relatively free access to those earthen works. Pushing hard, it didn't take long to open a wide gap in the flimsy barrier that let them get among the Sicyonians and deal out sharp death without hindrance. The hoplites from Sicyon were beaten then in short order, tossing their sigma-emblazoned shields and running in mortal fear toward the sea with their Argive tormentors in all-out, hot pursuit. The Spartan cavalry commander, Pasimachus, who was on foot since his and his troopers' mounts were useless in the current setting, saw this disaster in the making and rushed to help. He and volunteers from among his men picked up some of the discarded aspides in an attempt to arrest the chase. Xenophon reports that "at this point Pasimachus uttered the remark, 'By the twin gods, you Argives, these sigmas will deceive you,' and came to close quarters with them."[11] That observation was to prove both ironic and tragically prophetic as his opponents, who might otherwise have feared even badly outnumbered Spartans, boldly cut Pasimachus and the others down in the mistaken belief that they were mere Sicyonians due to the symbol on their shields.

Praxitas had held his much more disciplined Spartan spearmen steady on the site of their initial success. Upon seeing the Argives leave in pursuit, he ordered his men over the low wall and across the ditch to line up in phalanx with left flank anchored on the field-works and facing east toward the sector that their defeated allies had abandoned. They waited thus for the equally victorious Argive troops to return from slaughtering Sicyonians all the way to the nearby shore. Grown aware at last that the Spartans were unbeaten and maneuvering in their rear, the Argives hurried back on the double through the barrier breach they had created only to have Praxitas immediately lead his reformed mora in a lateral sweep across the original battleground. This small phalanx, probably standing four deep along some 250m between the ditch to the north and a few flanking peltast supporters to the south, hit the poorly ordered men from Argos on their right, unshielded side as they streamed back onto the field. What followed was a thorough rout that sent the surprised and terrified Argives racing away, many with shields thrown in a desperate bid at escape.

The fleeing men reached the corridor's high barrier on the east and turned south along it toward Corinth and the prospect of refuge. That hope quickly evaporated, however, as they came up in that direction against the Corinthian exiles and the Sicyonian unit attached to their wing. It seems that these had doubled back in a reasonable semblance of order after realizing that the light infantry they were chasing was far too fleet of foot to ever be caught by heavily burdened hoplites like themselves. Again threatened by leveled spears, the distraught and now partially shieldless Argives reversed only to once more be opposed by the Spartans coming on in pursuit. The trapped men surged frantically against the nearby wall, seeking by any means to get away. Xenophon described the horrific scene that followed:

> Some of them climbed up the steps to the top of the wall, from which they threw themselves down and were killed, while others, being pushed together around the steps were struck down and killed there. Still others were trodden under foot by one another and suffocated. The Spartans were not at a loss whom to kill, for the god had given them at that time at least an opportunity that they never could have prayed for: a petrified multitude of their enemy had been handed over to them, stupefied and offering their unprotected side [the right], with not one of them intent on defending himself; indeed, they were all assisting in their own utter destruction. How could one believe this to be anything but a divine occurrence? At any rate, so many fell in such a short time that the inhabitants, who were used to seeing heaps of grain, wood, and stones, saw instead on that day heaps of corpses.[12]

Despite Xenophon's grim account of their seeming complete destruction, a majority of the Argives actually managed to survive. That interesting fact comes by way of Diodorus, who reported 1,000 dead for the losing side in this battle.[13] We can perhaps apportion 100 of those to the successfully fled Corinthians and peltasts at well less than 5 percent for each. If so, the Argive contingent lost only about 30 percent of its men on the day. The rest presumably managed to escape somehow, either over the eastern barrier wall or directly back to the city through and/or around the likely less densely ranked enemy force returning from its failed chase to their south. It was nonetheless a very costly defeat,[14] which the Spartans exploited to occupy Lechaion and then clear a course for their armies above Corinth by punching wide openings in the long walls.

The strategic value of this engagement in its time was significant; however, it is the presence of two major types of barricading devices that makes it of particularly note to the study at hand. We see here that high barrier walls meant to deny entry to the port corridor over the long term found convenient use as artificial terrain for anchoring flanks in the short term. And Praxitas also deployed field-works. These had the purpose of limiting and influencing enemy movement solely over the short haul; indeed, only on the day of combat. Yet though merely temporary in design and thus much more humble in scope than the barrier walls, these lesser works still had a major impact on determining the battle's ultimate victor.

Barrier Walls

Hoplites mostly interacted with "barrier walls" as obstacles to their primary role as shock combatants.[15] These are the sort of long-standing constructions that created the port corridor at Corinth (and more famously at Athens) and enclosed the perimeters of most ancient Greek cities of substance. Such structures were higher than a man could scale without a ladder and fitted with interior steps up to walkways from which missiles could be fired. They usually protected finite sites subject to siege like strategic fortresses and the aforementioned population centers.

Much more rarely, barrier walls out in the hinterland could bar a major pathway for invasion. By far the best example of these was the "Dema Wall" system that Athens built in the early 4th century as a hedge against intrusions from the Peloponnese.[16] It was a set of high stone barriers complete with fighting platforms, sally ports, and watchtowers that spanned a broad expanse between the slopes of Mount Parnes and the Aigaleos ridge. Characteristic to this fortification, and all true barrier walls, was that it required full-time garrisoning. If not occupied and actively defended, such expensive and time-consuming projects could merely be torn down as at Corinth. The Dema Wall called for service from some 5,000 men in this respect. These were for the most part mercenary peltasts to hold the parapets, but also included a modest contingent of citizen hoplites and even a small number of wealthy horsemen primed to charge forth if the opportunity presented itself.

Beyond their value in creating havens from which a phalanx could sally and the fact that hoplites sometimes engaged in assaults on them (rather awkwardly up ladders to judge by a few extant artworks), barrier walls would seem for the most part to fall outside the specific topic of hoplite warfare that is the subject here. However, Praxitas' use of them as flank anchors points out that there were a number of occasions when they played an important role in more traditional phalanx combats.

A notable aspect of the engagement at Corinth is that it took place inside the city's long walls. This meant that the barriers' platforms were abandoned and thus posed no active threat to the enemy force that nestled alongside. The same thing can be seen in two examples of anchoring on barrier walls at Syracuse. That Sicilian city was under siege from Athenian forces in 414 and an odd contest developed outside of its western/landward perimeter. This had the Athenians trying to build a siege-wall completely enclosing that side of town (carrying out a "circumvallation" in military terms). The locals responded by extending counter-walls out from their gates. These latter aimed at intersecting the projected path of the enemy's structures so as to cut them short and preserve an overland path into the city.

The foregoing structures at Syracuse took various forms from earthworks to stone walls, but were undoubtedly much less ambitious than the very large features around the city or the ones connecting the port at Corinth. Probably barely tall enough to preclude foes from striking over the top with a spear, they would not have had parapets for missilemen like those loftier designs; instead, they must have featured "firing-steps" built-up on their inside base from which defenders could engage attackers below. And an interesting aspect is that they could be either single or double-walled. The latter seems to have been unique to structures subject to attack during construction. By creating a slim corridor in this way, those working within its enclosure could defend on both sides in conjunction with a mobile barricade that shifted forward across the construction's open mouth as each day's work extended its flanking barriers. It was, of course, much easier and faster to throw up a solitary wall and the Syracusans chose in the end to go that route in their desperate haste to preempt circumvallation. The problem with that tack, however, was that this less complex sort of edifice could not be defended from within. It required posting a phalanx nearby to keep the Athenians from simply pulling it apart. And, inevitably, this eventually led to a battle that the Syracusans lost while anchoring on the inner side of their counter-barrier on the left and against some incomplete enemy works on the right.[17]

The second episode of a barrier wall acting as a flank guard at Syracuse came the following year very near the end of the siege campaign. This marked the last significant overland attack by the Athenians prior to their withdrawal from the city and saw the invaders under the brilliant but unconventional general Demosthenes[18] make a bold nighttime assault on Epipolae. The attackers climbed undetected onto that plateau and marched down to strike in turn at a trio of Syracusan camps located there northwest of the city proper. They did this by using the barrier wall that bordered the upland on its western margin as both an anchor for their right flank and a guide for marching alongside in the dark. This once more was a case of the inner side of the barrier serving to fix a flank, precluding participation by defenders on the walkways above had that even been possible at night. The attackers caught their foes by surprise and achieved outstanding initial success, very nearly gaining a total and crushing victory before falling prey to a great deal of confusion in the dark. The ensuing chaos let Syracuse's hoplites recover their poise and mount a fierce counterattack against men grown not only unsure of their location, but unable to even tell friend from foe. The result was an utter rout that took a tremendous toll on both Athenian lives and equipment.[19]

These examples clearly support the thesis that barrier walls tended toward being passive elements utilized along their inside edge on those occasions when we can firmly document their presence during a phalanx battle. The only strong candidate for an engagement being fought next to the outer side of a barrier serving to buttress a flank seems to have been in 403 at Athens' port of Piraeus. Sparta's king Pausanius led a large "surge" of troops there to put down a rebellion against the pro-Spartan oligarchy imposed on that polis after its surrender in the Peloponnesian War. Entangled in a running skirmish with light-armed rebels while scouting, he ended up in a large battle as both sides sent more and more of their men into action until it had grown into a full-blown contest of phalanxes. The Athenians were engaging a foe with much greater manpower[20] and fixed their flanks within a narrow passage in the direction of their base as a hedge against envelopment. This site most probably lay between Piraeus' barrier wall and the coastal Halae Marsh a modest distance below it.

Our extant account[21] gives precious little detail about the actual fighting at Halae Marsh/Piraeus and fails to mention any participation by missilemen behind the crest of the barrier wall there. In fact, though, it seems clear that the rebel light infantry had been largely (if not entirely) committed outside the barrier during the extensive earlier skirmishing. One would thus expect its presence on the rampart to have been minimal at the very best. Had there been any supporting fire on the north side of the Athenian line it perhaps added just a bit toward protecting that flank. And as things evolved, it seems to have been the opposite end of the insurgent array that finally gave way. Pausanius' hoplites, forming a "very deep phalanx," apparently forced their way through at a point inside the swamp-side flank, where: "Some of the Athenians [those on the far right] were pushed back into the mud ... while others gave way, and about 150 of them were killed." If this truly was an instance of anchoring against the outside of a friendly barrier, then it certainly didn't deliver victory. Still, since the wall-side did remain unturned, maybe that approach contributed a considerable benefit all the same, preventing an otherwise likely double envelopment and helping to keep the losers' body count relatively low.

One last example of anchoring a formation against preexisting artificial barriers needs to be noted here, though it does not involve a wall high above the surface as per all of the preceding, but rather manmade waterways cut into the ground. This came in 361 when Sparta's Agesilaos II was campaigning with a Greek mercenary legion in Egypt on behalf of local rebels attempting to break from Persia. Having escaped circumvallation by means of an unexpected sally,[22] he enticed a pursuing force into a corridor between two deep irrigation canals full of water. The wily old Spartan (in his 80's at the time) kept fleeing until his foes had chased well into that narrows. Suddenly, he faced his men about to form a phalanx, "drawing up the front of his battle equal to the space between the two ditches."[23] Agesilaos had 10,000 or so troops,[24] some 6,000–8,000 of them likely being hoplites. His spearmen could thus have arrayed up to twelve-deep across at least 500m. The opposition is said to have had more manpower, and had certainly acted as if that was the case by pursuing so aggressively. But through his use of the canals as lateral anchors, Agesilaos rendered their superior numbers of no value. He thus reduced the ensuing fight to a heavy infantry shock-action in which his savvy professional hoplites had great advantage, and their charge delivered a decisive victory.[25] Absolutely unique in the nature of its barrier devices, this engagement deserves note here if for no other reason than that it joins the battle at the Long Walls of Corinth as an outstanding example of a phalanx fixing both flanks against available manmade features.

Regardless of whether the wall at Piraeus played an active part in the hoplite battle there, we know that such barriers definitely did do so elsewhere. In those cases, their impact came not when they rested alongside, but rather when one rose up behind a phalanx. So placed, their firing platforms could provide excellent support for hometown spearmen facing heavy-armed opposition. Peltasts, slingers, and archers positioned atop such high walls could easily reach out farther than their opposition counterparts below and punish an approaching phalanx for a goodly interval before it was able to strike back with its own missiles. Local hoplites might thus stand fast close beneath their city's perimeter fortifications and wait to engage foes at least somewhat weakened during their advance. Perhaps rather more often, they got to watch completely unharmed as the enemy either failed to close (lest they come under a barrage) or withdrew without a fight (so as to avoid taking further damage). Indeed, fleeing troops sometimes sought refuge under cover of such highly placed missilemen, at least on those occasions when the pursuers had no missile troops of their own. Xenophon described one of the more comical episodes of this sort of desperate tack:

> ... the Argives who were at the gates shut out the horsemen of the Boeotians who wanted to enter, through fear that the Lacedaemonians would rush in at the gates along with them; so that the horsemen were compelled to cling, like bats, tight to the walls beneath the battlements. And if it had not chanced that the Cretans [Sparta's mercenary bowmen] were off on a plundering expedition to Nauplia at that time, many men and horses would have been shot down by their arrows."[26]

A likely instance of the prospect of going up against a barrier-backed phalanx giving a commander pause took place outside Athens in 410.[27] The Spartan king Agis, who had earlier established a base in Attica at Decelea, marched from that site "up to the very walls of Athens" to threaten the city. But the Athenians marshaled to meet him and formed up in a phalanx close to the Lyceum gymnasium, which sat just below the outer wall on the southeastern side of town. Agis, seeing his foe's formation arrayed near that lofty structure, seems to have had no enthusiasm for advancing within the reach of missiles that he would have no way to return. Swallowing his pride, that famously aggressive leader wisely elected to withdraw rather than commit to a fight under such unfavorable conditions. Another instance of a Spartan commander showing this sort of caution when facing a high barrier perhaps occurred a few days prior to the engagement at Halae Marsh discussed above. At that time, Pausanius made an initial probe of Piraeus' defenses and, though the presence of an Athenian phalanx is not certain, we are told that "he kept his forces well away from the wall, about the distance from which the battle cry is raised."[28] Wariness of the enemy's potential for inflicting missile fire from the heights above would seem the most obvious reason for this positioning.

Agis in fact did not get away without loss at Athens in 410, as he suffered rearguard casualties from skirmishers harassing his retreat. Nonetheless, his decision not to take harm from the barrier wall before ever getting within spear-reach of the opposing phalanx seems prudent in light of what happened in 381 at Olynthus.[29] Sparta's Teleutias, having heatedly chased some enemy peltasts very close to the wall of that city in the Chersonese, paused on the spot to array his hoplites. It's interesting to note that he had avoided coming under fire from the same wall just a year earlier,[30] when he waited for a phalanx beneath it to advance out to his more distant station. But this time, he had incautiously come well within range of the missilemen above, and his formation soon began to take serious hurt from their near point-blank attack.

Teleutias' spearmen rapidly fell into disarray, raising shields and shifting about in frantic attempts to block or dodge the lethal shower. Seeing this, the Olynthians' hoplites sallied into their confused and milling foes. Teleutias fell in the fight that followed and those on his wing eventually gave way. And with those Spartans, the army's best troops, on the run, it wasn't long before the already unsteady remainder of their phalanx took off as well. The pursuit that came next must have been fierce. Diodorus cited 1,200 killed among the losers, and it's possible that this only counted Spartan nationals, while Xenophon claimed losses included "*that part of the army that was especially valuable*"[31] in confirming a crippling defeat—one brought about by the Olynthians exploiting a rare and deadly combination of barrier wall and imprudent opponent.

Field-Works

Praxitas at the Long Walls of Corinth took advantage of those already standing eponymous structures to ward his flanks from foes with superior numbers that could form a much wider array. Yet having thus restricted his front, he also then had his troops reinforce that interval with a ditch and low wall. And this last move was vital to his ensuing victory. Though those devices failed in the middle of his line, they gave critical aid to both wings, helping them survive poor odds to carry the battle in the end. Designed to bolster the leading ranks or extend the width of a phalanx, field-works functioned not only to simply stiffen the line, but also to influence the opposition toward areas of strength and away from weak points. They differed from high barriers in important ways: (1) they usually aimed at affecting an engagement immediately to hand rather than providing a long-term defense; (2) they often were used in rural locations along with restricting topography; (3) they were relatively less substantial, as befitted features destined to be fairly quickly abandoned for which only modest hours of labor could be devoted/justified; and (4) they displayed a much wider variation in components and basic designs than was the case with barrier walls.

The first instance in our sources of what appears to be hoplites strengthening their position by means of a field-work involved felled trees. This was in 510, when Sparta's Cleomenes led an expedition into Attica in alliance with local rebels to oust the Peisistratid dictatorship then ruling Athens. An earlier, amphibious attempt to do this had met defeat by the tyranny's Thessalian cavalry over cleared ground on the plain of Phaleron, but Cleomenes marched overland and cut down trees to impede and best those same horsemen.[32] We lack details; however, it is likely that this records the crafty Spartan's use of a wooden barricade or "abatis" to secure and/or lengthen at least one wing of his phalanx. Perhaps most significant for the course of history, this action might very well have informed the tactics used by Cleomenes' Athenian allies two decades later in their fabled victory over Persian invaders at Marathon.

Most reconstructions of Marathon have placed the initial contact in that engagement out on the open plain there; nonetheless, our sole ancient description of the battle site actually conflicts with that setting. This comes by way of Nepos:

> ... the [Greek] army was drawn up at the foot of the mountain in a part of the plain that was not wholly open ... the purpose was to protect themselves by the high mountains and at the same time prevent the enemy's cavalry, hampered by the "tree-hauling" [arborum tractu] from surrounding them with superior numbers. Although Datis [the Persian commander] saw that the position was not favorable to his men, yet he was eager to engage ... and began the battle.[33]

There have been various proposals as to just where the Athenian position might have been when the action opened at Marathon. Yet regardless of the exact spot, it would appear to have occupied a narrows of some sort if Nepos is to be credited at all. And that would have been the perfect place to employ the kind of wooden field-work (abatis or otherwise) with which the Athenian democrats defending there would have already been quite familiar from their service alongside Cleomenes in 510. This somewhat revisionist version of Marathon (actually dating from at least the early 20th century[34]) has certainly seen a good deal of passionate debate over the years; still, it at a minimum offers the strong possibility of another impromptu wooden field-work having aided hoplites under serious threat from opposing horsemen. And if true, it played a significant role in what was perhaps the most famous phalanx battle of them all!

The rather broad variability of field-works clearly shows itself in another engagement from the early 5th century.[35] This saw Phocian hoplites cover over and thus hide amphorae within a shallow trench at some distance in front of their phalanx,[36] which stood across an entry pass into Phocis' eastern marches at Hyampolis. Their opponents from Thessaly there sent their cavalry charging to get within javelin range of this stationary line of spearmen only to have hooves break through the thin camouflage, smash the delicate pots beneath, and send riders crashing down aboard mounts with broken legs. This was obviously a very unique example of a trench related field-work; all the same, ditches likely contributed elsewhere to hoplite actions, doing so in tandem with backing walls in a variety of restricted venues.

The trench and mound-wall combination seems very much a natural one in instances of earthen field-works, since the digging of one could provide building material for the other. A possible example of this kind of construction comes from the area around Thebes during the Boeotian War. At the same time that the Dema Wall was going up in early 378, the Thebans too built a defense system, which was some 20km long and enclosed the most valuable land near their city.[37] Unlike the Athenian stone structures, this work comprised a series of ditches and earthen mounds reinforced in lengthy stretches with wooden elements of some sort. Though we don't have a lot of detail on this configuration, the more substantial intervals were probably true barriers similar in concept to a counter-wall devised with ditch and wooden palisade at Syracuse in 414 (except that was constructed under threat and thus double-walled).[38] However, it appears that shorter sections of the arrangements at Thebes were more modest and required a substantial muster of troops if they were to be properly defended. This suggests something much more in the nature of field-works, perhaps not all that different from those thrown up by Praxitas at Corinth. At any rate, when standing before a hoplite array, these proved adequate. Indeed, though they would ultimately be compromised, that was not due to any inherent flaw in their design. It seems that the Spartans simply arose early one morning and crossed over before the Thebans had time to finish breakfast and put their phalanx into the field![39]

The best-known phalanx battle in which trench and mound field-works might have made an appearance was in Asia Minor at Issus in 333. The Persian king Darius III's troops had formed up there with a dry streambed between themselves and the army of Macedonia's Alexander III ("the Great"). Darius bolstered his position by building a modest barrier of some kind in back of the gentlest and most easily crossable portions of the stream's bank.[40] The exact nature of this construction is unclear, but it appears that during the ensuing battle it did not keep the forward ranks of hoplites in the Persian phalanx[41] from engaging in shock combat with hoplites (hypaspists) and pikemen serving Alexander. This suggests that it was most likely a modest ditch and low earthen wall combination very similar to the one of Praxitas in 392. In any event, it failed to secure success for its users, being no more effective against the Macedonians than the Sicyonians' works had been against their Argive foes at Corinth.[42]

Where stones of appropriate size were readily available, defenders could incorporate them into sturdy walls without the need to dig a trench. This seems to have been the field-work standard in such boulder strewn locales as at the foot of mountain slopes and alongside rocky riverbeds or in urban settings with plenty of stony building materials ready to hand. Our best documented example of this type of feature in action took place during the Athenian retreat from Syracuse in 413.[43] Seeking to gain the highlands to their north and safe passage thereupon out of danger from pursuit, the Athenians tried to force their way up a canyon leading to a prominent cliff face known as the Acraean Bald Rock. However, the Syracusans had anticipated this move and "fortified the pass in front" of that topographic feature. They then deployed a phalanx behind their field-work that was "drawn up many shields deep." This "fortification" was undoubtedly a wall compiled from local rock talus and low enough to permit fighting with spears over its top. Meeting defeat from the efforts of the thus well-warded Syracusan hoplites and their missilemen on the heights behind, the Athenians withdrew to regroup. That's when they caught some of the enemy starting a new field-work near the mouth of the canyon, intending to seal them front and back within a narrow death trap. Chasing that work party away, the Athenians quickly abandoned their attack and retreated back onto the plain.

The men from Athens would fare better against another Syracusan field-work just two days later. Having escaped close pursuit by means of a stealthy night march, they came up against a small body of the enemy blocking further advance at a crossing on the Cacyparis River.[44] This contingent had built a wall (no doubt of stream boulders and much like the barricade at the Acraean Bald Rock) and strengthened it with a "palisade" of some sort (possibly stakes or other wooden impediments). This time, though, the Athenian hoplites were able to force their way past the blockage. That probably reflects a relative paucity of defenders on hand, which allowed the attacking spearmen to strike much more heavily above the wall. Driving back their thinly spread opponents, the Athenians were therefore free to attend directly to the field-work, pushing through it to put the then exposed defenders to rout.

The foregoing kinds of stone works sited in rural locales were actually not much different from those erected in urban settings save for the construction materials. We have an excellent example of one of these that sat across the narrow isthmus leading from the mainland portion of Syracuse onto the small island of Ortygia. This came into use in 357 during a civil war that saw the citizenry under its leader Dion seek to oust long-time dictator Dionysius II.[45] Shutting up the tyrant's mercenaries on the island, the rebels "raised a wall to invest the castle [island fortifications]." This counter-feature appears to have been a low, fighting-structure much like the ones discussed above in the Athenian retreat and at Corinth. And in this setting, it must have consisted of shaped stones repurposed from nearby buildings or incomplete constructions in the city. Dionysius apparently saw an opportunity in the relatively modest nature of this device and "sent the garrison of mercenaries out to make sudden sally against Dion's works." This attack caught the rebels by surprise and hit them "so furiously that they were not able to maintain their post," thus allowing the tyrant's men to break through the cross-wall and engage in an intense melee on its far side. Dion would eventually succeed in rallying enough manpower to repulse the mercenaries in a long and exhausting fight. It seems that the rebels were then able to inflict significant casualties on their foes as the failed field-work now played a different role, hindering the mercenaries from making a rapid escape back onto Ortygia.

Before leaving the subject of field-works, it's worthwhile to explore how such a seemingly valuable defensive device and its underlying concept might have gone unused in one of ancient Greece's most revered battles. This was the "Phocian Wall" at Thermopylae. That had apparently been constructed earlier in the 5th century in connection with the same Thessalian conflict in which the Phocians employed the amphorae-filled trench discussed above. Said to have incorporated a gate,[46] this might have been a true barrier wall. However, the distance from Phocis and seeming requirement of full-time garrisoning for such a feature suggests a mere field-work as more likely—though perhaps an especially robust one meant to support a seasonal campaign rather than just a single engagement.

The Phocian structure was in ruins when Leonidas and his army arrived to block the Middle Gate at Thermopylae against Xerxes' huge Persian invasion force in 480. And hurriedly fabricated, Leonidas' rebuilt version of the Phocians' wall seems to have been no more than a low field-work regardless of what its original nature might have been. It would thus have had little value against foes like the Persians, who relied heavily upon missile fire rather than the sort of spear-dueling and othismos that a low wall was designed to protect against. This makes it probable that the Spartan king ordered its restoration more as a way to keep his troops occupied in advance of the pending enemy attack than as a serious defensive measure. And, indeed, that interpretation along with the wall's likely limitations make the best sense out of Leonidas' insistence over the ensuing three days of combat that his phalanx engage well forward of this work in a more open part of the pass. There, his men could shelter from arrows in the lee of the enemy formation as well as apply othismos, which the field-work would have denied.

But perhaps more intriguing in the case of field-works at Thermopylae is the lack of them on the Anopaia path along which the Persian Immortals would eventually flank and defeat Leonidas' position in the coastal pass below. The same Phocians who had built the barrier at the Middle Gate apparently on this occasion left an even narrower passage completely unfortified. Possibly this was because they saw such additional effort as unnecessary, given that they should have had more than enough men to block the way with shields alone. Or maybe they too thought a low field-work would be more of a hindrance than aid to their phalanx fighting style when engaging an enemy prone more to the bow than spear. Whatever the reason, it's certainly one of the interesting "what ifs" of the ancient world to contemplate the effect that a good field-work on that mountain track might have had on subsequent history.

Artillery

Artillery in the form of stone and bolt throwing catapults came into use in the Greek world in the early 5th century. These were first devised in southern Italy[47] and mostly served both besieger and besieged during investment operations. Still, the potential for such devices to alter battlefield fundamentals was recognized early on, most notably by the Spartan king Archidamus (son of Agesilaos). Seeing a catapult from Sicily in action for the first time, he exclaimed "Great heavens! Man's valor is no more!"[48] This would turn out to be a rather severe over-reaction in light of those devices subsequently seeing only extremely limited use on battlefields. There is actually but a single outstanding instance of them playing a critical role in an open phalanx engagement. This was in 354 in Thessaly, where Phocis' warlord Onomarchos set up an ambush of Philip II of Macedonia.[49] Drawing the Macedonians into a box canyon, the Phocian punished their formation with fire from catapults previously sited on the enclosing hillsides. This so damaged and disrupted the targeted array that it utterly collapsed when then charged by the phalanx of Onomarchos. Philip's army was so badly hurt and shaken by this defeat that it nearly went into revolt, forcing him to withdraw for the rest of the campaign season.

The catapults involved here were non-torsion cross-bows ("belly-bows") some 9m in length and capable of hurling both bolts and rocks, with the latter weighing up to 2.3kg.[50] It's probable that Onomarchos had fabricated these by copying one or more prototypes looted from dedications made at Delphi.[51] Other indications that these sorts of devices found application in the open field come from the expeditions of Philip's son Alexander, who used them in at least two actions to cover his forces while crossing rivers against opposition.[52] The catapults are described as "siege-engines" in both cases. This strongly implies that their employment outside of an investment must have been exceptional. Yet it's likely that other irregular use of stone and bolt throwing devices took place on occasion since we know of one other certain attempt to do so. That was in 207, when the Spartan tyrant Machanidas planned on opening an engagement by disrupting the opposition with fire from siege machines placed ahead of his troops.[53] This stratagem came to naught due to the Spartan's foes charging immediately upon perceiving their danger and thus preempting his barrage. All the same, it demonstrates that creative commanders beyond Onomarchos and Alexander at least contemplated the use of field artillery.

Since applying artillery outside of siege campaigns was clearly unusual, this makes it much more of a curiosity than a fundamental factor in any study of hoplites at war. Yet before leaving the topic of "other devices" that played roles in phalanx battles, it's important to note that this was definitely not the case with other types of constructions falling into that category. Not only do we have multiple citations for a number of these, but even those reports should not be considered truly representative of how often they came into play in ancient combats. Indeed, more than many other aspects of phalanx fighting, they seem likely to have been particularly shorted by our available sources. This was perhaps due in part to the ancient Greeks seeing them as unmanly in that they provided artificial substitutes for traditional battlefield virtues. The caprices of survival are surely a factor as well, rendering relevant works either fragmentary or utterly lost. And we also need to consider that ancient authors undoubtedly assumed their contemporary readers were already aware of such familiar elements. This must have affected many descriptions of sallies from behind barrier walls that consist of no more than a handful of words. How often were those actions accompanied by supporting missile fire from the backing ramparts? That sort of wall-based aid was probably commonplace, something most ancient readers would have known, but about which we today can only speculate.

The incomplete status of our extant sources has had just as great an impact on underreporting the use of field-works. This is profoundly illustrated by those all too rare instances where we have access to more than one account. Thus, Herodotus does not report on field-works in his description of either Cleomenes' campaign in Attica or the battle of Marathon, and it is only via Frontinus and Nepos (both perhaps drawing on the much earlier Ephoros) that we learn of those possibilities. Likewise with regard to the field barrier at Issus, Curtius[54] says nothing of this; therefore, it is solely from the later Arrian that we know of its presence. Even the field-works at the Long Walls of Corinth, where we opened the present inquiry, play no role in Diodorus' accounting of that battle, making it most fortunate we have Xenophon's more complete description including this detail. If Herodotus, Curtius, and Diodorus alone had come down to the present, then we would be completely ignorant of the realities and possibilities for the use of field-works in all of the foregoing engagements. One can only wonder how many other examples of such devices in operation are now lost to us due to the vagaries of possessing but a single source or the lack of any surviving record whatsoever.

Part II. The Men

5

Culture

Hoplite warfare developed through the early 5th century in the context of an overwhelmingly agricultural society. It thus largely featured part-time militias resolving conflicts over cultivatable border acreage. Spearmen also played leading parts in factional violence within poleis, though that was less common. In both cases, the cultural milieu of hoplite battle was that of amateur warriors, most of them farmers. Not that there weren't variants among militiamen. Most notably, Sparta developed a strict caste system with elite spear-fighters at its top; and a few other states maintained smaller bodies of select hoplites (epilektoi) at public expense. Yet, these were all essentially still citizen forces intimately steeped in militia culture. Later in the 5th and into the mid-4th century, political/economic interests and related conflicts escalated beyond those between individual states or modest alliances to involve extensive coalitions. This period saw the previously rare hiring of spearmen from outside a polis rise in frequency, with a few phalanxes even becoming dominantly mercenary. The roles of citizen soldier and paid fighter were blurring and finally merged when the Macedonians raised a national host cored by locals serving full-time for pay; a practice that would spread along with their imperial conquests. The cultural climate in which most hoplites labored now featured large professional armies aligned with mostly royal paymasters. Conscripted spearmen remained vital only to poorer states unable to hire a wholly paid force. It was a far cry from the days when militia phalanxes were at their height and single poleis like Argos and Sparta had ruled the battlefields of Greece.

Sepeia (494): Borders and Blood

Southwestern Greece hosted powerful city-states that were among the leaders in the development of hoplite warfare. Combative peoples speaking the Doric dialect of Greek (thus known as Dorians) dominated many of these poleis, having migrated from the north sometime c.900 or before.[1] Prominent among the Dorian centers was Argos, which sat low on the Argive Plain in the northeastern Peloponnese. The origin of the Grecian phalanx is murky to say the least; however, it most likely came in the wake of the economic rise of yeomen farmers, whose mass formations of foot let them replace aristocratic horsemen as the backbone of their states' militias.[2] Argos seems to have been the epicenter for this evolution in combat as it was there that the hoplite's signature shield so crucial to the phalanx proper might have been finalized.[3] This device greatly enhanced the effectiveness of close-order infantry and gave rise to the first true phalanx, which might well have been an adaptation by the Argives to optimize fighting on the broad plain hosting their city. And whether inventors or early adopters that perfected a "Doric" formation that was taking shape more haphazardly among their ethnic kin, the Argives plied it well in gaining regional sway by the early 7th century.

But even if the Argives had indeed gotten off to a faster start in the deadly art of phalanx fighting, Corinth and Sparta were at worst not far behind[4]; and both contested Argos for valuable border acreage. Corinth disputed Argive control over the district of Cleonai along its southern frontier and Sparta sought to wrest away the rich farmland of Thyreatis. Located between Sparta and Argos mid-way down the west side of the Argolic Gulf, the latter was to inspire a struggle lasting better than two centuries. An initial armed clash in this contest took place c.719[5] and appears to have marked a failed Spartan bid to oust the Argives from the area. Argos would then go on to cement its dominance over Thyreatis some half century later with a decisive victory over Sparta at Hysiae (c.669).[6] But the Spartans came back in the spring of 545, seizing Thyreatis and defeating the Argive army in a hard-fought action when it responded.[7] This long and violent history served as the backdrop for a climactic and particularly brutal engagement that took place in 494.

Argos had rebounded strongly by the end of the 6th century, defeating Corinth c.500 in what was likely an attempt by that polis to seize Cleonai.[8] This highlighted growing Argive capability that made it ever more apparent to the Spartans that their ascendency was in jeopardy; and they eventually moved to take preemptive action. One of Sparta's kings, Cleomenes I, led out his national host and, either dissuaded by an ill omen or (perhaps more likely) finding the Argives well positioned overland, he moved up the Argolic Gulf from Thyreatis by ship to land just south of Argos near Nauplia in the territory of Tiryns. The Argives marched to intercept and caught Cleomenes near the village of Sepeia, where they camped "leaving very little space between the two armies"[9] and set up to offer battle. Cleomenes, however, was not of a mind to accept. The reason for this is not recorded; however, Sparta had much more to lose than Argos, including not only outlying properties like Thyreatis, but supremacy in the Peloponnese as well. It is therefore probable that the king was unsure of his chances for success and wanted to secure some kind of advantage before committing to a battle in which the consequences of failure would be quite severe.[10] At this point, we have two different takes on the lead-up to a final clash of arms.

Herodotus recorded the best-known account of Sepeia.[11] This claims that Cleomenes played a waiting game for several days, perhaps deploying as if to fight on occasion, but refusing to make a final advance into combat. The wily king looked for an opening and noted that his foe mimicked all of the Spartans' moves: deploying when they did, retreating in parallel, and taking food at the same time. Knowing that an army might be caught fatally unaware around mealtime,[12] he issued the usual horn signal for breakfast. But instead of taking their own meal, Cleomenes had his men charge the Argive encampment, catching the enemy by surprise and slaughtering them in great numbers without effective resistance.

The problem with this version of events is that under the attendant circumstances it is highly improbable that the battle-savvy Argives would have failed to force Cleomenes into a conventional action in their favor. They could have done this by simply advancing on his position, which sat so close upon their own. It's of course possible that they preferred standing in place to receive an attack; that was a sound means of reducing the risk of envelopment from the Spartans' favored maneuver of cyclosis.[13] But such an argument seems rather weak. Plutarch's description[14] of the trickery preceding the battle actually appears to offer a more reasoned alternative, though it does serve up an unlikelihood of its own. His variant has the Spartan monarch make a seven-day truce with the Argives, presumably for the purpose of discussing a settlement to avoid unnecessary bloodshed. This is something quite possible in that the Spartans were to prove willing to avoid combat in this manner on several later occasions when their phalanx was on the verge of battle.[15] The Spartan hoplites at Sepeia then launched a nighttime sneak attack after only two days had passed, using the pretext that the cease fire agreement had specified "days" and not "nights." The only questionable element in this tale is that the strike came after sundown, when poor visibility is unlikely to have allowed for so highly effective a result as is universally reported. A more probable scenario combines both foregoing traditions; this suggests that a truce did indeed keep the Argives off the offensive, but that Cleomenes then attacked during a daytime meal to gain an easy triumph over an unsuspecting and almost defenseless opponent.

Regardless of exactly how the Spartans set up their victory at Sepeia, it was followed by notable atrocities. Cleomenes and his spearmen pursued and trapped a number of Argive hoplites within a sacred grove nearby. They then began calling these men out by their names (supplied by local turncoats), saying that they had been ransomed as per a common procedure of the day that set a standard fee for doing so. But each man that emerged was swiftly murdered. After fifty or so had lost their lives in this way, the remaining fugitives discovered what was going on and refused to move. Cleomenes then impiously had his helots set the grove on fire and burnt those still within to death.

Tomlinson has criticized Cleomenes' methods at Sepeia as "un–Greek acts of treachery and sacrilege."[16] And so they would appear to be in light of the usual standards openly espoused within the militia society of his time. It is abundantly clear that Cleomenes was indeed a cunning and most ruthless individual; something that eventually led to his being held in low esteem by Spartans and foreigners alike. Yet battlefield realities were often much darker than public cultural expressions ever dared to portray lest they tar the community's image and damage the pride/morale of its military going forward. Moreover, the things he did were in many ways harbingers of other surprise attacks and atrocities to come.[17] These grew increasingly common in the Grecian world as its wars became wider in scope with more diverse objectives.

Inter-Poleis and Intra-Polis Wars

The fight over Thyreatis was part of a border dispute of exceptional scope and duration; however, such bouts concerning frontier territory on a more modest scale sat at the center of most combats between poleis amid the opening three centuries or so of hoplite warfare. This can be seen in what was the very first clash between hoplite armies[18] recorded in the literature, which occurred during the war fought by Chalcis and Eretria for possession of the Lelantine Plain on Euboa c.710. Thucydides called that conflict somewhat unusual in having participation by a few allies at a time when "what fighting there was consisted merely of local warfare between rival neighbors" that he typified as "the usual border contests."[19] And it was those kinds of disputes between lone states (aided at most by an ally or two) that served as the leading "casus belli" for Greek armed conflicts into the mid–5th century.[20]

There were, of course, other factors inspiring city-states to declare war; yet these seem most often to have been only supplementary to land issues. After reviewing the literature on the causes and aims of Grecian warfare, Hans van Wees concluded that most Greek authors accepted the idea of three primary motivations for war: self-defense, honor, and profit.[21] However, one can logically argue that the first of those was subordinate to the others in being no more than a reaction to one of them being directed against the defender. And van Wees noted that "honor often conveniently coincided with profit"; while even in the case of material gain, "booty, ransom, extortion and enslavement were a useful means of meeting the cost of warfare rather than a primary goal of war." His observation then that "wherever there were boundaries between states, land was a cause and goal of war" forms an important bottom line. Victor Davis Hanson similarly studied the literature to find that "a variety of sources state explicitly that Greek warfare arose over border disputes." He saw this as fundamental within a hoplite system requiring that wars "be fought over local, tangible issues, most often borderlands under dispute, in places where land was of the utmost material and spiritual concern to the local farmers and the agrarian community at large."[22]

Excellent farmland as on the Lelantine Plain and at Thyreatis obviously offered a rich prize to its winner. Yet "eschatia" was more often the object of these border clashes; a term describing the marginal nature of both the ground's locale and its quality. Usually mountainous,[23] eschatiai lay on the fringes of a polis' developed expanse, where they served as outlets for expansionist ambitions that could stem from as simple a cause as population growth. Ancient Greek farms were quite small in area, generally less than 9ha (about 22ac).[24] They therefore had little potential for division among more than one heir; while their modest area combined with the region's limited rainfall and often rocky soil to make it hard to accommodate any significant increase in the number of mouths to feed. Tremendous social and economic pressures would thus come to bear in otherwise prosperous times that saw the populace expand. This pressed poleis to find more cropland; acreage that could accommodate second sons and others facing the prospect of otherwise living at a level of bare subsistence and grown desperate to provide better circumstances for self and family. A few states exported their excess masses into distant colonies; however, most tried to exploit eschatiai. This set them to developing their own marginal land and making attempts upon contentious acreage along their borders that at times lay within the traditional domain of a neighboring polis.

Border clashes could spawn multi-generational struggles for control of highly valued areas like Thyreatis, but were usually resolved in the short term by means of a single phalanx engagement. These were fought during brief summer campaigns and reflected a highly practical militia culture in tune with the priorities of its mostly farmer hoplites.[25] Such actions produced limited casualties, with few dying before one side or the other broke and with protocols calling for pursuit to cease at the edge of the plain of battle. And damage to property was likewise small—often nil—being confined at worst to a bit of ravaging by the initiating party to goad their foes into action. It is important above all to understand that these were not acts of invasion and conquest. As remarked upon by van Wees, "it was rare for a city to go beyond occupying disputed border land and seize the enemy's entire territory."[26] The object of these battles was almost always the gaining of mutually recognized rights over the specific and modest acreage at hand. And this was to be pursued within combat parameters that would limit immediate costs as well as long-term disruption for winner and loser alike in recognition that those roles might well be reversed the next time around.

Bouts of intra-polis violence were distinct from the foregoing border clashes. These were political in that they were insurgencies seeking to oust a ruling power; still, they were usually economic struggles as well. Such upheavals largely featured disparities among a polis' wealth-classes at their hearts. We thus time and again see a small aristocratic faction (royal/tyrannical or otherwise oligarchic) set against a larger and less affluent portion of the populace. The latter invariably included those whose intermediate income qualified them to be hoplites. And a majority of lower class residents often joined the spearmen's fight, apparently judging it more beneficial to their own interests. It was the hoplites (the best-armed within their faction) that then resolved the conflict. They most often did this by battling similarly equipped men hired by the opposition and/or lent to it by sympathetic allies.

The first of these insurgent clashes to match armies with phalanxes seems to have been at Pallene in 546. This saw the exiled Athenian tyrant Peisistratos return to Attica and defeat his democratic enemies by catching them unready for a fight after their midday meal.[27] The tyrant did this with an army that included his own Athenian supporters and hired troops as well as both volunteers from the island of Naxos and a contingent from Argos. Herodotus claimed that the Argives were also paid fighters; however, Tomlinson has reasonably argued that, rather than being true mercenaries, these were militiamen sent "on the understanding that their expenses would be met from Peisistratos' private fortune."[28] Regardless, it's ironic that some of the Argive hoplites so successful through trickery at Pallene must have lived to see their descendants fall for much the same ploy at Sepeia half a century later.

The sneak attack at Pallene is unlikely to have produced anything approaching a proper phalanx contest; however, such did take place in connection with other uprisings. This was the case on Sicily at Syracuse. That Corinthian colony saw no less than three internal hoplite engagements during the 5th century, and all pitted popular factions led by the polis' militia spearmen against hoplites and other mercenaries that were either serving under or had past attachments to the city's dictators.[29] And Syracuse was by no means unusual; indeed, it was very much the norm for intra-polis unrest to see hoplites come to grips. Some good examples of this include: a pair of clashes within Sparta's realm against Messenian rebels (465 and 463); hoplites battling during a civil war on Corcyra (427); a major engagement resolving an insurgency in western Macedonia (423); two pitched battles at Athens during its Spartan occupation (403); and a grand action that concluded Cyrene's civil war in North Africa (400).

It is notable that ancient Greek revolts tended to feature pitched battles rather than the kind of terror and guerrilla campaigns that so often accompany modern insurgencies. This is attributable to dominant aspects of hoplite culture as well as weapon technology and geography.[30] The development of the phalanx and its great utility in the border wars between city-states deeply colored their martial culture, which focused almost exclusively on maintaining units of close-ordered spearmen.[31] This combined with the practical benefits of phalanx combat—which was typically brief and took but a small toll in lives and property—to make pitched battle the preferred means of resolving all disputes, even internal ones. There was no arms race; weapons were more or less the same on both sides in intra-polis clashes. Hoplite gear represented the premier military technology of the day and was normally available to all involved.[32] There was thus no need for insurgents to resort to hit and run tactics in facing foes with superior weaponry. Finally, poleis were quite modest in areal extent. This made them poorly suited to host guerilla forces needing lots of space for maneuver and concealment, or to pursue lengthy campaigns of attrition. It is no wonder then that intra-polis as well as inter-poleis wars were usually decided in set battles between hoplites.

Citizen Militias and Epilektoi

The hoplites that cored Greek militias came from those with sufficient assets to afford the equipment required for phalanx combat. Authorities measured this set amount against the size/output of their land for the farmer majority and the value of other property/income for the minority in urban trades. These spearmen had middling wealth between that of the poorer folk working very small plots or engaged in low paying, non-farm professions and those sufficiently well-off to serve in the cavalry[33] as well as the super-rich that could supply a warship and its crew to their polis. However, hoplites were definitely not "middle-class" as that term is generally understood today; they were, in fact, among a polis' wealthier residents.

Estimates indicate that out of 60,000–70,000 free adult males in the poleis of 5th century Boeotia only 12,000 (16–20 percent) met hoplite qualifications.[34] We can also draw from Thucydides' tally of the forces available to Athens at the outbreak of the Peloponnesian War in 431.[35] This suggests that there were 29,000 heavy spearmen if we include age-reserves and resident aliens (metics). Exempting a likely 3,750 metics,[36] that would represent about 15 percent of some 172,000 citizens (those whose parents were both Athenians),[37] with all hoplites making up only 8 percent or so from an entire male population of around 315,500.[38] It's thus clear that the men standing in the ranks of Greece's militia phalanxes must have been relatively affluent.

A city-state going to war called up its militia from names kept on a public roster (*catalogos*). These draftees filled as many tribal/geographic organizational units as would likely be needed for the task at hand.[39] Those mustering for duty gathered at a pre-designated location (*syllogon*), bringing along their own gear (*panoplia*), food for several days in the field (cheese, olives, and onions were common staples), and a personal attendant (*hyperetes*). The latter was to help the spearman carry his equipment (especially the heavy aspis) and generally render aid on the march and in camp. Those among them thought to be most reliable (probably from a freeman minority) were also to serve as skirmishers (*psiloi*) when it came time to fight. So prepared, the hoplites formed up in column behind their equally amateur generals (*strategoi*) and marched toward the field of battle. Greek citizens did this as a civic obligation without pay for over a quarter of a millennium, and then for but very small compensation from the mid–5th century on.

This militia system had some clear strengths. Materially, it put no significant financial burden on the state; since, in purest form, conscripts provided their own arms, provisions, and even manual support. And the format of mutual service and comradeship among fellow citizens at work and hazard was of great cultural value, enhancing their sense of civic pride and unity. Yet, the amateur nature of the entire enterprise from lowest private soldier all the way up to commanding general was an obvious weakness; at least, whenever facing savvy opponents such as the Spartans with their full-time warrior elites. Any answer to this problem that called for a polis to abandon its own ways and adopt something like the radical lifestyle in Sparta was out of the question, and no other Greek state would ever go that route; however, some did seek a compromise solution. This was the epilektoi—modest numbers of spearmen maintained and highly trained at public expense to supplement the regular militia.

The concept of organizational units with picked fighters seems to have had a long history in Greece. The names of select hoplite contingents in 5th century Sparta (the "hippeus" or horsemen) and Thebes (the "charioteers and footmen") reflect this, referencing a time when mounted aristocrats were a city-state's most elite warriors. Heavy spearmen had fully usurped that role in most of the Greek world by the 6th century, and it was they who dominated special force teams of the classical era.[40] These units of epilektoi included the Argive One Thousand, the Six Hundred at Syracuse, Thebes' 300-man Sacred Band, the Arcadian Eparitoi, and two contingents at Elis (the Three Hundred and Four Hundred).[41] Such men took full advantage of state financing to drill to a level that could at its best let them match Sparta's finest.[42] This prepared them to operate either on their own or in stiffening the otherwise amateur ranks of their polis' phalanx. Epilektoi in the latter role mostly served as promachoi (front-fighters). These stood in the forward lines and had both the greatest exposure to danger and responsibility for victory. But though enjoying public funding, epilektoi remained very much citizen soldiers. They were thus little if any different in culture from the militiamen who fought alongside them; having great devotion to their native polis and being fully indoctrinated in all of its martial values.

Coalition Wars and Mercenaries

Temporary cooperation of a few friendly poleis sometimes present in the early phalanx era's border wars began to give way to broader, more stable arrangements going into the 5th century. This trend got its start with the network of mutual defense treaties that Sparta developed in the late 6th century, creating what's known today as the Peloponnesian League. And then in 480, there came the grand alliance of a great many Greek states that succeeded in fending off Xerxes' invasion. This banding of poleis was fragile and short-lived; however, it gave rise to a long-lasting descendent in the Delian League. The Athenians initially led this confederation of largely outlying maritime states as a ward against further Persian aggression; but they set about forging an empire as that threat faded and eventually reduced what had been allied equals to a status much more like that of vassals.[43] This was highly profitable. Athens made wanton use of monies flowing from direct tribute,[44] League-related acquisition of gold and silver mines in Thrace,[45] and the domination of trade throughout the Aegean basin in financing projects like the Parthenon and other impressive works that put its soaring prosperity and prestige on display for all to admire.

Even in its early stages, Athens' efforts to gain control over more and more markets for its lucrative endeavors began to reach into the Greek mainland; and this was a key element sparking the so-called First Peloponnesian War in 461. Larger and more complex considerations were starting to supplant borderlands as the root cause of conflict. Not least of these were a fierce trading rivalry between Athens and Corinth, a key Spartan ally,[46] and an obsession with homeland security among the Spartans themselves. The latter made them highly sensitive, if not actually paranoid, about the idea that Athenian-style democracy might spread into the Peloponnese; where Sparta sought "to secure their [the allies'] subservience ... by establishing oligarchies among them."[47] Still, the first Peloponnesian War was not really a single bout between the wider Spartan and Athenian spheres of influence. It consisted instead of a punctuated interval of only loosely related conflicts; with land issues, though no longer as important overall, continuing to play a major role here and there.[48] It was thus only with the start of the "Great" Peloponnesian War in 431 that the Greek world's two grand coalitions finally came to blows all at once and in earnest.

Like epilektoi, mercenaries in the form of hired hoplites were by classical times an old story among the Greeks. There is a tale of hoplites ("bronze men") from Ionia and Caria in Asia Minor landing in Egypt to fight for pay and help raise the lesser king Psammetichos to become pharaoh in the late 7th century.[49] Yet these hirelings generally came from the edges of the Greek world and served foreign monarchs with treasuries sufficient to meet their cost. The relatively poor agricultural communities that characterized most poleis located on the Greek mainland and elsewhere would never have seen clear (or even have been able) to waste resources buying fighting men that those states' similarly armed militias could provide at little or no cost. It was only with the rise of tyrannies that mercenary spearmen began to appear in poleis so governed; their despotic rulers able to accumulate enough wealth to hire soldiers from the outside to aid their conquests and protect from internal uprisings. And even then, these were usually no more than modestly sized contingents of bodyguards. It was the rare tyrant like those that first came to power on Sicily in the early 5th century and later in Thessaly that could accumulate wealth sufficient to contract truly large mercenary contingents.[50] Elsewhere, it was only initially with outside funding and then by repeatedly raiding riches stored in the shrine at Delphi that the warlords of Phocis were able to finance sizeable armies manned primarily with hired spearmen.[51]

The paid hosts of Thessaly and Phocis were yet in the future when the Peloponnesian War broke out, while the poleis of Sicily had largely joined that island's leading city of Syracuse in once more drawing their troops from citizen lists. Militia culture was therefore still very much the rule among Greek militaries—something that wouldn't change even by the war's end. While taking on soldiers from outside a polis increased in the late 5th century, this mostly involved light-armed men rather than hoplites. That followed upon Greek commanders assigning greater importance to skirmishers as support for their phalanxes, and for executing a variety of detached operations. These were all missile troops whose skills benefited tremendously from years of practice with their weapons; thus, outsiders of known ability with those specialized tools of war came to be highly valued and increasingly filled the light-armed contingents of those states able to afford them. Yet pitched battles remained common[52] and very much the domain of amateur heavy infantry; therefore, most professional hoplites could find employment solely in small batches.[53]

Draftees thus still dominated phalanxes as the 4th century got underway, but their motivations for making war had changed. This was not a case of abandoning militia mores so much as an evolution within them. Economic concerns had grown far past simple disputes over local borders, and these complex issues of commerce had ties to contrary political philosophies. This pitted democracy against oligarchy, and inter-poleis conflicts became more like intra-polis ones. The latter had largely been socio-economic, setting income classes against each other. Now, inter-poleis wars began to stem from the same politics of wealth. Yet, these weren't struggles to determine which class would rule a state; rather, they were contests between entire coalitions that fell on opposing sides of those same factional divides.[54] Hoplites were now deeply vested in their chosen governmental form and its related economic system and most no longer fought limited battles over scraps of land on their borders. They instead waged wide and near total wars on behalf of that favored political view, making phalanx actions less decisive as just one among many ways to exhaust a foe in such comprehensive contests. Hoplite culture was therefore much changed, with its still mostly amateur combatants grown nearly tribalistic in their contempt for the other side's political/economic institutions.

Professional Armies and Imperial Wars

Sizeable contingents of mercenary Greek spearmen in the early to middle 4th century served as mostly seasonal hires among Thessalian warlords, whose lands had no hoplite tradition of their own. Longer lasting employment could be found with the Persians and their foes overseas, who had a healthy respect for the European heavy infantry that had often bested Asian armies in the past. Flush with royal cash, they usually offered contracts covering the duration of entire conflicts, which could last several years. The most secure jobs of all, however, were on Sicily. Resurgent tyrannies at Syracuse and some lesser poleis had sufficient means in the form of ready funds or land grants to put a great many mercenaries on long-term retainer. These last were the closest thing among the Greeks to a standing, professional army; yet, even those troops were generally not of sufficient strength to fight a major war without calling upon citizen levies for much of the required manpower. And throughout the overwhelming majority of states in the Greek world, hired spearmen were but temporary supplements to local militia. Pay for such hirelings was much like the small allotments given to draftees for their time in the field and came to little more than base subsistence[55]; therefore, even for poleis that did take on a few professionals to beef up their campaign efforts, war-making remained a fairly low-currency transaction.

The ascension of Philip II to the throne of Macedonia would change all of that. Taking charge upon his brother's death in 359, Philip shortly thereafter created Greece's first full-time, professional army.[56] This was a natural consequence of the young king's invention of a modified phalanx that relied upon close cooperation between elite hoplites, pikemen, and shock cavalry with strong skirmisher support. Philip must have quickly realized that to make this system work at top efficiency called for spending much more time on drill and campaign conditioning than any short-term conscript could ever spare. He thus had to raise a standing army; however, if he was to do so by pulling his countrymen from their private occupations, he must adequately compensate their resulting loss of income. On the plus side, that would provide collateral benefits by elevating the local economy, discouraging desertion, and buying the good will and loyalty of his troops. But it would also be quite expensive in mandating what we today might call a "living wage"—a rate well above the minimum mercenary and militia stipends of the era.[57] When Philip elected to put this costly scheme in place, it then became an unsung driving force behind his subsequent strategy of extensive territorial expansion. All his other ambitions aside, the Macedonian monarch now had to go out and seize the sort of vast wealth required to finance his army. He was thus fortunate that his new war machine proved most adept at achieving such conquests.

Philip succeeded in absorbing nearly all of Greece using his reformed armament, which was manned almost exclusively by professionals. These included his well-paid Macedonians as well as a great many mercenaries. The latter were direct hires in his earliest campaigns and then mostly provided by subject allies in Thessaly. Alexander III followed and went farther still in adding all of Persia's holdings to the empire. He accomplished this with an army that was only professional in part; however, that segment of Macedonians and contracted troops provided his prime combatants, leaving the large contingents of amateur Greek allies also present to serve in secondary roles. And even these last turned mercenary when they chose to stay on for pay after the conquest of Persia had brought their initial voluntary commitments to an end. After Alexander's demise, his Macedonian successors and others went on to design fighting forces along similar lines.[58] Most of this new set of leaders set themselves up as royal despots with support from hosts of professional soldiers. A majority of troops thus serving did so within standing armies, but some in Ptolemaic Egypt and Seleucid Asia spent long periods stockpiled as reserves among a variety of special military settlements (*klerouchoi*). There, they, their sons, and their sons' sons sired generation after generation to follow into the family trade of military service.

Greek armies of the post–Alexander (Hellenistic) era engaged in what is best characterized as imperial warfare. This took place between competing realms or within a single realm either between rival warlords or against an internal revolt of some segment of its subject population. Hoplites and other combatants now fought for pay rather than patriotism. And they were also attached to a single ruler with recent and fluid holdings instead of to a polis or other entity of long standing. These vital circumstances conspired to produce a much altered military culture from the one that held sway among the militias of old or even during the following interval of coalition wars.

One of the most obvious expressions of this evolved ethos was the phenomenon of mass troop revolts in the field. During the era when it was primarily amateur citizens on voluntary campaign, such uprisings simply didn't take place. If a war was unpopular, the militia would never agree to march out and fight; and if a leader proved incompetent, then his soldiers could remove him through political/legal action when they got home. Nor were troop revolts a factor within mercenary-rich armies of the coalition period. A paid "free-lancer" took his money and his chances, not being tied down to a particular place or employer. If he didn't like the way things were run, he could either just walk away from a campaign[59] or, should he choose to stick it out, refuse future contracts with anyone he thought inept. We thus don't hear of mercenary hosts ever rebelling; indeed, it seems that men kept re-upping at Phocis in the mid–4th century despite the absolutely awful battle record of its last couple of warlords. But things were markedly different for those in the imperial era's national hosts. Risk to their livelihood compelled them onto campaign under orders from rulers that had never won an election and who stood aloof from any established form of regulation. Those wanting to express dissatisfaction with such leadership therefore had no practical recourse other than to threaten or actually carry out an armed rebellion. And the best place to do that sort of thing was in the field, where the dissidents were fully gathered and had weapons ready to hand.

Such mutinies began to spring up at the very dawn of Greek imperial warfare, afflicting its first true master. That was Philip II, who in 354 had to return home or face a revolt by his new model army in the wake of two defeats in Thessaly.[60] And Philip's heir Alexander was forced to end his Indian campaign and retreat under similar duress in 326, when his exhausted host refused orders to advance against yet another large enemy gathering.[61] Still, he fared better than Perdiccas, the next to try and control Macedonia's empire. Having come up short in a pair of costly crossing attempts over the Nile in 321, his command rebelled, killed him, and made peace with the other side.[62] A similar fate befell Eumenes of Cardia, another of Alexander's successors, who in the winter of 317/16 lost the battle of Gabene and then his life to a mutiny by his most esteemed body of men, the hypaspists.[63] And lest these betrayals in the field appear confined to only Macedonian-centered armies, there is the Syracusan tyrant Agathocles, who had to make a desperate escape by sea from troops grown seditious during a disastrously failed campaign in North Africa.[64]

But no matter how prone to revolt imperial Greek armies might have been, the heavy infantrymen in their phalanxes appear to have had a strong taboo against changing sides once committed to engage. It seems, in fact, that there is only one recorded instance of that happening over the course of the many centuries and hundreds of battles encompassed by the age of hoplite warfare.[65] There are several examples on the other hand of mounted contingents going over to the enemy at the point of combat.[66] It would have been much easier of course for horsemen to escape battle than for heavy infantry. That reflects a rider's greater mobility and common positioning on the edges of a battlefield. His dominant missile-firing role was also a factor, allowing him to avoid the short-distances and physical entanglements of shock action. Still, the powerful cultural restraints that Greek military ethics imposed on spearmen[67] must have been a major factor as well in keeping them loyal to the stratiotai ranked about them. This was undoubtedly true in hoplite warfare's earlier days and was more than likely the case to at least a residual degree even in its final, imperial years.

The culture of Greek spearmen clearly underwent a great deal of evolution between the time when they were farmers voluntarily taking up arms to acquire or defend a few hectares of marginal land for the good of their polis and that of professional warriors serving some vast imperial conglomerate at the whims of a self-proclaimed king. Yet much seems to have endured as well. The hoplite "peltast" closely ranked with his comrades against Roman legions in the last great phalanx battle at Pydna in 168 had much in common with his "men of bronze" predecessors facing neighborhood foes centuries earlier. Not only were his signature spear, shield, and tight formation much the same, but so was the way he knew he had to fight: face-forward, steadfast, and, most of all, ever true to the brothers-in-arms at his side.

6

Physicality

Greek hoplites came from a hardy population of modest stature whose physical endeavors produced strong, durable warriors. The nature of their dominant occupations, as well as a fondness for athletics, tended to make them fit for the rigors of battle, with it being widely held that certain aspects of gymnastics in particular correlated closely with combat capability. And whether inspiring or inspired by the pursuit of such activities, the concept of physical perfection was a major element in Grecian art and its portrayals of well-kept bodies engaged in either sport or war. Amid that environment, the Spartans and a few small units of elites in other poleis drilled regularly to hone both their physiques and martial skills.

But they were the exceptions. The average Greek spearman was a hard-working and highly independent farmer; indifferent to anything deemed a waste of time, he felt that daily toil in his fields, along with a bit of athletic exercise and some private weapons practice with friends and/or kin, was enough to keep him prepared for battle. After all, that kind of fighting was familiar, something he and his forebears had often experienced over the years. And the Doric phalanx that ruled in the early days of polis warfare was key to creating this attitude, being a fairly simple tactical system that at minimum made no complex demands upon its stratiotai. It was therefore only in later days, when relatively raw conscripts began to more frequently encounter better prepared and sometimes professional foes exhibiting higher level abilities, that standard training gained favor. Still, no matter how superbly fit or finely drilled a man might be, there remained the unavoidable risk of taking a wound that might maim or kill. That was a grisly reality that hoplites had to face going into every action from the very first border clash between small neighboring militias to the last grand engagement of vast imperial hosts.

Mantinea II (362): A Decisive Draw

In the fall of 362, Epaminondas of Thebes faced his old nemesis, the wily old king of Sparta, Agesilaus, on the plain of Mantinea in a battle for hegemony of the Greek world. He had engaged the Spartans in a cat and mouse game of strategic maneuver, but Epaminondas was foiled at each turn by the quick reaction of his foes. Finally, with his term as Boeotarch, one of the seven leaders of the Boeotian League, coming to an end, he knew he must bring his foes to battle or risk trial by his political opponents at home. Seemingly the whole Greek world from Crete to Thessaly had ranged alongside either Thebes or Sparta. The battle would be the largest clash of hoplite armies, and the outcome would hinge on the tactical maneuvers of each side.

Much as Sparta and Athens had formed the greatest rivalry among 5th century poleis, so Sparta and Thebes became premier foes going into the 4th. Each headed a large coalition: Sparta with its net of allies in the Peloponnese and Thebes with the Boeotian League in central Greece. Sparta was politically an arcane mix of monarchic, oligarchic, and democratic elements that was difficult to export, so when extending their hegemony in the 5th century they tended to support narrow oligarchies that could be relied upon to be friendly and tow the Spartan line. Boeotia tended to favor democracy and would take up the mantle of its champion as they eclipsed Athens in power. This made it all too easy for each to see the other as an existential threat; thus, though cooperative during the Peloponnesian War, they soon found themselves on opposite sides when the buffer of their mutual hatred for Athens was removed. The breach began with covert Theban support for resistance to Sparta's occupation of Athens in 404–403; and it then escalated onto actual battlefields in the next decade during the Corinthian War. Briefly reconciled in the mid–380s,[1] the relationship between Sparta and the Theban mainstream crashed for good in 382. That's when Spartan troops aided the overthrow of Thebes' democracy, replacing it with a very narrow oligarchy (*dunasteia*). That new administration then closely aligned with Sparta, going so far as to add troops to its distant foreign ventures.[2] Three years later, when Theban exiles joined rebels still on the ground at home to violently oust the oligarchic regime and a Spartan-led garrison, the stage was set for all-out war. Restoring democracy, the Thebans and their Boeotian allies found themselves on the defensive in a fight with Sparta that played out exclusively on their own soil over the next four years.

This conflict (the Boeotian War) matched what were perhaps the two most physically fit and well-trained hoplite hosts in all of Greece. Spartan citizens (spartiates) exercised and drilled from early youth within a state-run system of instruction and indoctrination called the "agoge." The end product of this strict and often brutal process was a phalanx led by excellently conditioned and highly disciplined elite warriors. Not only exceptionally adept with their weapons, these men were masters of maneuvering in formation as well. Unlike the common hoplites of other poleis, every spartiate was expected to be able to form up alongside any group of men and understand their place in formation. Their abundant success on actual battlefields rendered them well tested and supremely confident.

The Thebans, however, had some countervailing assets of their own. Most notably, these included a large population with a long-standing tradition of sports and physical training. And their general Epaminondas had labored to keep the latter habit alive among the city's youth throughout the *dunasteia*. Another local leader, Gorgidas, then recruited an elite contingent to take full-time drill at state expense. This was the Sacred Band whose 300 picked spearmen were able within a few years to face even spartiates on even terms.[3] The only thing initially lacking from an optimum restoration of the Theban war machine was a bounty of positive combat experience.[4] Epaminondas and his close political ally Pelopidas remedied this by building the ferocity of their troops as one does fighting dogs, providing them foes of escalating difficulty. First there were victories over

Spartan-led armies at Thespiae (378) and Tanagra III (376); and then, a triumph over an all-Spartan force at Tegyra (375).[5] With their hoplites now seasoned and self-assured, the Thebans had become a real threat to Sparta—something that many would in time come to lay at the feet of none other than Agesilaus:

> [Lycurgus ordered] that they [the Spartans] should not make war often, or long, with the same enemy, lest they should train and instruct them in war by habituating them to defend themselves. And this was what Agesilaos [their king] was much blamed for, a long time after, it being thought that by his continual incursions into Boeotia he made the Thebans a match for the Lacedaemonians.[6]

The Boeotian War came to an end in 375 when Thebes' key supporter Athens, worried now about the rising strength of its erstwhile ally, made peace with Sparta. The Athenians dragged a reluctant Thebes into the truce as well; however, hostilities broke out again when Sparta objected to Theban intervention in neighboring Phocis. This brought about the battle of Leuctra (371),[7] which saw Thebes gain a crushing victory through the innovative tactical maneuvering planned by Epaminondas and the quick reactions of Pelopidas in command of the Sacred Band that put an end to Spartan influence outside the Peloponnese. As Greece's new preeminent military power, the Thebans then mounted invasions into Spartan territory. These had fair success; yet, Sparta remained unbowed and able to exert itself locally with a phalanx that was still much feared.[8] When the Arcadian Federation led by Mantinea chose in 362 to defy Thebes as well, Epaminondas marched yet another army into the Peloponnese.

On learning that the Spartans' army was ranged around Mantinea, he sought to defeat them indirectly and end the war by taking the famously un-walled Spartan polis while its army was in the field. But the Spartans had been warned by allied runners and were able to mobilize those of their forces still at home. Such ardently defended territory was a tough nut to crack, even when it came to its scattered urban concentrations, where each roof top could provide an effective platform for missilemen. And when resistance did not crumble quickly before their probing attacks, the Thebans broke off to avoid being caught between still intact defenses and the hurriedly returning Spartan field army.[9] Epaminondas withdrew northward, thinking to find Mantinea now vulnerable due to the Spartans having left to rescue their homeland. But he then found himself thwarted again when Athenian cavalrymen came heroically to the city's aid.

When his strategic maneuvering failed to bear fruit, Epaminondas decided to meet the Spartans in open battle. Here he used his command of tactical maneuver to provide every advantage to his men. First he marched as though withdrawing and then made as if to camp for the night. However, his foes didn't entirely let their guard down in either case and he elected to form up for a face-to-face fight where they were deployed on the plain across the narrowest part of the valley that hosted Mantinea.[10] With his troops shifting out of marching column into line of battle, Epaminondas could see his opponents' array in the distance; and he perhaps noted that it reflected a profound reduction in Spartan authority since his victory at Leuctra nine years ago. The Mantineans and other Arcadian locals held their right wing—a position that in the past would have gone to the Spartans even on Mantinea's home soil. But now, things were different; Sparta was no longer hegemon and had to be content with the spot next left in line. Beyond the easily discernable red-clad Spartans, well-regarded spearmen from Elis and Achaea held forth, and then it was militias of lesser note filling in the remaining center portion of the phalanx. On the Mantinean coalition's far left, there stood a large muster of Athenians.[11] That secondary post of honor was one they often took when in an allied capacity. Evaluating this with an experienced eye, the Theban general must have seen that his 30,000 or so infantry would hold a significant advantage in numbers over some 20,000 foot-soldiers on the other side.[12]

Epaminondas' own deployment put his best troops, the men from Boeotia, on the left just as they had been at Leuctra. The Tegeans and other Arcadians then ranked next in line.[13] The weaker allies occupied through the center of his phalanx, while troops from Argos manned the far right. Xenophon says that Epaminondas "strengthened the ram-like formation around himself [on the left wing]," and that he then "led his army forward like a trireme, with the "ram" [left wing] foremost ... preparing to fight with the strongest part of his army, and [having] placed the weakest units far away from him [at center]." This is more or less consistent with an "oblique order" used at Leuctra that featured a deeply filed left wing of the battle line and withdrawn ("refused") center and right. However, there were some significant differences in the Theban general's situation here versus Leuctra, and these had major impacts on his pre-battle arrangements.

At Mantinea II, unlike at Leuctra, Epaminondas had the larger phalanx.[14] Combined with the fact that he now faced spearmen from Athens on the enemy left who were sure to be more aggressive than the notoriously battle-shy Spartan allies of 371,[15] this both encouraged and allowed him to deploy his center and right wing at greater depth than before with some contingents standing at 12 shields or possibly even 16. That gave the Argives in particular a better chance to rebuff the advance of the Athenians by exceeding their strength of file. More importantly, the placement of the dread Spartan contingent inside that of Arcadia on the other end of the line was another key difference. At Leuctra, the Sacred Band foiled a Spartan attempted outflanking maneuver (cyclosis), either by a quick improvised charge into the Spartan lines as they attempted to move men across the field or by moving out from behind the Theban ranks to outflank them, depending on various readings of modern scholars. In this battle, the posting of the Spartans inside of the Mantineans and the close proximity of the steep flanking hills made Spartan cyclosis unlikely. The Sacred Band thus surely stood foremost in Epaminondas' deeply filed Theban strike force.[16]

With their light infantry and cavalry screening off each wing, the opposing formations came to grips, both sides closing into contact on the western side of the front and the Athenians initiating action to the east. The ensuing hand-to-hand combat was long and stubborn in those key areas of contention on either wing, with Diodorus calling it a "mighty, stupendous struggle."[17] In the west, the fighting pitted "the most capable foot-soldiers of that time, Boeotians and Lacedaemonians," who, with their lines "drawn up facing one another, began the contest, exposing their lives to every risk ... [thus] the battle raged severely for a long time and the conflict took no turn in favor of either side."[18] Xenophon gives us no real detail at this point, while the much longer account of Diodorus turns implausibly romantic.[19] However, the deeply arrayed wing contingent of Epaminondas was finally able to shatter the opposing Mantineans and other Arcadians, pushing them back out of formation and breaking their cohesion.[20]

Meanwhile, at the other end of the battleground, Athenian and Argive hoplites initially fought to a stand-off, and it was their flanking light foot and cavalry that had then proven decisive. The mounted Athenians on that wing performed well; still, they had to give way to stronger opposing light foot.[21] This success was, however, quite short-lived, as the riders and hamippoi from Elis sitting in reserve beyond the Athenian rear immediately charged in to resume the fight. Taking the Boeotian auxiliary force by surprise, these reinforcements put it to flight before their spearmen comrades could be fully enveloped.[22] This stood the situation on its head, since it was now the Eleans who were able to fall upon a freshly exposed enemy flank. Invigorated by so complete a reversal of fortune, the hoplites from Athens added their weight in a renewed effort and, under attack now from side and front, the Argives ceded the field.

Epaminondas had broken the ranks of Arcadians arrayed against him. His troops had performed the same feat at Leuctra against the finest of Spartan units, crushing the head of the snake so the body withered. However, his victory here came against units ranged alongside the Spartans. He had the snake not by the head, but by the neck, and it may well have bit him in its death throes.

It appears that the Thebans were following their traditional tactic of using concentrated force to pierce the battle line of their foes much as they had done at Tegyra, Leuctra, and even Coronea. But, as we might expect when fighting so close to home against a foe that had just marched on their city and families, the Spartans did not break immediately just because a unit alongside gave ground in the manner of their allies at Leuctra. The ensuing Theban advance thus had to expose its unshielded side in passing along a shielded file of vengeful Spartans still standing stubbornly in place; and it was on that dangerously vulnerable flank where Epaminondas himself must have marched.

Diodorus tells us that, "the Lacedaemonians, when they saw that Epameinondas in the fury of battle was pressing forward too eagerly, … charged him in a body." And Plutarch reports "Epaminondas had already routed the van of the Lacedaemonians, and was still eagerly pressing on in pursuit of them, when Anticrates, a Spartan, faced him and smote him." Xenophon then notes that "although the opposing phalanx had fled before them, their hoplites did not kill a single man or advance beyond the spot where the collision had taken place." These disparate traditions can be reconciled if we accept that the Thebans routed the Arcadian element of the "Lacedaemonian phalanx" opposite them, but as they passed, the Spartans followed their own traditional tactic as Xenophon recommended for Coronea and struck the unit passing through in the flank. This attack by the Spartans, fighting on two fronts in a crumbling battle line, could not snatch victory from defeat; however, it could crush the head of the Theban snake by killing the Theban leader arrayed on the right of his formation. We thus have both a penetration and rout followed by an inability of the Thebans to either give pursuit or wheel to roll up the enemy flank because the Spartans there held their ground and continued to fight.[23] Xenophon tells us at this juncture that "the rest of his [Epaminondas'] forces could not properly exploit their victory," and though "the enemy cavalry was also put to flight … Epaminondas' cavalry did not pursue them, and so they killed neither cavalry nor infantry, but timidly slipped away through the lines of the fleeing enemy, just as if they had been defeated."[24]

It soon became apparent that the Athenians were victorious on the other side of the battlefield. This disappointing intelligence came from infantry that had been directly supporting Thebes' horsemen on the west. Those foot soldiers had acted more aggressively than their mounted compatriots and gone across for the purpose of finishing off the enemy left. But they found the Athenian spearmen and their auxiliaries in full control over there, and a majority then lost their lives before making an escape.

Likely due to a combination of exhaustion and approaching darkness, neither side regrouped for a second round of engagement, and the battle thus ended in a draw:

> [The] god so arranged it that each side set up a trophy as if victorious, and each side was not prevented [from doing so] by the enemy; each gave back the dead under truce as if victorious, and both received back their dead under truce as if defeated. And though each side claimed the victory, neither side was seen to have gained anything—no city, territory or increased rule—that they did not have prior to the battle.[25]

In fact, though, this clash had actually been decisive in one very important sense— it turned the tide of Theban ascendancy. The death of Epaminondas was a cruel blow to Thebes' military capability. Gorgidas had retired or died prior to Tegyra (375) and Pelopidas had fallen at Cynoscephalae (364), leaving only Pammenes now active among the talented commanders that had enabled Theban hegemony. And that general's last significant campaign, an expedition into the Peloponnese in 352 to help restore order at Megalopolis, would mark an end to the significant exercise of Theban authority outside Boeotia.[26] But regardless of this longer term perspective, the engagement at Mantinea in 362 still constituted a most impressive accomplishment by the hardy hoplites of Thebes. They had carried their side of the field there against top-notch opposition, doing so in no small part due to "their superiority in bodily strength."[27]

Physical Attributes and Ideals

Studies on the remains of ancient Greek males indicate a mean height of 162–165cm (5ft 5in–5ft 6in) with an estimated body weight of 60–65kg (132–143lbs).[28] Since many of these were somewhat affluent individuals that had relatively costly burials, they might well over-represent the more privileged and thus better nourished. Nonetheless, the data remain useful for evaluating the physiques of hoplites, whose assets normally set them among the wealthier citizens in their poleis.[29] There are, in fact, suggestions that some picked elites might have stood above even the upper limits found in these studies of wider populations.[30] And though such measurements show Greek hoplites to have been significantly smaller overall than today's western males,[31] they were by no means diminutive compared to others of the ancient Mediterranean region. For example, estimates on the mean height of Roman men in classical times indicate a range of 162–170cm (5ft 5in–5ft 8in) that broadly overlaps that for ancient Greeks.[32] To put this in perspective, we might relate the phalanx spearman to a modern welterweight boxer like Floyd Mayweather, Jr. At 173cm (5ft 8in) and 63.5–66.7kg (140–147lbs), he would have fallen well below the maximums indicated for Greek hoplites—a modestly sized, but still quite formidable man.

There are many surviving artworks from ancient Greece that prominently portray athletes and warriors with superbly toned bodies. That characteristic is quite reasonable when the subjects are sportsmen, who must have spent years crafting their musculature in a quest for competitive advantage. However, the invariable application of that same standard of physical beauty to soldiers seems suspect. Were Greek fighting men always so exquisitely configured? Given the normal range of body types in any real population, should we not expect to see a few skinny or chubby hoplites? In fact, we know that the latter existed per the reported attitude of Epaminondas, who "always showed repugnance toward fat men."[33] And if exercise-loving Thebes (see Physical Training below) had overweight soldiers, we can be sure that other poleis had them as well and, no doubt, in even greater numbers.

The images we see in classical Greek art of nearly naked, trim, and finely toned hoplite bodies are thus idealized beyond any likely reality, while the counterpointing distaste shown by Epaminondas for unfit men was both common and present well beyond Thebes. This last can be seen in how the Spartan king Agesilaos inspired his troops by exhibiting the weak-looking bodies of their Persian foes in 395:

> [Believing] that contempt for the enemy would impart strength to his men for the battle, Agesilaos ordered the heralds to sell naked those barbarians who had been captured in the plundering raids. When the soldiers saw the skin of these captives, which was white because they never took their clothes off, and when they saw too, that these men were soft and unused to toil ... they concluded that fighting such men would be no more difficult than fighting women.[34]

That Agesilaos' men, who came from many poleis, so readily developed contempt for these barbarians as warriors based solely on their appearance says quite a bit about the prevailing attitude toward male bodies across the full breadth of Greek culture. And of key interest here, that standard of muscular perfection seems to have been applied to hoplites above all other types of fighters. This is evident in the criteria that the same Agesilaos used to evaluate the various arms contingents in his army. That he might encourage better conditioning, he gave out prizes for the cavalrymen who were best at horsemanship. Likewise, awards went to those archers and peltasts showing the most skill with their weapons. But among the hoplites, the top prize was awarded on a very different basis—it went to "the one who was found to be in the best physical condition."[35] This reflected a strong belief at Sparta that physical fitness was vital to a spearman's combat ability. Men who won at the Olympic or other major games were therefore routinely accustomed to gain an honored place in line beside the king in battle.[36] And all spartiates exercised daily, not only at home, but even when on campaign. The state mandated this for them "that they take more pride in themselves and have a more dignified appearance than other men."[37]

While Sparta was alone in the extent and intensity of military training among its citizens, the idea that basic physical fitness was a boon in battle was dominant throughout most if not all of the Greek world. Hans van Wees' extensive examination of Grecian warfare led him to conclude regarding evidence for weapons training and formation skill outside of Sparta that "there is not a whisper until well into the fourth century"; all the same, he found that it is "well attested" that hoplites "took mainly informal, private exercise, most of it aimed at general physical fitness rather than specialist combat skills."[38] This was clearly thought to improve physical aspects of combat performance, yet the intent to hone one's looks for their own sake must have been present as well. That, of course, would have been partly a matter of self-image, meshing with the worship of romanticized physiques on display in artworks scattered all about a city's private and public spaces. These men might well have prized their appearance so highly that it's even been suggested they could have feared disfigurement in combat more than suffering a disabled limb.[39]

But this was not just a matter of simple vanity. An important motivation for optimizing one's appearance was that it had potential to intimidate any foe that saw a fit-looking man as being more dangerous. And that most likely included a majority among one's fellow Greeks. The function of intimidation on the field of combat was to induce undue caution in the enemy. An overly cautious opponent was less prone to aggressively exploit any opening in your defenses while being more likely to expose a weakness of his own due to untimely hesitation. There were many ways to achieve this effect. We thus hear of the slow and silent advances of elite warriors like the Immortals of Persia and the Spartans that sent a terrifying message of serious, lethal intent; likewise, there were the clamorous nationalistic paeans with which most Greeks advanced into battle, hoping at least in part to cow the other side. But these were collective efforts, while making oneself look dangerous was something a man could achieve solo. This tack certainly was not unique to Greek hoplites, since the sort of awe in which men tend to hold well-formed foes seems inherent to the human species.[40]

A wide range of studies have shown that animals will signal dominance to rivals in a variety of ways. Studies on humans have shown that we respond to cues such as beard length, voice pitch, face shape, and even scent as indicators of dominance and masculinity.[41] The reason we have evolved to assess dominance is that we make use of this to find our place within the pecking order of our social unit with the least amount of conflict that could cause injury and destroy group cohesion. This requires that we can reliably calculate the likely outcome of an encounter based on an assessment of our opponent. Of paramount importance is that our opponent cannot cheat and present himself as more fearsome than he is. In order to be what a behavioral biologist would call an "honest signal," the trait must be costly to create metabolically, like height or physique, or signal an internal biological state, like the prime stage of life and high testosterone levels in the growth of a full beard. Studies have shown we react strongly to the presence of a beard on a man as a signal of dominance and aggression, though interestingly not sexual attractiveness.[42] Beards are an excellent case study in signaling between Greek men because they have passed down to us a category of beardless youths, and boys who are just getting their beards as non-threatening to men and the prime target of pederastic attention. In fact, the bearded youth was something of a comic trope as a sneaky copulator whom you could not trust with your wife! On the other end of the age scale, we have the greybeards, whose grizzled facial hair signaled they were past their prime as combatants, though presumably more wise than younger men.

As humans we can move culturally beyond the confines of biology. We therefore see the rise of adornments and armor that alter the appearance of men. The use of lofty horsehair crests on spearmen's helmets made them seem taller and wide shoulder pieces (epomides) gave a robust, "broad shouldered" appearance. Perhaps the ultimate expression of this "dress-for-success' trend was the "muscle cuirass." By mimicking a state of low body-fat and extreme development, this lent an air of perfection to anyone's torso. All of these devices combined with the Greek hoplite's efforts at conditioning to help mold his image into that of the ideal fighting man. Such accouterments are less direct, but still tied to an honest signal.[43] If you could afford expensive armor, you must be of high status. If of high status, either you or an ancestor was probably a proficient warrior. So this may be less of a "cheat" than it seems, and ostentatious warrior might rightly be considered dangerous.

Physical Training

Of course, physical training in Greece was not just focused on appearances; it aimed at improving actual fighting ability as well, though not perhaps in the way most of us might expect based on modern practices along similar lines. There, in fact, seems to have been a common attitude among ancient Greeks that many aspects of combat skill were more instinctive than learned. Even Xenophon, otherwise a strong proponent of training,[44] seems to lean that way in having one of his protagonists comment:

> [We] have been initiated into a method of fighting [with spear and sword], which, I observe, all men naturally understand ... not learned from any other source than instinct ... I never learned except from instinct even how to take hold of a sword ... this method of fighting [that] awaits us ... demands courage more than skill.[45]

Xenophon's attitude in this was perhaps largely shaped by his youthful acculturation at Athens; a polis that had quite an attraction to amateur militarism. Its great leader Pericles praised that attitude, noting that "where our rivals [the Spartans] from their very cradles by a painful discipline seek after manliness, at Athens we live exactly as we please, and yet are just as ready to encounter every legitimate danger."[46] Xenophon attributes to the laws of Lycurgus the strict diet and exercise regime that led Xenophon to say: "So it would not be easy to find healthier or handier men than the Spartans. For their exercises train the legs, arms and neck equally."[47] Thus, to best carry the hoplite to battle and bear the weight of shield and spear as well as helmet. To compete effectively, the veteran hoplite Socrates called upon his fellow Athenians to pursue private training[48]; so, while there was certainly a loose attitude toward such exercises, they were not ignored entirely. Elsewhere, training was taken more seriously, as at Thebes. The legendary strongman Hercules was that polis' iconic hero, and questing after "Herculean" physical prowess was very nearly a religious act there. Even so, Thebans initially seem to have put more emphasis on generic fitness than on acquiring specialized skill-sets for the battlefield.

Epaminondas advocated a training regimen at Thebes that focused on those aspects of sports that increased agility (velocitas); something that he himself had made a priority from youth.[49] And it seems that only after the great victory over Sparta at Leuctra did Theban physical training to gain skills specific to combat become near universal.[50] Though any city so entranced by the labors of Hercules undoubtedly must long have spawned many a muscular imitator, this increased militarism seems to have even further boosted enthusiasm for strength-related exercise; hence, within a decade comes the tale of Thebes' muscular potency at Mantinea II as noted earlier. And Diodorus would go on to say in a similar vein that in their struggle against Philip II at Chaeronea 24 years later: "the Thebans were superior [to the Macedonians] in bodily strength and in their constant training in the gymnasium."[51]

When it came to athletic training related to combat specific expertise, there were at least a few competitions that showcased skills of direct use on the field of battle. Running, throwing the javelin, and archery were such sports. While all of these skills most obviously applied to light infantry, good for peltasts and bowmen, it must be remembered that the overhand strike with the hoplite spear engaged all of the same muscle groups as the javelin throw. One sporting event more closely associated with heavy infantry was a foot race in elements of (and sometimes full) hoplite panoply.[52] It appears that this contest was normally held at the very end of gaming sessions as a nod to it being the event most closely connected to real military fitness.[53] Yet even here, the abilities called upon would have had value only to a spearman no longer in formation—one fighting singly, in pursuit, or in flight. The truth was that success for a polis' phalanx was much more dependent on the stoic endurance of its stratiotai than on the feats of speed or even strength normally emphasized in athletics. Thus, it was only competitions like wrestling and boxing involving a sort of mock combat that had significant worth for hoplites. These called for a combination of strength and agility not dissimilar to that needed in a closely ordered spear-fight.

Team sports existed in ancient Greece. Our sources are late, but if they can be believed, there were a wide variety of ball games. Of these, two played at Sparta stand out as excellent training for hoplite combat. Sphaeromachia, or "battle-ball," was an odd mix of American football and volleyball. Starting at a line at mid-field, a ball was tossed back and forth over the top of a clash of two lines of players who each sought to push the other backward.[54] Another game was played on a small island and is attested to by Pausanias in his description of Sparta:

> At the sacrifice the youths set trained boars to fight; the company whose boar happens to win generally gains the victory in Plane-tree Grove. Such are the performances in the Phoebaeum. A little before the middle of the next day they enter by the bridges into the place I have mentioned. They cast lots during the night to decide by which entrance each band is to go in. In fighting they use their hands, kick with their feet, bite, and gouge out the eyes of their opponents. Man to man they fight in the way I have described, but in the melee they charge violently and push one another into the water.

These games have in common the central theme of gaining and holding ground. Whether through sheer violence or physical pushing of the other boys, this ability is obviously one that would be crucial on a hoplite battlefield.

In fact, though, there was a rather lesser known form of exercise that best invoked this skill-set: dancing in battle gear. Dance in general was largely a male activity among the Greeks, who held it in high regard as both entertainment and, in the most knowledgeable military circles, something highly conducive to combat ability. Nowhere was the latter better appreciated than in that hotbed of Grecian martial virtue, Sparta:

> The Lacedaemonians also demand that the gymnasts have a knowledge of tactics, because they recognized in the contests a preliminary training for war; and this is not surprising, since the Lacedaemonians constantly associated even the dance, the most carefree amusement of peace times, with war, for they danced in such a manner as if to evade or throw a missile, leap up from the ground, and manipulate the shield cleverly.[55]

And though the Spartans might well have been the leading proponents of this fusion of the aesthetic and martial arts, it seems certain to have been a part of the training regimen elsewhere as well. At least that was the case in neighboring Arcadia.[56]

Along with the armed dances, group dancing would have provided men with training in mass movement. It has been suggested that the ability of to move in unison was a major advancement in human evolution, holding our groups together through "muscular bonding."[57] Group dance and processions can be seen on many vase images and were an important feature of celebrations such as the Carnea at Sparta. If you have ever witnessed a "cattle-call" audition for dance roles, you will know that professional dancers show an almost uncanny ability to process complex steps and memorize routines on the fly.[58] It would not be hard to teach a cohort of such professionals elements of drill that would normally take extensive practice.

As to the sort of drills in arms and maneuver that are more recognizable today as proper constituents of military training, these were essentially confined through the 5th century to a modest number of elites like the spartiates, epilektoi, and, perhaps, the very best of mercenary spearmen under longer term employment that allowed them to drill as a unit.[59] But going into the middle 4th century, attention to that kind of specifically combat-related preparation had begun to see fresh adoption by a good many poleis. This was probably to no small extent the result of those states reacting to having had their poorly schooled militia phalanx come to grief against better trained men; though, as discussed for Thebes, inspiration could arise out of a quest for more and even greater battlefield victories as well. Athens finally adopted mandatory training for its spearmen in the late 4th century.[60] This called for all citizen youths to undergo schooling in arms from the ages of 18 through 19; and the state equipped each man with a shield and spear after the first year that they might practice their use.[61] With even the Athenians now on the training bandwagon, virtually every hoplite then taking the field, amateur and professional alike, had the benefit of at least some formal drill.

Hunting was considered an important training ground for men.[62] In hunting men must travel over hard, broken terrain, suffer life exposed to the elements, use weapons, and most importantly kill a living creature. But beyond stalking of lower animals, the ultimate form of such "live-target" training for combat was the fighting of other men, with nearly incessant quarreling over borders among Greek poleis creating plenty of opportunities for hoplites to engage other warriors. Combat training through real battle was the norm at Athens,[63] and probably among most other city-states even if not so well-practiced there. However, intense drill was the more favored method of instruction at Sparta. Yet even that polis, known for its reluctance to unnecessarily risk a sparse citizen roll, took advantage of scattered episodes of border and other fighting to provide valuable training venues.[64]

Wounds and Death

No matter how fit or well trained a hoplite might endeavor to become, he could never escape the risk of taking a serious wound. That was a hazard to which he knowingly exposed himself each and every time he went into combat. Phalanx battle was a grimly brutal, physical affair; one waged face-to-face with steel-tipped/edged weapons that struck with all the power their wielders could muster. The damage thereby inflicted fell into three broad categories: (1) blunt force trauma that broke bones and concussed the brain; (2) incisions from the sharp edges of spears or swords; and (3) punctures that could run deep into the body from missiles of various sorts or, much more commonly for hoplites, hard-thrust spearheads.

Sadly for our purposes here, the surviving ancient literature on hoplite warfare provides little by way of statistical data for evaluating the frequency with which these types of wounds occurred. Mostly what we have are figures on battlefield deaths; and those are suspect as being exaggerated for an engagement's losers and incomplete at times even for the victors. Still, total casualties for a few of Alexander the Great's battles in the late 4th century offer some possible insights. These suggest that actions "not hotly contested" saw a ratio between the wounded and dead of about 5-to-1, while in those where "the fighting was severe" this rose to as high as 12-to-1.[65] These proportions are likely applicable to hoplite warfare in general, which was waged both here and elsewhere with similar weapon technology. However, it should be noted that they are probably accurate only for successful phalanxes like those from which they derive. In the case of a defeated formation, the ratio of wounded to killed would have been much lower. This reflects merciful/practical dispatching of many among the losers' fallen; the dead under those circumstances likely being roughly equal in number to the wounded who escaped or had been spared for ransom or enslavement.[66]

As scant as our information is on the rates of wounding in hoplite engagements, the data on its means of delivery and bodily locations are sparser still. Beyond a few anecdotes on famed individuals like Epaminondas, this comes primarily from one fictional source, the Iliad of Homer. Likely composed c.750 in the early days of the phalanx, this epic poem recounting events in the ninth year of the legendary Trojan War describes some 147 battle wounds. Of these, 123 (84 percent) are inflicted on their ilk by heavy spearmen almost surely modeled upon hoplites of the author's day, the remainder being evenly divided between those from arrows and sling bullets.[67] Taken with caution as having at least some basis in actual combat contemporary to its writing, this work sheds useful light on how and where wounds came about in Greek heavy infantry fighting. The primary weapon that these early hoplites used to inflict damage on their foes was a long spear. That device accounts for 106 (86 percent) of the Iliad's recorded wounds; though it must be acknowledged that spears in that period were not only thrust as in classic phalanx combat, but thrown as well. The secondary weapon of choice was the sword, which rendered all of the other hoplite-generated wounds described by Homer. As to where victims took damage, about half (51 percent) of it was in the chest. Many (24 percent) of the other hits described came to the head, with only a few injuries to neck (10 percent), arms (8 percent), and elsewhere (8 percent). However, given that combat accounts in the Iliad are largely (78 percent) of the lethal variety, it can be safely assumed that real fighting in its era must have seen a great deal of non-fatal wounding, especially to unarmored hands, arms, and thighs. It's just that such relatively "minor" injuries lacked sufficient drama to warrant the poet incorporating them into his narrative.

It's not likely that many hoplites died right away on the spot. Barring a rare near instantly fatal blow to head or heart, most of those who went down must have kept breathing for a while after hitting the ground. And many more among the wounded remained upright and vital enough to make their way from the killing field, doing so either on their own or with help from comrades. The leading cause of death in the immediate aftermath of combat was a deadly combination of shock and blood loss, which within the hour would have claimed the lives of about half of all destined to succumb to their wounds either on or off the field.[68] Nor were all of the injured who escaped such a quick death by any means "lucky," since serious infections (peritonitis, tetanus, gangrene, and blood poisoning) would kill just as many in a lingering and often horrific manner during the following days and weeks. Setting aside injured men on the losing end of a fight dispatched by the enemy where fallen or during pursuit, around 30 percent of the other wounded were destined to die by the time all was said and done.[69]

That the butcher's bill for phalanx battles was not higher than even the foregoing suggests is largely due to the ameliorating effects of ancient Greek medical care. Primitive as some of its practices might appear by modern standards, they were often effective and, in some cases, even superior to methods common well into modern times.[70] Treatment of wounds for the most fortunate came by way of an experienced doctor (*iatros*). If an injured man managed to get back to camp or a nearby allied city, there were probably physicians waiting to render assistance[71]; while at or near the battle site, it was professional medical practitioners among the other combatants that could render such expert aid.[72] Much more often, though, the task of trying to save their comrades fell to those common hoplites closest to hand.[73] All of these various medics recognized the concept of the first or "Golden" hour, when attention to severe injuries was most critical to survival,[74] and thus took quick action if at all possible. Not only might this benefit a valued companion in trouble, but it could serve the state as well should an otherwise lost hoplite gain sufficient recovery to fight for his polis on another day.

Given the aforementioned limited nature of the phalanx's athletic demands, even a man sustaining substantial permanent damage might well resume his place in the ranks. Philip II, blind in the right eye and with one leg so withered by a spear wound as to require a smaller greave, was thus still able to accompany his hypaspists into battle at Chaeronea. And it was well recognized in the Spartan hotbed of military virtue that a man lamed by old wounds was still to be valued in battle.[75]

But despite all of the foregoing efforts to condition men's bodies for war, to train for success and survival in combat, and to care for those suffering wounds, the bloody battlefields of ancient Greece still claimed lives in great number. From the beginning of the 5th century through the end of the Hellenic era in 323, armies with exclusively hoplite heavy infantry fought at least 269 significant battles. These killed around 200,000 (11–12 percent) of the spearmen engaged and left about twice as many badly wounded. Fatality rates for the victors' hoplites ran a little over 5 percent of those deployed, while the slightly smaller (10 percent fewer spearmen on average) armies of those defeated suffered 19 percent losses at just above three killed for each one taken out on the winning side.[76] There is no more graphic description of what those grim battlegrounds must have looked like than that offered by Xenophon after taking stock of the carnage that he and his fellow hoplites had wrought at Coronea in 394:

> Now that the fighting was at an end, a weird spectacle met the eye, as one surveyed the scene of the conflict—the earth stained with blood, friend and foe lying dead side by side, shields smashed to pieces, spears snapped in two, daggers [swords of the famously short Spartan variety] bared of their sheaths, some on the ground, some embedded in the bodies, some yet gripped by the hand.[77]

Xenophon had witnessed this sort of abattoir before during his time as a commander of spears for hire, but never on nearly so vast a scale. One wonders if he also walked the similarly dreadful site of Mantinea II. That grisly field lay a mere 55km (34mi) from his home at Corinth and had hosted the conclusion of a campaign in which his sons had fought and one had died. Had he indeed stood on that recently contested earth, Xenophon could have looked across its blood-soaked western end, where the late Epaminondas and his Thebans had laid claim to their costly share of success. And from the same spot, he could have just as easily passed his eyes over the other side of the battleground. There sat the trophy of captured arms that his surviving son and the other Athenians had erected to mark their own so-called victory. An elderly man now of nearly 70 years and mourning the loss of a child, his thoughts must surely have been much like those of Arthur Wellesley, the Duke of Wellington. Another saddened old warrior, that sage general would more than two millennia later pen an eternal truth that: "Nothing except a battle lost can be half so melancholy as a battle won."[78]

7

Psychology

Beyond physical and tactical factors, a hoplite's state of mind could have quite a profound effect in combat. Some of this was a matter of training, past experience, or the deliberate design of commanders; and elements so introduced were long in the making. Others were chance occurrences during a given action and thus solely of the moment. A few of these mental components were cultural and therefore unique to society in ancient Greece; but most reflected basic aspects of human nature and have been manifest on every battlefield throughout the centuries up to the present. Yet that very universality caused ancient writers for the most part to ignore such things, considering them to be "common knowledge" among their contemporaries. And that truly was a much greater reality then than in our modern world. While only a small professional minority usually sees military service in this day and age, a good many citizens of the classical era experienced combat as members of their polis' militia. That would have put them into intimate contact with the psychic side of war in all of its guises in that every armed action must have exhibited a multitude of these key psychological facets in varying degrees. Perhaps our best insight into how such factors could impact embattled hoplites comes from a linked pair of early 5th century engagements.

Cimolia I/II (458): Without Warning

Athens was a major power on the rise in the mid–5th century. Mining and trading wealth and the influence it bought had already gone far to put the polis on the upswing, but Athens' leading role in the defeat of Persia would add great impetus to the trend. The Athenians over the course of that long conflict had come to take hegemonic control over Greece's anti-Persian marine coalition, the Delian League, beginning to treat it as their personal fiefdom. Most of the organization's member states were like Athens in being Ionian Greek with democratic governments; and, largely located around the Aegean Basin, they gave the Athenians sway eastward all the way to the coast of Asia Minor. But, expansive as this realm was, they hungered for more. After Athens had further secured its eastern front with a climactic victory over the Persians on both land and sea at Eurymedon (c.466), it therefore sought to expand its influence to the west and north, reaching into the Greek mainland to form new alliances. Sparta and its league of allies, which were Doric Greek rather than Ionian and hosted oligarchic factions hostile to

Athenian-style democracy, saw this as a serious threat to their security. And that pervasive fear plus a variety of local issues ignited a series of "brush fire" wars with the Athenians over the next decade. Though separately initiated, these conflicts always pitted Athens against states in the Spartan sphere; they are thus often referred to collectively as the First Peloponnesian War.

Prominent among the components of this larger conflict was the Saronic War of 460–458.[1] That clash expanded from beginnings in a dispute over borderlands (eschatia) that Corinth had with its neighbor to the east at Megara. The quarrel led to limited violence in which the Corinthians soon gained the upper hand through a round of successful raids and skirmishes. The Megarans were disappointed in their hegemon at Sparta for its lack of support as this took place[2] and therefore broke away to seek a relationship with Athens instead. The Athenians agreed, no doubt feeling that this would boost their landward authority and provide greater security in the direction of the Peloponnesian frontier. They proceeded to help Megara build long walls to its port and installed a garrison in the city. Sparked by these troubling signs of Athens turning its ambitions from overseas toward the Greek mainland, fighting soon spread to include others nearby; in particular, the island polis of Aigina, which then came under siege from the Athenians. Both sides saw a number of ups and downs before the war climaxed in 458. That's when the Corinthians at last made an all-out effort to take control of the originally contested territory in the Megarid.

The entire regular ("field") army of Corinth was likely involved in this operation along with a small contingent from Sicyon. The Corinthian citizen militia would have supplied nearly 5,000 hoplites of prime age (20–49),[3] while the Sicyonians added perhaps 300 more.[4] And those heavy-armed troops would also have had a body of javelineers (psiloi) in tow; these coming from among the crowd of attendants accompanying their column.[5] This all combined to produce a force large enough to utterly cow the Megarans, who could hope to muster no more than 3,000 or so spearmen of their own.[6] The Athenians, though, would normally have been another matter entirely. They had the potential to throw well over 10,000 citizen hoplites into the field.[7] And the prospect of facing such a host certainly seems to have dissuaded the Corinthians from going on the offensive up until then.[8] Their present courage to attack derived from "the belief that with a large force absent in Aigina and Egypt, Athens would be unable to help the Megarans without raising the siege of Aigina."[9]

The ruling powers at Athens viewed this development with a great deal of frustration if not outright alarm. As the Corinthians had noted, they had most of their regular forces tied down at the moment: on the Aigina investment and in support of a revolt against Persia in North Africa. Troops involved in the latter campaign were simply too far away to recall even had that been desirable. At the same time, withdrawing from the siege would mean wasting the considerable effort already put into it. Yet responsibilities toward allied Megara and the fact that Corinth's aggression was unfolding so close to the homeland clearly demanded a strong response of some sort. The Athenians turned in the end to Myronides for a solution. An experienced general of good repute,[10] he seems to have been sitting among the polis' old-age reserves.[11] This savvy veteran came through brilliantly, devising a bold approach that employed an unexpected element to add substantial psychological assets to Athens' over-extended arsenal. His strategy would deliver a victory otherwise so seemingly unlikely that it was destined to become a somewhat gilded patriotic myth in later years.

Myronides' first order of business before intervening in the Megarid was to find sufficient manpower to match the considerable enemy presence there. He had three sources for this: citizens of the youth and old-age reserve, resident aliens, and allies. The reserve consisted of the two youngest year-classes (18–19 year olds) and the ten oldest (those 50–59). These might have composed up to 20 percent of all hoplites (the "zeugitai"), perhaps numbering better than 2,500 at this time with youths and older men in about equal proportions.[12] Alien residents ("metoikoi" or metics) were obligated for military service at Athens according to their wealth in the same manner as the citizenry; though mostly serving in a reserve capacity to man defenses[13] (thus being less capable "static" troops) rather than on field campaigns. Occupying separate units from those of the regular army,[14] these men had risen in strength during the 5th century, their population growing as Athens' economy expanded and foreigners immigrated in consequence of its burgeoning business and labor opportunities. They formed a ratio of about one for every six citizens at the time of the invasions from Persia[15]; however, that would approach one to four by 431[16] and probably was well on its way there even in 458. We can thus project that Myronides could have called upon a corps of metic spearmen at least equal in size to his reserve contingent at some 2,500 strong. As for allies, there is no record of Athens fielding them in this crisis; yet it's inconceivable that the Megarans did not take part on their own soil. It therefore seems almost certain that they contributed a full prime-aged muster of around 3,000 hoplites (though no doubt holding back their own reserves to guard at home).

By drawing from all of these sources, Myronides could gather more than 8,000 hoplites—possibly more, had other unrecorded allies been tapped. If so, he actually had a significant advantage in simple numbers[17] over the 5,000 or so spearmen in the field for Corinth. So it wasn't manpower that was the old boy's chief concern; rather, it was the overall quality of most of his troops. The Megarans were certainly neither well seasoned nor accomplished[18]; his metics were largely untested in open combat, having primarily been mere static defenders in the past; and maybe half of his age-reservists were green youths. That left only a little more than a thousand "old sweats" among the citizen reserve who were experienced soldiers of proven ability.[19] His challenge was to optimally exploit the sort of swagger from past battlefield successes that such veterans could bring to the fray, while at the same time finding a way to undermine similar confidence on the other side. That would give his men an edge "from the eyebrows up" and better allow their superior but little practiced numbers to prove decisive. He did this by marching direct from the city to surprise the Corinthians, who were looking for any threat to involve an Athenian redeployment from Aigina.

The Athenian and Corinthian phalanxes came to blows at Cimolia, which sat somewhere in the western Megarid region under contest. Our sources[20] give no details on the engagement save that both armies claimed to have won, with each gaining success on part of the field. Not expecting to see action and facing a larger enemy force, the Corinthian spearmen must have been shocked and shaken as they readied to fight. Beyond this handicap to morale, they also had to make physical adjustments in compensating for their lesser manpower. This called for filing thinner than normal to avoid flank overlaps conducive to deadly double envelopment,[21] which further added to their discomfort going into battle. Yet, despite all these challenges, they were still able to defeat the hoplites posted on the opposition's left. Those were probably the Megarans,[22] who would seem to have either suffered flanking from enemy rightward drift as the formations closed or simply couldn't stand their ground as adequately filed and more capable foes speared and pushed through by main force.

The Athenians, however, fared much better, routing the thinly arrayed and wavering spearmen of lesser note that they faced on the other end of the field.[23] And it was probably the youth and old-age reservists that did this. The older men were far and away Myronides' most reliable soldiers; therefore, placing the metics in the center of his formation, he would have assigned those veterans to the rightmost position of greatest responsibility. There, they probably mixed within the forward ranks to provide a steadying influence on untried youths standing alongside. Such "grey-hairs" also more than likely manned the rearmost couple of ranks so that they could hold strong against any othismos pressure that might intrude from the front.

Neither of the triumphant wings seems to have done much pursuit[24] and the Corinthians headed home. That left Myronides and his men alone in the field, where they put up a display to celebrate their share of success before retiring into Megara. This turn of events was significant in that possession of the ground after a battle and the setting up of a trophy there were widely viewed in Greek society as the true mark of victory. And when news of what the Athenians had done got back to Corinth, those that had initially thought themselves victorious became subjects of scorn, with perhaps the most painful taunts issuing from their own elderly reservists who chided them for losing to a bunch of old men and boys. Responding to these insults, the Corinthian militia returned to Cimolia a mere twelve days after leaving so that it might erect a competing monument. Yet all that would bring was another lethal dose of surprise mobilization from Myronides and his makeshift host of irregulars.

Sallying from Megara, the Athenians caught their foe even less prepared than before (perhaps laboring under the illusion that they had gone all the way back to Athens). Men constructing the new trophy lost their lives in short order and the attackers then descended upon the main body of Corinthians camped nearby. Again, we have no specifics on the ensuing fight, but this time the hoplites from Athens gained a decisive triumph on all fronts. Myronides must have made some changes to his array for this second action in adjusting for casualties taken earlier. Those steps quite possibly included tucking the spearmen who had previously done poorly (likely his Megarans) into the less exposed center of his formation and replacing them on the left with troops confident from having succeeded in the first fight (a split of either metics or age-reservists). He could thus have more competently engaged the opposing phalanx across its entire width. And had the Corinthians cut down at the trophy site been largely members of the skirmisher class on work detail there, he might also have been able to put a large advantage in light-armed strength to work against weakly screened enemy flanks. We can do no more than speculate about such tactical details; still, whatever they might have been, Corinth's hoplites suffered a thorough rout. This not only drove them from the battlefield, but also inflicted an atrocious slaughter on part of their company, which fled blindly into a ditch-bounded field to be trapped and shot down without customary quarter under a hail of stones and other missiles.

Myronides' accomplishments here would raise him to command of the regular army in the days ahead. Moreover, they would grow in the telling and retelling into a legend that inspired Athens' citizenry by suggesting that even its "oldest and youngest" could beat another polis' best men. Many psychological effects were on display in these engagements. Among them are those of training (or lack thereof), past combat experience (both its quantity and quality), surprise from unexpected mobilizations, disrupted routine, fighting on home soil (the Megarans), societal shame, and the fostering of atrocity. Some of these enabled combatants, motivating them through obligation or boosting their confidence. Yet others served to disable, crippling men with doubt and/or fear. Such factors affecting the mental state of hoplites before, during, and after battle were in no way unique to Cimolia; rather, they and more of the like were part and parcel of every ancient Greek combat.

Tradition, Training, and Combat Experience

Among the psychological inputs that impacted hoplites before they ever went into action were the martial traditions of their society in general and their polis in particular. These were instilled from childhood with a view toward shaping a man's wartime priorities. Known collectively as "paideia," these emphasized duty to the state and their fellow citizens, conditioning soldiers to muster, march into battle, and more than anything else stand firm in the ranks (*en te taxei*) while enduring the dire stresses of phalanx fighting. It was a process that took many forms: tales of glorious battles of old, urging men to do the like and gain their own small share of immortality in histories yet to be written; anecdotes to encourage emulation of praiseworthy behaviors and avoidance of contemptible ones; patriotic poetry and plays putting forth models of what was right and honorable; and public celebrations of the polis' militia and its heroes that inspired participants to meet the same high benchmarks should the time ever come for them to be similarly tested under fire. This produced strict tenets of obligation that were widely held within the community. And these not only had a great influence on those so prepared when they faced combat, but also saw the social shaming and even the imposition of legal sanctions upon anyone not living up to them.

Imparting factual history as well as anecdotal stories must have begun within the family at home and then been greatly reinforced during any formal education that males enjoyed up to and past their age of first military service. This was undoubtedly done at much greater depth and intensity within Sparta's famed "agoge" system of training and indoctrination[25]; but it had weaker equivalents at all other poleis. Nor were adult citizens immune to continued schooling in their communities' standards of what a "good man" (agathos) should do to display "manly virtue" (andreia), "courage" (arete), and "patriotism" (patris). We thus see the maxim of "passive courage" critical to disciplined phalanx fighting embedded within popular entertainments. Verse of the Spartan poet Tyrtaeus provides an outstanding example:

> Let him fight toe to toe and shield against shield hard-driven, crest against crest and helmet on helmet, chest against chest; let him close hard and fight it out with his opposite foeman, holding tight to the hilt of his sword, or to his long spear ... here is a man who proves himself to be valiant in war.

> With a sudden rush he turns to flight the rugged phalanxes of the enemy, and sustains the beating waves of assault. And he who falls among the front ranks and loses his sweet life, so blessing with honor his city, his father, and all his people, with wounds in his chest, where the spear he was facing has transfixed that massive guard of his shield, and gone through his breastplate as well, why, such a man is lamented alike by the young and the elders, and all his city goes into mourning and grieves for his loss.[26]

Nor was it Spartans alone who were bombarded from cradle to grave with these kinds of behavioral ideals; thus, the Athenian playwright Euripides has Hercules' father declare: "Your spearman is a slave of his weapons; unless his comrades in the ranks fight well, then he dies, killed by their cowardice" and "the bow is no proof of manly courage; no, your real man stands firm in the ranks and dares to face the gash a spear may make."[27] Athens' Plato defined bravery in much the same way, using his character Laches (a hoplite general and friend of Plato's teacher Socrates in real life) to say "if a man is willing to remain at his post and to defend himself against the enemy without running away, then, you may rest assured that he is a man of courage."[28] This attitude was codified in the pledge young Athenians (epheboi) made to start their military training: "I will not desert the man beside me wherever I may be stationed."[29]

Lionized everywhere from private conversations to speeches at public venues honoring a polis' military feats and war-dead, the stoic bravery required of phalanx fighters was therefore a near universal criterion throughout the Greek world. And anyone falling short could expect punishment, ranging from informal disgrace to legally imposed shunning and even banishment. Much of our surviving record of this comes from Sparta, where those so dishonored might well choose suicide.[30] But similar mechanisms were at work elsewhere. This can be seen in the shaming that drove the Corinthian militia back to Cimolia with such unfortunate consequences. It's also on display in the insults aimed at Athens' Demosthenes for tossing his shield in flight at Chaeronea. Of course, poleis varied in the intensity of such sanctions. This is obvious in that what was mortal disgrace for the Spartan survivors of Thermopylae seems to have been no more than a political embarrassment for Demosthenes.[31] Nonetheless, such deeply ingrained concepts of honor and obligation must inevitably have been much on the minds of many if not most hoplites as they took to the field for combat.

The foregoing forms of cultural conditioning might all be best categorized under the broad heading of "psychological training"; but what about the effects that "physical" training had on a hoplite's state of mind? We're talking here about the positive impact of certainty (or the negative aspects of its absence) that a man had in his martial abilities as well as in those of comrades standing all about him in formation. Intense drill surely gave those hoplites who received it greater confidence that they and their fellow spearmen could prevail in a phalanx battle, which in turn encouraged them to endure in the ranks until just such a victory was achieved. This was thus something of a self-fulfilling phenomenon, with those who believed they could win often then doing so in reality. Yet it would take a considerable amount of drill to instill that kind of confident determination; something that was rare in the realm of Greek militias. Their amateur members usually saw very little training beyond informal weapons practice with relatives and/or close neighbors.[32] So this sort of drill-yard experience was restricted to only troops with access to more generous training via state support; essentially, these were the Spartan equals/

spartiates and supplemented elites (epilektoi) in a few other poleis, with the latter mostly being rather small contingents.[33]

A key element if such instruction was to produce phalanx warriors both capable and confident was the instilling of an extremely positive self-image in its subjects. Any practice that might introduce a trainee to doubt and fear about his abilities would be counter-productive and could well trigger him to exhibit losing behaviors under the later duress of actual combat. As one modern study has noted about training: "Conditioned fear can be extremely difficult to extinguish. It cannot be eliminated through passive deterioration or even active attempts to do so. Even if it seems that it has been extinguished, stress may cause it to reappear."[34]

The very best hoplites were thus not only well drilled and certain about their physical skills, but also had a mind-set equally honed by positive reinforcement on the practice field to always expect success. And nowhere was this kind of psychological conditioning more evident than at Sparta. Spartiate spearmen were supremely assured and took on all comers with a high rate of success; something due in no small part to their simply refusing to accept the possibility of failure. Notable here is that they did this on occasion almost entirely on the basis of culture and training. That reflected long intervals when their polis concentrated on internal affairs to the exclusion of significant foreign engagement with its opportunities for combat.[35]

Yet, even though the Spartans' strong traditions and exceptional amount of drill were able to accomplish much on their own, the ultimate asset that any hoplite could carry into a fight remained his prior positive experience on a real battleground. In many ways this was similar to what supportive training could do as noted above; however, the impact of past exposure to success in the field was much more powerful. This was because it reflected confidence that had been driven deeply into the spearman's psyche by the sort of extreme pressures one could never truly duplicate outside the milieu of life or death combat. The most effective spur to victory was therefore merely having won in the past. This is something well illustrated by the Athenians' military prowess in the 5th century, a time when they disdained to do much in the way of formal training but often went to war. Success beginning with its stunning victory at Marathon in 490, Athens fought more actions in that period than any other polis and won better than two-thirds of them.[36] As opposed to Sparta's acumen gained on the practice field, the Athenians acquired their martial skills in actual combat. This was something the always casualty-conscious Spartans must have seen as a foolish risking of precious citizen lives; still, it was effective as well as compatible with Athens' larger population, wholly civilian occupations, and less regimented lifestyles.

Of course, just as bad drill practices might damage a hoplite's potential in future battles, so a defeat in the field could also prove disabling going forward for anyone managing to live through it. It is, however, difficult to document this. A polis with a long history of combat failures might well have fallen victim to many other negative circumstances, ranging from various manpower issues to just plain old bad luck. All the same, obvious parallels to the well documented effects of negative training seem to argue against that kind of coincidence, making it overwhelmingly likely that men once beaten were then more prone to quit fighting when tested again. And experienced commanders must have made this a prime consideration in selecting troops for posts within their phalanxes to minimize reliance on such questionable allies. Investing their trust instead in others with stronger traditions and/or better training and/or a pattern of past battlefield success, they would have agreed in total with Xenophon, who wrote: "I am sure that not numbers or strength brings victory in war; but whichever army goes into battle stronger in soul, their enemies generally cannot withstand them."[37]

Divine Signs, Home Soil, and Battle Companions

Beyond traditions, training, and experience; other significant factors colored the attitudes of hoplites as they took to the field and marched into battle. These included their religious beliefs, the personal importance of the ground under contest, and relationships with men ranked around them. Theirs was a world full of omens for good or ill; where the consequences of victory or defeat could go far beyond a hoplite's own fate to have a rapid and substantial impact on hearth and family. And those standing and fighting alongside a man were no strangers; more even than the closest companions, they were often his father, brothers, and other kinsmen.

Hoplites anxious about the immediate future as they marched off to war were sensitive to anything they might construe as an ill omen. Whether devoutly religious or a bit on the skeptical and atheistic side, they might well quit the field at any significant sign that the gods could be against them; the faithful trusting in such portents while doubters no longer had faith in now unsteady true believers, who would be standing alongside if it came to a battle. We thus see even armies led by hard-headed Spartans retiring after enduring an earthquake. Taken as a sign of possible disaster to come, Sparta's generals were either reluctant to continue and risk the wrath of earth-shaking Poseidon or knew that troops from other poleis and vital to their expedition's success were unwilling to do so. Spartan armies turned back without giving battle under such circumstances in 426, 414, and 402; though, both the Spartans' admiral Eurybiades and their sage general/king Agesilaos were able to talk earthquake-frightened forces into seeing temblors as good omens on two occasions; the former before the battle of Salamis in 480 and the latter in 388 while campaigning against Argos.[38] Nor was it just the Spartans and/or their allies that took fright when the ground shook or a tsunami rose, since we know of at least one Athenian raid coming to grief due to the psychological effects of an earthquake; this taking place on the island of Aigina c.505.[39]

Solar and lunar eclipses could also give otherwise hardy hoplites pause. The Spartan general Cleombrotus (father of Pausanius, the victor at Plataea) led an army back from the Isthmus of Corinth, where it had been at work on defenses against the Persians then close to hand in Attica, doing this after his men had seen a partial solar eclipse (on October 2, 480).[40] And Athens' Nicias delayed retreat from Syracuse for an astounding (and perhaps fatal) 27 days (thrice invoking the lucky number three: $3 \times 3 \times 3$) after an eclipse of the full moon on August 27, 413. Most of his men were "deeply impressed by this occurrence" and "urged the generals to wait." However, so long a delay seems to have been beyond any reasonable deference owed to the gods; thus, we see Thucydides' subsequent criticism that Nicias "was somewhat over addicted to divination and practices of that kind."[41]

Though earthquakes and eclipses don't appear to have affected an ongoing battle as far as our surviving records indicate, there were other omen-like events that did intrude in the midst of fighting. These included storms. Certainly, violent weather could have a significant physical impact on an engagement, as well demonstrated by the battle at Crimisus River[42]; however, most of our recorded examples seem to be much more indicative of psychological effects. Pausanius related a legend that the destruction c.465 of an Athenian-sponsored army of Greek colonists at Drabescus in Thrace was due to it being "struck by lightening."[43] This would seem a likely indicator of a storm hitting at or near the battle's start to unnerve the hoplites as a prelude to their slaughter by barbarian foes. More clearly documented, we have Thucydides' account of a storm striking during the opening action at Syracuse in 415. Imparting "claps of thunder with lightening and heavy rain," this "did not fail to add to the fears of the party fighting for the first time, and very little acquainted with war."[44] Some probably saw the storm as a troubling divine signal while others were merely further shaken within the grip of acute stress related to their first combat. At any rate, the tempest seems to have had its greatest effect upon the rather less combat-savvy Syracusans, who would ultimately quit the field in defeat. Interestingly, it would be the Athenians who then suffered from a storm that was taken to be literally "ominous" during their retreat from Syracuse two years later. This was at the Acraean Bald Rock.[45] Athens' hoplites there, struggling to attack a well-reinforced position, were hit by "claps of thunder and rain." This unexpected event "still further disheartened the Athenians, who thought all these things to be omens of their approaching ruin."[46]

But perhaps the most common battlefield happening that might have been seen as an ill omen was the death of a commanding general. It's debatable whether the blow to morale that accompanied a leader's loss was inspired by religious concern (the gods striking at those they despised) or by the secular fear of now having to fight without his tactical and spiritual guidance. Both these elements were most likely part of a unique and potent mix for each individual within the fallen general's host. Yet it's not clear any psychic damage that the loss of a leader inflicted on his men was ever enough on its own to insure their defeat. A case can certainly be made among the Greeks that "defeated commanders usually died in battle"[47]; yet, that in no way shows that it was their demise that led to the defeat rather than the other way around.

As in so many martial matters, there might have been a divide on how a general's death was viewed between the Spartans and hoplites from other, less battle-wise poleis. Spartan deployments commonly list multiple officers, forming a chain of command that let another take over should the present leader go down. This played out in full on the island of Sphactaria in 425. A small Spartan force there surrendered under Styphon, who was in charge because "Epitadas, the first of previous commanders, had been killed, and Hippagretas, the next in command, left for dead among the slain, though still alive; and thus the command had devolved upon Styphon according to the law in case of anything happening to his superiors."[48] And though not always recorded in detail, such a system seems to have been in place among the Spartans from at least the early 5th century until past the end of their hegemony. This is apparent from Thermopylae (480), Leuctra (371), and Megalopolis (331). Spartans in all those actions continued to fight effectively (even if in a losing cause for other reasons) well after their kings went down, with pre-designated subordinates stepping up to assume the mantle of command. Other phalanxes therefore might or might not have fled in panic upon the loss of a general, but that was something for which Spartan hoplites seem to have been organizationally and thus mentally well prepared.

Fighting close to home is another factor long thought to have heavily affected the psychology of Greek hoplites. A popular view on this is well summed up by Mitchell: "[Long-distance expeditions] placed the advantage in battle firmly with the defending force ... which could concentrate on the simple matter of defending their own land, on a site of their own choosing. They also could draw on superior psychological motivation. Defending one's own territory was at the heart of Greek warfare ... the ones with the most to lose could be expected to fight most doggedly."[49]

There were certainly logistical advantages to engaging in one's homeland or upon other familiar ground (see the discussion below on surprise attacks). But how valid is the idea of having a psychological edge when defending native soil? This seems to have become "common wisdom" (perhaps based largely on the failings of Persian invaders 490–479, the final action at Thermopylae being their sole victory, and quite a costly one at that). However, analyses of the wider Grecian battle record during the 5th century, when polis militias were at their height, strongly suggest that the opposite was more probably true. Save for when springing an ambush, hoplites actually seem to have been at a measurable disadvantage when engaging near home. It appears that, even including victims of surprise attack, an invading force fighting similarly sized opponents on their own ground was half again more likely to be victorious than the locals.[50] Why would this seemingly counterintuitive tendency be the case? Any answer to that query is certainly speculative, but we might propose that it involves a native hoplite's lack of confidence due to fear for the extended consequences of defeat.

Our best ancient support for this thesis comes from a speech that Thebes' general Pagondas gave before the battle of Delium in 424. That was an action his men would have to fight beyond their frontier, since the opposing army of Athens had already crossed over the Oropian border and out of Boeotia: "The party that is attacked, whose own country is in danger, can scarcely discuss what is prudent with the calmness of men who are in full enjoyment of what they have, and are thinking of getting more ... people who, like the Athenians in the present instance, are tempted by pride and strength to attack their neighbors, usually march most confidently against those who keep still, and only defend their own country, but think twice before they grapple with those who meet them outside their frontier and strike the first blow if opportunity offers."[51]

The effective differential in psychology when it came to combat on native ground might well have boiled down to the factor of men acting "confidently" just as Pagondas said. The fact was that it took a great deal of certitude for a hoplite to march into someone else's backyard to fight. But having done so, he was then distant from his own people and property, which were secure back home and so gave him naught to fear for save his personal safety, something that was probably of relatively modest concern to a confident man. And that contrasted sharply with the feelings of those facing his aggression. They were beset with a multitude of terrors; and not simply for their own well-being, but much more with regard to the future of dependents, crops, and other items of value should they lose. For men thus conflicted, it might readily appear better to run at the first sign of potential failure. That would at least give them a chance to escape and see to their farms and families, when to stay and quite possibly die risked forfeiting all those precious things in addition to their lives.

In short, fear of loss might frequently have trumped any urge toward "dogged" resistance as per that implied by Mitchell and others. That overriding concern then would become a likely precursor to defeat. Of course, there can be no doubt that tradition, training, and past positive experience of combat as outlined above could overcome this sort of diversion of focus onto personal risks. They could therefore keep a hoplite steady in the ranks against even the most dreadful odds. All the same, the weaker that such elements were among a given body of men, the greater the probability that some would yield to fear and break away from a battle, taking down their entire array in the process.[52] And the data indicative of relatively poor performances by hoplites fighting on home soil would seem to suggest that this failure-prone outlook was rather more often the case among defenders than not.[53]

Yet, though terror of a personalized sort might oft times have conspired to send men fleeing from the field of combat, the equally personal aspects of companions and relations sharing risk in a communal effort seem to have inspired them to keep on fighting. The strong sense of obligation that warriors feel for their comrades-in-arms is well documented among modern soldiers[54]; and it was obviously no less potent for ancient Greek spearmen. Indeed, their style of close-order warfare made the concept of "fighting at one's side" as literal a reality as could ever be possible. Moreover, unlike the norm today, when armies represent spotty recruiting within huge and largely urban populations, polis militias were near-universal drafts from smaller and mostly rural communities. Their tight-knit musters thus included neighbors, friends, and family members alike. A hoplite among those ranks necessarily stood between men that might well include his father and brothers, not to mention many if not nearly all of his other male acquaintances (and perhaps even a lover[55]). As such, he must have been under tremendous pressure to hold fast in battle; not only to protect friends and kin, but also in full knowledge that those same fellow fighters would surely later condemn him should he prove wanting. Their acceptance and approval in fact comprised the most powerful mechanism for enforcing his polis's martial traditions and standards for bravery.

Surprise Deployments and Attacks

Myronides' tactic of deploying by surprise at Cimolia was one that he would put to good use again the very next year. Now in command of Athens' regrouped regulars (save for a few still in Egypt), he marched them and a large contingent of allies into Boeotia to confront a Spartan-led army that had been operating there along with the locals to resolve a land dispute at Doris (important to the "Doric" Spartans as the legendary fount of their race). This led to a battle just north of the Attic border at Tanagra. The combat ended in disputed fashion with both sides carrying their respective rights as so often happened in engagements between well-matched phalanxes. Diodorus[56] actually called it a draw; however, Thucydides[57] seems to have been more accurate in declaring a victory for the Spartans due to their remaining on the contested ground when the fight was over.

That came about when Myronides withdrew rather than face a second round of combat against a Spartan wing that had defeated the Argives holding his left (losses there accounting for most of those he took on the day).

Sparta chose in the battle's wake to sign a four-month truce with the Athenians that would allow its troops to go home for some rest and healing. But that fatally ignored Myronides' flair for doing the unexpected. Instead of resting his own men as anticipated, the crafty old general took them back into Boeotia only 62 days after the end of his last foray. He acted without his allies this time so as to move with the utmost speed and secrecy, and that caught the Boeotians ill prepared for a fight. Hastily gathered and now without Sparta's help, they took a crushing defeat against the invading phalanx very near to Tanagra at Oenophyta.[58] This battle put Boeotia in thrall to Athens for a decade (until Coronea I in 447[59]); and given lesser manpower versus Tanagra that was similar for both sides, its outcome must have stemmed in no small measure from the unsettling psychological effect that the Athenians' surprise deployment had on their foes.

Though a master of its form, Myronides was far from the only general to exploit the tactic of surprise mobilization. A survey of significant Greek battles in the 5th century indicates that just over a quarter featured an army moving into the field unexpectedly. And it seems to have been highly effective, with 85 percent of those so deploying then claiming a victory. But it is important to note that there seems to have been a strong factor of amateurism at work in these results. When we look at the following century, there are very few surprise mobilizations to be seen (they preceded less than 5 percent of the era's battles), though they were just as effective on those few occasions when used.[60] Much like other methods requiring a naïve and/or inexperienced opponent (as per mid-combat maneuvers[61]), catching a foe off guard with a deployment seems to have become much harder to do over time as Greek hosts became better trained and more professional.

However, a clear distinction exists between unexpected mobilizations and actual surprise attacks. The former dealt an enemy psychological trauma prior to engagement; while the latter did its psychic damage only at the very time of combat and usually provided physical bonuses as well. Suddenly taken unaware and unprepared, victims of surprise attack often couldn't get properly arrayed to fight; and even when they did, they remained emotionally unstable, overwhelmingly subject to panic and swift defeat. Another key difference is that, while unanticipated deployment was a tactic equally useful for aggressors and defenders, ambushes were far more effective on native soil. There, the perpetrators could often use proprietary knowledge of local terrain to great advantage. Surprise assaults therefore not only delivered success in the field at a high rate, but they did so best of all for defending forces. In fact, armies able to employ a surprise attack in their homelands won about two battles for every one that they lost.[62] And that tactic seems to have been a threat to even the savviest foes. Though ambushes and the like went down some in frequency from the 5th to 4th centuries as Grecian armies improved with regard to scouting and intelligence gathering, they remained far from uncommon and were just as deadly.

That surprise assaults were part of the classical hoplite's repertoire from the beginning is indicated by one of the more outstanding examples of the genre occurring as early as 494 at Sepeia. And it seems that the Spartans there were already infamous for martial trickery if we are to judge by a Delphic prophecy given to Argos in warning prior to the engagement. Thus apprised and probably already aware of the risk from past experience, their Argive foes "were not afraid of open battle, but rather of being conquered by guile"[63]; yet they fell to a sneak attack all the same. Other instances of surprise attack during the 5th century include many from Demosthenes of Athens, who was every bit a maestro of that method as his polis fellow Myronides had been of unexpected deployments.

Demosthenes' list of devious enterprises includes: (1) springing an ambush to wipe out enemy troops at Ellomenus in the onshore territory of Leucas in 426; (2) besting a Spartan-led phalanx at Olpae in the winter of 426/5 by sending a contingent of his men against its rear from hiding in the midst of battle; (3) catching a relief force of Ambraciots in their beds with a dawn assault a few days after Olpae; (4) devising the surprise foray onto the island of Sphactaria that defeated the Spartans there in 425; (5) leading a team of peltasts from hiding to help capture the long walls at Megara in 424; and (6) authoring a nearly decisive but ultimately failed nighttime sneak attack on Epipolae at Syracuse in 413 (see below), which Thucydides aptly described as "a piece of audacity" that the enemy "never expected."[64]

Most worthy of note among 4th century proponents of unexpected assault is Sparta's long-serving leader Agesilaos. He executed a devastating ambush against a pursuing army near Sardis in Lydia during his 395 campaign against Persia in which a hidden force hit his Asian foes in the rear after they had formed up for battle.[65] He also carried out a river-assisted ambush of Epaminondas at Amyklai in the winter of 370/69.[66] In fact, Agesilaos' very last action in 360 at the Egyptian Canals was preceded by a surprise attack. This was a sudden and unexpected sally that let the aged ex-king and his mercenary legion break out of pending entrapment through a gap in a nearly completed barrier with siege wall and ditch.[67] Agesilaos, like Myronides, Cleomenes, Demosthenes, and many other commanders, gave his hoplites both physical and psychological advantages through the use of deceptive tactics. And though that approach did not invariably deliver victory for all who tried it, it did so at a rate sufficiently high as to ensure its prized place in the tactical tool box of any truly competent Greek general.

Confusion, Combat Behaviors, and Battle Trauma

One of the most powerful of psychological phenomena that intruded onto ancient Greek battlefields was confusion and its consequences. Unclear about what was going on about them, men could latch onto mistaken beliefs about the reality of their situation for either better or worse. This came about in various ways, often by accident, but sometimes due to a commander's machinations; yet, it almost always exacted a high cost in blood when striking amid the inherent chaos of a mortal combat. The critical dynamic empowering battlefield confusion to do good or ill was the same one present in most of the psychological factors discussed here: the relative balance of confidence versus fear. Simply put, anything that increased a hoplite's belief that he was winning tended to inspire him to greater exertions and increase his chances for victory; while anything causing him to doubt his phalanx's performance would tend to make him fearful and might discourage further putting forth a maximum effort, thereby upping the odds that his side would lose.

We thus see Athenian spearmen on Syracuse's Epipolae in 413 falling prey to a misunderstanding that turned their pending triumph there into a devastating loss. In the midst of carrying all before them in a night attack under Demosthenes, a few frontfighters from Athens took a modest reverse from a small group of defenders. Shouts of joy and despair spread out from this action, infecting all within hearing distance. Bewildered about what was actually transpiring, the attacking force that had earlier been "flushed with victory" then "fell into great disorder and perplexity" such that "all in front was now in confusion."[68] With the defending Syracusans revitalized and "cheering each other on," the Athenians suffered a costly defeat; and one that had been prefixed more by them being beaten in their minds than on the field.

The confusion that so dramatically reversed the role of victor and vanquished in this case was obviously enhanced by poor visibility despite there being a full moon that night. Yet much the same thing could come to pass in sunlit conditions. This reflects the practical reality noted by Thucydides that even by day a "fog of battle" was present due to "no one knowing much of anything that does not go on in his immediate neighborhood." This was endemic to the close-ordered and claustrophobic press of phalanx combat and so familiar to veteran commanders that they could actually take advantage of it as per Myronides of Athens' ploy at Oenophyta in 457: "The Athenians and Thebans were deployed for battle. Myronides ordered the Athenians to run at the enemy beginning from the left, when he gave the signal. He signaled; they ran. When they had advanced a little way, Myronides ran to the right wing, and shouted loudly: 'We are winning on the left.' Encouraged by this report of victory, the Athenians attacked more eagerly. While the Thebans, dismayed at the news of defeat, turned to flee."[69]

The clever old general won what Frontinus described as an otherwise "indecisive battle" by means of "inspiring courage in his own men and fear in the enemy." Such unfounded fear could not only disable armies against their foes, but might even lead to incidents of self-destructive "friendly fire." This was the case at Epipolae, where the bested Athenians "coming into collision with each other in many parts of the field, friends with friends, and citizens with citizens, and not only terrified one another, but even came to blows and could only be parted with difficulty."[70] Hoplites from Athens had earlier slain their own during the raid on Aigina c.505, where earthquake-rattled men "lost their minds" and "began to kill one another as though they were enemies."[71] And that kind of fratricide could even strike on the verge of victory. The Thespians at Delium in 424 were "surrounded in a narrow space and cut down fighting hand to hand"; yet, "some of the Athenians also fell into confusion ... and mistook and so killed each other."[72] Nor were Athenians alone in so suffering, since we know that Syracusans took similar self-harm while campaigning against Carthage in 307. That incident saw them panic and flee their camp upon the unexpected return of some deserters; and "those who happened to meet fought each other as if they were enemies."[73]

It's worth noting that these recorded instances of self-imposed casualties must represent only some of the most egregious examples. Given limits on a hoplite's vision and hearing when wearing a Corinthian helmet, the din of spears and swords clashing on shields, the similar gear worn by both friend and foe, and any boosting of confusion by the occasional unforeseen event, we can be quite certain that at least a few Greek spearmen wounded or killed their own in every battle where the contending front-ranks became entangled. Mass slaughters being rare, these were for the most part personal tragedies and known by a polis' citizen soldiers to be an inherent part of waging war.[74] Like so much else about their experience of battle, it therefore went largely unremarked upon as being no more than commonplace.

More deliberate, but no less a product of the frenzy accompanying close combat, was the commission of battle-related atrocities: going beyond the widely accepted protocols of honorable fighting to inflict harm on a helpless foe. Such acts have been elements of warfare in all ages, but often reflect individual propensities rather than a culture-wide characteristic. And among the ancient Greeks, this was more connected to light-armed pursuers[75] than hoplites. Still, we have some clear cases of spearmen committing deadly mass transgressions against others of their ilk.

As noted earlier, atrocities followed upon the Spartan victory at Sepeia in 494.[76] And the Athenians' actions in slaughtering the Corinthian spearmen penned inside an enclosure during the pursuit following Cimolia II seems nearly as dishonorable. With Myronides' hoplites barring the entryway to cut off any escape, those troops should by accepted custom have been allowed to surrender and then buy back their freedom; but instead, the Athenians massacred them with missiles.[77] There is also the case of Athens' Pericles on Samos in 440, who tied his captured hoplite foes to posts, taking them down after ten days only to bash their heads in with clubs.[78]

The psychology of these and other known mass killings by hoplites of helpless members of their own class[79] most often reflects truly intense inter-polis hatreds/rivalries: Sparta and Argos, Athens and Corinth, etc. These clearly raged at levels far hotter than the norm for most Grecian conflicts. Yet, though rare (at least in their reporting), such atrocities reveal how hoplites really waged war: not always treating their defeated adversaries with honor or even reasonable humanity.[80]

The terrors unleashed in exceptional cases of battlefield confusion and atrocity were in truth no more than distilled and thus slightly more potent exemplars of the sort of mental trauma that came along with every life or death engagement. Combat stress and its constant companion fear affected all but the most resistant of hoplites as they headed into battle. Holmes[81] catalogued common physical reactions to these psychological demons as recorded among modern soldiers; symptoms no doubt just as familiar to their ancient counterparts. These include: a violent pounding of the heart; a sinking feeling in the stomach; a feeling of weakness or stiffness; vomiting; and involuntary urination and/or defecation.[82] But more impactful in the long run than such transitory physical expressions of battleground stress were the psychic blows a hoplite received once embroiled in combat. These grew out of his seeking to kill someone, seeing close friends and family die horribly, and witnessing the indifference of command and fortune to what he believed was fair and right.

Grossman has documented the apparent genetic tendency for human beings to abhor the act of killing their own kind. The dominant observation that he makes is that "throughout history the majority of men on the battlefield would not attempt to kill the enemy even to save their own life or the lives of friends."[83] Conditioning methods can significantly boost men's tendency to engage in lethal acts,[84] as can the environment within closely bound elite units (comparable to Sparta's spartiate lochoi or the epilektoi in other poleis) and modern weapons crews. The last let a soldier be both somewhat anonymous in his actions while receiving absolution for them from his immediate fellows, benefits that the Doric phalanx also seems to have provided:

> [T]he phalanx succeeded by turning the whole formation into a massive crew-served weapon ... each man in the phalanx was under a powerful mutual observance system and in the charge it would be hard to fail to strike home without having others notice that your spear had raised or dropped at the critical moment. And, of course, in addition to this accountability system the closely packed phalanx provided a high degree of mob anonymity.[85]

The Greek military system was therefore well-designed after many years of evolution; it combined tradition, training, and peer pressure within the perfect close array that let those inputs do their best in motivating hoplites to fight in an aggressive manner despite all the terrible strains inherent to mortal combat. Still, a few men broke down, such as Epizelus of Athens; we are told that this fellow lost his sight at Marathon "though he had not been struck or hit on any part of his body" in what appears to be a clear-cut case of psychosomatic ("hysterical") blindness brought on by seeing a spearman standing alongside struck down.[86] Yet this sort of trauma on the immediate field of battle seems to have been rare (Herodotus set Epizelus' tale apart as being "amazing"). Most of the time, hoplites were able to function effectively in service of their phalanx for as long as it remained intact. But if ancient Greeks did a good job of handling psychic challenges before and during combat, then what about when the fighting stopped?

Modern studies suggest that only a very few soldiers are able to take an enemy's life without remorse,[87] and there is no reason to think that was any different for hoplites. It must have been just such remorseless and deadly men among his polis' draft that led one observer to write: "Out of every one hundred men, ten shouldn't even be there, eighty are just targets, nine are the real fighters, and we are lucky to have them, for they make the battle. Ah, but the one, one is a warrior, and he will bring the others back."[88]

Yet for everyone else in the phalanx, even among those other "real fighters," the grim struggle to slay or be slain would have done great violence to their psyches. Grossman has proposed that killing (or even attempting to kill) a fellow human is a leading cause of what today is called Post Traumatic Stress Disorder (PTSD); and there is no reason to doubt that violations of such a cultural and likely genetic imperative did indeed deal hoplites significant mental harm. Another factor that appears to have been most impactful on the post-battle psychology of Greek spearmen was having family members and/or close comrades die in combat; this then adding to other battle-related hardships and seeming injustices to fuel a very damaging perception that things had unfolded without regard for "themis." The hoplite's concept of themis covered the full sweep of commonly held moral and social conventions.

Jonathan Shay has rendered "themis" into the modern idiom as "what's right." He has proposed that when soldiers feel their experience of war has violated themis, they then develop an "indignant wrath" (*menis*).[89] And it is such rage that he believes was "the first and possibly primary trauma that converted subsequent terror, horror, grief, and guilt into lifelong disability [by way of PTSD]." Direct evidence for similar psychological distress among ancient Greek warriors comes from Gorgias of Leontini, who wrote during the Peloponnesian War period that men upon "seeing frightful things [in war] have also lost their presence of mind at the present moment," falling into "groundless distress and terrible illness and incurable madness."[90]

Lawrence Tritle has made a highly detailed case for the presence of PTSD among classical Greek fighting men by drawing from Xenophon's tales in the *Anabasis* regarding Clearchus of Sparta. An experienced hoplite and renegade governor, Clearchus led Xenophon and his fellow mercenaries in 401 during their famous march into Persia on behalf of Cyrus the Younger. Tritle documents Clearchus' many disturbed behaviors, citing him as "the first known historical case of PTSD in the western literary tradition."[91] Others that he suggests are strong candidates for having had PTSD include the Athenian general Demosthenes and Alexander the Great.[92] And it's important here to realize that these famous men are surely no more than the tip of what must have been an iceberg of common hoplites suffering from PTSD. The identities of those thousands are now lost to us through a paucity of source material and the relative anonymity within it of all save a few highlighted individuals; yet nearly all Greek citizens of the day were acutely conscious from personal experience of both the severity and the scope of the damaging effects that combat could have on the minds of men.[93]

It seems clear in all of the foregoing that understanding the psychology of hoplites is every bit as important to comprehending how they made war as the physical aspects of their armaments, formations, and tactics. Just as Greek spearmen exposed their bodies to terrible hazards and long-term crippling in manning their phalanxes, so they likewise put their mental health at risk. And it was awareness of that complete spectrum of dangers that inspired Pindar to say: "Sweet is war to the untried, but anyone who has experienced it dreads its approach exceedingly in his heart."[94]

Part III. The Phalanx

8

Hoplite Formations

The group efforts of hoplites on the field of combat were made within the confines of their chosen battle formation, the phalanx. A close-ordered arrangement of long ranks and relatively short files, these arrays stretched across the narrow valley-floor battlegrounds of Greece and advanced into violent contact with each other as well as other, barbarian formations to let the first two ranks of their hoplites spear into the opposition. Meanwhile, those in file behind stood ready to move up in replacement for the fallen or to aid a collective push against the enemy front. This was a fighting method that at its most basic made few demands upon those in its ranks (stratiotai) other than that they resolutely persevere in struggling ever forward into the opposition. It was thus perfectly suited to the sort of amateur hoplite militias fielded by most Greek states. But Sparta was an exception. That polis had a singular societal structure that allowed its citizen spearmen to drill and gain much greater formation skills. And in time, others raised elite units at state expense and/or hired mercenaries able to drill frequently and thereby improve the performance of their own phalanxes.

A major variation on the original or "Doric" phalanx emerged in the mid–4th century at Macedonia under its king, Philip II.[1] But even this new "Macedonian" phalanx had the same fundamental mechanics, varying only in providing better support for the hoplites that led its attack wing (just as in the older Doric array) by using pikemen as defensive specialists on the formation's defensive wing and shock-capable cavalry flankward. In all its forms, the phalanx was formidable at the fore, presenting a near-overlapping line of shields behind the fearsome lancing of hundreds or even thousands of weapons; yet, it was highly vulnerable elsewhere. Men on the flanks, especially on the unshielded right, were easily beaten if struck from the side, while assaults on the rear invariably proved successful. This led to taking great care in arranging formations toward preventing the enemy from overlapping or otherwise circling around a flank for such advantaged strikes. The Spartans excelled at this developing unique methods to both promote and avoid flank overlaps. Still, even those long-time masters of phalanx combat could fall prey to either an especially astute foe or a bungled maneuver.

Mantinea I (418)—Not Skill, but Courage

The initial phase of the Peloponnesian War[2] raged for a full decade before Sparta and Athens agreed to terms in the spring of 421. But this settlement, known as the Peace of Nicias for the Athenian general that was its chief broker, was destined to fail before long with both sides at fault. The expansionist Athenian policies that had led Sparta and its alliance partners to declare war in the first place were very much still in play; while on the flip side, the Spartans proved incapable of meeting their obligations under the treaty. The latter called for major concessions to Athens by other members of their coalition; and when Sparta couldn't compel those allies to abandon self interest and comply, Athens reneged in kind.[3] The rising tensions that resulted would eventually see Spartan and Athenian hoplites standing once more on opposite sides of a battlefield; and though that did not in itself entirely break the negotiated "peace" for good, it certainly served to foreshadow its rapidly approaching demise.

The engagement's immediate cause actually lay in bad blood between Sparta and Argos. Those long-time rivals[4] had last come to blows during the so-called First Peloponnesian War,[5] but had signed a 30-year truce in 451. This agreement kept Argos neutral as Sparta and Athens fought the Archidamian War; however, its pending expiration was a looming concern for the Spartans.[6] Though Sparta was eager to sign a new accord, talks fell apart as its increasing frictions with Athens led the Argives to reconsider. They chose instead to join former Spartan coalition members Elis and Mantinea in concluding a partnership with the Athenians.[7] Elis then shut Sparta out of the 420 Olympic Games in its territory, while Argos and Mantinea became more assertive. The Argives attacked Epidaurus in a bid to detach key Spartan ally Corinth, which had strong security and economic interests there, even as Mantinean surrogates began to intrude along Sparta's northern frontier.

These conflicts led to mobilizations in 419; however, the contending parties failed to come to conclusive battle.[8] And this mostly bloodless kind of maneuvering resumed the next summer when Sparta's king Agis responded to continued attacks on Epidauros by taking a huge army into the field. That expedition also failed to produce a decisive combat; a four-month truce emerging instead when neither the king nor his Argive counterpart[9] proved willing to risk so important a confrontation under the circumstances then present.[10] The lack of official sanction for this agreement from their home governments led both poleis to immediately criticize it; each side thinking that the advantage would have been theirs had an engagement taken place. Therefore, upon hearing that their allies at Tegea were being menaced by Mantinea and would defect to Argos if help was not forthcoming, the Spartans sent Agis out again. He marched under close observation and a vow to be more aggressive this time.[11]

Agis entered the territory of Mantinea and began plundering to bring the locals out to fight. And that reaction was not long in coming, with the Mantineans in the company of reinforcements from Argos and their other allies stationing a large army on a "lophos" (free-standing hill) near the Spartan camp.[12] Agis called off an upslope attack at the last minute[13] and withdrew southward across the Tegean border. He then had his men plug several sinkholes that provided underground drainage for streams around Mantinea in an effort to entice the opposition onto less challenging terrain.[14] Fearing that the city would flood if this was not remedied, the Mantinean force came off its high ground, camped for the night, and then arrayed for combat the next day.

Agis had headed back to his former campsite near Mantinea that morning, unaware that the damming operation had already lured his foes from their upland. A dense stand of oak trees blocked both the old and new enemy positions from view as the king approached (apparently without benefit of advance scouts)[15]; as a result, he and his column emerged from behind that screen to the utterly stunning sight of a large phalanx of hostiles standing just ahead and ready for combat.[16] Thucydides claimed that "a shock like that of the present moment the Spartans do not ever remember to have experienced"; nonetheless, "they instantly and hastily fell into their ranks ... their king directing everything according to the law."[17] Agis' well-drilled troops thus overcame their initial surprise and were soon equally aligned for action.

We have an outstanding description of the preparations at Mantinea I from Thucydides,[18] who was not only contemporary and a likely visitor to the site, but also had personal access to king Agis as a highly informed eyewitness source.[19] Both sides deployed to fight in the long, tight rows and modest depth that defined the classical phalanx as first devised by Greece's Dorian warriors and honed to near-perfection during better than three centuries of combat. Men took post by polis and sub-unit in the company of friends and family; each array's hoplites (stratiotai) with their long spears at the ready and standing so near to comrades alongside as to touch shields edge to edge. This let those at the fore create a wall of hard-polished bronze that flashed in the bright mid-morning sun. Backing these front-fighters (promachoi), others held close-ordered files; those first behind set to add their lances directly to the coming fray, while men farther to the rear and constituting the bulk of their armies stood in waiting. If someone ahead went down, they would move up in replacement; alternatively, they might be called upon to press into their hollow aspides and shove ahead in mass.

There was some small variation in arrangement along the lengths of the facing formations as indicated by Thucydides' note on the Spartans that "they had not been all drawn up alike"; each contingent arraying as per the dictates of its commander, though "they were generally ranged eight deep."[20] Sparta's allies would surely have been just as discrepant in this regard, though, again, a depth of eight shields must have dominated. Agis' phalanx had Sparta's most trusted perioeci, the Sciritae, in its secondary post of honor far left. Next right was a collection of liberated helots comprising both veterans who had won manumission after serving in northern Greece during the Archidamian War and others granted freedom since.[21] An Arcadian contingent came next, and then the bulk of the Spartan army filled out the center toward the right wing. The remaining Arcadian troops were on that wing with the Tegeans at their far end; however, hegemon Sparta reserved the most prized station on the extreme right for itself, with a crack Spartan battalion (lochos) holding that unshielded and vulnerable flank.[22]

The opposing array featured the Mantineans in the rightmost position of honor as befitted an action to be fought on their behalf and on their home soil. Next came a lochos of their best Arcadian allies and then a unit of elite hoplites *(epilektoi,* trained at state expense) from Argos to complete the right to center. At center-left were all the remaining Argives, with allied levies from Cleonai and Orneai alongside. Finally, the rest of the Arcadians stood right of a force of seasoned Athenian spearmen that had the distinction of holding the far left flank. It is highly likely that the resulting phalanx had files of eight shields deep for the most part; however, the minor irregularities in this practice already noted for the Spartans opposite must have been a factor here as well.

Such modest lack of uniformity was no doubt inherent within any formation deploying units from many different poleis, each having its own military customs.

Our sources lack values for the contenders' total manpower, leaving us with no more than Thucydides' vague note that "the Spartan army looked the largest."[23] It would appear that the native Spartans on hand included eight of the polis' ten "field grade" lochoi. Two other lochoi had initially marched from Sparta, these making up "the sixth part of the Spartans [when added to the ten units of all citizen regulars], consisting of the oldest and youngest men." But these reservists had likely come along only to fill in for two regular battalions guarding at home against raids from Pylos and any surprise advance from the Argive coalition.[24] Agis therefore felt free to dismiss them after being joined at Tegea by an adequate alternate force of allies. This suggests that his subsequent array featured six Spartan lochoi at center, another (the Sciritae) on the left, and one more far right.[25] Adding in 1,000–1,500 helots then made for 5,200–5,700 Lacedaemonian hoplites in all. With the Tegeans and other allies numbering maybe 4,000–5,000,[26] Agis might thus have had 9,200–10,700 spearmen.

The opposing heavy force was much the same size. It included the 1,000 epilektoi from Argos as well as a unit of "the older men of the Argives"[27] plus their "five companies [lochoi] so named" of regulars. At around 500 men each like their Spartan counterparts, those last six units would have provided 3,000 hoplites to which we can add something like 500–1,000 more from Cleonai and Orneai.[28] The Mantinean levy might have been modestly larger than that of the Tegeans,[29] while the other Arcadians perhaps provided another 1,500–2,000 heavy infantrymen. Finally, the Athenians had brought 1,000 hoplites, including some settlers from Aegina.[30] This all indicates that there were 10,000–11,500 spearmen with the Argive coalition; the lower figure supporting Thucydides' second-hand impression that it was the smaller force, but otherwise suggesting a modest numerical edge.

The cavalry on hand for both sides took post off their flanks in league with all the foot skirmishers that they might guard the ends of their hoplite arrays; and the phalanxes then began to move at each other across the flat. There was a differing character to this on either side, with "the Argives and their allies advancing with haste and fury, the Spartans slowly to the music of many flute players—a standing institution in their army ... meant to make them advance evenly, stepping in time, without breaking order, as large armies are apt to do in the moment of engaging."[31] A strong tendency existed for phalanxes to drift rightward in so closing as each man instinctively edged nearer to the protective shield of his line-mate on that side. Moreover, the crack team of Spartans on Agis' far right was likely amplifying that trend, dragging those to its left along in a conscious bid to outflank the opposition. This was a favorite Spartan ploy,[32] but it came with a drawback in that it could cause one's own left to fall dangerously inside the enemy's extent as it likewise pulled rightward. And that's just what Agis saw in the offing as his troops marched resolutely at the raucous foemen ahead.

The Spartan king's response to this risk was to send a runner to the Sciritae and the helot contingent with instructions that they make all efforts to hold even with the Mantineans on the enemy's right extreme. This, of course, would cause a space to develop between the helots and Arcadians next right; so Agis also ordered two lochoi of Spartans to fill that pending gap by shifting over from their current position farthest right within the main Spartan deployment.[33] However, that last command was either misinterpreted or simply ignored[34] to the effect that a huge opening remained within Agis' left wing when the battle fronts finally came together.[35]

Agis' attempt at clever maneuvering had backfired badly, leaving his formation's integrity seriously compromised and putting his army on the brink of complete disaster. Yet this was not to be, as "the Spartans, utterly worsted in respect of [tactical] skill, showed themselves superior in point of courage."[36] The *Mantineans*, their picked allies, and the Argive epilektoi quickly took advantage of the breach in Sparta's line to enclose the helots' exposed right flank, putting them and the Sciritae to rout and driving the fleeing mob rearward in a hot pursuit that carried all the way to Agis' encamped baggage train. But elsewhere it was quite a different story. King Agis was in the center of the field within a lochos that included an elite 300-man bodyguard; and these led the way as the Spartans bested the select veterans and other Argives opposed there to send them packing. And the same fate befell the Argive allies and Athenians trying to hold their formation's far left; these being worsted if anything more swiftly still as the elite Spartan lochos on that side led their Tegeans allies in wrapping around those outflanked foes to chase them off with only the screening efforts of Athens' horsemen on that end preventing a serious slaughter.

Both armies were now in effect cut in two, each with right wing triumphant and left wing in flight. But having failed once to successfully exploit his Spartans' unique talent for battlefield maneuvering, Agis would now invoke those skills yet again; and this time they would prove decisive. Turning his victorious hoplites aside, he allowed the defeated Athenians and Argive regulars to get away without further damage, instead reordering his spearmen to march laterally across the field. This fresh advance caught the Mantineans and epilektoi from Argos unprepared on the return from their chase and they fled. The Spartans essayed no more than a perfunctory pursuit,[37] but still brought down "many of the Mantineans," though "the bulk of the picked body of the Argives made good their escape."[38]

Losses for the Argive alliance came to some 1,100 hoplites (roughly 10 percent), while the victors lost only around 3 percent in the form of 300 from Sparta itself, its allies suffering no appreciable casualties.[39] The Spartans set up a trophy to mark their triumph and stripped the enemy slain. Their own dead were carried to nearby Tegea for internment, while those of the enemy were returned under truce. It had been very much a "soldiers' battle" in which Agis' magnificent fighting men had recovered his opening blunder and gone on to once more confirm their status as the most preeminent masters of the phalanx formation among all the Greeks.

Early Formations

John Keegan in *The Face of Battle* noted: "Inside every army is a crowd struggling to get out" and that "…a crowd is the antithesis of an army."[40] It is not surprising that this is stated in a chapter on Waterloo, because that battle took place at a time when discipline was fetishized as a means of making large conscript armies—often composed of reluctant soldiers—do entirely unnatural things, like stand in formation amid billowing smoke and invisible death. The reasoning behind predicting imminent rout when disciplined ranks and files transform into a seemingly leaderless crowd is ontological, because every man in the army was taught that the loss of the order imposed by their commanders presages defeat. But what if there had never been order imposed from officers to men in "top-down" fashion? What if instead, the men fought as a crowd and order started with them as a "bottom-up" process?[41]

Modern science has shown how order arises out of seemingly chaotic interactions between individuals.[42] Imagine the endless drill required to teach an army to create the spectacle of dressed ranks marching in well-ordered files, and compare that to seeming perfect symmetry of motion in a swirling flock of starlings or a school of fish. Order in the latter swarms emerges from the bottom as individuals react to each other according to stereotypical rules. These individuals can perceive only their immediate surroundings and have no knowledge of the greater formation they are a part of. We are told that this was the environment of the hoplite in battle, where "each man hardly knows anything except what is occurring to himself."[43] It is important to remember that this was true for the officers in the phalanx as well as the rank and file. In animal swarms, it is easy for us to appreciate the bottom-up order inherent in crowds, but in humans we imagine it does not exist because we expend so much mental energy imposing order from the top down.

In order to launch a bayonet attack, an officer of the type Keegan had in mind must rely on discipline to form his men in a group and get them moving in the same direction, hopefully running intently towards the enemy. The men's fear of death pressures them to shy from combat, but their greater fear of the consequences of breaching discipline keeps them moving forward. What then of the dreaded rout? When an army breaks, the men move away from their enemies as a group, hopefully doing so with vigor. Now, the fear of breaching discipline is eclipsed by a greater fear of the enemy. What took hours of drill and discipline to achieve in the direction of attack emerges unbidden during retreat. It is thus in defeat that the natural self-organization of a human crowd becomes obvious; though, as Keegan suggests, it was there all along.

Van Wees looked to tribal combat in New Guinea as a model, describing early hoplites as a "motley crew" that moved into battle as a disorganized and dispersed cloud of intermingled spearmen and missile troops.[44] Early hoplites did not drill endlessly to maintain rank, yet it is a mistake to think they could not achieve order that would be difficult to distinguish from the product of top-down discipline. The rules fish or birds follow that give rise to bottom-up order are very simple. Animals in swarms have an urge to follow others of their kind and to maintain a "comfortable" distance. They like to be surrounded by others in their swarm, but not so close that they foul each other. When working well, those simple rules give rise to the amazing coordination we see.

Early hoplites likewise had uncomplicated rules, which were directly dictated by the nature of their arms and armor. A man in a missile duel with a large shield is an island of protection behind whom those without shields would naturally shelter, if at all possible.[45] Another man, with his own shield, is able to cut down on the angles his foes can use to strike at him by simply standing near the first shield bearer. This would become even more attractive as hoplites became more heavily armored and could rely less on nimbleness to avoid incoming missiles. Once the benefits of moving swiftly in and out of missile range became reduced, the drive to move into mutually supporting groups that concentrate firepower would be great. The rules for hoplites thus need not be more complex than: men with shields tend to stand beside men with shields to protect their flanks and archers tend to stand behind men with shields. If we were to fill a battlefield with men following these rules, the result would not be a widely dispersed crowd of intermingled troop types, but rather a formation resembling the Germanic shield-wall or late Roman fullkum.[46] This type of formation puts more heavily armored men, who may throw missiles themselves, in front of unarmored missile troops to act as a wall or screen.[47] Segregation like this is natural to tribal war bands in which richer, better equipped men lead a troupe of progressively poorer and lighter equipped warriors into battle. It would actually take more discipline to keep troop types evenly mixed than to clump in this manner.

A major rift between scholars of hoplite combat centers upon the notion that there was a sudden revolution in hoplite tactics directly tied to the adoption of the panoply and contemporary political reforms.[48] The orthodox view holds that the hoplite drills and close-ordered phalanx tactics of the classical period originated in the 7th century with the introduction of the new elements of panoply. The opposing view sees hoplites fighting in an open order not much changed from centuries before during the Archaic period. The gulf between the orthodox view of spearmen making an organized, mass attack that had a component of physical pushing and the heretical depiction of a crowd of individuals fighting alone or in small groups with missiles disappears on the self-organized battlefield. In a self-organized swarm, it is the individuals within the mass that organically give rise to that proximity.

One advantage of the large diameter of the aspis is that it acted as a literal meterstick. Men did not need to make any judgment on their frontage beyond lining up shield rim-to-shield rim. In human crowds, as in schools of fish or flocks of birds, individuals are completely interchangeable. Early hoplites would have formed in units based on aristocrats and their family and retainers, yet the individual men need not have had assigned posts in rank and file. The result is that nobody has a specific place in the formation and the group is highly fluid. Men can move to the front line or beyond to throw missiles at the enemy or challenge a foe, and then fade back into the group and retire out of combat; and such "milling" is commonly seen in all but the densest of crowds[49] as single men or small groups easily break out from the mass, and just a swiftly melt back into it.

The downside of this sort of freedom of movement is that men can skulk away and shirk combat just as easily. The late 7th century poet Tyrtaeus codified the memes of such self-organization. He urged young men to "remain beside each other" and "encourage the men beside them"; and perhaps more importantly, he warned these youthful warriors not to skulk behind the line of battle and leave their older comrades behind to die in their place.[50] It was this fear of being called out as a coward that drove men forward in the early phalanx rather than a fear of officer's punishment. Social ostracism can be a far greater motivator than simple death. The Spartans had temples to both Eros and Phobos, love and fear. This is the love of messmates and the fear of letting them down or being perceived a coward. And so influenced in its deployment, a crowd of hoplites would have looked very much like a classical phalanx.[51]

A battle line would be made up of a series of individual crowds of men based on kinship or fealty that were held together by ties to the poleis or treaty. Such crowds need not be formed in tight squares, because a linear formation emerges spontaneously when opposing lines approach each other and their forward progress is halted. The presence of throwing spears in the arsenal of early hoplites makes it likely that any initial encounter occurred beyond spear length, but probably no more than 15–20m given the limited range of thrown spears. Opposing shield walls at this distance could either move forward, allowing the light missile troops behind to engage the enemy, or move back out of missile range. Heroic men might step forward into the dead space between walls and fight. There would always be a threat at this distance that one side would charge to use their retained spear. This might be triggered by a perception one side was losing the missile duel or might reflect men no longer able to bear the stress of being under the enemy's barrage. If the men in the front-line then stand shield-to-shield, the literal pushing of mass-on-mass envisioned by the orthodoxy could easily ensue as men pile up from behind, making this development a constant threat even if not intended.[52]

The foregoing may go some way towards explaining the origin of phalanx tactics. If battlefields in the early period were dominated by well-armed and trained aristocrats and their retainers, then a mode of battle that requires individual skills like missile combat or spear fighting would have been predominate. But as the battlefield filled with citizen farmers, with disposable income for quality armor, but not the free time required for extensive training, two concurrent pressures altered the way battles were fought. First, the increase in numbers without the appearance of a more efficient command structure demanded that these additions reinforce through increasing a unit's depth rather than its length of its front. That would in turn have radically changed applicable tactics in that missile troops cannot reliably shoot over more than about four ranks.[53]

If you are facing a more skilled opponent in any martial art centered on striking like boxing, you really only have two choices: move out of range or move in to clinch. In this way too, the best plan for an army of semi-skilled men to fight those of greater skill is to rely not on their weaker weapons ability, but rather their hopefully superior mass. This means that you must get in close and negate your opponents' skill with the spear by crowding them. The inability for rear-rankers to throw over the heads of those in front or bring their spears to bear would have relegated them to providing no more than moral support; however, if this crowd and its ability to push were weaponized, then you could effectively use every man in your phalanx as a direct combat asset rather than just those skilled fighters at the very front.

This "crowd-as-weapon" concept is the focus of the great ongoing debate among scholars on the nature of othismos, which is the pushing by groups in battle. Bardunias had suggested that surviving such pushing required protecting the diaphragm from constriction, a requirement fulfilled by the Argive aspis.[54] If true, then the shape of the aspis would have been optimized for this role soon after othismos began to occur.[55] As long as there was a threat of othismos occurring in battle, the aspis could not be altered in a manner so severe that impeded its anti-asphyxiation function. For this reason the aspis, of all the hoplite panoply, remained virtually unchanged for centuries.[56]

The Hoplite Phalanx

A self-organized crowd can be both flexible enough to allow all of the missile combat and personal challenges seen in the pre-hoplite era and yet spontaneously form into compressed masses akin to phalanxes upon contact with the enemy. But in a crowd, men who were free to move forward and back were also able to flee at the first setback. This could be mitigated by forming men up next to their relatives or in smaller units, where leaving would be noticed. Hoplites in the 6th century (and perhaps through the early 5th) formed along lines of sociopolitical distinction. Each of the ten tribes of Athens, for example, may have made up a large unit called a *taxis*.[57] Herodotus could thus speak of the hoplite battle-line through the descriptive term "parataxeis" in which individual taxeis literally lined up alongside each other. Each taxis would have had a leader (*taxiarch*) and a pecking order that must have disseminated throughout the ranks. Any line of more than one rank had a built-in differentiation of file-leaders (*promachoi*), those who support them, and a closer (*ouragos*) at the back of each file.

The file-leaders must of course be brave men and superior fighters that they might effectively form their formation's cutting edge. And second rankers would be second only to the file-leaders in valor as they were separated from the front line only by those elites and might be called upon to step up in replacement should one of them go down. In contrast, a file-closer did not need exceptional fighting prowess: instead he must be steady and able to urge on the men ahead while keeping them from turning to precipitate a rout. Yet there is no need to see in these various duties a true officer corps nor any notion of numerical homogenization between units.

One might imagine the social maneuvering that went into determining where kin-groups stood along the front of the deployed taxis, as well as the order in which each taxis lined up on the field. From early times it seems that the place of honor was at the forward edge of the right wing. The reasons for this will become obvious as we delve deeper in this chapter and the next, but it is enough to know that men in this position led the marching column and were responsible for positioning the army on the battlefield. The resulting depth of the battle-line may not have been uniform, instead being decided by the manner in which the kin-groups that made up the smallest recognizable unit (lochos) shuffled their irregular number of men into line. All that was needed to form the ordered ranks and files that made up the classical phalanx was for each man to know who he stood behind, and for the front rankers to know who to stand beside.[58]

This simple set of rules lay at the very heart of hoplite drill. As Xenophon tells us: "The formation is so easy to understand that no one who knows man from man can possibly go wrong. For some have the privilege of leading; and the rest are under orders to follow."[59] Nevertheless, the greater the ratio of actual officers to followers, the more flexible the deployment of the phalanx could be; and the Spartan army at the height of its intricacy was unique in possessing an extensive officer corps. Xenophon describes a Spartan command structure that consisted of a mora of 1,152 led by a polemarch, which was divided into four lochos of 288, each led by a lochagos, eight pentekostyes of 144 led by pentekosteres, and sixteen enomotia of 36 hoplites led by enomotarchs who conveyed verbal commands. The Spartan enomotia was a reflection of the fundamental social grouping of mess-mates of a broad age spectrum within what was called a *phitidion*.

Because of this, the actual numbers of men in each enomotia was determined by the age-classes of men called up in each muster.[60]

The fundamental formation of such units at Sparta was established in the line of march long before going into battle. The subdivisions would march to the battlefield in a long single file line that contained all of these elements embedded in their proper order. Deployment was a matter of the first man in marching column standing on the spot that would become the rightmost station of the battle-line; then each enomotia was brought up alongside the one before it to form a common front. Because files of 36 men were viewed as too deep for normal combat by the Spartans, the enomotia normally divided into equal sub-files, each moving up alongside their enomotarchs. In this way, an officer could easily determine how deep his phalanx would be. For example, Xenophon states that enomotia could be formed in a line of 36, but also sub-divided into either three files of twelve (a common depth for Spartans in the 4th century) or six files of six that was utilized if a phalanx was seen to be too short.

In his *Cyropaedia*, a fictional account of the training of the Persian King Cyrus, Xenophon presents a picture of idealized hoplite drill. He relates a tale of an aspiring taxiarch bringing his command to dinner and showing off its good order:

> And once he saw another taxiarch leading his taxis up from the river left about in single file and ordering, when he thought it was proper, the second lochos and then the third and the fourth to advance to the front; and when the lochagoi were in a row in front, he ordered each lochos to march up in double file. Thus the dekadarchs came to stand on the front line. Again, when he thought proper, he ordered the pempadarchs to line up four abreast.[61]

What he describes is a quite simple process called "doubling." Approaching in a single line, the taxis of 80 hoplites first split into four equal lochoi of 20 men. The leader of the first lochos (its taxiarch) stood fast and the following lochagos veered to the left to bring their lochoi up parallel, leaving a gap between units such that three more hoplites could form up along the front of the phalanx in the interval. At the taxiarch's command, an officer called a dekadarch (leader of ten) would lead the rear half of each lochos up to the left, allowing a space one hoplite wide between himself and the lochagoi. The taxiarch then commanded that the pempadarchs (leaders of five) bring the rear half of each file forward and take post beside and between the lochagoi and dekadarchs respectively.

On a real battlefield under normal circumstances, this process might have flowed more naturally if each lochos fully deployed down to files of ten or five immediately upon reaching its station. This would eliminate the need for lochagoi to calculate spacing for three hoplites to fill in later. Instead, if successive dekadarchs and lochogoi simply lined up at arms-length from each other (measured either by lateral reach with the right arm or by aspis width), then space for the pempadarchs to move up would be left between them (see figure). Xenophon goes on to confusingly say that "they assume a front of sixteen men and a depth of six." This must mean that pempadarchs led six men and dekadarchs twelve, coinciding with his description of the depth into which the Spartan enomotia can subdivide into teams of three or six, though this changes nothing in our understanding of the previously laid out drill.

Seemingly complicated maneuvers could easily be conducted using this fundamental system of organization[62]; and with the enomotia as its basic tactical unit, the Spartan

8. Hoplite Formations

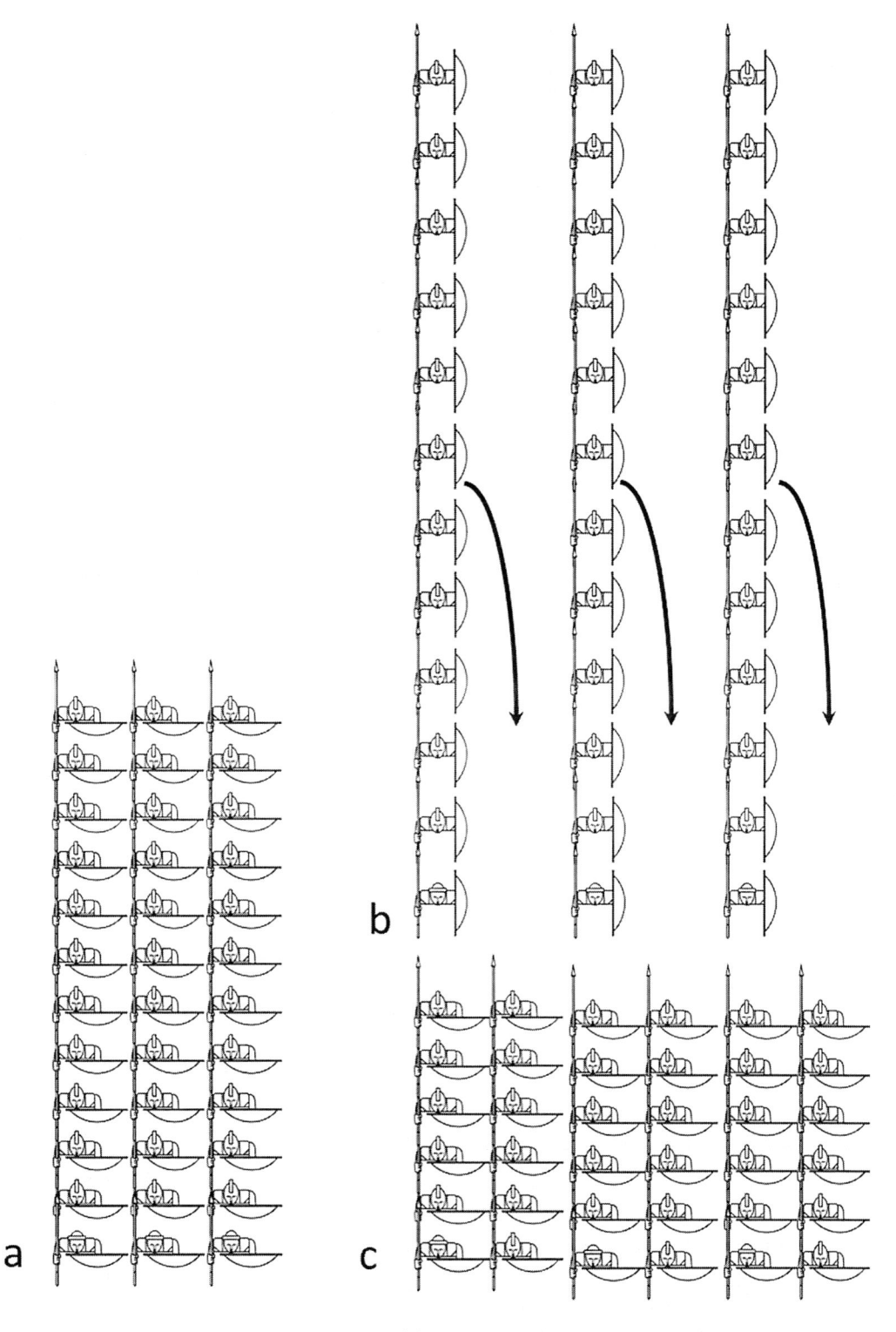

Spartan enomotia shown deploying into either (a) three lines of 12 at close order, (b) three lines in opened order, or (c) doubling the three files into 6 files of 6 at close order.

116   III. The Phalanx

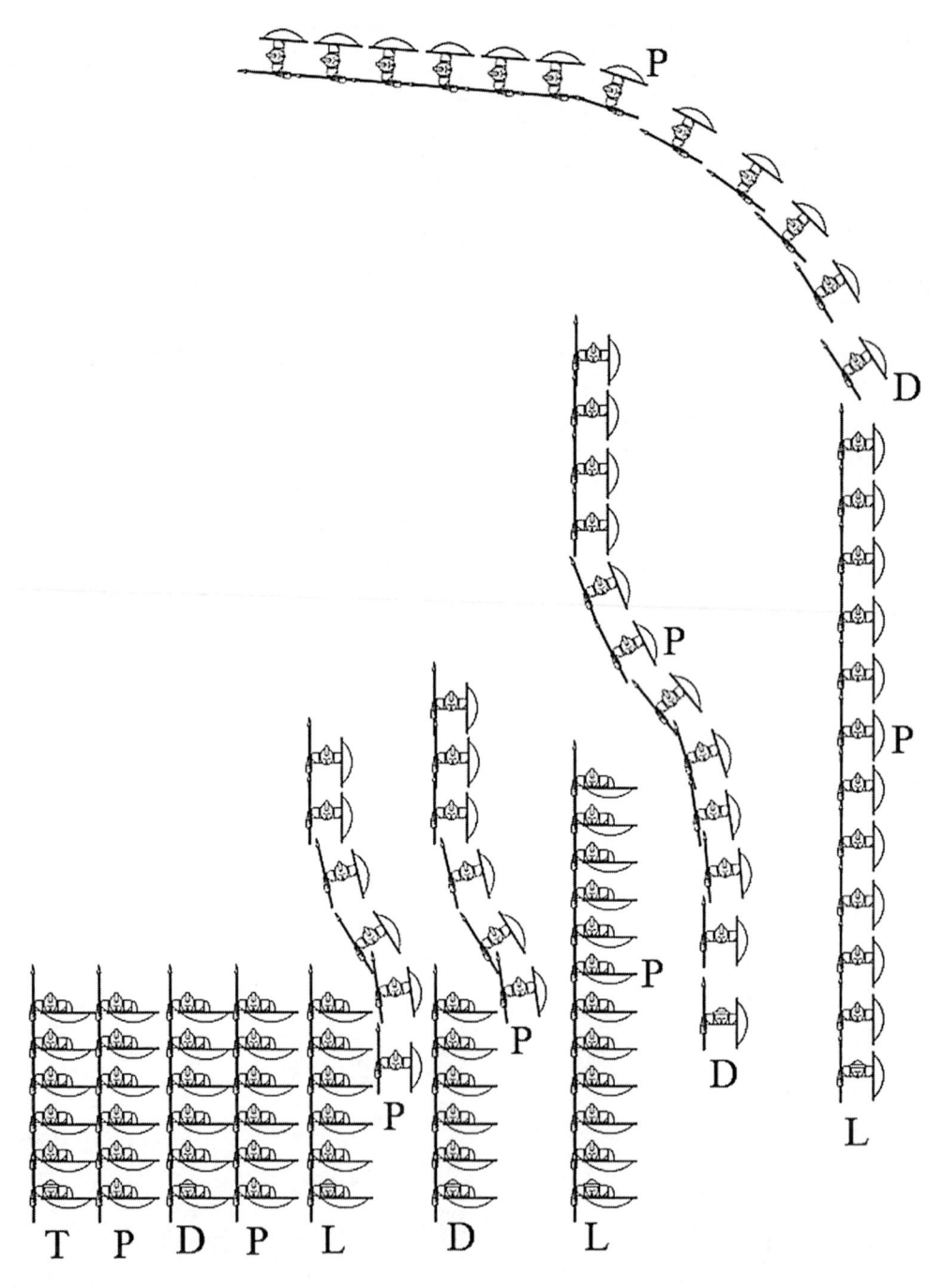

Doubling files in the dinner drill described by Xenophon. From an original formation of 4, the Taxiarch (T) is the first man in the line of march and forms the head of the right-most file. The other 3 lochoi deploy from the single file line towards the left, each leaving 6ft between him and the next man (L). Within each deployed lochos, the dekarch leads his half of the file up parallel to the front (D). After this, the pempadarchs (P) lead their quarter-files up to the left to render 16 files of 4 men at 1m frontage. Xenophon describes each doubling as a discreet command for the whole force, but in practice, each lochos may have deployed fully as it arrived on the battle line.

army had the flexibility for speedy deployment to meet sudden threats. It could rapidly deploy to the fore per the above, yet just as easily wheel each enomotia to the right or left and form up at the required depth. And if a battle-line was threatened from the rear, or had to otherwise turn around like Agesilaos did at Coronea II,[63] they could do so through a process called countermarching. This was, in fact, an incredibly easy maneuver calling for the file-leader to simply turn around and walk down the length of his file as each man he passes turns to move behind him. The file-leader then stops after moving until the last man in file can turn around and join the file.

Frontage

The amount of space each hoplite has available to him between men along the front of the battle line is important in determining how he fought and how well protected he was by those beside him. Perhaps the simplest spacing hoplites could take would be the width of the aspis, using that device as a literal meter-stick. Men formed up shield rim-to-shield rim would have enough room to fight, yet still benefit from the protection of those standing alongside. A frontage of 1m is larger than it might seem, for example, two spearmen can move past each other chest to chest in a frontage of 1m/man. It's perhaps more likely, though, that shields overlapped to some degree. A shield wall of overlapped shields limits the mobility of each man, but presents a far stronger barrier overall to enemy weapons and pushing.[64] The defensive benefit of overlapped shields and the cost to individual movement depends on men standing in very close order. Hoplites that just overlap the off-set rim of their aspides would still have mobility while still presenting an interlocked line to anyone attempting to push through them. If shields overlapped with the shield rim of one resting on the face of the other at the point where the thickened side-wall section begins, they would present a frontage of roughly 72cm/man, with a frontage of 60cm/man cm probably being the minimum a hoplite could take and remain combat effective.

Cawkwell suggested that men fought in a frontage of 2m/man, consisting of the 1m width of his shield and another shield's worth of space between him and the next hoplite in line.[65] At this spacing the hoplite enjoys great freedom of movement to dodge and plenty of room for wielding his weapons. Unfortunately, his

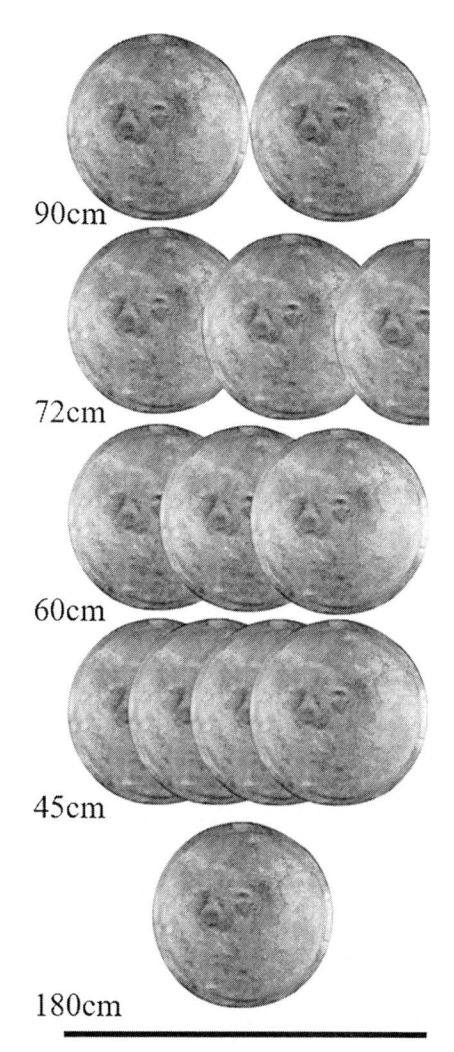

Shields overlapped to the degree demanded by differing frontages. All measured against the 180cm scale at the bottom.

opponents would have equally greater freedom to strike at him. The main benefit of forming a line of men for battle is that the men beside you protect your sides and cut down the angles from which attacks can come at any one man. Spear fencing mainly requires space for back and forth movement at your opponent rather than lateral sidestepping; and for this there is no need for a 2m/man frontage. Perhaps most importantly, it is difficult to imagine how men maintained such a large gap between themselves during a charge into battle that would have encouraged their convergence.

Matthew, on the other extreme, advocates a frontage of 45cm/man for hoplites in close order based on his interpretation of Hellenistic military manuals.[66] This is, however, an anachronistic application of non-hoplite tactics, since a hoplite with a 1m-wide aspis cannot assume a frontage of 45cm and still present his shield face-on to the enemy. A 45cm frontage only became possible when the Macedonian phalanx appeared, and then only for those within it who wielded sarissai (pikes).[67] Men armed with a long pike like the sarissa must use both hands to hold it. This naturally forces them to stand side-on with the left hand forward and requires a smaller shield than an aspis that let them pack belly-to-back at a mere 45cm apart. Matthew's figures on this issue is misleading in that he never actually shows hoplites formed at 45cm apart, but instead presents a stance running closer to 60cm/man. If we redraw his figure comparing four hoplites at "45cm" to three at 90cm separation to show the spears directly opposing rather than staggered, it is obvious that for a true 45cm frontage there has to be a ratio of two spears for every one spear at 90 cm (or, in the case of this diagram, 4-to-2). There are, in fact, four spears for the closer order for every three held by the 90cm hoplites, which represents a frontage of 60cm/man and is in line with the theoretical minimum for marginally functional hoplite combat.

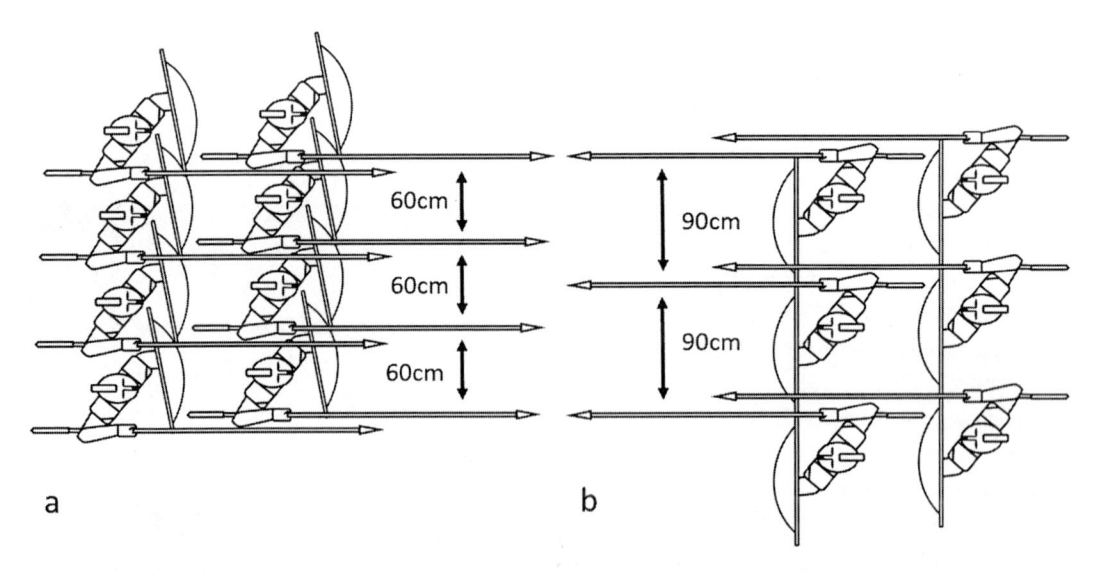

Matthew's diagram of hoplites in "45cm" frontage squared off against hoplites at 90cm frontage redrawn to align the spears so as to show that his "45cm" is actually 60cm frontage. He additionally scaled spacing along the file so that two ranks of the closer ordered men faced only one rank of men at 1m frontage. Both the 45cm frontage and the linkage of depth and width are anachronistic Hellenistic elements he misapplied to hoplites.

8. Hoplite Formations

Tied to the question of how far aspides overlapped is the question of how they overlapped. The most commonly used method of overlap by modern re-enactors is for the hoplite on the left to bring his aspis in front and over the aspis of the man on the right. This is simple to do and makes it relatively easy to disengage by just turning the shield forward and pulling back. The drawback of this method is that, if overlap is more than around 72 cm/man, then a hoplite has the rim of the aspis of the hoplite to the right between his chest and his own shield, which may well become a liability in the tight press of group combat.

If a hoplite merely keeps the aspis in front of his chest and stays behind the half of the shield that is jutting out from the man on his right, then a wall naturally forms that can be termed right-over-left. Tests of this method show that it is no more difficult to advance in than left over right, and, in the press of crowded combat, the hoplite's diaphragm is completely protected behind his shield. This approach show that it is more difficult to disengage with this stance, requiring a turn to the right; however, this actually reflects a benefit, because each man is standing behind not only his own shield, but a portion of that of his line-mate to the right as well, and it is very difficult to break through a line made in this fashion. To gain a similar level of strength in a left-over-right arrangement, you would have to brace that portion intruding from your neighbor's aspis with hand or arm and thereby greatly restrict any use of a weapon.

Iconography is of little help in illuminating this issue, because all of the images that look to show left-over-right overlap (like that on the Chigi olpe) appear to portray men advancing with their aspis presented edge-forward, while those showing right-over-left are probably just moving in single-file.[68] Sekunda has suggested that hoplites formed phalanxes with their shields staggered over-and-under on the basis of images of Geryon, the three-bodied titan.[69] But this method actually shows no benefit over the others pre-

Images of hoplites from the 2015 Archaeon Dromena at Marathon, Greece. Hoplites with aspides overlapped left-over-right (a) and hoplites overlapped right-over-left (b). Note they are not at equal frontage.

viously discussed. While it might seem that such staggering is the natural outcome of doubling files; the fact is that any method of overlapping is so simple to carry out that there is really no need to see a limitation due to doubling.

Depth of Files

Depth of files was governed by two factors: how much depth each hoplite required and how many hoplites formed a file. The depth a hoplite needs has often been linked geometrically to the width allotted his frontage; however, this is a mathematical nicety that had no application to hoplite formations. Men are wider through the shoulders than from front to back; therefore, a hoplite requiring 60cm–1m of width for frontage only needs some 45cm of depth at an absolute minimum. In spear fighting, hoplites may have required more than 1m to rear back and thrust forward. Frontage is largely static after it is initially set because there are hundreds of hoplites on either side which need to be moved in order to change it on more than a local level. Depth is not so constrained, probably changing over the course of a battle as files crowded forward or backed away from their file-leaders.

The number of men in files was never standardized, though the battles of the 5th century tend to show that eight shields was a common formation depth.[70] Before this time, it is possible that the phalanxes formed shallower to allow men to easily throw spears over those ranked ahead. Commanders could use the method of doubling described above to tailor the depth of his phalanx to match battlefield conditions. If fighting foes more lightly armed than hoplites, then files of four may have been all that was needed.[71] If a longer battle line was required, men could be formed thin, as when conducting a siege or some other action in the presence of barriers.[72] When more depth was required, as might be the case with an exposed flank, hoplites could be stacked to form greater depth of file.[73] As we have seen, by the 4th century Spartans were regularly forming at a depth of twelve men. The Theban general Pagondas famously formed his men at a depth of 25 hoplites at the battle of Delium in 424.[74] The latter started a trend in Theban tactics that culminated in the "not less than fifty shields" depth of Thebes hoplites reported at the battle of Leuktra in 371.[75] Thebes' use of excessive depths was consistent enough that allied poleis attempted to limit its files by agreement to only 16 lest the phalanx become so short that it was easily outflanked.[76]

Increased depth was probably attained by simply bringing units up to the right of those before them at the battle-ready frontage of 1m/man, rather than by leaving space for further doubling. This can be seen in the manner by which Spartan enomotia formed files of six or twelve. By the same logic, a pair of files of eight would yield a file of 16 when doubled-up. It is also possible that a commander would deploy down to a common file depth, but stack two or more deployed units with one behind the other. This is probably what was done with the Theban phalanx and the Sacred Band in some fashion at the battle of Leuktra.

There are many benefits to forming taxeis in depth rather than maximizing width with a shallow formation. The first is morale. Men in combat receive emotional support knowing that someone quite literally "has their back." Moreover, it would be difficult for the men in the first couple of ranks engaged in spear fencing to force their way back through the ranks behind them.[77] While this explains forming in more than a couple of ranks, it is still hard to see morale benefits as the prime reason for forming files of 25 versus 16. Perhaps a better explanation would be that is easier to move men in deep columns than wide lines.

Comparisons are often drawn between hoplite "columns" and those employed by the French in their revolutionary and Napoleonic armies. This comparison fails because there were very different combat expectations for these later-day troops than for ancient hoplites.[78] The aim that the French formations had during advance was to pass through the enemy's fire so as to then threaten his line (of which few ever managed to stand their ground when on the receiving end of a bayonet charge); and should their arrival fail to break their foe, the French soldiers than would redeploy three-deep ranks to return fire of their own. Although many taxeis of hoplites broke prior to actual combat, it is unlikely that a commander would actually base his depth solely on the hope they would do so.

As a practical matter, there is no indication that a hoplite taxis could re-deploy in the very face of the enemy; therefore one deep column would be severely limiting its frontage in order to rapidly bring men to a spear-fight for which the majority stuck in the numerous after-ranks would be quite useless.[79] The real reason for this deep stacking, beyond morale factors and the like, is that hoplites so formed could literally push, file-against-file/taxis-against-taxis, with great strength. This has been called a "reverse tug o' war,"[80] with Luginbill stating that this interpretation stems from the plain reading of the texts.[81] Such a physical shoving match—to which the term *othismos* is applied—has been likened to a giant rugby scrum seeking to push the opposing section of the phalanx out of alignment with the rest of its formation, forcing it to rout.

9

The Phalanx in Action

There was a dominant pattern to phalanx battles that almost always produced a well-documented sequence of events. This opened with an advance into combat. Most of the time this movement was carried out by both sides, though circumstances of favorable positioning or inadequate depth of array might lead one combatant to receive a charge in place. Spartans were exceptional among hoplites in moving forward at a slow pace measured in time to the playing of flutes, a practice that badly disconcerted its target as a display of professionalism and deadly intent. Most other spearmen were prone to battle calls/chants as they rushed toward the enemy; yet, even these would slow at the last to begin fighting at a brief distance. This phase featured the dueling of spears as men in each array's front two ranks thrust and parried in the quest for an advantage. Any extended action along these lines eventually led to the breaking of spears and ever increasing employment of shorter weapons (spear stubs and swords) all along the battle front until the struggle might devolve into shield-on-shield shoving in addition to continuing strikes over the top as still able.

The contest at this point could become one of concerted shoving (othismos) with entire files pushing in a desperate effort to move forward. This featured the hoplites leaning chest-first into the hollow of their aspides to avoid suffocation as they pressed and were crushed from behind into the man ahead. Inevitably, one side or the other would either be physically forced out of order or suffer from a sense of pending defeat and fall into disorder out of sheer panic or exhaustion. This moment marked the turning point of the battle as one of the formations routed, disintegrating as rank after rank peeled off from the rear and ran for their lives. As this developed, the victors might choose to pursue and punish those in flight or let them go and loot the dead and dying as their sole possession of the battlefield now gave them the right.

There were unusual engagements, however, where the foregoing train of events might not play out fully, the reality being that a rout was actually possible at any stage of the action. Some phalanxes broke and ran at (or even before) first contact with the enemy, and others endured but a brief duel of spears before yielding the field. Often the normal pattern would progress in opposite directions on each end of the battleground, with one army victorious on one wing and its opponent on the other. This was usually resolved immediately with another engagement. However, in one truly exceptional case, such a second action saw one army break the center of the opposing phalanx only to go from victor to being pursued. That happened when the enemy failed to fall apart on either side of the penetration and turned about to give chase.

Coronea II (394): They Killed and Were Killed

Sparta had collaborated with the Persians to gain funds for naval resources that were a key in forging its victory in 404 over Athens to conclude the Peloponnesian War. Part of that arrangement had been to cede Ionia's Greek poleis to the Persians under terms of the ensuing peace settlement. The Spartans, however, soon began to rethink that concession. They did this not only due to criticism received for having abandoned fellow Greeks abroad, but also, rather more cynically, in light of the opportunities for wealth that Grecian Asia Minor had to offer. This inspired Sparta to support Cyrus the Younger's attempt on the Persian throne in 401. When that failed, the Spartans in 399 dispatched Thibron to take control of Ionia as governor (harnmost), providing him with a force sufficient to core an uprising against the Persians. With alternating periods of fighting and truce, this campaign had only limited success; and in 397, Dercyllidas, successor to Thibron, signed a cease-fire freeing Ionia from Sparta and Persia alike. Still, the siren call of Asian riches remained persuasive. The Spartans thus used what seems to have been fear-mongering about a pending Persian attack on Greece as pretext in 396 to send yet another army into Ionia. And marking its serious intent, this one went out under their recently crowned and highly aggressive king Agesilaos II.

But even as the new Asian campaign was unfolding, things began to heat up back in Europe. Thebes had emerged as a major competitor for prominence among the Greek states and was causing trouble. Perhaps encouraged in part by monies flowing out of Persia as a means to divert Sparta's attentions,[1] the Thebans pushed Opuntian Locris to expand on a border dispute brewing with neighboring Spartan ally Phocis. This triggered an armed Phocian retaliation followed by a counter-strike out of Boeotia. And when Phocis then asked for aid from its hegemon in turn, Athens, fearful that Sparta was again reaching too far afield, threw in with the Thebans, who had supported its rapid recovery after the Peloponnesian War. This all eventually brought about the defeat of two Spartan-led armies (at Haliartus and Naryx in 395[2]), the beginning of what is known as the Corinthian War,[3] and a call for Agesilaos to return with both troops and a trove of plunder[4] that could help sustain Sparta's looming war effort.

Agesilaos headed toward Greece at speed in the summer of 394 and reached Amphipolis on the eastern edge of Thrace.[5] It was there where he heard of his polis' great victory at Nemea River.[6] It's also likely that this is where he got instructions from home (via Dercyllidas, who was on his way to take over in Ionia[7]) that he should move to subdue all of the Boeotians currently under Theban leadership.[8] Crossing Macedon and Thessaly, he bested the latter's mounted Theban allies[9] and transited Thermopylae[10] to arrive in northern Boeotia and camp near Chaeronea.[11] He received reinforcements there in the form of a mora that had marched all the way from Corinth and a lochos that was half of another mora already in place at Orchomenos.[12] The last had come to help in the company of a levy of hoplites from that local ally.

The Spartan king's foes now moved at last to block him, seizing the first reasonable chokepoint to the south just southeast of Orchomenos on the northwestern outskirts of the town of Coronea.[13] They deployed there across a modest plain below the Cephissus River, placing their more vulnerable right flank against swampy terrain bordering Lake Copais to the east and with Mount Helicon at the rear as a potential fall-back haven.[14]

We have no ancient figures for this Theban-led force's manpower; however, modern estimates of around 20,000 men seem reasonable and have been widely accepted.[15] As to the phalanx's order of battle, we know only that the Thebans held its anchored right wing (likely with the other Boeotians immediately to their left) while a contingent from Argos was on its open (or at least poorly fixed) left flank.

Agesilaos sent his light-armed troops forward to skirmish as he scouted the enemy and arranged his spearmen into a contending formation. His hoplites were equal in number to those on the other side at maybe 15,000 in all, with Xenophon noting that "the opposing lines of battle were exactly matched in strength."[16] The cavalry arms were also equivalent, but Sparta's king did hold a significant advantage in light infantry.[17] His phalanx set up with the Spartans at its right end followed leftward by some helot spearmen and then the former mercenaries of Cyrus the Younger. A spartiate named Herippidas now led the latter while their past commander, Xenophon, was serving as a lesser officer in the ranks. Next left stood Ionian Greek militiamen and then Aeolian and Hellespontine contingents. The king's remaining levies filled from there to the point where the Orchomenians sat near Lake Copais, holding that secondary post of honor in their own land.[18] Thus arrayed, Agesilaos recalled the skirmishers to take station off his more exposed right flank and prepared to open battle.

The phalanxes initially faced each other at a separation of several hundred meters, spreading out to the west from the lake environs along a front that was probably close to 2km long at a common average file depth of eight shields.[19] These arrays then almost simultaneously began to move, marching slowly at first in a silence broken only by the creak of leather and stiffened linen gear amid the soft footfalls and rustle of thousands moving through low grass and brush. Xenophon tells us[20] that as the fronts closed to less than 200m the Thebans on the east gave vent to their polis' signature war cry (paean) and broke into a fast walk/trot until reaching "close quarters" against the troops from Orchomenos arrayed opposite. They stopped there to begin a vicious spear-fight (doratismos). And on Agesilaos' side, Xenophon and the other Cyreans under Herippidas shortly thereafter sped up as well when they got within less than 100m of the enemy; their charge carrying the Ionians, Aetolians, and Hellespontines along with it. All of these hoplites quickly reached "spear-thrusting distance" and likewise halted to begin striking with their long lances.

Spear duels thus commenced unevenly as the various opposing segments of each phalanx came together somewhat piecemeal and clashed all along the front—everywhere, that is, save on the far western end of the action. There, the Spartan king and his crack Lacedaemonians had so unnerved the opposing Argive contingent with their signature measured approach that it "did not even await the charge of Agesilaos and his men but instead fled immediately toward Mount Helicon."[21] Yet, quick as this success by the Spartans had come, it proved barely faster than those gained by others elsewhere across the field. These not only included Herippidas and his hirelings, who rapidly broke their opposition to complete a rout of all enemy forces within sight or sound of the king,[22] but the opposing Thebans/Boeotians as well. Those hardy spearmen had easily put to flight the Orchomenians and others at the battleground's eastern extreme and then continued on to menace Agesilaos' baggage train.

Interrupted in the midst of celebrating what at first seemed a near-bloodless victory, the Spartan king reacted immediately when informed of the Thebans' success and their positioning to his rear. He regrouped those of his men that had refrained from pursuit and remained on the field ready for another fight; these likely being his highly disciplined Spartans and well seasoned mercenaries.[23] Leading those crack troops along to form up in phalanx once more, he had them face north across the ground that their Orchomenian allies had abandoned, and through which the men from Thebes would surely pass to regain their own camp. Nor was that return long in coming. Apprised that the Spartans were also triumphant, the Boeotians hurried back and redressed their own ranks to then boldly close on Agesilaos' reformed array with the intention of breaking through to join their flown compatriots in the highlands beyond.

A second battle now ensued, which, though smaller in scale[24] than the opening clash, was much more intense and prolonged. And as this brutal contest dragged on, an increasing number of slender spears broke. This forced their owners either to reverse the remnant still in hand and ply the attached butt-spike like a short lance or to call upon the sword sheathed at their side as a weapon of last resort. Inevitably, the combatants closed tighter and soon were literally "thrusting shield against shield."[25] That led to those behind compressing as they pushed with their aspis, which were held tight across the chest, against the back of the man ahead in the tactic known as othismos. Front-fighters (promachoi) used whatever weapons remained to them, wielding them overhand as best the crush allowed. Meanwhile, their comrades behind (but before the final rank[26]) were mashed as one amid the terrible press, seeking any increment of forward progress possible in hope that it would lead to victory, and all the while, panting raggedly for breath within the hollows of their aspides. These desperate efforts played out as a horribly claustrophobic scrum in which "there was no shouting, nor was there silence, but the strange noise that wrath and battle together will produce," as "crashing together their shields, they shoved [and at the head of the files] they fought, they killed and were killed."[27]

Ultimately the Thebans, rightly famed as paragons of physical strength among all the Greeks,[28] were able to hack and push their way through the opposing formation. Having thus created a breach, some of their lot poured through it in the direction of Mount Helicon[29]; still, "many were killed as they tried to retreat there"[30] when the Spartans and their mercenaries caught them from behind. Diodorus reports that the entire engagement cost the lives of 600 Boeotians and their allies, while 350 fell on the other side.[31] If correct (and all lost hoplites as was common in such tallies), this would actually have been quite a modest butcher's bill by then current standards, amounting to only 4 percent for the losing army and barely more than half that for the winners. This seems to belie Xenophon's subsequent dire description of a heavily gore-soaked and corpse-strewn battleground.[32] But his horror becomes more plausible when it's considered that he was really talking about just the relatively small area that had hosted the engagement's final phase. Perhaps a majority of those lost on the day had bled out and left their bodies within that limited space to create a truly appalling scene.

A good deal of criticism has gone Agesilaos' way for his decision to seek a second frontal engagement at Coronea II, beginning with a rebuke from his battle-companion Xenophon.[33] Though he veiled this behind some artfully distanced praise that "one might say, that Agesilaos had proved his courage beyond a doubt," Xenophon made it clear that "the safest course … would have been to let the troops marching against him pass through and then attack them from behind" instead of engaging "head-on." Maybe Agesilaos believed that only a face-to-face beating would take the Thebans out of the war for good; to wit, they had come back once already from a non-frontal whipping at Nemea River. We'll never know. All the same, Hamilton has judged the victory to have been "dubious" given that a full-scale invasion of Boeotia did not follow, "as apparently he [Agesilaos] had been instructed to do."[34] And Cartledge is harsher still in his opinion, saying that "our final judgment on Agesilaos' generalship at Koroneia should be far less laudatory [than that of later classical writers]." After all, "he had done nothing but place his men where the enemy would have to fight them or run away"; and moreover, he had failed strategically in that "Sparta's position north of the Isthmus of Corinth had not been restored to what it had been before Haliartos."[35] The fact is, though, that Sparta never again had to face Thebans (or any other Boeotians) during the rest of the Corinthian War. Indeed, the next time Spartan and Theban hoplites stood on the same field (at Mantinea Plain in 385, and then doing the same in 382–381 at Olynthus I/II) the latter did so as subordinates of Sparta. It might be fairly suggested on that basis that the positive strategic impact of Coronea II for Sparta may be seriously underappreciated.

Yet all such wider implications aside, the battle was a manifest tactical success for Agesilaos and his polis. Though badly wounded, the king was still on the contested ground at day's end; therefore, those that had fled had no choice but to ask him for a truce if they wanted to recover their dead—one of the most prized privileges for the victor in Grecian warfare. Agesilaos went on to erect a trophy of captured arms on the spot where the fight had turned in his favor, leaving it behind to formally document his triumph as he headed home to a hero's welcome.

The Advance

Most hoplite armies consisted of men called up in amateur levies according to tribal units (*phyle*) or, later, geographical units (*demes*). These musters formed taxeis of about 700–1000 men, which were then subdivided into lochoi of 100 or more. For much of the hoplite period, we do not know if these men were in well-ordered ranks and files or a less rigid massing of some sort. Taxeis drew up alongside one another upon arrival on the battlefield, with the first forming what would become the right of the battle-line and the others adding on to the left in order of march first to last. Thucydides called the resulting linear array a "parataxeis" (literally multiple taxeis formed parallel along a line), noting how exceptionally well-trained Spartans could efficiently take this form even under great duress.[36] Beginning with those well-drilled Spartans, we see growth through the late 5th century in the use of skilled mercenaries and units of picked citizens trained at state expense (epilektoi) likewise skilled in the phalanx.[37] In the Spartan army, the basic tactical unit was the sworn band or enomotia of 32–40 men, wherein each man knew his assigned place. Less is known about the elite units of other poleis, such as the 1,000 Argive epilektoi or the Sacred Band of Thebes, but we can assume they approached the Spartan model in drill and on the field of battle.[38]

Ancient authors usually recorded a phalanx's number of ranks in terms of "shields."

9. The Phalanx in Action

This "file depth" seems to have often been up to the unit commander and commonly varied from 4 to 16, with 8 or 12 being the norm for most of the period under discussion. Environmental constraints, like a narrow road, could force units to form in deep ranks by stacking smaller units; and Thebans in the late 5th and early 4th century notoriously deployed in files of 25 or even 50 for major battles.

Men formed their ranks with a frontage of 1m/man according to the standard width of their aspides. A frontage wider than this could not be maintained during advance as there was no way to measure separation between shields and men would naturally come together as they advanced; however, in cases where hoplites stood to receive a charge rather than advance, they may have formed-up with shields overlapped at a frontage of roughly 60–72cm/man.[39] The depth that each man required is a not readily ascertainable, as it need not be tied to frontage given that the distance between successive men in file might far exceed what they took up along the line of battle. This allowed for some freedom of movement throughout an already deployed phalanx. We thus read of officers being accompanied onto the battlefield by servants as shield-bearers[40]; and there is no need to imagine extra space allotted to frontage to allow either these aides or light troops to pass. Hoplites were able to get out of the way by side-stepping in front or behind their comrades in an adjacent file.[41] The same likely applied to entire units; these forming avenues within their arrays without breaking the battle-line by simply moving forward to allow light troops passage behind their rear rank. It is possible that whole sections of the line were left staggered in this way until the battle commenced.

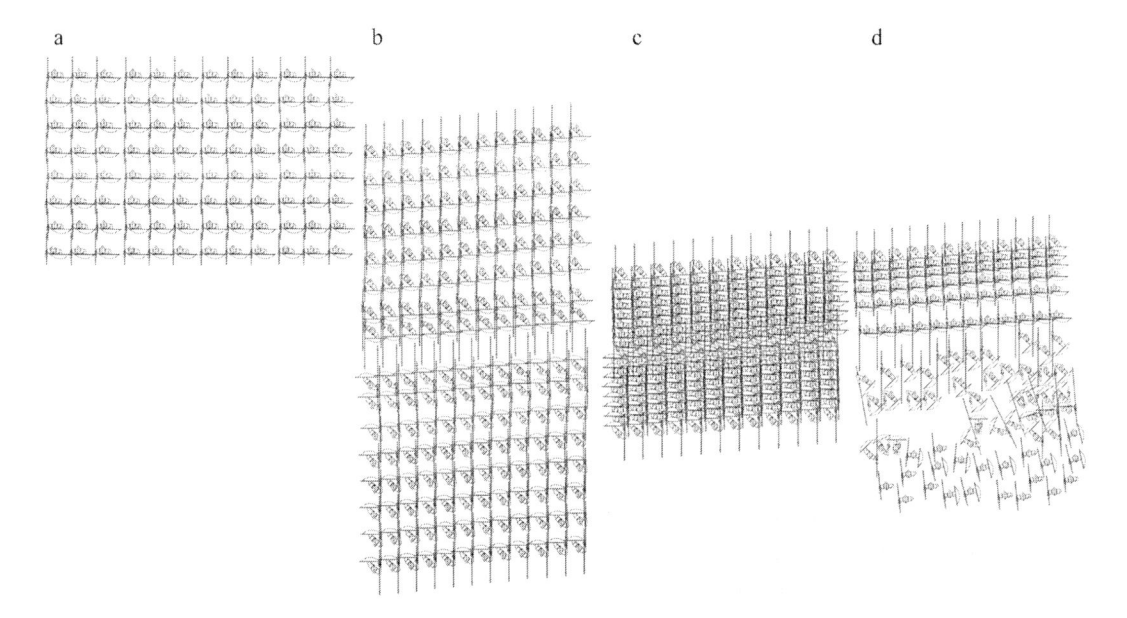

Phases of battle. Hoplites deployed into ranks and files readying for the signal to charge (a). After the charge, men have converged to the right and spear fencing ensues across an interval of space between opposing phalanxes of about the reach of a spear (b). Othismos emerges as warriors move to fight shield on shield and the crowded men push (c). When one side breaks, hoplites flee from the rear, often dropping their aspides (d). Some men are left fighting as their fellows run. As the routing ranks pull back, the front ranks of the victorious side loosen their formation and are no longer in othismos as they move in pursuit.

The ability of armies to array and maintain morale and the appearance of discipline once so formed was crucial. This was, in effect, the opening clash between opposing formations, a psychological battle of wills. Any sign of fear or disorganization signaled vulnerability to the enemy.[42] Conversely, an army that showed that it was steady could make the opposition rethink engaging.[43] Remaining calm in the ranks while facing impending death is no easy thing to do, and impossible to fake. This renders it an "honest signal" to the enemy and allows them to predict the outcome of a clash and make a rational decision as to whether to fight or break off. In order to bolster morale, leaders could walk along the front haranguing the men.[44] Offerings could be sacrificed and hopefully foretell good fortune ahead. And while Spartans did not put their faith in rousing pre-battle speeches, they supported each other from the bottom-up by passing words of encouragement and singing traditional songs within the ranks.

In a prelude to the battle to come, the opposing light troops or cavalry would often skirmish in the space between the opposing phalanxes. This action could screen their hoplite formations from opposition scrutiny. In the case of early hoplites, they may have taken advantage of the pre-battle setting to move out from the phalanx and taunt the enemy, perhaps challenging champions from the other side doing the same. And the outcome of any resulting duels or the light-armed skirmishing between the lines of later days could have a very real impact on the ensuing battle in terms of morale and the possible disorganization of the battle-line.[45]

Communication within the phalanx was a mix of bottom-up and top-down processes. The fundamental means of information transfer was between individuals. Much of this was non-verbal, with men jostling each other into position. But passing of local information was handled by commanders to ensure that the phalanx was fully deployed and ready for battle, even when they themselves could not view the whole line. Starting with the commander, a watchword was sent down the line. Xenophon tells us this was "Zeus Saviour" at the battle of Cunaxa.[46] When it reached the end, the last man passed back a response "Victory" towards the general. In this fashion, the commander could be sure each man in line had been part of the assessment of the phalanx's readiness. While this exchange of information was thorough, and faster than sending a runner down the line, it required time for the message to transit both ways. For prearranged instant commands, like an order to advance that required simultaneous action, the commanders signaled with trumpets (*salpinx*). Intermediate between these extremes would be localized signals like the men's songs or the sound of flutes.[47]

Ancient Greek battlefields were notoriously flat and not overly broad, which made it easier for men to keep some semblance of order. Hoplites would sing the "paian" in unison to boost morale and aid coordination as they advanced. This paian was a religious song and each culture had its own; Spartans, for example, may have sung a hymn to Castor.[48] We read thus of disruption when armies of mixed origin sing Doric or Attic paians that were like those of ethnically similar troops among the enemy forces.[49] The paian could also be used as a generalized rallying call, sung whenever men were required to focus their attention.

Once the salpinx sounded, men advanced. Marching in step would have been beyond most armies, but Spartans moved to the sound of pipes to help them keep pace. Here we have another point of communication between armies. An ordered advance over even flat terrain is difficult to maintain and the signal sent by an army that can do as much is one of good order. At this point, men would bring the shield up in front and the command would be passed for the first two ranks to lower their spears at the foe. Much ink has been spilled on how hoplites lowered their spears from their shoulders and lifted them up into an overhand strike. This was based on the presumption that the spear was held with the thumb pointed towards the spear-tip in the manner of an underhand strike and needed to be clumsily rotated in the hand. Reenactment has shown another solution. The spear was never held in an underhand grip during the advance, but with the thumb and fingers pointed downwards instead. This is seen on vase images, the best of which is attributed to the "Achilles painter."[50] In order to level the spear, it is simply raised upwards and, as the spear falls forwards, the hand rotates with it. The hand never leaves the shaft or changes grip. Such initial lifting of the spear can be done straight upwards in the ranks; therefore, this maneuver requires no more space than that occupied by the hoplite himself and could be done once combat ensued as rear rankers moved forward to fill gaps due to casualties.

When the armies had closed to around 200m apart, most phalanxes shouted an ululating war cry and charged at the run. They did so for psychological reasons, channeling nervous tension into the attack and frightening the enemy with their rapid advance. Coordinating a charge along the chain of units that made up the phalanx seems to have been difficult, and gaps often formed as some hoplites charged sooner than others. Xenophon describes difficulty in maintaining a measured and orderly advance during the battle of Cunaxa, where one section of the phalanx broke into a running charge and the whole line was then drawn into it.[51] Spartans did not charge at the run, instead approaching in a slow, orderly fashion that caused any unit ranged alongside to invariably pull away as they charged. The result of this and similar variances in advance is that a phalanx rarely encountered its opposite as a unified front. For these reasons, Thucydides tells us that large armies broke their order in the moment of engaging.[52] He also describes phalanxes drifting to the right as they move forward because men seek to shelter their unshielded right side.[53] This could very well be a factor, yet such drift most likely resulted to a larger extent from men attempting to advance with their torsos twisted in the act of holding their aspides in front of them. In test marches with lines of hoplites, it has been shown that the right-most man has to maintain a bearing based on a pair of visual points of reference ahead and physically jostle those on his left back into position in order to maintain a line of advance's integrity.[54] This is perhaps another reason that generals were stationed on the right, since that allowed them to control the lateral movement of their phalanxes.

It is likely that the entire phalanx contracted during advance. Hoplites bunching as they moved would have been a natural reaction for fearful men just as it is among other animals. The Strategikon, attributed to Maurice, describes the ease with which men can converge laterally just prior to contact with the enemy.[55] Men who began the charge at a spacing of just over the diameter of their shields might now find that their aspis overlaps to some degree, perhaps 60–72cm/man, with that of their neighbor. Two approaching phalanxes would end up thus overlapping on the right due to the effects of drift and/or contraction toward the right, the effects of either would have been difficult to distinguish for those on the battlefield.

Much of the order lost during the charge must have been regained as units reformed a battle line upon contact with the enemy. The alternative is that whole taxeis ran tens of meters past already engaged units next to them in line when their own directly fronting foes were either delayed or the famously slow moving Spartans. Both phalanxes would have slowed as the enemy loomed large ahead as the same fear that drove them to charge would now keep them from running blindly into a hedge of enemy spears. Tests of two ranks charging rapidly at the 2015 Archaeon Dromena in Marathon demonstrated that hoplites could charge a simulated enemy at a moderate run with leveled spears and pull-up at spear range without ranks colliding.[56]

It has been argued that opposing phalanxes crashed directly into one another as hoplites used their spears like medieval lances in a fierce, initial collision.[57] This notion is largely based on a mistaken belief that charging would add impetus to a pushing match that was thought to ensue soon thereafter. However, Bardunias has shown that if disorganized men charged at speed into the enemy it would have resulted in a weaker mass collision than had they stopped and formed-up densely before engaging.[58] And if men did not regularly stop and fight with their spears, then it is difficult to understand the many references to one phalanx breaking when the two had closed into spear range. Hoplites converging at even a modest 5mph (a brisk walk) would cover that distance in less than half a second.

How quickly the charging lines shook out into a semblance of formation upon contact may have been yet another form of message exchanged between opponents, projecting a measure of their relative combat ability. When we read of an army breaking immediately prior to contact, as often happened to foes of the Spartans, it may not have been through an irrational loss of nerve. If one side were to engage in better order than the other, then it would enjoy a distinct advantage. Thus, hoplites slowing from a run to face a well-disciplined enemy advance could have made a decision that their own phalanx was not coming together swiftly enough to repel their foes' first onslaught. This gut-level "calculation" would have emerged spontaneously, expressed in different ways by each man as some attempted to hold steady and others tried breaking away. The mass can be swayed towards standing if men feel supported by those arriving behind them; yet the reverse could be true in that men deciding to run will influence those around them to break as well. Here is where individual heroics or cowardice can make a substantial difference in the outcome, because a single man holding position bravely can form the nucleus of a stand, while one coward can cause a chain of men to turn from battle and initiate a general rout.

At Spear Point

In an early phalanx, where men carried throwing spears, the whole process above may have been more compressed. Lines might have formed just beyond missile range and men may have advanced more slowing into the range of thrown spears.[59] Only when missiles or nerve was exhausted would the shield-walls converge. What followed once men were within the range of thrusting spears was described by Sophocles as a "storm of spears."[60] While taunting their foes, the first two ranks of the opposing phalanxes would assume the three-quarter stance common to most combat arts and strike overhand across a gap accommodating the 1.5m or so reach of a dory. The overhand motion results in a much stronger thrust than stabbing underhand, and would be less likely to impale the men behind.[61] When striking from behind a wall of shields, the overhand strike not only ensured that your arm was always above the line of shields but also allowed a wide range of targets. Strikes would be aimed primarily at the man directly opposite you, as basic human nature would focus a hoplite's attention on that most immediate threat. But if a hoplite noticed one of the men to either flank of his foe had left an opening, his long dory allowed the exploitation of such targets of opportunity. Because of this, adjacent hoplites had to be mutually supporting or a man could be killed through the failure of those alongside him.[62]

Obvious targets for the spear would have been the face, throat, upper right chest, and shoulder for men in a wall of shields. In an overlapping line of shields, the ability to move the shield is greatly curtailed, though bringing the shield up so that the rim protects the lower face is possible and can be seen on vase imagery. The length of the spear and the space between the front lines meant that low strikes are delivered at flatter angles than often imagined, rendering the thighs, groin, and lower legs viable targets as well. With overlapping aspides, the sides of the body and abdomen are protected by adjacent shields. Any disruption to the phalanx, such as when a man died and the man behind had to move up, could leave the right side of a hoplite open to attack. The second-ranker would then have to act fast to reestablish the front line of interlocking shields and eliminate any local superiority enjoyed by their foes. The prime role of the second-rankers would have been to attack where they could reach, but their spears also defended the men in front.[63]

The fundamental mechanic of a phalanx is that individuals are mutually supporting. This limits the mobility of individuals. If a small gap forms in the enemy line, hoplites would be loath to leave their own formation to exploit it. Lines bend forward or bow backwards, but there is no indication of individuals breaking into the enemy ranks. Such heroics, though perhaps disrupting the enemy line, would also be disruptive for the hoplite's own formation and ultimately suicidal for himself. There is a common perception of furious striking back and forth between the phalanxes, and such flailing can be seen in many forms of mock combat today; however, when weapons are sharp and death is on the line, everything changes. A hoplite is never more vulnerable than when he is striking a foe, since to strike with force, he must expose a large portion of his body and focus his attention on the enemy. Spearmen must actually have spent much of their time simply defending themselves with their spear shafts. Many of their strikes would have been half-hearted jabs intended to threaten rather than damage. There would be the ever present risk of a spear getting stuck in their foe's aspis or a committed blow being deflected and unbalancing the attacker. Only when a clear opening presented itself could a full-force strike be attempted. Of course, there must have been much individual variation, with some men making few, if any, committed attacks. But even these would fulfill their role in the phalanx by maintaining the integrity of its line. Although the trading of blows between individuals may be irregular, as a group there would be a constant clamor of spears. It was this frequency of attacks averaged along the front that kept distance between the two lines rather than static, out-thrust spears.

Spear fighting could go on for some time, and often one side must have given way as a result, but we know that battles could move to close range.[64] It is difficult to imagine men easily forcing their way past multiple ranks of spears, but hoplites often broke their spears, forcing them to rely on a sword. A sword-armed man would be highly motivated to close within the reach of his foe's spear; something that was perhaps easier to do as fatigue set in. There would be no need for the "referee with a whistle" suggested by Holliday[65] to signal this change to a new phase of battle as that would have been a natural transition emerging out of the rational decisions of individual hoplites. Once swordsmen had closed with spearmen somewhere along the line, phalanxes would collapse into each other like a zipper closing as the latter, finding themselves suddenly shield-to-shield with the enemy, abandoned now useless long spears in favor of their own swords.

Othismos

Once the front rank men were shield-to-shield, rear rankers could bring pressure to bear. They would close up swiftly, initially just supporting those in front, but then gradually pushing them tight together. All ranks would now cover their chests with their shields and a crowded condition, "othismos," occurred. The orthodox position, championed by Grundy, Hanson, Luginbill, and Schwartz, portrays othismos as lumbering masses of men that charged directly into the formation of their foes and shoved in unison in a manner reminiscent of a rugby scrum.[66] Frasier, Van Wees, Krentz, and Goldsworthy describe hoplites dueling with spears.[67] They hold that any "push" was either a figurative description or uncoordinated shield-bashing. Bardunias has suggested that both sides of the argument are wrong and correct in equal measure when the physics and mechanics of large masses or crowds are applied to hoplite combat.[68]

The word "othismos" was a noun that derived from "otheo," a verb meaning to thrust, push, or shove. Modern definitions of othismos treat it as a verb; for example, Liddell and Scott render it as either "thrusting, pushing" or secondarily "Such a noun would have to be defined as "a state wherein thrusting, pushing, jostling, or struggling occurs," i.e. "a dense crowd" in common parlance. This is exactly parallel to the way that the noun "press" (a state of dense crowding) is derived from the verb "to press jostling, struggling."[69] Note that we are not taking about a crowd in the sense of many people or a throng, because the Greeks had other words to describe that; instead, this is essentially a traffic term like jam or deadlock, implying that many individuals are locked together and cannot move past each other.

The term "othismos" appears in three contexts within our surviving ancient literature. First, it is used to describe hoplite battle. Thucydides describes fierce combat by noting that it is accompanied by "othismos aspedon."[70] This terminology has been held up as the clearest evidence for othismos being a literal "pushing with shields," though a more precise reading might perhaps be a "deadlock of shields" that emphasizes opposing ranks coming together and pushing. Arrian did not address opposing ranks; instead he used othismos to describe the crowding of second-rankers in a phalanx against the backs of those at the very front so that they can also bring the enemy with the modest reach of their swords.[71]

Second, othismos is used in situations familiar to anyone studying crowd disasters. In the worst of these, people are asphyxiated or squeezed either hard enough or long enough to cause them to lose consciousness or die because pressure on their chest and diaphragm prevents them from breathing. Xenophon, Plutarch, and Appian all cite othismos as occurring when a crowd of men attempt to exit a gate.[72] And Polybius describes Aegiratans routing Aetolians fleeing into a city by saying that "in the confusion that followed, the fugitives trampled each other to death at the gates ... Archidamus was killed in the struggle and crush [and within] the main body of Aetolians, some were trampled to death."[73] It is important to note here that it is a maxim among those who study crowd disasters that most deaths attributed to "trampling" are in fact due to asphyxia while still standing.[74]

The third use of othismos occurs where literal pushing could not occur. When Plutarch describes ships as being in othismos, he refers to crowding rather than mass pushing.[75] In many cases, "othismos" is completely figurative. Herodotus twice uses othismos to describe an argument.[76] This is often translated as a "fierce argument"; however, traffic terms are commonly used to describe arguments. As a case in point, we regularly call for an arbiter when two sides in negotiation come to an impasse or a "log jam." And similarly, in one of Herodotus's examples, the Tegeans and Athenians at Plataea found themselves at an impasse in negotiations after having put forth competing claims to an honored place in their allied army's formation.

Each of the above usages contains elements of impasse, crowding, or crushing. What the ancient Greeks did with battlefield othismos was to harness the force of a panicked crowd and turn it into an offensive weapon. The modeling of how force is generated in crowds is in its infancy, but its destructive potential is shown by the many tragic deaths caused by crowds colliding during sports events or fleeing in panic.

Schwartz, the latest champion of the orthodox view, describes "tremendous pressure" having been generated by hoplites who "stemmed their left shoulder against their shield and thrust it against the shields and bodies of the enemy with all their might; and the ranks behind them in turn stemmed their shields against the backs and right side of the man in front in a 3/4 stance."[77] This is the most glaring problem with the current portrayal of othismos. Tests of othismos by re-enactors in accurate panoply have shown that hoplites cannot both stand at a "three-quarter stance" and sustain "tremendous pressure." When pressure is applied to hoplites by those behind them in file, they are forced to collapse frontally into the rim of their shield. The lion's share of force is generated by the mass of the men as they lean forward against each other like dominos rather than by muscles used in pushing.[78]

The outcome of a collision of ranked hoplites is not simply a matter of the number of men on either side. Most of the force applied by the rear ranks will simply be absorbed by the mass of their own men in front. In order to maximize the pushing force of a crowd, the distance between bodies must be minimized to the point that individuals lose control of their own movement and the group becomes a single mass pushing in synchrony. In crowds of this density, shock waves are produced that can tear off clothing, lift people off their feet, and propel them 3m or more through the air. These forces are generated by a domino effect of people leaning against each other and pushing in the same direction all at once. Such stress has been shown to exceed 1000 lbs of force and be capable of bending metal retaining structures.

Men pushing in a crowd-like manner during othismos tests at the 2015 Archaeon Dromena in Marathon, Greece. Note the first 6 ranks that are pushing have assumed a vertical, leaning posture and the manner in which the abdomen is covered by the aspis to guard against asphyxiation. Only the last man, number 6 in this image, has the freedom to push hard with his legs.

Tests conducted with files of hoplite re-enactors in accurate panoply in the fall of 2015 show how mass is added to the forward press as successive hoplites are added to the file. A compression sensor was affixed to a large tree with bailing wire. A test hoplite pressed his aspis against this sensor and pushed. Once his individual level of mass transferred was recorded for about 20 seconds, the next hoplite in file pushed against the back of the foremost man and the new value recorded.[79] This process was repeated for a total file length of ten hoplites and run in three bouts to derive an average mass transfer for each length of file. In this initial set of tests, hoplites were instructed to push in the crowd-like manner described by Bardunias,[80] forming up belly-to-back with the aspis supported against the left shoulder, upper chest, and left thigh. Average pushing weights are shown on the graph, but the maximum force generated by a single file of ten men was 247 kg (544 lbs). This is surely an underestimate of ancient reality in that a lone file like this must spend some of its energy on maintaining lateral stability and not falling out of line. In the large masses of men within an actual phalanx, files standing alongside would have forced centrally located files into alignment and eliminated their need to expend energy staying in line. And, indeed, when a shorter file of six men pushing against a compression sensor as above was flanked on each side by six man files and all pushed together, mass transferred through the central aspis reached 368 kg (811 lbs).

Contrary to Matthew's claim that neither the aspis nor its holder could survive such a press, it should come as no surprise that not a single re-enactor hoplite was lost during our testing. Moreover, the aspides[81] being tested had to support pressures approaching

Average Mass Transfer

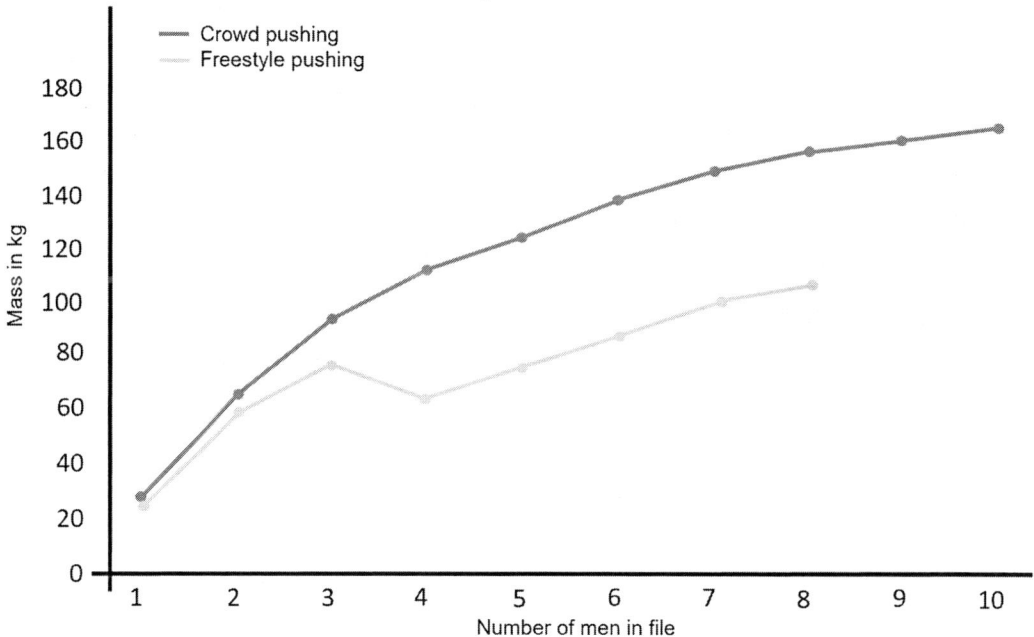

Average Mass Transfer for files of men pushing as each new hoplite is added to the total effort.

a half a ton and transfer it through a 1 × 2in (2.5 × 5cm) metal sensor to the tune of over 400lbs/sq.in. Yet, though the sound of grunting men and creaking shields loudly filled the air, not a single aspis was deformed and those involved testified that their aspides allowed them to breathe even at the height of the crush.

A second group of eight men who had not been part of the crowd-like pushing test were allowed to push freestyle for three bouts, generally by pushing side-on and getting low to the ground as a man would do naturally in pushing an object when by himself. Interestingly, it can be seen from the graph of mass transfer that there is no appreciable difference in the way mass was added for the two hoplites. For this freestyle group, the amount of force actually went down with the addition of a fourth man and did not reach the same level until a sixth man came aboard. The reason for this is that rather than efficiently transferring force through the men ahead as in crowd-like pushing, the rear ranks foul those in front and actually decrease the overall pushing force. In fact, the reason that mass begins to be transferred efficiently as the sixth through eighth man add on is that the foremost ranks have been inadvertently pressed into a crowd-like condition. The maximum mass recorded for freestyle pushing was 128kg (281lbs), somewhat less than the average force produced by files of 8 men engaged in crowd-like pushing. Thus, the crowd-like group could sustain a level of force higher than what for the freestyle group was a momentary pulse, and produce pulses of their own that were over 100kg (220lbs) more weight.

The manner in which mass is added may indicate why hoplite file depth evolved as it did. The graph of mass transfer shows that there is fairly linear increase in mass from the first three hoplites. There is then an inflection point after the fourth hoplite joins, with less mass subsequently for each further man and a second point of inflection forming after the eighth add-on to indicate a plateau being reached. Past the eighth man, each new addition contributes less than 10kg each to the total mass. This probably explains why eight shields was the most common depth in Greek phalanxes, since adding more hoplites than that yielded only a slight increase in mass per man. Very deep files, like those of 25 men among the Thebans, would have contributed little additional force compared to that provided by alignments of only twelve or 16 shields.

Why then were such long files ever created? It seems likely that these might have aided combat in two ways. First, the above data is average mass, but all crowds are subject to random shockwaves of force that peak when individuals briefly align perfectly to produce an optimum moment of truly concerted leaning. Great depth may have made this otherwise rare occurrence much more frequent, resulting in perhaps the same average, but much higher "highs" and lower "lows." But rather more importantly, a great mass of men solidly behind the front of a file acts as a physical wall, helping keep those at the fore tightly pressed tight into a crowd-like state and making it difficult for them to turn in flight or incrementally give ground. In fact, when men in file are pushed back into those arrayed in depth behind them, they cause the rear ranks to pack tighter still and be even more efficient at resisting the opposing force. Great depth may thus have enabled a slow ratcheting advance as the mass followed on the heels of any forward movement of their own file, while at the same time increasing resistance to repulsion from opposing files.

We are told that the Spartans did not excel in combat because of the martial arts teaching of combat trainers (hoplomachoi), but instead because of their skill at singing and dancing.[82] The reason for this is obvious should we accept the model presented above. If accidental synchronicity of effort is what builds lethal shock waves in crowds, then Spartans who trained to coordinate their motions through group dancing and rhythmically chanted songs would have had an advantage in producing and amplifying forces during the othismos. Coordinated pushing can be seen in the Oscar nominated documentary *Winter on Fire: Ukraine's Fight for Freedom*, directed by Evgeny Afineevsky. During the revolution that took place in 2014, riot police moved in to disperse demonstrations, breaking down barriers and pushing into the demonstrators with rhythmic pulses of force. Because they pushed as a crowd, this yields a good analog for hoplite othismos as described above. In this case, the police were thwarted in their efforts. That was due not only to the arrival of additional protestors, but also because those resisting them linked arms to form a human chain. This suggests that it might have been when they were losing an othismos contest that hoplites used the second grip seen on many aspides to lock themselves together. Employing these handles had no value for maintaining cohesion when moving forward and was actually detrimental in preventing use of a weapon. However, when being pressured backwards and forced apart as their line bulged rearward, hoplites in the rear ranks might well have found locking together via such second handles to be a highly useful tactic.[83]

Theban success in battle was explained in part by skill in wrestling, which develops a kinesthetic sense and the ability to read and anticipate motions. It is thus possible that at the height of their power, the Thebans were, in fact, emulating the past evolution that had driven the first hoplite-farmers and tradesmen into deeper formations and mass combat to make up for a disadvantage in weapon skill compared to aristocrats and well trained retainers. The Thebans were countering Spartan skill at coordinating shock waves and propagating them along files with sheer mass. Increased file depth is an advantage in this type of contest; however, the best answer to why 50 ranks of Thebans at Leuctra didn't immediately drive a mere 12 ranks of Spartans from the field seems to rest in the difficulty of coordinating concerted pushing from such deep files along with a need to constantly repack them as they advance.

The crowding of othismos and periods of active, intense pushing could last for a long time as men leaned ahead like weary wrestlers. But peak pressure is only maintained if the opposing phalanx offers resistance. Should it move back, those advancing must pack-in tight again before transfer of maximum force can be resumed. This had to start at the back of the files; there was never a point at which front rankers could simply jump back and let their foes fall forward. Just as packing was a gradual process, so was unpacking. The whole mass would thus move in spasms and waves like an earthworm. This must have driven one to give ground until enough intervening room was created to permit a resumption of more open combat. At the point where one side broke, they were no longer in othismos, because it requires near equal pressure from both sides to maintain the force that keeps men in the crowd state. If the side that backed off did not give way completely, this could reboot the cycle of combat phases as a prelude to multiple cycles of othismos.

Along with the characteristic aspis, a second element of the panoply associated with the emergence of hoplites is the sauroter, a specialized butt-spike for the spear. The sauroter has been linked to phalanx combat through its use as an auxiliary weapon, and dispatching potentially dangerous wounded men that were being blindly trampled as the crowd advanced would be an important function. But it may also have enabled the spear to be used as a staff in steadying the men in the rear ranks and allowing them to add the strength of the right arm in pushing.

Othismos did not signal an end to weapons play. Swords could still be used in the press, as the raised right arm would have had just enough room to brandish a weapon in an overhand strike over the "V" formed by overlapped shields. Due to the way hoplites align when packed tight, they end up fighting the man ahead and to the right. The downward stabbing strike of a spear from the rear ranks would require very little range of motion to find targets, while the point-heavy chopping swords commonly used relied on a snap of the wrist more than a broad slash to the same advantage. The most deadly weapon in this press would be the short Laconian enchiridion when stabbing in a downward strike from above as can be seen on vase imagery. This type of combat would be a sort of vicious knife-fight, with men benefitting from the aid of those behind to help deflect blows or bind up enemy weapons. That the Spartan dagger-like enchiridion could have been developed as a specialized weapon for the othismos is perhaps indicative of Sparta's role in perfecting this phase of combat.

If the othismos gradually became the phase of battle that decided a majority of hoplite conflicts, this may explain the late 5th century trend towards reduction or outright abandonment of body armor and trading enclosed helms for the high-peaked pilos, which provided greater protection from overhead strikes. Most of the body is screened by other men's bodies in the crowd, and any benefit of armor would be outweighed by the need for increased stamina and the ability to breathe freely and hear commands. In fact, one of the greatest protective factors a front ranker enjoyed would have been being in such close proximity to his foe, whose allies are highly constrained in striking you with blows that might hit him as well.

The goal of this phase of battle was not to break into the enemy line—for this they would be better forming a wedge of some sort—but rather to force the whole taxis opposite back out of alignment with the rest of their line until its hoplites succumbed to exhaustion and a breakdown of cohesion. Hoplite battle was a struggle to maintain ownership of a battlefield, and winners were generally those who remained on the field in control of the enemy dead[84]; and forcing the enemy army back was the swiftest way to accomplish that task. Perhaps this was the hoplite's priority from the phalanx's earliest roots, its predecessor on display in images of Homeric struggles over the bodies and expensive armor of dead heroes.

Rout

When hoplites could no longer sustain the rigors of pushing, the rear ranks of the phalanx would turn and flee. A phalanx breaks from the rear, because only these men have the freedom of movement to turn and leave; all the same, their decision to run is based on information passed back from the front. Men who are packed in tight and pushing are subject to waves of force moving back through the press. Whether in othismos or while spear-fencing, they are also conscious of their own rearward movement and mentally characterize giving ground as "losing" the struggle. This perception is the product of expectations, for if they were peltasts, they would expect to give way and then turn back for another attack. This dichotomy of expectations shows the real target of hoplite combat. Men in a close formation of ordered ranks and files can hold ground against men formed less densely or massed with less order, though this comes at a cost. Maintaining cohesion is difficult, and reforming orderly ranks a daunting task. The focus of hoplite combat was an attack on the cohesion of the enemy phalanx. This can be achieved through attrition, yet is far more elegantly, and safely, achieved through breaking the enemy's will to fight. Thus, we have seen the transfer of information between phalanxes that amounts to a psychological battle. This is not simply an assault on the bravery of individual hoplites, though hoplites are the receivers of such information, but rather on the mass of men as a whole.

There is a group mentality at work in calculating the probability of victory or defeat. Limited information is perceived by each hoplite, such as "I am being pushed back" or "I am being jostled by the men to either side in a way that indicates they are nervous." An individual's internal values, such as fatigue, anger, fear, and confidence, weigh into their ensuing calculation of how well the battle is going for good or ill. The hoplite then outputs behaviors that pass on signals to all of the hoplites around them. The crowd psyche that emerges from the aggregate calculation process among all the hoplites may well be far different from that of any one of them. Small setbacks may turn into disasters based on a runaway feedback loop between men who add their own fear to the information they receive and behave in a manner that amplifies the unease of the others around them.

Conversely, brave men may dampen down a signal which would otherwise lead a rational person to rout. Hoplites in the rear ranks are the ultimate receivers of this mass communication. And their decisions to break ranks or not will be governed by each man's perception of the aggregate behaviors of those around him.

What followed could be a free-for-all as men on the victorious side might break ranks as well in order to target the backs of routed foes. Krentz estimated that defeated armies generally lost between twice and three times the casualties of victorious armies.[85] Much of the difference in losses must have occurred after one side routed and the other gave chase. It is now that lessons of hoplomachoi (martial arts masters) were of most use.[86] Men who had been holding up their arms throughout battle could now opt for underhand strikes. This type of combat may be what artists have in mind when painting many of the vase images we see. Hoplites did not press pursuit for long, allowing many to save their lives by dropping their heavy and awkward shields to outpace those in pursuit.[87] Safer still was making a stand with compatriots and letting the victorious hoplites find easier prey as Socrates did after Delium.[88]

The aim of battle for most of the hoplite period was simply to defeat the taxis ranged opposite. There are many instances of the men of a poleis fighting what amounted to their own battle amid the greater conflict.[89] Chasing a routed taxis so far that the victorious unit removed itself from the greater battle was common. In almost every hoplite battle there was variation in the success of the individual units involved, with some winning and some losing on each side. Even when a victorious taxis had punched through the enemy phalanx and had the opportunity to turn and take the enemy units still fighting from the rear and changing the outcome of the greater conflict, this was almost never done. Part of the reason for this stems from the very real difficulty in re-directing a largely amateur formation; still, the contest of battle appears to have been primarily between units ranged opposite and there was no expectation that they should do more than win their local conflict.

The aftermath of battle was shaped by the customs and religion of the ancient Greeks. A winning phalanx would hold the battlefield and the bodies of the dead. At least from the mid 5th century on, they would set up a trophy made from the panoply of the enemy dead as a sign that they claimed victory.[90] The defeated force for its part would send heralds to request permission to collect their dead for burial, and thereby formally admit defeat.

10

Special Tactics

The weapons, armor, and phalanx formation of hoplites all had designs meant primarily to combat similarly outfitted and arrayed enemies. Yet, other sorts of warriors were almost always present as friend and/or foe on the battlefields of Greece, and they were dominant among many foreign opponents. Such troops included various forms of lighter infantry as well as horsemen, pikemen, and swordsmen, the latter two becoming factors especially later in the history of hoplite warfare. These posed a wide array of very different challenges than those which hoplites were used to from their own kind, leading Greek spearmen to devise special tactics for operating either alongside or against those other species of fighters as was needed. There were also settings wholly unsuited to the phalanx that likewise called for unique tactics, most notably when hoplites were retreating while under attack, serving shipboard as marines, or making a contested amphibious landing. All of these differing tactical conundrums and their specialized solutions were so wide ranging that no single battle ever came anywhere near to hosting a full spectrum. However, one well-documented action during the Corinthian War seems to have had more than the usual number of them in play.

Lechaion (390): Death from Beyond Reach

The Spartans captured Corinth's port of Lechaion in 392[1] and then operated one of their own regiments out of there for most of the remainder of the conflict. It seems that many of the conscript hoplites in the mora that held that station early in the summer of 390 were natives of the district of Amyklai, and these men were at that time granted a leave by their king, Agesilaos, so that they could go home and attend an important local festival dedicated to the god Apollo.[2] Leaving Lechaion in the hands of its standing garrison, the 600 or so other spearmen in the regiment joined with cavalry (a unit of perhaps 100 riders at most) to escort their compatriots on the road toward Sparta via Sicyon. Once well past Corinth, the mora's remnants turned back for the port as their horsemen continued on a bit farther with the festival goers. All had gone well until then, but this return march near the coast soon came under observation from Athenian forces close upon the city below. Those foes marked the Spartans' clear deficiencies in numbers as well as skirmisher support and went into action.

Callias of Athens led the attack in command of a sizeable hoplite force (perhaps a tribal levy or "taxis" of around 1,000). Alongside were fellow Athenian Iphicrates and his mercenary peltasts at maybe 800–1,500 strong.[3] Callias and Iphicrates came up suddenly on the Spartan column and deployed their men in a manner well suited for dealing with heavy foot lacking a proper light-armed screen by having the peltasts race out in the lead. Probably marching four abreast and seeing the enemy closing fast, the Spartans showed no panic; instead, they quickly and with admirable discipline made a quarter turn to the south. This put the sea behind them and presented a stout front instead of their unshielded right toward the approaching attackers. Even so, the ensuing barrage of missiles hit hard, laying low several in their ranks.

Damaging as this opening round was, the well-drilled men from Sparta took it in stride, and sending their servants/attendants on to Lechaion with the initial victims, those remaining prepared to counter-attack. This was something they undoubtedly approached with some confidence due to their kind (and perhaps these very men) having bested the same javelineers in neighboring Arcadia. Though Iphicrates' peltasts had soundly defeated other spearmen there, they "were so frightened of the Spartans that they would not approach within a spear cast of the hoplites because once on a previous occasion the younger Spartans, even from that distance, had managed to capture and kill some of them."[4] But whatever cockiness that lent the Spartans was quickly dispelled. Their skirmisher foes weren't about to allow such heavier-equipped opponents to catch them this time around; nor were they alone as before. With Callias' spearmen in support nearby to the rear, any Spartan that pursued that far would see his swift-footed quarry come under protection from a long line of shields and lances.

Thus, when the Spartan commander signaled his fleeter hoplites to dart out in the sort of loosely ordered charge that had worked so well in Arcadia, it failed utterly. The javelinmen had kept beyond a short-run's spear-reach and took to their heels at the first sign of an enemy rush. They then downed some of their pursuers with parting shots during the chase that followed. Whether winded or just having come too close to the bulwarking Athenian phalanx, the running Spartans finally gave up and turned around only to have Iphicrates and his crew reverse back into range and take out a few more of them from behind. This deadly cycle played out several times, with both the Spartans' numbers and speed of foot dwindling as attrition took a steadily mounting toll. While this was happening, the cavalry that had been with the Amyklaians came on the scene, returning to base after having completed that escort duty and seemingly unaware of what had befallen its beleaguered infantry comrades.

The Spartans added these horsemen to the effort as they tried once more to get the better of their tormentors. But Xenophon, who was both an ex-cavalryman and later author of note on horsemanship, claimed that when the peltasts gave way as before it was the riders that now "bungled the attack."[5] This was because "they did not pursue the enemy until they had killed some of them but, rather, kept an even pace with the hoplites in both the attack and their retreat." The javelinmen therefore continued to bleed and discourage their foes as the pattern of failed defensive sallies continued in much the same way. Nearing total exhaustion with ever fewer effectives and facing an enemy growing bolder with each new series of attack and retreat, the Spartans fell back to a position on a small hill not far from the shore. The hoplites were "now at a loss as to what to do … suffering dreadfully and enduring wretched deaths while unable to harm the enemy in any way."[6] It was at this crucial juncture that the Athenian phalanx finally began to advance on them. There would be no suicidal final stand on this day, as the last of the Spartan spearmen (many if not most wounded) broke and fled before their new hoplite opponents could come within reach. A few retreated with the cavalry to Lechaion while others dove into the sea and swam out to friendly boats that had come to their aid from the port. They left behind a scattering of tossed shields and some 250 of their dead; who, at better than 40 percent of those engaged, had fallen without landing so much as a single recorded blow on their killers.

This was certainly a much smaller action than those in which the Spartans had dealt defeats to their coalition foes at Nemea and Coronea back in 394; and their casualties were a mere quarter of those they had inflicted in the modest combat between Corinth's long walls at Lechaion just two years earlier. Still, the huge disparity in relative losses and the Spartans' final flight were considered quite shocking at the time. Fair or not, when some 350 of Sparta's elites[7] chose to escape rather than fight to the death, it put considerable tarnish on the image of super-human valor that Leonidas and his men had bought so dearly with their martyrdom at Thermopylae.[8] Agesilaos demonstrated this clearly when he posted another mora to the port and marched the defeated troops back to Sparta, creeping around or through each city along the way during off-hours to avoid parading their shame.[9] Yet the reality was that his hoplites at Lechaion had actually shown incredible discipline in standing fast as long as they did under such truly appalling and hopeless conditions. Their defeat was not due to any deficit in courage, but rather to special enemy tactics that were well matched to both the resources and situation at hand.

Light Infantry and Horsemen

By far the most common threat that a phalanx encountered from light footmen or mounted foes was that of having them enfold a flank in the midst of fighting another hoplite array. That calamity subjected its spearmen to attacks from the side/rear; and when those thus put-upon instinctively turned in response, the opposition heavy infantry was frequently able to push through their formation as it then fell into disarray. Such success on the flank(s) could even allow for recovery of a concurrent defeat along the main battlefront (see Spartolos below).

One could counter the threat of a light-armed turning in the right terrain by abutting both ends of a hoplite line against topographic features difficult to navigate. However, such ideal settings were most rare; much more often, it was only possible to secure a single end of the formation. In fact, the overwhelming majority of engagement sites actually lacked practical barriers of any sort.[10] Greek generals facing mobile enemy components in this kind of open country normally turned to their own light-armed troops for flank protection.

Large numbers of attendants typically accompanied the army of a Greek polis into the field that they might carry gear and supplies and otherwise assist the hoplites on the march and in camp. Most of these were perhaps slaves, but more reliable younger relatives and poorer fellow residents made up a sizeable minority. And in contrast to mostly non-combatant servants, these went into action along with the phalanx.[11] Such picked men were known as "psiloi" or "gymnesioi" ("naked" or lacking armor) and primarily carried javelins (short, slender throwing spears) rather than the make-shift weapons (farm tools, clubs, rocks collected for throwing, etc.) of their attendant comrades. Many of these auxiliaries in later years added a small shield. This device was called a "pelte" (hence its users were styled "peltastai" or peltasts) and derived from the crescent-shaped targets of Thracian javelineers, whom the Greeks first encountered as foes and then pursued as both allies and mercenary hires. It became common over time for peltasts and the like to form dedicated units rather than be drawn individually from the crowd of attendants. In addition to the majority of light foot, nearly all Greek horsemen carried javelins as well; and poleis having a mounted militia contingent often teamed it with the psiloi/peltasts posted to their phalanx.

A general would send his cadre of light-armed fighters out to skirmish in the no-man's-land between armies as he assessed the opposition and deployed his phalanx in response. He then had them retire to positions off either side of his hoplites; there, they could neutralize any attempt by their enemy counterparts to threaten a flank. Should their spearmen partners carry the field, they would give swift chase to bring down as many fleeing foes as possible. Conversely, in the case of defeat, they would form a mobile rear-guard to dissuade the opposition from giving like pursuit. Such cooperative special tactics between light and heavy-armed elements of Greek armies were so ubiquitous and successful that our ancient sources took them for granted and it's thus quite unusual to find an account that mentions them. Light-armed contingents canceled each other out most of the time, leaving battle decisions solely in the hands of their hoplites. We therefore know about this aspect of phalanx fighting mainly from those few instances where flank protection failed spectacularly.

It is actually the 4th century that yields the bulk of our references on flank turnings (or their attempt) by auxiliary troops. Xenophon's and Diodorus' descriptions of the action off the Theban right wing in the battle of Mantinea II (362) offer some of the best documentation,[12] detailing the posting of horsemen and foot skirmishers on the flanks of both phalanxes. The ensuing engagement saw the Thebans nearly carry the light-armed fight on their right only to meet defeat due to the timely intervention of an opposition mounted reserve. And we get briefer glimpses into similar tactics in two of Philip II's victories. The earlier of these was an action against Illyrians on Lyncus Plain in 358. The Macedonian king's cavalry[13] there "pressed on from the flank and rear"[14] around "the enemy left"; and then, "by throwing their whole line into confusion,"[15] his phalanx was able to carry the day. Philip's mounted Thessalian allies did much the same five years later at Crocus Plain, besting the flank screen on the unanchored landward side of a Phocian phalanx to clear the way for a devastatingly successful envelopment by the Macedonian heavy infantry.[16] Such a mobile assault on the enemy left coupled with a strong push from elite hoplites went on to be a highly characteristic method of Philip's son Alexander and his immediate successors.

The relatively sparse record of this tactic in the 5th century undoubtedly reflects a strong focus of histories covering that era upon hoplite combat rather than any real shortage of occurrences. This is indicated by such skirmishing on phalanx flanks showing up in reports on a few battles that garnered more attention than usual due to unique circumstances. The earliest of these was an engagement on Cyprus in 498 during the Ionian Revolt. This pitted hoplites from the Greek poleis on that island against Persians and their Phoenician Cypriot allies. The rarity here was that the horsemen screening on the flanks of the Grecian phalanx were charioteers. These rode in two-man vehicles that had teams of javelineer footmen in support. Fighting in front of the city of Salamis, the Greek chariots faired well against opposing cavalry on at least one wing only to have some of their number switch sides and deliver a traitorous flanking and ultimate victory to Persia.[17]

Two additional 5th century examples come from the Archidamian War. One was an opposed landing at Solygeia in 425,[18] which saw the defending hoplite array suffer a decisive mounted flank turning; and the other is actually our best-described instance of a Greek army going down after failure of its light-armed troops. This was in 429 during the first major hoplite battle of the war when a phalanx from Athens met a sally from the city of Spartolos in the far northeastern Grecian region of Chalcidice.[19] The match-up involved fairly equivalent heavy-armed manpower. However, the Athenians' auxiliaries were weaker than the local light-armed force[20]; and though their phalanx thrashed that of Spartolos, they suffered defeat. With the enemy's flank screens in full flight, the victorious northerners were at that key moment joined by more javelineers from allied Olynthus and, buoyed by this reinforcement, they went on the offensive against the now unsupported Athenian hoplites. Those spearmen, like the Spartans at Lechaion, tried to strike back. Yet, "whenever the Athenians advanced, their adversary gave way, pressing them with missiles the instant they began to retire." This went on until the opposing horsemen "riding up and charging them just as they pleased at last caused a panic" and the rout was on. Athens' spearmen fled under a lengthy pursuit and 430 (better than 20 percent) ended up losing their lives on the day.

Though it began by featuring typical flank actions, the light-armed attack at Spartolos evolved into a frontal confrontation between skirmishers on one side and hoplites on the other. Missing from this scenario in contrast to the somewhat similar engagement at Lechaion was cover for the light-armed from a phalanx standing to their rear, the local heavy array that might have so served having fled the field. Fortunately for the men from Spartolos, their Athenian foes were clearly not practiced in the sort of out-running counter favored in such situations by the Spartans; instead, they made slow advances in formation. That allowed their more mobile opposition to stay beyond spear-reach while spewing a deadly rain of missiles. During the same war, however, we do have an excellent example of a phalanx providing a backing bulwark for a successful light-armed attack on fellow hoplites. This took place on the small Peloponnesian island of Sphactaria in 425.

Athens sent a force under Demosthenes onto Sphacteria with the goal of dislodging a modest band of 420 Spartan hoplites stationed there.[21] Coming ashore just before dawn, the Athenians took the island's defenders by surprise, wiping out an advanced post and moving to surround the main body of enemy spearmen formed up near the center of the island. Demosthenes arrayed his 800 hoplites in phalanx at a distance to the south and posted his skirmishers in 200-man parties to rises ahead of his heavy line.[22] The Spartans then "serried their ranks and pressed forward to close with the Athenian hoplites in front of them." But this was to prove fruitless as their foes refused to cooperate, "remaining stationary instead of advancing to meet them." Meanwhile, Demosthenes' high-placed archers opened up; and his javelineers, slingers, and stone-throwers charged down in packs to join in the bombardment. The embattled spearmen darted out to repulse "the light troops wherever they ran up and approached too closely; yet they retreated fighting ... easily getting away." Tiring with many wounds and no small number of dead, the Spartans withdrew under duress to put their backs to a ruined fortification near the northern tip of the island; however, the enemy closed about and eventually brought them under fire from above and behind. With the situation now hopeless, the Spartans finally surrendered. The action had taken the lives of 128 of their polis' rare and precious hoplites (just over 30 percent of those engaged) at very little cost of any kind to Demosthenes' landing party.

The special tactic of supporting light-armed sorties with a phalanx acting as a rearward redoubt as on Sphacteria and at Lechaion saw use in several prominent engagements thereafter that pitted hoplites not against their own kind, but rather foes dominant in cavalry. The earliest of these took place in 368 along the road from Pherae in Thessaly into Boeotia, where a retreating Theban invasion force came under fierce mounted attack. The hoplites from Thebes were too slow to either catch or escape from the Thessalian horse and light foot, and had soon suffered a number of casualties under a nearly continuous shower of javelins. The former general Epaminondas was serving as a spearman in the Boeotians' ranks and they turned to him for help, appointing him commander on the spot. That proved a wise move. "Selecting the light-armed men and cavalry, he [Epaminondas] took them with him, and, posting himself to the rear, with their aid checked the enemy pursuers."[23] By this tack, he "provided complete security for the heavy-armed men in the front-ranks [of the phalanx behind]," who were then able to safely retreat. Significantly, this incident took place when the future Macedonian king Phillip II was a youthful hostage at Thebes. Undoubtedly hearing much about so successful a tactic in the ensuing months of his captivity,[24] it is not surprising that he later put it to good use on his own account.

Though our only report appears confused, it is likely that Philip employed a bulwarking phalanx at the rear of light-armed forays in defeating the cavalry of the Scythian king Atheas in 339.[25] This action took place on the Dobruja Plain on the west side of the Euxine (Black) Sea. Shortly thereafter, Philip likewise engaged a force strong in horsemen from the Thracian Triballi tribe as he was making his way back to Macedonia. He once again arrayed his phalanx rearward and led an out-rushing attack on the enemy riders and peltasts with his own mobile contingents. This time, however, he was facing a foe that countered using a similar ploy, falling back from Philip's charge behind a line of footmen armed with spears of great length ('sarissai'). That opposing infantry reserve halted the king's pursuit and dealt him a serious personal injury, one of their lengthy lances piercing his thigh to kill his horse.[26] The Macedonian phalanx then responded much as Epaminondas had in 368, falling back by stages as its screeners skirmished behind the withdrawal.[27]

The campaigns of Philip II's son Alexander provide another, well documented example of light-armed troops charging opposing cavalry while a phalanx stood redoubt. This came about near the newly founded Macedonian city of Alexandria Eschate in the far Persian northeast.[28] Challenged by mounted Scythians arrayed across the Jaxartes

River, Alexander laid down a catapult barrage to allow his men to cross and set up their phalanx on the far bank. After a sally from that formational bastion failed using horsemen alone, he then "mixed the archers, the Agrianians [peltasts], and the rest of ... [his] light-armed troops in with the cavalry and led them against the Scythians" to gain a resounding victory.

There is another aspect of Alexander's tactics worth discussing relative to the use of bulwarking phalanxes against mounted foes. This involves his setting up hoplite arrays in his larger battles to back up another phalanx rather than just out-striking skirmishers. We see this best at Gaugemela (331). Alexander deployed his leading light and heavy elements for that battle in typical fashion; however, "he also posted a second line so that the phalanx could become double-fronted."[29] This rear array held most of his Grecian hoplites. They were under order "to wheel about and meet the barbarians' attack if they saw their comrades [in the leading phalanx] surrounded by the Persian army [composed overwhelmingly of cavalry]." And though lacking the same kind of detail, our surviving accounts show him using phalanx redoubts in his two other major engagements in Persia as well.[30] This special tactic seems to have gone out of fashion at Alexander's death, not finding use among his successors. Their abandoning the concept of a heavy-armed rear bulwark probably came in response to foes much less generally unbalanced toward mounted operations than Alexander's Persians.[31]

Based on a rare insight gained at Granicus River, it would seem that Macedonian practice was to intimately mix its mounted men and foot skirmishers.[32] This was the preferred technique among the most cavalry-savvy Greeks; javelineers being so attached to well regarded Thessalian, Boeotian, and Sicilian horsemen.[33] Philip II might have adopted this practice from Thebes or nearby Thessaly, though his native cavalry had perhaps long used the same approach. We have an account of Theban/Thessalian routine from Mantinea II in 362. The Thebans arrayed their riders on the wings for that battle and "stationed infantry among them."[34] Xenophon saw this as superior, noting that the other side's horsemen stood less effectively in ranks "without any infantry intermingled among them." These differing dispositions then played out in Thebes' favor:

> At first they engaged in a cavalry battle on the flanks ... as the Athenian horse attacked the Theban they suffered defeat not so much because of the quality of their mounts nor yet on the score of the riders' courage or experience in horsemanship ... but it was in the numbers and equipment of the light-armed troops and in their tactical skill that they were far inferior to their opponents. Indeed they had only a few javelin-throwers whereas the Thebans had three times as many slingers and javelin-throwers from the regions about Thessaly ... [that] practiced from boyhood this type of fighting and were wont to exercise great weight in battles because of their experience in handling these missiles. Consequently the Athenians, who were continually being wounded by the light-armed and were harried to exhaustion ... turned and fled.[35]

The need for hoplites to include light footmen with any cavalry assigned to their flank screens would seem to stem from the innate inferiority of the saddle as a missile platform. A peltast or slinger, not to mention a foot archer, could easily outrange a man handicapped by having to hurl his javelin from a seated position on horseback. Moreover, the combination of rider and large mount made a vastly easier target to hit than a man on foot; while a wounded horse was likely to become a liability to continued effectiveness of its master, and the death of so costly an animal threatened his pocket book. It thus makes a lot of sense that light infantry were invaluable to cavalry, countering light footmen by killing them and/or exhausting their supply of missiles to allow the mounted troops to more safely close into range. And it's worth noting that just such considerations must have applied at Lechaion toward keeping the Spartan horsemen there from straying too far from the protective shields of their outrunning hoplite compatriots. The sort of risk they were facing is illustrated by the experience of Spartan cavalry that joined young spearmen rushing up a slope in Acarnania the very next year. These hoplites pursued and killed many of their peltast foes until, approaching a backing enemy array, they came under heavy fire that "wounded some of the Spartan cavalrymen and killed some of the horses."[36] This opposition was only dispersed when the Spartan phalanx came to close quarters and threatened a shock fight; something that had not been a realistic option at Lechaion.[37]

The Theban-allied skirmishers at Mantinea II (as well as the Athenians on Sphacteria) included men armed with the shepherd's sling. This device was common in the hilly Greek interior; where it served in repelling predators from that region's stock herds. The island of Rhodes was also known for its sling-savvy herdsmen and eventually became a prime source of outstanding mercenary slingers. The weapon was well suited to charge-and-retreat fighting on phalanx flanks and in frontal assaults as per Sphacteria. Another shining example of slings used in this manner came just a few weeks after Spartolos in an action near Stratus in the Grecian northwest. Locals from Acarnania there withheld their own spearmen and beat back a column of hoplites by "slinging at them from a distance"; it being noted that "the Acarnanians are thought to excel in this kind of warfare."[38] In fact, though, the sling's longer range versus other missile weapons also gave accompanying hoplites an additional choice. Keeping their distance, they could stand their slinger contingent immediately forward or behind their line and pelt foes beyond javelin and even bow range. This tack saw use by Cyrus' hired Greeks in their long retreat after Cunaxa in 401–400.

The withdrawal of this legion of Grecian mercenaries suffered under Persian arrows and slung stones. Eyewitness Xenophon noted "that neither our Cretan bowmen [using simpler bows] nor our javelin men can reach them in reply; and when we pursue them, a long chase … is out of the question, and in a short chase no foot-soldier, no matter how swift, can overtake another foot-soldier who has a bow-shot the start of him."[39] The Greeks realized that their hoplites included a number of Rhodians familiar with the sling, and they organized a 200-man squad to provide a better defense. These men used small lead bullets that could travel twice the distance attainable by their enemy counterparts, who used larger natural stones; the Greek slingers ranged out "farther even than the Persian bowmen."[40] This relatively small band of slingers went on to considerably aid an ultimately successful retreat.

Yet, despite any such superiority of Rhodian slingers over the archers of Persia, it was bowmen that most often provided a "stand-off" defense for Greek hoplites. These were usually mercenaries, often from Crete, but Athens was an exception. The Athenians had native foot-archers that they employed both shipboard and in tandem with their phalanxes. Perhaps created after facing Persian missilemen at Ephesos (498) and Marathon (490), these were hundreds strong.[41] Our first mention of them is an account of their exploits against Persian cavalry prior to the battle of Plataea in 479.[42] There, they were in the company of a 300-man contingent of picked spearmen, that unit apparently being accustomed to working with the archers during phalanx actions. How the bowmen and hoplites did this is unrecorded; however, it's likely that the latter formed a fronting wall of aspides to shelter the missilemen behind, not unlike then current Persian doctrine.[43] Of course, when engaged in operations of lesser scope, archers would not have had select hoplites along and must have stood with any other light foot on hand. This would have been the case among the modest forces involved in landing operations that drew bowmen from their ships' marines. Regardless of how disposed, all archers made terrible close-in fighters; still, their arrows could reach out much farther than a javelin to keep a foe so armed from getting into range of their hoplite companions for as long as their fire held up.

The limitations of bowmen in screening hoplite arrays against more shock-capable light-armed attacks were starkly exposed during Demosthenes' Aetolian campaign in 426. That Athenian general had come ashore and advanced into the interior above the Corinthian Gulf with a strong hoplite force. He had his marine archers in tow, but had taken the field without waiting for a contingent of allied peltasts. His column eventually came under attack near the village of Aegitium from local tribesmen armed with javelins. Demosthenes was unable to engage with his heavy infantry, whose every advance was countered by an enemy withdrawal; the hoplites having to endure a fresh barrage each time their foes then ran back into range. Demosthenes' bowmen were able to partially fend off such attacks for a while, reaching out with their arrows to discourage the greater mass of Aetolians from coming near enough to strike. However, not being equipped to run out in close pursuit, they couldn't drive off the opposition, but only keep some of it at a distance. This was a tactic doomed to fail in the long run, if for no other reason than that the Athenians' supply of shafts was not endless. The archery officer eventually fell to a javelin, causing his men to panic and scatter, which left their phalanx exposed with no screen of any kind. Defeat followed as the hoplites "worn out with the constant repetition and hard pressed by the Aetolians with their javelins, at last turned and fled."[44] Demosthenes survived the ensuing slaughter, but 120 of his Athenian spearmen did not.

One other special hoplite tactic useful against light infantry and horsemen is worthy of discussion: formation of a defensive box by an army's spearmen. Most of our references to this ploy involve Greek forces on the march, and usually in retreat. The Spartan general Brasidas employed this technique in 423 during a withdrawal from western Macedonia. He "formed his hoplites into a square with the light troops in the center ... posting his youngest soldiers to dash out wherever the enemy should attack, he himself with three hundred picked men in the rear to face about during the retreat and beat off the most forward of their assailants."[45] This was essentially a reversal of the normal dynamic, with the spearmen acting to screen their skirmishers instead of the other way around. And the Athenians pulling away from Syracuse a decade later essayed much the same: "the army marched in a hollow square ... the hoplites being outside and the baggage carriers and the bulk of the army in the middle."[46] The famous Greek retreat after Cunaxa in 401 also did this, Xenophon noting that it was best "to march with the hoplites formed into a hollow square, so that the baggage train and the great crowd of camp followers may be in a safer place." Later though, "the Greeks found out that a square is a poor formation when an enemy is following,"[47] since it became disordered in negotiating narrows; that led to adoption of a more open marching order with van and rear guards.

There was also an unusual incident involving a chariot attack in which the concept of a defensive square proved wanting. This took place near Dascyleium in the northern Asia Minor province of Phrygia in 395. A large Greek raiding party there came under attack from Persian horsemen supported by two chariots with scythes attached to their axles. We are told that the Greeks "gathered into a tight formation," which was very likely a square with the hoplites outermost. However, when the chariots bore down on it, this array came apart, its members running in fear only to be all the more easily cut down by pursuing horsemen.[48] The lesson here: no tactic, no matter how special, is ever any better than the men executing it.

Pikemen

Greek hoplites came across pikemen no later than the early 5th century; doing so in Thrace, where a small number of fighters used the sarissa (pike), perhaps mostly as an anti-cavalry device.[49] The Greek general Iphicrates, no doubt having seen this weapon while campaigning in that region, may have adapted it for phalanx use in the early 4th century.[50] Most likely he did this out of necessity in expanding the line infantry element of a mercenary force he was leading in Egypt.[51] Iphicrates' innovations failed to catch on in Greece; however, they seem to have had more influence in Macedon. There, his adopted brother, Philip II, made sarissai integral to the new style formation that he first took into battle in 358. And it was almost exclusively within and against this reformed version of the phalanx that hoplites interacted with sarissophoroi (pike-carriers or phalangites).

Participation by hoplites in Philip's combat array has been a subject of much debate. This reflects a lack of detail in our sources for the period of his rule; as a result, we have had to draw mostly upon less explicit data to get at the issue. As it turns out, though, these are quite diverse and appear to be consistent in indicating that the hypaspistai (hypaspists) serving a leading role within the Macedonian phalanx were almost surely hoplites in the old Greek mold. Evidence includes terms and passing references from the better-documented career of Alexander III, who inherited Philip's military machine intact.[52] This is telling in that the son did not differ from his father in terms of front-line infantry operations.[53] We also have a number of pictorial displays showing Macedonian soldiers in hoplite gear.[54] And finally, there are archaeological finds that support the concept of native Macedonian hoplites.[55] Of particular note here is that some of these are directly related to Philip himself.

Hypaspist hoplites were Philip's (and Alexander's) best shock troops; select men, who drilled to the highest level of performance as full-time professionals. The method by which they worked with the pikemen in their battle formation was very much like what a polis' best spearmen had often done in the Doric phalanx. That was to rout an opposing wing by penetration or turning around its end, wheeling then to roll up the entire enemy line from the now exposed flank. In the older array, the men to the left of such elites were fellow hoplites of lesser caliber; these had the task of holding steady in place while their picked comrades carried the day. The Macedonian phalanx assigned that same role to its sarissophoroi; standing on the center through left of the formation, their long weapons held opposition spearmen at bay before several progressive rows of pike-points.[56] In addition to working with phalangites on their left (as well as allied spearmen there in some instances), Macedonian hoplites also operated in tandem with horsemen and light infantry on their right. The main tactical innovation here was that these mobile troops included elite cavalrymen[57] bearing a lance (*xyston*). That tool gave them the ability to join their heavy infantry in the sort of shock action usually required to break an opposed enemy left wing.

But while Macedonian hoplites adjusted their tactics to work in synch with non-traditional fighters like pikemen and shock cavalry, opposing Greek spearmen do not seem to have been as creative in response. Most of the time, they appear to have simply persisted in their standard methodologies and fought the new Macedonian array very much as they had any other phalanx in the past. That approach at first seems to have produced rather close-run results. The opening contest between the old Doric and new Macedonian systems took place in Thessaly in the winter of 357/56 and went to Philip; however, he very likely had the key advantage of a much larger force in that action.[58] More representative of the competiveness of the initial Greek versus Macedonian match-up was a series of combats that followed in the same area in 354.[59] First, the Greeks (Phocian allies and mercenaries) left the battleground and Thessaly to Philip; but then it was he who had to withdraw from a rematch after those same opponents had been reinforced. Neither side was able to punish the other sufficiently to achieve a truly decisive victory. This led to a third engagement that summer in which Philip's main foe, Onomarchos, finally employed some innovative tactics, ambushing him with an artillery barrage before charging into his disrupted phalanx to put it to flight.[60] Sadly for the opposing Greeks, this was a "one-off" event and Philip was able to return the very next year to crush and kill the Phocian warlord at Crocus Plain. The Macedonian king would engage three more Doric arrays during his career; but none of them had generals as clever as Onomarchos and all went down to defeat.[61]

There was a dramatic improvement in the Macedonian phalanx's battle record against Greek foes following the winter of 354/53 (two wins and two losses before versus four victories without defeat afterward). This suggests that an upgrade to its equipment and/or methods had likely taken place; and the nature of any such retooling has implications for the types of special hoplite tactics it was designed to counter. As it turns out, the only real change displayed by Philip's later arrays is adoption of a sarissa longer than that of Iphicrates' reforms.[62] Finds from Chaeronea indicate that these were in use by 338[63]; however, just how early they might have been adopted is not known and 353 would be at least a fair possibility. Their introduction then would have been exactly what Philip needed to restore confidence to a twice-beaten and badly shaken army, one that had gone into revolt to literally drive him from the field after Crescent Hills. This indicates that hoplites could sometimes force their way past a hedge of shorter pikes to strike the men behind, the resulting disruption perhaps having muted the success of Philip's earlier victories before handing him a close-run defeat in the second action of 354. Regardless, whether they went into use the next year or some time later, longer sarissai made that tactic much less effective.

The only other special approach for spearmen against the pike-armed portion of a Macedonian front was to set up behind ground difficult for sarissophoroi to cross. This saw use at Issus in 333. Greek mercenary hoplites in Persian service deployed there in back of a streambed with minor field works to receive an attack from the phalanx of Alexander the Great.[64] One of the regiments in the middle of the sarissa array became so disordered trying to negotiate those impediments that the opposing spearmen were able to get through its fronting pikes. They killed 8 percent of the regiment's nominal complement (120 men), including its commander. But this did the mercenaries little good in the end, since their foes at the same time were turning the Persian left wing. That immediately trumped any tactical advantage the Greeks had gained toward the center of the field as Alexander rolled up the hoplites' formation and cut off their penetration from the rear. Nor was their partial success to become a model for the future. An army facing such a hostile setting would normally simply refuse to engage, withdrawing to find a more acceptable battle site. In this case, however, Alexander's foes had come upon him from behind, cutting off his line of supply so that he either had to attack where they chose or face being starved into submission. That kind of unusual circumstance, key for the tactic's employment, was never to repeat.

With elongated sarissai taking frontal penetration in their sector pretty much off the table, hoplites had to look to other places where they might get the better of a Macedonian phalanx. One obvious approach was to simply outfight the elite hypaspists on its right wing. However, given the exceptionally high quality of the full-time professionals that occupied the right wing of most Macedonian arrays, this was a tough proposition for even the best of opposing hoplites. And to make matters worse, Greeks appear to have persisted in assigning their finest fighters to the more traditional station of honor on the other end of their line; thus, they were set up for stalemate against nearly impenetrable ranks of overlapping pikes. Oddly enough, Macedon's hypaspists presented a challenge not unlike that in the past from crack Spartan spearmen likewise standing on their right wing. One would think that the old Theban trick against Sparta of massing picked troops at great depth on the left would thus have been just as sound an approach here.[65] Yet no one seems to have tried it as far as we can tell from our meager records. Notable in this regard is that the Thebans themselves fought their lone set battle against a Macedonian phalanx at Chaeronea by standing far right, where they accomplished very little despite fielding the Greek coalition's best hoplites.[66]

Denied a reasonable chance to penetrate pike-hedges and unwilling or unable to properly test hypaspists face-to-face, there was no real prospect for Greek hoplites to beat a Macedonian phalanx by main force along the formation's front. Their only hope then was to carry out or threaten some kind of flanking action. Our best documented instance of this working comes from Lamia in the spring of 322.[67] Greek mounted and foot skirmishers there in Thessaly took the unusual tack of leading their army's fight, doing so in front of passive heavy formations. They were thus able to decisively defeat the opposing cavalry and light foot before the enemy's phalanx could come to action against their own; the Macedonians then pulled out of the field rather than engage without proper flank screens. It seems, though, that this tactic was dependent upon failure by its targets to act aggressively with their line infantry. And it fell short on that account a few months later at Crannon.[68] With the opening skirmish there again going badly, the Macedonian commander precipitously moved his phalanx forward to initiate and win a shock battle much more favorable to his mix of arms.

At about the same time that the Macedonians were losing the field at Lamia, another of their armies met defeat down in Attica. The admiral Micion had landed there with a large force of Macedonians and mercenaries from a fleet of 110 triremes,[69] suggesting 4,400 heavy footmen at 40 per ship. Phocion sallied from Athens to intercept him near the village of Rhamnus, that aged general having some 5,000 hoplites as well as perhaps 500 horsemen plus a sizeable contingent of psiloi. It seems that Micion had some handicaps. To begin, there were the spearmen on his right wing; these were common mercenaries somewhat less capable than elite hypaspists. Even more critical, though, were his flank screens. Those lacked cavalry and had rowers doubling as sub-standard foot skirmishers. And once engaged, Phocion "entirely routed the enemy, killing Micion and many more on the spot."[70] This likely saw Athens' much superior light troops roll around the opposing right where Micion stood, encircling it to leave no avenue of escape as their hoplites pushed through to seal the victory.

The tactics used in other successes by Greek hoplites over pike-bearing formations are hard to pin down with the scant data to hand. We can certainly set aside a Phocian triumph over Philip's mercenary commander Adaios in 353.[71] That would seem to have come against hired spearmen rather than Macedonians including phalangites. And the victory of Agis of Sparta over Corhagus in 331 was likely inflicted upon hoplites as well.[72] All the same, there are later examples of hoplite armies besting true Macedonian phalanxes at Amphipolis in 316 and Apollonia in 312. And the most probable method behind each was an outflanking by superior light-armed troops; their spearmen then finishing with a drive into the now disordered enemy front.[73] Adding these to other hoplite successes over sarissa-bearing formations makes it clear that such arrays, while certainly formidable, were far from invincible. The correct combination of circumstance with well-applied situational tactics could and did give Greek spearmen some reasonable opportunities to come out on top.

Swordsmen

Swordsmen posed a very different challenge than that of sarissophoroi, since their weaponry had a much shorter reach and required fighting in looser order so as to allow for swinging it. Greek hoplites first encountered such warriors[74] when Syracuse sent Sparta a force of mercenaries to help fight Thebes in 369. These were 2,000 Iberian and Celtic foot soldiers and 50 horsemen with mounts that arrived on more than 20 triremes that included some configured as transports.[75] The infantrymen were mainly shock fighters with long slashing-swords, who also used throwing spears for preliminary bombardments. For protection, they relied on large, oval, center-grip shields, with the Celts being otherwise unarmored. The Spartans employed these men in detached raiding; and Diodorus claimed they did well "in hand-to-hand fighting and in battles and many both of the Boeotians and of their allies were slain by them."[76] In fact, though, much of that might reflect outstanding work by the hirelings' modest mounted contingent, which contemporary cavalry expert Xenophon held in very high regard.[77] They actually appear to have fought only one pitched action against hoplites. That took place at Sicyon in the upper Peloponnese, where the mercenaries "met the Sicyonians in battle in the plain, and defeated them, killing around seventy."[78]

Details are lacking for the fight at Sicyon; however, unless the Sicyonians panicked unduly in the face of an initial wild charge by their foes, it would seem more likely that the mercenaries' riders turned a flank against those horse-poor Peloponnesians to trigger the victory than that it was due to sword-play along the line of battle.[79] This particular mercenary contingent left Greece at the end of a five-month term of employment; however, what was probably a very similar force came from Syracuse in replacement the next year. That group went into the field with the Spartan phalanx and joined it in an engagement in Arcadia near Melea that became widely known as "the Tearless Battle" for causing no Spartan casualties. The hired men might have been deployed on the left wing of Sparta's phalanx; but even if so, they saw very little if any real combat there. The opposing hoplites were unready to fight and "only a few of them waited until the Spartans were within spear range, and these were killed … the rest fled and many of them fell at the hands of the pursuing cavalry and Celts."[80] The swordsmen ended up contributing more or less as skirmishers in the post-battle phase, giving chase much as was usually the role of peltasts in Greek armies.[81]

The relative ineffectiveness in close combat of these kinds of swordsmen with little or no armor seems to be confirmed by their poor battlefield performance during an invasion of Greece by Celtic Galatians (Gauls) nearly a century later. Those barbarians were just as unable to break through hoplites at Thermopylae in the winter of 279/78 as were Persians 200 years earlier; possibly doing even worse in that they took serious damage but killed only 40 Greeks.[82] The invaders' casualties came from Grecian spears as well as missiles from the south-bounding heights. And they then suffered a heavy defeat against Greek spearmen on the road to Delphi.[83] A phalanx frontally assaulted them there even as peltasts circled around to open fire from behind. Fleeing, the surviving Gauls rallied, only to leave Greece rather than face fresh Boeotian and Athenian armies. The winning tactic in both battles was for hoplites to engage and create a static front while missile troops showered the swordsmen's poorly protected bodies from directions other than those faced by their shields. It seems that the Gauls were simply not equipped to answer that approach.

But there were significantly more potent swordsmen elsewhere in the Greek world; something that Pyrrhus of Epirus found out to his cost in Italy. That monarch and warlord received an invitation in 280 from the Greek colony of Tarentum in the far Italian south to cross over and intervene in a pending war with the Latin city-state of Rome. Pyrrhus, instructed as a youth under Alexander the Great's old general Antigonus and his son Demetrius, had a fine army at his disposal. This force not only had benefit of his recent Hellenistic training and famed genius for tactics, but actually boasted roots in the Macedonian military system going all the way back to Philip II.

It is likely that Pyrrhus' uncle, Alexander, had earlier reformed his nation's fighting force from a tribal system of heavy spearmen. He was the younger sibling of Philip's queen, Olympia (mother of Alexander the Great), and his brother-in-law had taught him much during a 14-year stay at his court in Macedonia prior to making him king of one of Epirus' three main tribes in 341. Alexander then created a tribal confederation that accepted him as its military leader. He must have spent the next seven years transforming his host along the lines of Philip's before going to Italy in 334 in response to a call for help from Tarentum. He had initial success there in fighting a coalition of barbarian tribesmen on that city's behalf, but he fell in action in 332 to bring his bold overseas venture to an unfortunate end. Pyrrhus was now taking up a similar challenge, doing so with the army Alexander had built and that he himself had further tuned since coming to power.

It seems almost certain that the host Pyrrhus took to Italy included elite hoplites. Contemporary Hellenistic armies on the plains of Asia had come to rely upon cavalry off their flanks to gain combat decisions; therefore, their infantry now tended toward being primarily defensive and mostly pike-equipped. However, there is no indication that this trend had spread to Europe. On the more restricted terrain that often dominated there, it made more sense to follow Philip II's highly successful lead. And that called for balancing the mix of arms so as to be able to carry a field by either mobility on the wings or frontline shock, whichever was most appropriate on any given battleground. We can thus assume that both Pyrrhus' Epirote army and a force of Macedonians lent to him for this campaign[84] included select hoplites as per the hypaspists (though that precise term never appears).[85] These might have formed a ratio of something like one for every three sarissophoroi as per the formations of Philip and his son. And allied contingents from Tarentum,[86] other Italiote Greeks, and Hellenized barbarians provided Pyrrhus with even more spearmen. That left him with the task of integrating these varying troop types in the service of tactics effective against Rome's swordsmen.

The sort of special tactics that were to work to good effect against unarmored Celtic swordsmen a year later in Greece would not have been appropriate against the Romans. They were well-armored, which made them much less susceptible to missile fire and a good deal more difficult to stall at the front with a simple hoplite formation. Pyrrhus therefore approached his battles in Italy by alternating arms, flanking sections of spearmen with phalangites and vice versa along his phalanx.[87] Our accounts of his major actions at Heraclea (280) and Asculum (279) are much in conflict,[88] but they generally indicate that the infantry formations stalemated at Heraclea and exchanged the better of it along different parts of the line at Asculum.

Pyrrhus' tactical scheme apparently called for his interspersed pike arrays to protect against collapse of adjacent spear sections that, for their part, provided greater offensive potential to bleed the enemy. All the while, his cavalry would seek to turn a flank; and with the aid of elephants,[89] it did so to carry the day in both engagements. Yet despite Pyrrhus' overall success, the Romans were able to deal out more damage than anticipated in what must have been the spear-armed sectors. They even broke through some of his barbarian spearmen at Asculum to flank and put the Tarantine contingent there to flight such that its position had to be recovered with a mounted counter. Combats along the line of battle were thus lengthy as well as costly for both sides.[90] Still, though no easy go, Pyrrhus' scheme worked well enough to deliver a pair of victories against some very tough and dogged opponents.

The only loss Pyrrhus suffered against Rome came at Beneventum in 275. This was a modest action over hilly ground that followed upon a grueling night march with a picked contingent; and those factors conspired to preclude any duplication of his past successful tactics against the legions. Relevant here is that Pyrrhus' selection of his "best men"[91] for a detached strike element produced a spear-armed force. This is seen in Dionysius' observation on the subsequent defeat that:

It was bound to happen, as might have been expected, that hoplites burdened with helmets, breastplates and shields and advancing against hilly positions by long trails that were not even used by people but were goat paths through woods and crags, would keep no order and, even before the enemy came in sight, would be weakened in body by thirst and fatigue.[92]

Of course, the most important clashes between the Greek and Roman ways of war were yet to come during Rome's invasions in the Macedonian Wars of the 2nd century, which ultimately led to its conquest of Greece. That hoplites had any role in that struggle has been a point of controversy, with some seeing Greek militaries as having by then entirely abandoned them in favor of the pike. This is an idea based upon Alexander the Great's equipping his hypaspists with sarissai in India as indicated by their reported use of them at the battle of Hydaspes River in 326.[93] However, this would seem less likely a case of giving up the spear and aspis than one of cross-training to use the sarissa in given circumstances; namely, when facing elephants, against which the pike was by far a more effective weapon. Indeed, it has been proposed that Alexander had gone the other way as well, adapting his arms-mix to the needs of situational tactics by outfitting some of his pikemen with hoplite gear.[94] This suggests that Alexander's Asian successors' use of hypaspists and other elites as sarissophoroi may not have reflected a fundamental change in equipment so much as something done to meet specific tactical demands in their area of operation.

The foregoing implies that any Hellenistic tendency to favor the pike might not have applied elsewhere or even all the time in Asia. Thus, when ancient writers report an army to have adopted Macedonian arms, it might not mean their sole use of the sarissa. Rather, it may in fact have been a switch to a system of mixed arms that included hoplites much like the old Doric type, and an argument can be made that the well-known Spartan and Achaean military reforms of the late 3rd century could both have followed along that more complex line.[95] And the clearest evidence for continuing importance of hoplites to the Macedonian phalanx actually comes from its very last major battle on Greek soil.

The Macedonian phalanx of Perseus met invading Romans at Pydna in 168, going down to defeat due to disruption of its pike-front while advancing too quickly and/or over broken ground. This presented the opposition with gaps in the sarissa hedge, which they penetrated to get at and defeat the poorly protected phalangites behind. The Romans also bested the mobile screen on Perseus' left flank to roll up his line from that side as well.[96] We are fortunate to have a surviving depiction of the final stage of the battle in the form of a carved monument erected in honor of the victorious Roman general, Aemilius Paulus. That display shows legionaries taking down the Macedonian elites that held out to the very last on the phalanx's right wing; these appear to be using thrusting spears and carrying large, concave shields by the antilabe and porpax suspension system so characteristic of hoplite aspides.[97]

Livy gives us a unique and critical piece of information regarding the Roman casualties at Pydna,[98] noting that "by far the greater part of these were Paeligni." This refers to the Paeligni cohort that went up against the spearmen standing far right within the Macedonian phalanx. That contingent "incautiously encountered" those crack troops at the start of the battle and was unable to withstand their "dense formation." The Paeligni with "their first ranks being slain … were forced to give back,"[99] and the cohort next right, that of the Marrucini, surrendered ground as well.[100]

The reason for the success of these spearmen, whom we might style neo-hoplites in light of their somewhat modified equipment versus the hoplites/hypaspists of the past, seems fairly clear. Polybios claimed that the defensive ability of an unbroken phalangite array in this era of elongated pikes was so formidable because it projected five rows of sarissa points out front at half the lateral spacing per pikeman versus his sword-wielding Roman foes.[101] This required each legionary to battle past ten sarissai to get at a facing opponent. There would have been a similar (but in this case offensive) dynamic favoring the Macedonian spearmen. These could strike from their first two ranks at enemies engaging from only a single rank and saddled with twice the spacing distance. This gave the neo-hoplites a 4-to-1 edge in strikers all along their front. Adding this to the advantage in reach provided by their longer weapons must have ensured them of drawing more blood than they gave in close combat against Romans, though the latter could inflict more damage in return than against sarissophoroi.

Perseus' tactical design seems to have been to carry the battle with his heavy infantry on the right while holding fast on the left. Given the bloodletting by his neo-hoplites and the pikemen's ability to advance, this might not have been all that bad a plan had his men not let their front fall into disorder. That failure echoes what had happened to some of the sarissophoroi at Issus and to a lesser extent the Tarentines at Asculum. And Perseus' inability to recoup this situation as Alexander and Pyrrhus had done, plus the defeat of his left-side screen, sheds light on a key decline in capability over the last century. No matter how skilled the neo-hoplites might have been, the best tactics that spear-armed troops could employ against swordsmen called for cooperation from other arms; namely, mobile forces off their flanks or in reserve, especially horsemen.[102] The latter were expensive and seem to have become less numerous as Hellenistic armies fell into a convenient pattern of fighting ever cheaper and more formalized pike-duels against each other. That habit then cost them dearly when the Romans hit their shores and showed no interest in observing any such restrictive conventions.

Development of the neo-hoplites seen at Pydna could date from no earlier than the late 3rd century in that a variant of the old-school shield was possibly still in use at that time.[103] The picked men called "peltastai" at Cynoscephalae in 197 might thus have carried either that sort of aspis or the newer version lacking an offset rim; either way, they were probably spearmen, with Asclepiodotus stating that "their spears are much shorter than those of the hoplites [a term denoting pikemen for Asclepiodotus]."[104] Putting the peltastai within the wider context of historical Macedonian military practices has led Duncan Head to reasonably suggest that they might have been the "equivalent in status and perhaps equipment and role of Alexander's hypaspists."[105] Their numbers at Cynoscephalae (3,000) and posting (far right) mirror those of both Philip's and Alexander's hoplite elites in support of that idea. It seems that the tactics attempted there were very much like those essayed at Pydna nearly 30 years later, attempting to turn the Roman left wing primarily by means of shock infantry action. And they were no more successful, the failure this time being not the least due to a bungled deployment that saw the phalanx's right wing exposed to a fatal flanking when its leftward equivalent was late getting onto the field.[106]

Hoplites might have continued to exist at and beyond the edges of the Mediterranean world after 168, perhaps briefly seeing action for Carthage before its final fall and persisting for a time in distant backwater outposts of Greeks far to the east.[107] However, Pydna marked the end of their four century or more run of real prominence, bringing the hoplite era to a close as late Hellenistic militaries began to abandon the phalanx in favor of Romanized ways of war.[108]

Shipboard and Amphibious Assaults

Greek hoplites served as marines (epibatai) aboard their poleis' triremes, which called for different methods than used ashore. Still, they retained their thrusting spears and aspides; that gear being useful for a combat mode that had opposing vessels come together for an open order shock fight across their decks. Yet such equipage was not the norm elsewhere. Marines of the most highly regarded fleet of the day at Phoenicia, though otherwise outfitted like the Greeks, used javelins along with small, rimless shields better suited for throwing.[109] And the marines of most other nationalities were missile-men as well.[110] These could be quite effective against epibatai, shooting them down from beyond spear-reach.[111] It was likely just such experiences that led Greece's most astute seamen at Athens to counter with archers on their own triremes. Yet, Greek warships, even those of the Athenians, continued to employ spearmen despite the short range of their weaponry. Ameliorated by an increasing reliance on ramming tactics that made marines less vital, this reflected the great operational value of projecting force onto the land from offshore. That called for epibatai, either alone or with other hoplites carried as passengers, to hit the beach in amphibious assaults.

One might hark back to the mythic thousand ships at Troy to begin a discussion of Greek amphibious operations; but the truth is that sophisticated use of hoplite landing forces really started in the 5th century. This began as a mere transport option that moved large armies by sea rather than marching them overland. That was something that only a few ship-rich poleis could do on their own and therefore more often a coalition effort as per the previously described Mycale expedition.[112] Athens later exploited its exceptional naval assets in widespread amphibious raiding as a way to counter contrasting Spartan dominance in land warfare.[113] This let the Athenians strike at distant targets, even those deep in hostile territory, without risk of interception by more powerful armies during a long, cross-country trek. It also eliminated any concern for choke-points along the way. But perhaps the best tactical aspect of such seaborne deployments was that they frequently caught the opposition completely by surprise.

Given a long beachfront, it was possible to avoid set defenses by simply moving farther along the coast before coming ashore. It was thus rare for a landing to meet resistance on the beach. And even then, battles usually developed in a fairly conventional manner if a portion of the invading party could offload. Our best described instance of a landing effort meeting opposition partway through the process was in 425 near Solygeia on the eastern Peloponnesian seaboard.[114] The targeted Corinthians there had posted troops to the area in anticipation of a raid; and, seeing Athenian triremes pulling onto the shore, a large contingent quickly closed in battle formation to catch about half the invaders still aboard ship. The Athenians addressed the situation by forming up the right wing of their phalanx and advancing into combat; they then brought the left wing in to join the action once it too had landed.[115] Athens would score a victory when its cavalry, last to unload and farthest away, finally arrived on the field and turned the Corinthian right flank. Therefore, despite being quickly met, a landing force might still prevail if it could get some assets ashore, keep discipline, and eventually feed the rest of its men into the fight as if they had been in reserve all along. These were surely tactics born out of desperation, but sound ones nonetheless.

Even more difficult for an amphibious effort was for it to encounter foes already in place before any sort of beachhead could be established. Such a confrontation was unavoidable if the landing area was small, making it impossible to shift to an alternate site. That was the situation facing Athenians trying to come ashore on Psyttaleia during the final stages of the naval battle of Salamis in 480. Their objective was to eliminate a body of Persian sparabara holding out on that small island; however, those intended targets had bows as well as spears and directed a shower of missiles at the triremes upon their close approach. The Greek answer to this was for archers and stone-throwing crewmen to lay down counter-fire. That suppressed the Persian barrage just enough to let the ships offload their hoplites. Meeting no shock resistance, but only arrows against which their large shields and stout armor offered good protection, the Greek spearmen formed up in phalanx, advanced into direct contact, and made short work of the lighter-equipped Asians.[116]

Covering hoplites with shipboard missile fire was also the opening gambit of an attempted Spartan landing at Pylos in 425.[117] But that assault had a very different kind of reception waiting for it. A small defending force was able to deploy heavy spearmen backed by javelineers along those brief stretches of the peninsula's rugged coast that were suitable for beaching a ship. Athens' Demosthenes reminded his defenders there about the known difficulties of such operations:

> [Y]ou as Athenians who know by experience what landing from ships on a hostile territory means, and how impossible it is to drive back an enemy determined enough to stand his ground and not be frightened away by the surf and terrors of the ships sailing in, to stand fast in the present emergency, beat back the enemy at the water's edge, and save yourself and the place.[118]

The Spartan ships could back just a few at a time into the limited landing space. And when the embarked hoplites tried to come down gangways at either side of their sterns, they failed to get ashore; those that survived javelin fire during single-file descents along the narrow planks had poor footing and were outnumbered by a team of opposing spearmen waiting on firm ground at the bottom. It was, as Demosthenes had predicted, an "impossible" task that failed miserably.

Though the masters of Greek naval warfare at Athens clearly held a poor opinion of mounting amphibious assaults on positions held by hoplites, there was at least one role in which they felt such an action was justified. That was as a tactical diversion meant to keep the enemy from defending a more important landing site elsewhere. Such was the task in 410 at Kleroi (Cleri), a beach near Cyzicus on the Asian shore northeast of the Hellespont.[119] This saw the Athenians divide their naval force into three flotillas and use one of these (20 ships with Alcibiades, leaving 20 with Theramenes and over 40 with their admiral, Thrasybulus[120]) to draw out and engage a Spartan fleet. But Sparta's commander, Mindarus, grew aware of his foes' true numbers during the ensuing combat and broke away to beach his triremes. That let him join some allied troops that he might make a stronger stand onshore.

Alcibiades chased into the shallows and his archers provided cover as their hoplites and a few oarsmen waded in to grapple several grounded vessels that they might be towed back to sea and captured. Repeated attempts to do this failed, but they did occupy the enemy's attention, allowing Thrasybulus to land unnoticed nearby. And when that new threat came marching down on Mindarus, he had no option other than to split his modest manpower between two fronts. It was a fatal dispersion of strength that would cost him both battlegrounds in the end. Thrasybulus won the inland share of the contest after Theramenes arrived with reinforcements. Meanwhile, Alcibiades and his marines forced their way ashore to overrun what had become a seriously undermanned position around the beached triremes. Mindarus lost his life there and his crews fled after setting fire to their ships to deny them to the victors. It had been a particularly complex engagement, one carried across the board by Athenian hoplites fighting to good effect in a trifecta of habitats: aboard ship, in the water, and on dry land.

As the diversity of action at Cyzicus makes clear, Greek hoplites were versatile enough to be highly effective in a much wider range of settings than their reputation as simple phalanx fighters might imply. It was merely a matter of finding the right special tactic that would optimize their utility in any given situation. They were thus able to do battle both with and against light infantry, horsemen, sarissophoroi, and barbarian swordsmen, doing so in a broad array of terrains and circumstances.

11

Phalanx Maneuvers

Grecian phalanxes, like all battle formations, had inherent strengths and weaknesses, which more astute commanders duly recognized. This put them to work developing maneuvers for their arrays toward maximizing the former while exploiting the latter. These evolutions covered a wide range of tactical objectives. They included the flanking of enemy lines, pulling away either before contact or in the midst of a losing fight, reengaging after withdrawal, and even repositioning to initiate a second round of combat. Some counter-moves were developed as well. Given that these were not easy tasks, the ability of a phalanx to operate in this way was entirely dependent upon the skill sets of its stratiotai. And it was only a small minority representing the very most capable and well-drilled of hoplites that could so maneuver. But what those kinds of elite spearmen were able to do amid the sound, fury, and lethal stresses attendant on an ancient battleground was often truly amazing. This was nowhere better demonstrated than during what might have been Greece's most fateful clash of phalanxes—one where its city-states fought to stay free against just such finely trained foes.

Chaeronea (338): Dancing with Death

Perhaps one of the most fitting matches of site to event in all history took place in September of 338 near the western Boeotian town of Chaeronea. Greeks engaged there in a crucial test for their venerable system of conscripted phalanxes across ground so famed for such actions that it had been called "the dancing floor of Ares [war]."[1] This saw a combined force of Grecian militias face off against the new model army of the Macedonian king, Philip II, who had brilliantly built upon past practices to meld full-time soldiers from his homeland and select mercenary manpower[2] into a truly deadly fighting machine. That martial juggernaut adopted gear designed to match its methods[3] and drilled intensely until able to execute phalanx tactics of old with an efficiency never before seen. Philip was now set to pit this fearsome combat instrument against the best that more traditional poleis could send against him. And his prize for success was to be nothing less than mastery of all Greece.

The soil on which this struggle would take place covered the flat between highlands to the west hosting the acropolis of Chaeronea and the swampy environ of the Cephissus River eastward. It was alongside the latter's easily negotiated course that Philip advanced into central Greece in search of a decisive confrontation. This was to be no accidental meeting; in fact, Philip had openly encouraged his foes to put forth their utmost against him. Having in 339 inflamed passions with provocations in the far northeast against both the local allies and vital grain fleet of Athens, the most powerful of his opponents, he had then marched brazenly into Boeotia and announced the intent to subjugate what was left of Greece in the coming year. This put his enemies there on notice so that they could gather all that they could against him. Confident of victory, Philip was cleverly taunting the Greeks into an all-out effort. He thereby sought to not only crush them in the ensuing battle, but also to leave them with so little in reserve that any hope of future resistance would be dashed as well. His was the boldest of strategies, and it would work to perfection.

It seems clear in retrospect that Philip had not only prodded his foes into the field, but had also discerned just where they must make their stand. Skilled phalanx tactician that he was, the Macedonian monarch knew that the Greeks would inevitably seize upon the plain below Chaeronea as the best choke-point along his route of advance down the Cephissus. It is notable here that he had gone to some length in highlighting that very path for them by using it the previous year. He had then put guerrilla fighters to work there over the intervening months lest it be forgotten. And even a marginally competent Greek general could see that the valley below Chaeronea was the optimum spot to deploy a phalanx. It supplied level, open ground well suited for hoplites. Moreover, he could block it completely with available manpower, its narrowest point spanning 2.3km between the bounding hills and river. And those last would then provide ideal terrain barriers next to which his spearmen could anchor against any threat of being flanked. What Philip hoped was that such a favorable environment for the Greeks' standard combat mode would encourage them to stand and be destroyed in open battle. He could thus eliminate the prospect of having to engage in a subsequent series of sieges that would surely prove costly in time and resources, and might even fail.[4] It also allowed him to customize a battle plan that would let his unique fighting force exploit both the picked ground and well-known enemy tendencies to the fullest. Philip's tactical approach would ultimately endure a stern test in a very closely fought engagement,[5] but just like his grand strategy for conquest, it would emerge triumphant.

The Macedonian king arrived at Chaeronea to find just what he had expected. The phalanx of the Greek coalition was blocking the entire valley, with its hoplites poised shield-to-shield along their ranks and in files twelve deep. The Athenians held the formation's left wing up against the hills. Some 10,000 strong, these men were inspired by Philip's recent outrages in the north against their polis' interests and were ready to fight, yet few among them had much combat experience. Elite hoplites of the Theban Sacred Band stood on the opposite end of the line to abut the marshland bordering the Cephissus. The reputation of these 300 men as the best fighters in the Grecian host had gained them that honored posting on the right extreme, where there would be no protection from a comrade's aspis should their flank be turned. The rest of what was a total 10,000 Boeotian League spearmen were next left: first the others from Thebes, renowned for their physical strength, and then each of the remaining federation contingents in turn. Practiced at war, the Boeotians could be relied upon to put up a good fight. Between these and the Athenian troops on the other end of the phalanx, there stood around 8,000 additional hoplites. They comprised 2,000 each representing Corinth, Megara, and the mercenary ranks[6] plus another 2,000 from elsewhere across Greece (including Euboa, Achaea, Leucas, Corcyra, and Acarnania). Most of these must have been awaiting the coming fight in apprehension, since save for the hired men, they were no more seasoned than the Athenians.

Supporting the Greek heavy infantry were about 7,000 light footmen. These were peltasts for the most part, armed with javelins and a small shield. There was also a modest contingent of cavalry, mostly from Athens and the Boeotian League and perhaps numbering around 2,000 in all. Apparently not sent out on this occasion for advance skirmishing, and otherwise denied access to the prospective battlefront due to its being completely spanned by their anchored phalanx in close order, these light forces took post flankward. Some of the foot skirmishers thus secured the west-bounding slopes while the rest joined their horsemen eastward across the Cephissus, where they could ward off any enemy attempt at a wide-looping encirclement.

As for Philip, he had marched with all of his infantry. This likely included about 24,000 shock fighters consisting of 6,000 hoplites and 18,000 pikemen as per a tally of national strength just four years later.[7] He also would have had 3,000–4,000 mostly peltast light infantry plus quite a few mercenaries. The latter came from his Thessalian allies (through whose lands he had passed on the way to Chaeronea) and might have totaled some 6,000 spearmen. This gave the Macedonian king only a very small numerical edge in battle-line infantry.[8] However, he could expect to actually enjoy a more significant advantage once the fighting got underway due to the battle-savvy of his Macedonians, who had the benefit of a tremendous amount of drilling and active campaigning over the last twenty years.

Yet as complete as Philip's roster of foot soldiers must have been, his accompanying contingent of horsemen appears rather minimal. It might in truth have come to no more than 2,000 riders,[9] with 800 of them lance-armed "Companions" and the rest late-arriving[10] Thessalian javelineers. If so, this further suggests that Philip had indeed engineered the location for this clash, and had then tailored composition of his deployment with an eye to maximizing its odds for success on that specific ground. He thus geared his inherently limited supply capacity toward supporting as large an infantry force as it could, recognizing that only that arm could be decisive within the bounded narrows at Chaeronea. Philip then had to compensate for this in turn by placing a practical cap on his cavalry. Though requiring enough horsemen to offset whatever mounted strength the enemy might put in play, it would be unwise to waste any of what resources he could carry on more, since additional horsemen were unlikely to be of much help on the ground that he had gone to so much trouble to arrange. Philip therefore seems to have settled for merely matching his foe's cavalry count. Nonetheless, he must have had full confidence that outstanding quality and vastly greater experience would let his veteran riders easily neutralize their Greek equivalents and meet the needs of his intended tactical scheme.

The battle opened with Philip's advance. Signal horns blared in command as the Macedonian's phalanx closed on the waiting Greek line to the south at a slow and deliberate pace that kept its long ranks well dressed. The king marched within the right wing of this array, which was held along its farthest extent by the picked hoplites known as hypaspists. These formed companies 1,000-strong, with the most elite of those (the

11. Phalanx Maneuvers

[Diagram: Battle of Chaeronea showing troop positions between the Cephissus River (north) and rough/upland terrain (south). Macedonian forces on left: phalangites (10-deep), mercenary hoplites (10 to 12-deep), hypaspists (12-deep). Greek allied forces on right: Sacred Band (12-deep), Boeotia (12-deep), allied and mercenary hoplites (12-deep), Athens (12-deep). Arrows indicate movement. Cavalry skirmishing noted north of river. Vertical Scale: 0m–200m.]

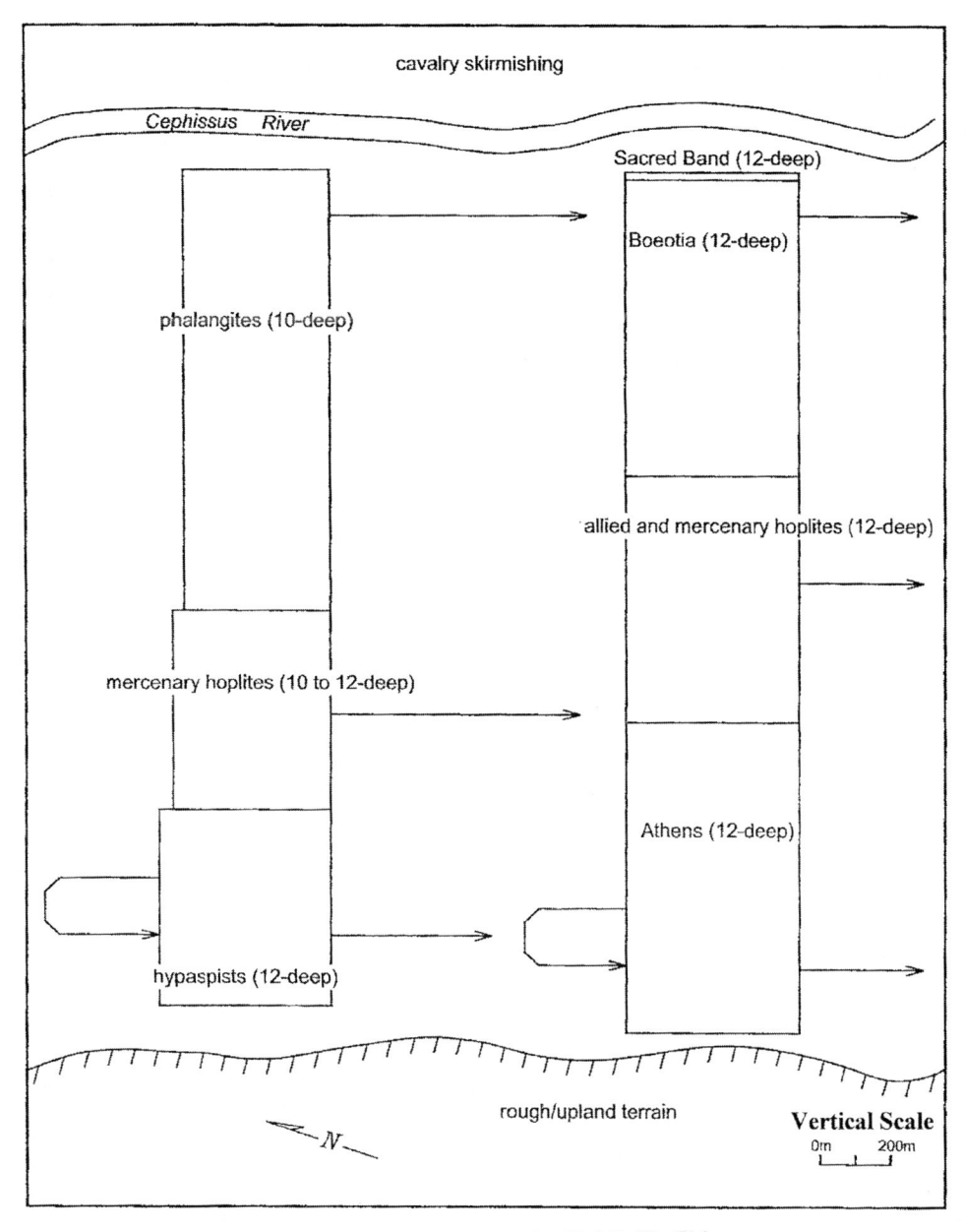

CHAERONEA (338 B.C.)

Battle of Chaeronea—338 BC (Joan Huckaby).

"agema") at line's end guarding Philip himself. Next left were the mercenary hoplites of the Thessalians to complete the phalanx's right/strike wing, having all its troops filed up to a depth of twelve. This left the corps of pike-armed Macedonians to make up the formation's left/defensive wing, stretching ten-deep under the leadership of the teenaged prince Alexander to cover towards the edge of the Cephissus. Philip's cavalry had already forded that stream along with a section of his light infantry to execute their task of stalemating the enemy horse likewise deployed in that battlefield periphery.[11] What remained of the Macedonian skirmishers then moved onto the high ground to the west that they might similarly match their enemy counterparts there.

Coming together with weapons at the ready in their forward ranks, the two phalanxes filled the air with war cries and the thunderous clash of steel on bronze as they engaged in a frenzy of dueling with their pole-arms. The long pikes of Alexander's phalangites dealt the best hoplites of the Greeks ever increasing frustration where they were assigned to carrying the battle on their right. It was going to take a frontal penetration to carry that part of the field due to anchoring on the river denying a bypass of the flank there to both sides. But the spears of the Greeks were simply too short to permit more than an occasional and brief reach past the serried ranks of points presented by the much lengthier Macedonian pikes. Thus, even though the fight wore on for some time,[12] only a very few of the prince's men went down. Yet though the length of the phalangites' weapons afforded excellent protection, weight, unwieldy dimensions, and restriction to weak underhand thrusting severely reduced their own potential to inflict damage on armored hoplites with large shields. Therefore, though Macedonia's pikemen could well have had slightly the better of it in the arms-length fencing on their end of the field, no one was actually making much real progress. This, of course, played out to the invaders' advantage, since their left wing was thus getting the job done of keeping the enemy's finest troops from gaining a decision so that their own elites might carry the day on the other side of the field.

Things were not, however, unfolding all that much differently over on the western part of the battleground. It was hoplite against hoplite there; and while the first two ranks of each phalanx could thus reach their foes with strikes that were spilling considerably more blood than was the case to the east where it was pikes versus spears, neither Philip's crack hypaspists nor his mercenaries had been able to quickly break the will of their less experienced opponents. As the fight dragged on in consequence, shafts had shattered and ever more spear-butts and side-arms came into play. Some finally began pressing shield-on-shield into facing foes, aided by those directly behind thrusting overhead where spears remained intact and from entire files pushing in othismos against their leaders' backs. Still, the stubborn Greeks would not yield.

It must have been Philip's original design for his select right-wing veterans to simply force back less savvy Athenian hoplites in opposition there, putting those unseasoned men into so great a panic that he could roll up the Greek phalanx as their flight left it fatally exposed. That was the most obvious and easiest route to victory. But when this didn't come to pass, the wily Macedonian leader put a back-up maneuver into action that the full-time nature of his national forces had let the hypaspists practice to perfection over the last year in anticipation of just such a situation.

At a propitious point, likely when sufficient weariness was setting in along the battlefront to create a noticeable lull in the action there, Philip signaled for his crack spearmen to begin an orderly withdrawal. Such breaking off in the midst of a fight was something only the very most skilled troops would ever have dared, and even for them it was likely to trigger disaster unless their foe proved either too tired or too naïve to properly react. The Athenians in this instance were not only somewhat worn down but quite green as well.[13] That gave the hypaspists the precious few seconds without pressure needed to step backwards in sequence from rear rank to front. And once having gained enough separation, they then boldly turned about to effect a rapid retreat. This left the hired men from Thessaly with a naked flank, which their first couple of files must have covered best as able by pivoting rightward while their former line-mates withdrew. Yet, dangerous as this must have appeared, it would turn out that the king was not in fact putting those allies at any great risk for very long.

The men from Athens thought that victory was nigh and rapidly overcame the surprise of their foes going all at once from vigorous attack to seeming flight. Shouting in triumph, they followed their enthusiastic general Stratocles in chasing after the Macedonians lest they get away.[14] And this pursuit soon became so rapid and intense that they fell into disarray. That was when Philip and his men, having reached a rising slope, suddenly spun about on signal to reverse direction.[15] Quickly redressing their ranks, they then advanced with lowered weapons and thrust a well-ordered front into the mob that had been on their tail. Athenian cries of joy turned into screams of mortal fear as the hypaspists began spearing men down right and left. Some 1,000 of the Greeks died on the spot and the rest scattered as many tossed shields to speed their exit. But even such acts of cowardice weren't enough to save another 2,000, who would fall prisoner before the rout was complete.

Philip's picked spearmen passed the position still held by their mercenaries and moved to wrap around the Greek phalanx where the fleeing Athenians had exposed its flank. This rapidly tore the coalition array apart from left to right, one contingent and then the next dispersing in turn much like a falling line of dominoes as the attack progressed laterally down their alignment. Disintegration flashed from rear to front within each unit, leaving men yet facing forward to be overrun where they stood while others turning to flee were cut down from behind. This wave of destruction eventually reached the Boeotians battling on the far right. Unable to pierce Alexander's pike array, those steady soldiers had held fast during a lengthy and possibly somewhat unequal contest; but with all hope now gone, they quickly chose to follow the example of their allies and seek escape.

Flight of their fellow Thebans left only the surviving members of the Sacred Band on the field to make a forlorn and final stand. Alexander's pike force was able to move steadily against those desperate hoplites' abandoned left flank to close about and break into their ranks.[16] And by this time, the Greek cavalry across the river must have joined in the general rearward rush, permitting the crossing of some Macedonian horsemen onto the main battleground to aid in pursuit and, perhaps, help dispatch the very last of the Sacred Band. Philip would later lament the passing of those keen Theban warriors, even as he savored the prospect of empire that their deaths and the utter destruction of their army now left open before him.

Envelopment Maneuvers

The most fundamental maneuver of the phalanx was aimed at flank envelopment. This called for angling an advance rightward so as to enable hoplites on that end of the formation to make a lateral attack on the opposition's left flank or even wrap around it sufficiently to strike at the enemy rear. That sort of thing undoubtedly must have initially come to pass unplanned as a natural consequence of how aspis-bearing hoplites tended to head into potential danger. Thucydides described the phenomenon in his exceptionally detailed account of Mantinea I (418):

> All armies are alike in this: on going into action they get forced out rather on their right wing, and one and the other overlap with this their adversary's left; because fear makes each man do his best to shelter his unarmed side with the shield of the man next to him on the right, thinking that the closer the shields are locked together the better he will be protected. The man primarily responsible for this is the first upon the right wing, who is always striving to withdraw from the enemy his unarmed side and the same apprehension makes the rest follow him.[17]

The tendency for hoplites to so drift during advance often led to mutual flanking in which the right wings of both phalanxes carried their part of the field. These experiences inevitably led the more creative among Greek generals to take extra precautions that they might better protect their left. Among the resulting adjustments were things like slower (therefore more controlled) advances, shifting leftward prior to advance, standing to receive an attack in place, etc. All such procedures were possible for the relatively unpracticed militias that served most city-states, which were slow to institute formal drills.[18] Sparta, however, was exceptional in that its singular caste of elite hoplites ("equals" or "spartiates") had both the time and obligation to train extensively. This gained them skills that included an ability to carry out complex maneuvers far beyond the capacity of any other Grecian military.

Basic among these Spartan evolutions was cyclosis.[19] This was a deliberate exaggeration of natural rightward drift giving extraordinary extension to Spartan right wings that could then enfold even the most wary opponent. Placing the best among its spartiates (doubtless the finest heavy infantrymen in the world at the time) on the far right, Sparta at its peak crushed one enemy phalanx after another, relentlessly rolling them up from an overrun flank. Mind you, this was a tactic that would often greatly expose their own left wings in turn. The Spartans addressed that by taking care to assign troops of superior quality from their homeland to the hazardous post at line's end on the far left. We therefore see from our most detailed account of their phalanx in action that the Sciritae battalion (lochos) stood there at Mantinea I.[20] Manned above-strength (600 soldiers versus the normal 500 or so), that seems to have been the most select unit below spartiate rank in the Spartan army.

Yet the same battle shows that additional steps might be needed to address the risk of counter-flanking endemic to cyclosis. The Spartan king Agis tried to shift the Sciritae farther left while transferring two other units from his right onto the other side of the field.[21] Either confusion or disobedience among his subordinates caused this perhaps overly bold move to fail. But cyclosis still delivered success as Sparta's picked men on the right were able to outflank and rout the opposition there.[22]

In time, a rival polis finally did manage to offset cyclosis in a crucial major engagement against the Spartans. This was Thebes in central Greece. That city took advantage of an exceptional generation of native generals to free itself from domination by the Spartans, going on to put an effective end to Sparta's long run as a great power. The key event in this saga came at the battle fought near the Boeotian city of Leuctra in 371.[23] Epaminondas of Thebes executed a tactical scheme there against Sparta's phalanx that placed his best troops at exceptional depth (filed at 25–50 shields versus only twelve-deep for the opposition[24]) and on his left rather than the customary right. He then either rushed this wing ahead with his Sacred Band in the leading ranks or maneuvered that elite unit from behind his left extreme to extend the wing.[25] The result in either case was that he caught the cyclosis maneuver before it could fully develop, aided fortuitously by the Spartans being slowed down due to interference from their own cavalry fleeing around that end of the line. Reluctant Spartan allies on the other side of the field declined to advance against the refused wing of Epaminondas and the battle turned into a lengthy slugging match between Spartans and Thebans. The latter were able in the end to exert a final, powerful wave of othismos and claim victory as they shoved their exhausted foes into retreat.[26]

With its chief national proponents at Sparta in eclipse, cyclosis seems to have played a rather less prominent role over the next few decades. It is conceivable that some mercenary units might have been sufficiently skilled to employ such sophisticated maneuvers during this period; however, there is no record of them actually doing so. Still, it seems that you just couldn't keep a good idea down for long. This recognizes that the tactical approach Philip II adopted soon thereafter can quite reasonably be seen as having a foundation in cyclosis. Philip merely replaced sole use of picked hoplites on his right/strike wing with equally elite hypaspists working in close cooperation with his homeland's signature shock cavalry. He thus introduced a mix of specialized arms into the equation, providing greater versatility and effectiveness with superior potential for his highly mobile riders to get outside an opposing battle-line and initiate a turning that could then be completed by his select spearmen. All the same, Philip's fundamental formula seems to have very much resembled that plied by the Spartans of old.

Of course, as Macedonian retooling of the cyclosis concept indicates, flank envelopments were not the realm of hoplites alone. They were possible for light infantry and (especially) cavalry as well. The Greek anchoring at Chaeronea was thus not aimed solely at precluding a mixed-arms sweep around the left. It also addressed potential flanking on the right. And that would have been primarily a mounted affair in that the opposing pikemen there were ill-suited for enveloping (they are not known to have ever attempted it). Nor was the act of fixing on a barrier always focused on envelopment by maneuver—even when only infantry was present. That was because outflanking could also occur due to a manpower discrepancy. Phalanxes could thin their files toward matching the line-length of a foe with greater numbers, but this had a practical limit[27] (generally at about four shields deep). Small armies unable to avoid an engagement might therefore suffer on one or both flanks from much wider enemy deployments, which required no maneuvering per se. This was surely what took place in many of our known and suspected instances of "double envelopment" in which a phalanx was enclosed on at least three sides to take exceedingly ruinous casualties.

Yet the most famous example of hoplites executing a double envelopment, at Marathon in 490, joins Chaeronea above to remind us that overlapping to make a flank attack was not the only way to envelop. One could achieve much the same effect by defeating an opposition wing by other means. The victors could then turn against the enemy center, assaulting a new and open "flank" that they themselves had just created. Battle mechanics from that point on would then be fundamentally identical to those already discussed for turnings by maneuver, rolling up the victim as a lateral attack went down his array. Hoplites at Marathon thus drove back both ends of an opposing Persian front to close about from either side and doubly envelop its center. And, as seen, the elite Macedonian spearmen at Chaeronea made a similar turning (though on but a single wing) to initiate their army's rout of the coalition Greeks.

Envelopments of all sorts appear to have decided a great many phalanx actions. Surveys covering significant 5th and 4th century engagements[28] suggest that more than a third of these likely included envelopments among their deciding factors. Moreover, this same data indicates that the ability of Greek armies to carry out such maneuvers seems to have gone up over time,[29] probably reflecting more frequent drilling of militias and the increased use of cavalry, native professionals, and mercenaries. We can often draw directly on our sources' statements in assessing whether an envelopment took place and can reasonably infer it elsewhere from casualty rates. Significant losses that are mostly confined to a single contingent are a good indicator that it was enveloped. More generally, a report of heavy casualties[30] to a defeated army that does not appear to have been extensively pursued is suggestive of envelopment. And if both sides took such costly hits, then it is highly likely that each suffered from an enveloping on one end of the field. As to whether a given envelopment was the result of flank maneuvering or of some other means, this can be very hard to determine in light of the near universal shortage of detailed battle descriptions in our sources. But indications of how long a fight went on might yield useful clues. An envelopment coming at the very onset of an engagement likely reflects the effect of an opening flank maneuver. Conversely, a lengthy combat suggests that any turning resulted from a wing giving way along its front due to excessive damage or some enemy ploy in that sector.

Withdrawal Maneuvers

Even more than maneuvering for the sake of flank envelopment, the sort of false retreat that the hypaspists carried out at Chaeronea was possible only for the best-drilled troops. This was by far the most complex and difficult way for a phalanx to withdraw and it must have come about as an outgrowth of less demanding evolutions. These allowed armies to refuse a pending battle or escape one already in progress. Yet even those undoubtedly simpler processes seem to have required skills well above what hoplite militias normally possessed. It is thus contingents with exceptional training and mostly under the greater sophistication of Spartan leadership that appear in our surviving record of such maneuvers in use.

Thucydides[31] provides us with an excellent example of a phalanx withdrawing at the very point of engagement. This took place in 418 near the Peloponnesian city of Mantinea when the Spartans under their king Agis were facing a phalanx from Argos that was deployed on ground "difficult to approach" (perhaps sitting upslope). Having brought his own front to "within a stone's throw" of the opposing line, Agis decided that his position was too unfavorable and withdrew. Sadly, we get no details on how he pulled this off. However, being so near to the enemy, the Spartans must have backed away while still faced to receive a charge, something no doubt initiated from rear rank to front much as was likely the case for Philip's men at Chaeronea. It was therefore only after getting out of reasonable range of any potential Argive rush that they turned their backs to make a faster departure. Once completely out of danger, Agis would then have simply reordered into a column and marched away. Such an escape from imminent battle must have been most unusual in the world of Greek militias. The reaction of the Argives shows this clearly, since they were "amazed at the sudden retreat of the enemy after advancing so near, and didn't know what to make of it." A state of surprise so profound must certainly have greatly aided the Spartans' withdrawal.

Two other known instances of Spartan armies backing away prior to a pending engagement involved Agesilaos II. The first took place near Thebes in 378 when that king withdrew after offering battle to a smaller enemy force that was holding fast on a height and had discouraged his attack over such unfavorable ground through a daunting display of discipline.[32] Agesilaos probably escaped here in a manner much like that proposed above for Agis. The second action came in the Peloponnese just west of Mantinea in 371. The Spartans eluded an encounter there with foes again better-poised on a facing slope, this time within a narrow valley.[33] Having aligned his men nine or ten shields deep "so as to present an armed front to the enemy," Agesilaos ordered his leftward contingents to turn, starting from their rear ranks, and reposition behind the still stationary right wing before again pivoting to face forward. This simultaneously let them pull away while doubling the depth of his phalanx. The king perhaps repeated this evolution once more and then had his greatly deepened formation make a right turn as he led it away. And it would seem that all of this was completed before his startled foes could organize to intervene or even mount a timely pursuit. Agesilaos appears to have cleverly improvised his escape here by combining a simple quarter-turn and flankward march with a file-deepening maneuver called "anastrophe" ("wheeling around"),[34] something in which his troops were obviously well-practiced.

However, another use of anastrophe on the island of Corcyra in 372[35] provides an outstanding illustration of how maneuvering in close proximity to a more aggressive foe than faced by Agesilaos could have terrible consequences. The Spartan commander there, Mnasippos, feared that one of his wings was too thin (filed at eight shields) and ordered it to double its depth.[36] But as this progressed and his front rank began pulling back, the enemy, instead of being confused and inactive, took that as flight. They therefore charged "so that the Spartans could not complete the maneuver … then the troops next to those attempting the wheel-around movement turned to flee." This time the Spartans had misjudged their enemy and maneuvered rashly. They thus ended up absorbing a ruinous loss that took Mnasippos' life and decimated his army.

The failed maneuver above did not actually involve an attempt to avoid battle, only a misconception of one; however, Sparta's defeat in 395 at Haliartus in Boeotia might very well reflect such a bid gone wrong. The ambitious general Lysander had disobeyed orders to await reinforcement and advanced with a modest host toward bringing that city into revolt against Thebes. Suddenly, a large Theban relief force arrived to confront him. There is no certain evidence in our sources[37] that Lysander was even able to deploy his phalanx at this point; still, the normal time demands of preparing for a hoplite battle might have let him get into some semblance of order as his foes likewise marshaled across the way. Seeing that he was badly outnumbered and likely to suffer envelopment, he could well have tried then to maneuver away from danger. If so, nearly all of his army, which was far below Sparta's usual standards in having but a handful of officers present along with a single contingent from its colony at Heraclea, simply ran away when the savvy Thebans almost immediately began moving forward lest their quarry escape. Lysander and his immediate companions were left alone on the field and quickly cut down; but his fleeing men took only modest losses, being able to reach some nearby hills to bleed and repel their pursuers with a deadly hail of missile fire and thrown stones. If Haliartus did indeed feature a pre-battle withdrawal maneuver, it would certainly add an exclamation mark to the idea that doing that sort of thing in front of an experienced and well-led opponent was to court disaster.[38]

It is worth remarking before leaving the subject of withdrawal prior to combat that a good and oft employed alternative to maneuvering your phalanx was to come to terms with the enemy. We therefore see a number of commanders arriving at negotiated truces even as their armies stood facing each other along a prospective battlefront. And no one seems to have been keener to seek such life-saving arrangements than the Spartans. Among our recorded examples is the Spartan monarch Agis coming to a mutual agreement to halt hostilities after an army of Argives and their allies had run him down in a chase across much of the Peloponnese. This came "just as the armies were upon the point of engaging"[39] in the summer of 418 and despite the Spartans having fielded "by far the finest Hellenic army ever brought together."[40] And such a pacific resolution is all the more interesting in that it was overseen by Agis, reputed to have been one of the most headstrong and warlike of all Spartan leaders.[41]

Another good example of this kind of peaceful withdrawal from pending battle came in 397 above the Meander River in Ionian Asia Minor. A huge hoplite phalanx led by Dercyllidas of Sparta was arrayed eight shields deep there on the verge of engaging Persian forces under the satraps Pharnabazus and Tissaphernes.[42] But the last of those had seen an Asian army suffer against the Greeks at Cunaxa a few years earlier and had no desire to repeat the experience.[43] Nor was his Spartan counterpart any more eager to fight. That was because Dercyllidas was facing action on an open plain where his much more cavalry-rich foes would enjoy a significant advantage. These mutual concerns led to a truce, which not only avoided the encounter at hand, but also put a halt (temporarily as it turned out) to the entire war. It is clear from the foregoing incidents that the Spartans were nearly as masterful at negotiating their way out of trouble as they were in maneuvering out of it. Using any and all means, they actually found ways to avoid fighting more often than any other Greeks and their reputation for bloodthirsty martial fanaticism would therefore seem much exaggerated.

Clearly then, there were practical ways to avoid coming to blows even after a phalanx had deployed for battle. But what about breaking off a combat already underway? Curiously, we have documentation of this as a prelude to reversing back into engagement (see below), but no explicit reference to it in terms of making a simple escape. Yet this must have happened; indeed, it is logical that the concept of "false retreat" most likely came about as a way to exploit a previously established practice. Even so, city-state militias, as we've seen, usually had no more than primitive maneuvering abilities. It was thus only the very most skilled of Greek armies that might have executed such demanding and dangerous evolutions. Sparta certainly had this sort of fighting machine by no later

11. Phalanx Maneuvers 171

than the early 5th century. And Thebes[44] followed by Macedonia developed something similar in the 4th century. We therefore must seek possible examples of successful mid-combat withdrawals[45] solely among defeats for those particular combatants. Moreover, the search needs to concentrate on those actions where the losers' casualties were light, potentially reflecting that a maneuver had discouraged effective pursuit.

The earliest candidate for Spartans having maneuvered out of a lost engagement might be along the road from Mantinea to Argos at Oenoe in 461. Celebrations of this otherwise obscure action were prominent at Delphi and upon the famous painted colonnade in the agora at Athens.[46] These marked a rare Spartan defeat in fixed battle at the very start of the First Peloponnesian War. It would seem that an army from Sparta was moving through the mountains toward Argos with the intention of intimidating it out of a new treaty signed with Athens. But a phalanx of Argives and Athenians had deployed with extraordinary rapidity to block the way. This held a choke-point that allowed it to anchor northward on the steep slopes of Mount Artemisius and against the Charadrus River torrent on the south. We have no description of what followed, but it appears to have been a set-back for the Spartans from which they withdrew without losses significant enough to be noted anywhere in the surviving literature. An orderly maneuver out of combat as per the opening phase of Philip's evolution at Chaeronea would therefore seem a strong possibility. Executed at the point that both sides were stalemated in the tight pass and approaching mutual exhaustion, the Lacedaemonians could thus have gotten away clean.

Maneuvering out of an ongoing combat must already have been a standard practice for the Spartans at the time of Oenoe based upon their earlier use of false withdrawals. And it would seem to have remained a basic element within their tactical kit for decades to come, likely being how they pulled from a battle gone bad against the Thebans at Amyklai in the winter of 370-69.[47] Of course, abandoning the field had a definite downside. It left the enemy free to brag, erect statues, and paint pictures marking their glorious victory as per Oenoe. But it also preserved precious Spartan blood. And that had a higher priority due to the severe shortage of citizen manpower inherent within Sparta's caste-based society. We thus see Spartans disdaining extended pursuit,[48] since that might put hard-to-replace hoplites at risk just for the sake of chasing already beaten men. This along with the previous discussion on avoiding combat by either negotiation or maneuver provides critical context for Sparta's application of its exceptional capacity for drill toward finding ways to save valuable lives amid pending defeat. And there could be another benefit as well, since keeping casualties low might encourage history to nearly ignore an otherwise embarrassing loss like Oenoe.

While mid-battle withdrawals almost surely formed the original basis for development of the sort of faux retreats employed by the Spartans and later by the Macedonians at Chaeronea, an even closer link might exist between the latter battle and a tradition of escaping combat by maneuver. This is Philip's defeat in his first meeting with Onomarchos of Phocis in 354.[49] That was in Thessaly, likely near Pherae, which was facing a threatened siege by Philip at the time. We unfortunately know little more than that Onomarchos claimed a victory; yet, the fact that Philip's army escaped to remain in the field indicates it sustained no more than minor losses. And such an association of exceptionally light casualties in defeat with a highly drilled fighting force strongly suggests that it might well have been an oft-practiced maneuver that allowed the Macedonians to slip from exhausted foes. If so, it was both an effective tactic in the moment as well as a foreshadowing of what was to come in the final fight for Grecian supremacy 17 years later at Chaeronea.

What then of the tactic of faking retreat from ongoing battle and then reversing to attack such as Philip is said to have done at Chaeronea? How often was so obviously hazardous a mid-combat maneuver actually employed? In fact, we have only two additional documented instances beyond the Macedonian maneuver in 338. Both show the Spartans making as if they wanted to escape an ongoing engagement only to then spin about and heavily punish their enemies. These were on the first morning at Thermopylae in 480 and a year later on the Greek right at Plataea. In the former, Leonidas' men "would turn their backs and feign flight all together" and "then suddenly turn around … and slay countless numbers."[50] And about the latter, Plato portrayed the "old sweats" Socrates and Laches as discussing how Spartans at Plataea "ran away" but then "they turned and fought … and so won that particular battle."[51] It is important to understand though that this kind of maneuver may well be underreported in our surviving literature. Notably in this regard, it shows up again in a treatise that Onasander dedicated to the Roman counsel Veranius in the 1st century AD:

> It is sometimes a useful stratagem for an army facing the enemy to retire gradually, as if struck by fear, or to about face and make a retreat similar to a flight, but in order, and then, suddenly turning, to attack their pursuers. For sometimes the enemy, delighted by the belief that their opponents are fleeing, break ranks and rush forward, leaping ahead of one another. There is no danger in turning to attack these men; and those who have for some time been pursuing, terrified by the very unexpectedness of this bold stand, immediately take to flight.[52]

While by no means a certainty, it seems quite reasonable that this philosopher and military writer might have been familiar with instances of false withdrawal maneuvers in addition to those few still extant today. This suggests that both that tactic and its likely prototype of simple escape from ongoing combat may have been much more common than our surviving sources can firmly attest.

Reengagement Maneuvers

It would seem that the fairly frequent occurrence of simultaneous turnings of opposing left wings in phalanx battles as a result of mutual envelopment should have led to a large number of drawn engagements. Yet these were actually rare.[53] The probable reason for this ostensible paradox is that the men involved in such twin turnings commonly reengaged with their opposite numbers, who were likewise still on the field. This then let them reach a more definite final decision in favor of one side or the other. And in these cases, our sources usually just report a simple victory or defeat. Discerning the presence of interim envelopments, if possible at all, must thus come via subtle clues as discussed earlier.

It is likely that most of these renewed engagements were pretty ragged and far from organized affairs. This was due to the difficulty of reforming for another fight under the powerful urge for soldiers to chase a beaten foe. Such behavior was clearly on display among the Athenians fighting Philip in 338. And it was something Onasander noted as a widespread bent that opposing generals could cannily exploit. Almost pure instinct was at work here, compelling those gaining the upper hand in a shock combat to pursue in a way often impossible to restrain.[54] Olpae in 426[55] provides a good example of such lack of restraint prompting a multi-stage battle. A phalanx there in the Greek northwest under Spartan command had fallen victim to a mid-battle ambush that routed its left wing. Ambraciot hoplites on the right, however, had enveloped their immediate foes and chased them well away from the battle site, utterly disregarding what was unfolding elsewhere. As a result, when these men finally sought to rejoin their army, they ran into unforeseen resistance from enemy troops still milling about on the originally contested ground. The Ambraciots fought their way free only with great loss, and their final flight from this renewed action turned what had been a potentially somewhat inconclusive result into a total victory for the opposition. There is no indication in any of this of a formal maneuver; rather, what we see is a much less organized reforming among previously victorious phalanx segments that unexpectedly found themselves once more at hazard. And it is this sort of essentially inadvertent pattern that seems to have characterized many, if not most, Greek reengagements.

However, just as natural rightward drift turned into cyclosis, so reengaging became a deliberate and deadly maneuver under Spartan leadership. The key in doing this was to instill sufficient discipline into your hoplites so that they would refrain from pursuing beaten foes to await further commands. Those orders might indeed unleash them to chase the enemy, but then again, the instruction could be to reform, facing in a new direction before launching a second attack.[56] Instances of this sort of designed maneuvering to renew engagements are well documented and include some of the most famous battles in Greek history.

The celebrated engagement at Mantinea I in 418 has already been mentioned in this regard. There, the Spartan king Agis, having enveloped and routed the Athenian contingent immediately opposed to his right wing, "ordered all the [Spartan] army to advance to support the defeated wing"[57] on the left/allied side of his phalanx. Details of this maneuver are sadly lacking in our surviving accounts; but Agis was apparently able to regroup his men into a new formation that targeted the previously successful enemy troops, causing them to flee once they saw "the Spartans in full advance upon them." We are fortunate in having better descriptions of what this reforming evolution must have looked like from a pair of battles during the Corinthian War in 394.

The first of these came at Nemea River in the northern Peloponnese.[58] The Spartan army and its allies there had confronted a larger opposing coalition force based around major musters from Athens and Boeotia. Both phalanxes veered rightward as they closed into action; the Spartan wing doing so in an extreme manner as per its well-established practice and an over-deep Theban contingent leading the Boeotians in an at least somewhat similar fashion across the way.[59] The Spartans easily bested the Athenians that they greatly overlapped on their end of the line and the Boeotians did the same to Achaean hoplites on their end to produce an exchange of envelopments. But at that point, the two victorious factions behaved very differently. The Boeotian brigade broke into a chase to punish its fleeing foes and pulled some of its allies along even as the highly disciplined Spartans held their ground to keep rank and file intact. The Spartan commanders then arrayed their men anew and sent them into the enemy troops as they came straggling back disordered from their ill-advised pursuit. Sparta's hoplites smashed the flank of each unit in sequence as they drove down the opposing line to complete a devastating rout that went on until nightfall. And the Spartan king Agesilaos then forged another victory by means of a reengagement maneuver; this coming just days later at Coronea in Boeotia. However, Agesilaos' share of success was much costlier for his troops in that his second attack plowed into a stoutly reformed enemy front rather than a disorganized and vastly softer flank.[60]

The foregoing clashes early in the Corinthian War plus the Spartan victory two years later at the "Long Walls" of Corinth[61] with its similarity to Nemea marked the height of this kind of renewed engagement maneuvering. It never again played a role in a prominent battle as far as our scanty records allow us to know.[62] Some of that, at least at first, was likely due to greater awareness among opposing generals of its potential use by their enemies. This led them to be more wary and avoid falling prey to such tricks if possible. But there were limits on how much they could truly control on a battlefield. The fact is that reformed attacks as well as simpler mid-combat withdrawals were highly dependent on cooperation from within the enemy ranks. Men who could avoid breaking into an unwise pursuit were not vulnerable to false retreats, while those that could recognize the real thing would make anyone maneuvering rashly pay a steep price. Gullible opposition simply faded away as armies became more professional and better-drilled until the sort of green troops fielded by Athens at Chaeronea were more or less extinct. Philip's faux retreat in that battle thus not only marked a brilliant example of such maneuvering by a Grecian general, it might have marked one of the very last as well. Yet it's important to remember that this drop in use over time of codependent evolutions was opposite the pattern for more self-contained flanking maneuvers. The trend toward greater tactical capability in Greek armies actually facilitated application of those ploys. Enveloping an enemy formation therefore remained a much prized goal throughout the entire history of Grecian warfare—and well beyond.

12

Use of Terrain

> Yet the Greeks are accustomed to wage wars, as I learn, and they do it most senselessly in their wrongheadedness and folly. When they have declared war against each other, they come down to the fairest and most level ground that they can find and fight there, so that the victors come off with great harm; of the vanquished I say not so much as a word, for they are utterly destroyed.[1]
>
> —Herodotus, *The Histories*

With these words Mardonios of Persia belittles the appreciation of Greek generals for the use of terrain. Modern scholars have often echoed his critique, finding no other explanation for the consistent choice of the few level plains in Greece as the places to join battle than in an agonistic type of warfare governed by so many strict rules that combat became sport. This belief is badly mistaken. The correct explanation is that what appears to be a gentleman's agreement to fight on flat land is, in fact, a display of enlightened self-interest on the part of each commander. A phalanx requires its troops to maintain formation and cohesion, and rough terrain degrades the ability of men to move in unison. If a phalanx fights best on level ground, then we should expect hoplite generals to choose such terrain for battle if they trust in the strength of their spearmen, even though this would also benefit a like-armed opponent. We therefore see most of the major phalanx battles, where the opposing forces approached parity in numbers and/or effectiveness and other troop types were either absent or cancelled each other out, occurring on the same few fields that were best suited to such deployments.

Mardonios was thus incorrect in his belief that Greeks ignored the value of topography. Their generals were actually well versed in the use of terrain, even if they sought to minimize it as a factor in many of their battles. When finding themselves mismatched to the enemy in terms of hoplite quality/quantity or in being outnumbered by swarms of light infantry or cavalry on the wings, commanders turned to terrain features to augment their forces. A good general could use landforms to keep his flanks just as safe as if protected by picked cavalry. He could harness gravity to provide impetus to the advance of his hoplites down a slope, or degrade the effectiveness of the most elite foes by forcing them to climb to face him. Whole armies could be shielded behind hills to conceal their advance, or elements could lay hidden in wait to launch a surprise attack. This inevitably led to landscape playing an important role in quite a few hoplite engagements.[2] An outstanding example of such exploitation of terrain came at Crimisus River, where Timoleon of Corinth led a badly outnumbered phalanx to fight off foreign invaders by taking every advantage it could of the lay of the land.

Crimisus River (341): Mud and Blood

Syracuse on Sicily was a foundation of Corinth and looked to that mother city in the mid–4th century for help to break from the tyrant Dionysius II. The Corinthians voted to send a mercenary force and to supply a general. Their choice was an odd one, which makes one wonder just how eagerly the citizens vied for the glory of relieving their colony. They chose Timoleon, an elderly general who had disengaged from public life twenty years earlier after freeing Corinth from tyranny by conspiring to kill his own brother the tyrant Timophanes.[3] Telecleides, the leading man in Corinth, tapped into the shame of this act to provide an inspired bit of motivation. He excoriated Timoleon that if he were to succeed in overturning this new tyranny as well, he would be remembered for his tyrannicide, but should he fail he would be known only for his fratricide.[4]

From the moment he assumed command, Timoleon proved to be a remarkable leader. He first succeeded in freeing the polis from its dictator and then went on to wage a wider campaign against other tyrants on the island. This proved costly in that it required compensation for a fair number of hired soldiers. Pressed to meet his payroll, Timoleon raided Punic territory for the funds he needed; something that Carthage rightly read as a clear violation of past treaties with Syracuse. The Africans responded by declaring war, and the campaign season of 341[5] saw them land an army in western Sicily.

Timoleon moved to mobilize against this peril and appealed initially to the Syracusan citizenry. But this produced only a disappointing 3,000 hoplite volunteers, leaving him with no choice but to turn elsewhere for more troops. Other poleis, perceiving a collateral threat from the invaders, stepped up and provided another 3,000–5,000 spearmen. And even the tyrant Hicetas of Leontini, with whom Timoleon had been warring, felt so endangered as to lend mercenaries to the cause. These brought Timoleon's hired hoplites up to 4,000 strong; therefore, he might have been able to field as many as 12,000 spearmen.[6] Adding 1,000 cavalry[7] and perhaps 1,000–2,000 light footmen, he elected to meet the enemy well away from Syracuse.

Plutarch tells us that Timoleon's decision to pursue a defense so far forward rested upon trying to better motivate his men to fight by denying them an easy retreat (or burial) should they suffer defeat. But it's clear instead that the highly experienced general was actually quite aware of terrain conditions around the Carthaginians' staging area in the island's distant west beyond an established ford on the Crimisus River.[8] He therefore chose to engage there with the idea of catching them not only unready to fight, but also toward compelling a contested river crossing that might go far in compensating for his lesser manpower.[9] However, it took eight days to march all the way across Sicily, and that gave plenty of time for doubters among his troops to begin questioning the wisdom of their leader's bold strategy. For as risky as attacking at so great a distance from home might have seemed at its first acceptance, the sort of rumor mill attached to any large group in the field had since exaggerated potential dangers to such an extent that the expedition now seemed suicidal to some. And, indeed, one of the mercenaries that had come from Corinth with the aged general denounced him, saying that "Timoleon was out of his mind and was leading his men to certain destruction."[10] But though this fellow deserted with 1,000 other hirelings, the rest of the venerable old strategos' men forged on, trusting in his well-grounded judgment.

Timoleon approached the Crimisus amid pre-dawn gloom and thick river-fog; the last rising up with a sun that shown dimly on a morning that was heavy with the threat of ominous storm clouds rolling in from the east. And he took care at this point to keep his army well hidden behind an intervening ridgeline from any unfriendly eyes and ears among the enemy that might be alert even at such an early hour. It was from the crest of that shielding highland where the veteran general and his scouts then secretly observed their foes below as best first light and mist allowed.

The Carthaginian force on display was clearly very large; however, our sources undoubtedly overstate its size.[11] Based on Plutarch's claim (also implied by Diodorus) that the Africans' infantry arrived aboard 200 warships (i.e. "oared," with supplies and mounts on sailing vessels), a figure of 30,000 foot soldiers appears most reasonable.[12] These likely composed ten divisions of 3,000 men apiece (nominal, perhaps averaging more like 2,750 at parade strength[13] with one select contingent, the "Sacred Band," maybe completely manned at 3,000[14]). A fair mix of weaponry might have rendered nearly two-thirds of the Punic infantry heavy-armed. That would suggest six divisions of shock fighters. One of these contained full citizens (the Sacred Band); perhaps two were of Liby-Phoenician residents ("perioeci") and the final three of Libyan mercenaries. All the heavies would have been spearmen very much like Greek hoplites. The remaining foot troops were contracted skirmishers. They included Iberians, Celts, Italian Gauls, and Numidians. Mounted strength maybe came to 3,000 riders at a tenth the infantry count. These were both cavalry and charioteers, with the last numbering at least 600.[15]

Timoleon had planned upon setting up across the Crimisus from the Punic camp so that he could use both the river's flow and steep bank to disadvantage any assault on his front. Thus, he must now have been greatly disturbed to find the enemy already in the process of fording. The chariots had led the way followed by the flower of their heavy infantry in the form of the Sacred Band and the Liby-Phoenician divisions.[16] This put around 10,000 fighters on the eastern bank, amounting to about half the Africans' shock troops and a third of their total manpower. Having lost his long planned upon position to this rapid advance, Timoleon needed to take quick action if he was to salvage the situation. He had two distinct tactical options at this juncture. The first was to deploy on the heights and wait for the enemy to come up to him. This was easy to do and would force his foes into a literal uphill battle. Yet it also would allow them to deploy their entire army. And it was that aspect that now led him to select the alternative of initiating action by means of a charge down to the river,[17] deciding that the opportunity to give his opponents less time for physical and mental preparation while catching them below full strength was well worth forfeiting any advantage to holding the high ground and risking an overly rapid and disorderly advance down the slope. And a victory over the enemy's advance elements would then let him occupy the riverbank much as he had originally intended. Sending his cavalry down to attack, Timoleon arranged his 9,000–11,000 hoplites into a phalanx probably eight shields deep, putting the mercenaries and best Sicilian spearmen on his right and the remaining allies on the left wing. This positioned his less reliable Syracusan militia in the middle, where it could be steadied by more capable soldiers on either side.

Suddenly realizing that an opposing force was moving against them, the charioteers rushed out and cycled back and forth in front of their infantry comrades; meanwhile, those surprised troops scrambled behind the horsemen's cover to get into rank and file that they might meet the looming menace. The Sacred Band elites must have taken their accustomed post on the right wing,[18] likely standing along a front of some 400 shields and thus filed eight deep.[19] With the Liby-Phoenicians aligned across the center and left of their array, the Africans seem to have had just enough time to properly receive the attack. They held their ground to engage in a clash of forces that, for all the differences in the overall strengths of the two armies, were remarkably similar in size at the actual point of contention.

Timoleon's cavalry could not penetrate the Punic chariot screen and he ordered it to withdraw sideward and threaten the ends of the opposing line. This caused the charioteers to move away as well that they might protect their flanks. Though the Greek horsemen had failed to inflict all that much harm upon the enemy, they had bought time for their phalanx to draw near and redress its ranks, restoring any order lost as it moved down the slope. Timoleon saw that the enemy front was now exposed and ordered the signal to sound for attack.[20] His hoplites closed into the Carthaginian line with weapons raised and the air began to reverberate to the clang of spears striking shield or helm amid the shouting of men both furious and fearful, a din punctuated now and then by a cry of pain when it was frail flesh rather than metal that received the blow. Evenly matched in equipment and formation width/depth, the Africans held firm against the Greek assault. They gave about as good as they got during the initial duel of spears as well as the sword-work and shoving of shields that slowly began to dominate the ever tightening action. Just then, the storm moving in from the east that morning broke over the battlefield with great violence.

All of the combatants were drenched in a driving rain, pummeled by hail, buffeted by strong winds, and dazzled by flashes of lightning accompanied by deafening blasts of thunder as the tempest raged about them; however, it was the Carthaginians who took by far the most damage. The west-moving gale blew directly in their faces, blinding and urging them rearward even as it pressed into the backs of their foes to if anything aid their momentum. Along with the deadly weapon strikes and powerful crush of hoplites already coming their way, this was simply too much for the battered Africans to bear and their formation began to come apart as a sense of panic raced through its ranks. And when the Punic phalanx's rearward elements unraveled in a fear-filled bid at escape, Timoleon and his hoplites surged ahead, spearing and slashing down hundreds of enemy front-fighters caught in place and unable to get away. The Carthaginian troops still on the far side of the Crimisus saw this happening and rushed to cross and join the fight. But their efforts as well as those of their fleeing fellows on the far bank were to meet fatal interference from one of the most primeval banes of fighting men—mud.

The riverbank hosting this battle was made of the sort of floodplain silt and clay common to the volcanic-rich terrain of Sicily. Once soaked by rain (and likely no small amount of blood and other body fluids from the combatants), intermixed clay near the surface would have begun absorbing moisture. This caused it to swell, which added to interstitial water in boosting the potential "lubricity" or slickness of the ground's uppermost layer.[21] And the churning of that interval by the feet of thousands of struggling soldiers had then broken down its normally stable internal structure to produce a viscous slurry of mud. Sliding atop still unsaturated sediment below, this slimy ooze made footwork increasingly difficult. Such treacherous footing was initially worst at the battlefront where modest separation between the formations gave ready access to the rain, which added to human secretions in completely soaking the soil even as the back and forth fencing of fighters stirred it up. Meanwhile, within the following ranks, the lesser amount of movement preserved traction a bit longer so that effective othismos continued at least briefly. As for the area behind the phalanxes, this was unoccupied when the downpour began and therefore remained firm; however, that changed as the Carthaginians started to run and their feet immediately churned the ground at their rear into a gooey mess as well.

Floundering across slick muck, the Africans became easy prey for their pursuers and many were taken down from behind. Others reached the edge of the Crimisus only to stall before its rising flood. These too were caught and killed, either where they stood in hesitation or in trying to reverse toward the landward slope. Nor did plunging into the flow prove any less deadly, with the raging torrent perhaps drowning even more than the Greeks slew. And the unengaged troops attempting to ford and get in on the action fared no better. Those not going to a watery grave in the racing river made its far bank where they fell victim to the same awful footing that had doomed so many of their fleeing comrades. There were in fact some tried and true techniques for soldiers of this era to improve their navigation across muddy ground.[22] But these applied to relatively level surfaces, and the Carthaginians here had to contend with a steep riverbank. Worse yet, their hoplite foes now held the crest of that slippery incline with spears and swords at the ready. Struggling up the grade, many must have slid back well short of success to further impede those below. And what of the "lucky" ones that did gain the top? They encountered the enemy spearmen in waiting, who swiftly thrust them back down, wounded at best and like as not dead or dying. By the time it was all over, thousands of the invaders had been lost, with their bodies either littering the red and sopping battleground or floating down the Crimisus. And thousands more that had somehow gained the river's east side or been trapped there earlier were now captives.[23] Those that escaped the slaughter retreated to their colony at Lilybaeum to the southwest, and Carthage moved soon thereafter to make peace on whatever terms it could get.

Timoleon led his hoplites to a victory over foes more than twice their number; doing so largely through his skill at putting the available terrain to optimum use. The wily Corinthian veteran began by hiding his army behind a screening upland. He then adjusted on the fly to an unexpected enemy advance with a quick attack, catching his foes divided and thus exposed to defeat in detail. Finally, he restored his pre-battle strategy by driving the opposition's vanguard into the Crimisus. That let him set up in a strong defensive position atop the river's bank and deny a crossing to Carthaginian reinforcements. Though employed exceptionally well by Timoleon, these and other types of terrain exploitation were actually fairly common in Greek warfare.

Terrain Anchors

At Crimisus, both Timoleon and his adversary deployed along rather than across the river valley. The steep slopes (upland and riverbank) initially sat at their rears as a result and played no role along the flanks of the contending arrays. That put the onus for securing those tactically vulnerable points solely on light-armed auxiliaries, especially mounted men in this case. While lateral terrain barriers did see significant use on Sicily, it seems that actions with phalanxes stationed either in front of or behind streams and parallel valley slopes were much more common there than on the Greek mainland. That was due in part to the humid Sicilian climate. This produced rivers and streams larger both in number and flow rate than did the more arid conditions in Greece. But it was of greater significance that armies on Sicily usually moved along or near the shoreline. Their routes thus ran perpendicular to watercourses flowing seaward out of the island's interior highlands. That reflected the location of Sicily's major population centers upon its lush coastal plain, which sent armies marching parallel to (if not actually along) the strand in moving from site to site. Efforts to block those advances often resulted in battles setting up across their routes; and therefore, parallel to major, river-cut topography (as at Crimisus). Lateral anchors within such a general orientation tended to be somewhat rare; and they usually occurred where a shoreline intersected the perpendicular downhill trend of the island's drainage and uplands (see "Himera I" below).

While Sicily had an elongate mountainous core enhanced by volcanic activity that sent rivers flowing more or less straight down to shape landforms and deposit a fringing coastal flat, the geomorphic setting in mainland Greece was quite different. It featured a series of tectonic uplifts (horsts) that channeled river courses down parallel down-dropped blocks (grabens), forming slender valleys between the lengthy highland trends. And many of Greece's poleis had inland cities within those valleys, where the rivers provided vital water and fertile floodplains for farming. Yet the same fault-aligned valleys served as easily negotiable pathways for invading armies. This resulted in attempts to block these avenues normally lining up crosswise, which put terrain boundaries alongside rather than behind or before the combatants.[24] And even along the shore, lesser sedimentation generated during the modest seasonal floods typical of Greece's dry clime formed terrain distinct from that of Sicily, where drainage rates were almost constantly high. Grecian coastal flats were thus narrower, actually being more subject to marine erosion than fluvial deposition much of the year. Hoplites certainly did at times deploy parallel to linear topographic trends on the Greek mainland; however, the physiography there conspired to make it more common that they set up perpendicular to the dominant landforms. And that frequently allowed them to employ many sorts of natural barriers to ward their flanks.

A Greek general could make use of a wide variety of terrain features that provided such anchors to the flanks of a force of hoplites. These included sheer cliffs and steep, talus covered slopes; rivers and streams, whether bank full, shallow flowing, or completely dry; swampy areas around rivers, lakes, or along the seashore; and even ocean waters themselves. The potential threats to flank security were no less varied. These might come from other hoplites seeking to wrap around a shorter front, light infantrymen sweeping past to direct missile fire into unshielded rear ranks, or mounted charges beyond a flank to likewise hit at a phalanx's highly vulnerable backside; and occasionally two or all of these might menace at the same time. It's therefore notable that each anchor type had unique characteristics that dictated just how effective it was likely to be in countering these different threats along the edge of a battle formation.

Two of the foregoing kinds of terrain barriers were used by King Leonidas of Sparta in what is undoubtedly the most famous hoplite action to involve the topographic fixing of phalanx flanks. This was at the coastal pass of Thermopylae in 480.[25] The Greeks there faced an opposing force not only large enough to outflank any heavy array they might field across unrestricted ground, but also so rich in light infantry and cavalry that those could easily overwhelm any skirmisher screen deployable off an open flank. This led Leonidas to make his stand in a very narrow part of the pass known as the Middle Gate. There, he could fix both of his flanks against topographic features: a sheer mountain cliff on one side and the Euboan Channel on the other. These were to prove highly effective anchors even though they differed significantly in the details of their individual blocking characteristics.

Steep and impossible to scale, the cliff-face on the Greek left was very much an absolute barrier, denying any access whatsoever around that flank. The marine waters on the right, in contrast, were more of an impediment (albeit a strong one) than a complete blockade. This recognizes that it was possible for men or horses to wade out beyond a wing that was itself sitting on dry ground. However, this posed two serious problems. The first was that neither man nor beast could wade through water that was too deep, and there was no sure way to judge just how close to land that point began. Any passable margin offshore might thus prove far narrower than was practical for an envelopment, something highly probable at Thermopylae in 480, when erosion rather than deposition was dominant as shown by how very slim the Middle Gate was at that time. Still, a man on horseback could negotiate greater depths than one on foot, and cavalry might be able to bring adequate numbers into play even on a fairly narrow offshore shelf if it were to charge in column. This brings us to the second problem with attempting such a maneuver—soft bottom sediment. The hooves of a heavy horse with rider would sink deeply into the semi-solid surface layer of the seabed, putting cavalry at a disadvantage in mobility relative to much lighter opposing foot skirmishers. It seems highly likely that the Persians judged these potential dangers as presenting an unacceptable risk for their valuable horsemen and therefore chose not to even attempt a mounted flank action at Thermopylae. That limitation contributed to Leonidas and his hoplites being able to stand firm within their terrain anchors well into the third day of combat; indeed, not yielding until the Persian Immortals managed to bypass those effective obstacles with an end-run above them along the Anopaia path.

The foregoing issues regarding shoreline anchoring at Thermopylae are equally relevant to assessing other engagements where seawaters are known or suspected to have served as a lateral barrier. These show them to have been effective for securing the ends of phalanxes against all manner of opponents, including hoplites, foot skirmishers, and horsemen. With regard to so barring heavy infantry envelopment, a good case exists that this took place in Thrace at Porus in 403. Though the exact location of that action is not known, it lay between Byzantium and Selymbria and thus almost surely along the shore-skirting route connecting those northern Aegean ports. The Spartan governor

Clearchus and a band of mercenaries advanced there out of Selymbria and fought a hoplite force from Sparta, which had landed at Byzantium intent on reining in his bid to establish a dictatorship in that city.[26] The site's name suggests a choke-point ("poros" being Greek for "passage"). This makes it highly likely that the renegade governor chose to set up his array in a narrows where he could fix it on rough/high ground to the left and water's edge on the right. If so, the sea appears to have been just as effective as the inland barrier in preventing a rapid flanking by the enemy's elite spearmen. And critically for Clearchus, it did so where he personally must have stood on his right wing. Despite the Spartan hoplites eventually carrying a grueling, drawn-out battle through main force, he was therefore able to escape collapse of his formation, elude what little pursuit there might have been, and ultimately find sanctuary in Ionia.[27]

We appear as well to have a likely instance of hoplites abutting a strandline as a precaution against light-armed footmen. This came on Sicily in the opening phase of the battle of Himera I in 480.[28] Taking place at very nearly the same time as the fighting at Thermopylae, this action also featured a Greek army attempting to stave off a much larger force of foreign invaders within a narrow coastal pass. In this case, however, the Greeks were actually the ones superior in cavalry; rather than fearing a mounted envelopment, their concern was to find protection from the opposition's much greater strength in infantry, both heavy and light. A massive Carthaginian army had landed in northwest Sicily and advanced toward Himera on the island's north coast. Allowing the barbarians to close and set up a fortified camp along the shore just west of town, the Greeks took advantage of that positioning to launch a full-strength sally. That let them fight in a slender passage separating the east-west trending shoreline and a high, north-south aligned plateau; this alley sitting between the Carthaginian encampment and the more open beach immediately beneath the walls of the city.[29]

A key factor here was that the invaders had lost their chariots and horses to a storm during transit from Africa. Still, they fielded a huge host. It might actually have held a 5-to-1 advantage over the Greeks in heavy infantry while possibly outnumbering them by 10-to-1 or better in foot skirmishers.[30] The garrison at Himera was desperate to avoid the horrors that would accompany a long siege and sought to repulse the enemy before it came to that. Wisely discounting the value of their modest cavalry force,[31] the Greeks conceded as well that, should they form up across open ground, there was no way to either deploy an adequately wide phalanx or effectively secure its flanks with their small available number of light-armed footmen. Only by engaging in a highly restricted setting could they have any chance for success. That had potential to reduce the contest to one of hoplites against their Punic equivalents; a scenario in which Grecian skill in close-order combat might somehow carry the day. But that was to prove a forlorn hope as the Africans soundly repelled the ensuing attack. All the same, the decision to anchor on sea and upland must have reduced Greek casualties by denying the swarms of enemy light infantry present any flanking opportunity and hindering their ability to pursue from a crowded post behind the Punic front-fighters. And the manpower thus preserved and then supplemented by a large allied reinforcement from Syracuse would prove valuable just a few days later in helping to hand the Carthaginians a devastating beating in a decisive second engagement.

Onomarchos of Phocis provides a fine example of shoreline anchoring meant to fend off cavalry in a phalanx contest that took place in 353 on Thessaly's Crocus Plain.[32] That engagement saw Macedonia's Philip II intercept Onomarchos as he marched to relieve a siege on the Thessalian city of Pherae. Possibly deploying overnight,[33] Philip cut off his foe before he could join up with the Pheraeans. This was critical in that it was their role to provide Onomarchos with nearly his entire mounted arm. Caught almost bereft of horsemen (he fielded only 500 from his own polis) and facing the Macedonian king who had some 3,000 riders in tow on a wide coastal plain, the Phocian warded his flanks as best he could. This called for fixing one end of his phalanx against the Aegean on his right while posting all of what little cavalry he had to screen his otherwise open left flank. That the seaward terrain barrier was daunting is implied by Philip's decision not to test it with his own riders; this despite having a 6-to-1 edge in mounted strength that certainly gave him that option. Instead, he placed his cavalry wholly on the landward flank. Those horsemen would eventually carry that end of the line in the course of a fight described by Diodorus as having been "severe" across the entire field. Yet, though Onomarchos lost both army and life in the rout that followed, the value of his seaside anchor is well shown in the fact that it was never turned.

Couplings of coastal highlands with shorelines to fix both phalanx flanks such as at Thermopylae and Himera were not only mirrored, but in fact greatly superseded by combinations of elevated ground and inland watercourses; this being particularly true on the Greek mainland due to its physiographic character as discussed earlier. Beyond the danger of braving its current, a river running full like the Crimisus was similar to the coastal shallows in that its water depth and muddy bottom could preclude envelopment from wading men or horses. But that last factor of fine-grained sediments was not normally the case in the mountainous settings most common in Greece. Streams there more often had a coarser flooring of pebbles, cobbles, and boulders.[34] Yet those harder floors presented their own unique threats to easy movement and were still useful as flank anchors; something that applied even when the associated watercourses flowed at no more than a trickle or were completely dry.

The difficulty with transiting mountain-fed streambeds was the extremely uneven nature of their surfaces. Covered with a jumble of rounded and variably sized debris prone to slide underfoot, these could not only reduce charges to a crawl in trying to ford them, but often inflicted crippling injuries to feet/ankles and unshod hooves as well. And stumbling over this sort of stuff was hazardous regardless of how much water was present. Challenging enough under dry or barely wet conditions in the normal summer campaigning season, such crossings were actually even more difficult when rocks were flow-covered and coated by the sort of slimy moss that flourishes in that moist environment.[35] It's no wonder then that such streams made excellent anchors for hoplite arrays, especially when they could be backed by peltasts or other auxiliaries able to answer a stand-off volley[36] and bombard anyone working over or around.

There are many instances on record of anchoring one flank of a phalanx along an upland slope[37] and the other with a watercourse. The previously discussed engagement at Oenoe in 461[38] is one of these. That showcased an array of Argive and Athenian hoplites just so anchored turning back an invasion from Sparta. Ironically, some of the Spartan spearmen that suffered defeat there must also have been at Plataea 18 years prior, when their general Pausanius repelled a Persian attack using the very same method.[39] He and his men had been retreating near dawn from a position facing their Asian foes on the other side of the Asopos River only to have pursuing cavalry close on their rear. The Spartan general responded by deploying his hoplites in a phalanx, wedging it between the rough ground of a ridgeline on his left and the Moleis, a tributary of the Asopos, on the right. This was late in the dry summer season and, lacking snow melt, the Moleis would have carried no more than a mere trickle of water. Nonetheless, its wide and boulder-strewn bed still provided an effective obstacle to envelopment. And with their flanks thus warded, the Greek spearmen went on to fend off the mounted threat and kill the Persians' commander Mardonios in doing so.[40] They then routed the enemy infantry force that had followed its cavalry into play against them.

A simultaneous action on another part the battlefield at Plataea demonstrates that, shy a convenient upland, a second streambed could substitute in anchoring both flanks of a hoplite array. This took place a little west across the ridge from where Pausanius made his stand, in an area known as "The Island," which was a slight rise of ground between two strands of a small, braided stream (the Oeroe). Much like Pausanius and his Spartans, the Athenians involved here had arrayed in phalanx to face a large force of cavalry chasing their withdrawal from along the Asopos. Caught on the flat, the Athenian general Aristides was able to fix either end of his hoplite array against the Oeroe branches, which ran nearly 600m apart[41] around The Island. Aristides also had the luxury of being able to deploy a large contingent of foot-archers[42] to pick off anyone trying to work their way across these barriers. This combination of fluvial anchors proved effective against the Persians' Greek allies: horsemen, hamippoi, and hoplites alike. The Athenians were therefore able to hold fast until retreat of the Persians that had been bested by Pausanius induced withdrawal of their opponents as well.

And Plataea has one more lesson to teach on the value of being in an anchored array. This involves what happened to a brigade of hoplites that tried to join in on the fight at The Island.[43] These troops, many from Megara and Phlius, descended toward that action from a slope to its southwest, moving too rapidly and in poor order with no protective terrain at hand. The same horsemen that failed to harm the well-fixed Athenians raced to attack this reinforcement. Unable to form up and lacking flank barriers even had they done so, the Greek spearmen lost some 600 of their number in a frantic flight back onto high ground.[44]

The final type of anchoring terrain used by Greek phalanxes was swampland. This type of barrier against flanking has already been discussed in other contexts at Piraeus/Halae Marsh (403) and Chaeronea (338).[45] It's pretty easy to see how such a surface could stop any attempt at envelopment cold, with the legs of soldiers or horses sinking so deep into the mire as to set them creeping if able to move at all. Another battle where these conditions likely applied to anchoring a hoplite formation took place in Boeotia at Tegyra in 375.[46] A small Spartan phalanx there rested its left against either the margin of Lake Copais or (perhaps more likely) a bog fringing that body of water. And the other end of the line might have found a similar anchor, possibly setting against a finger of marshland common in the vicinity.[47] As it turned out, these barriers actually seem to have held; yet, the Spartans went down to defeat anyway when the smaller contingent of Theban spearmen standing in opposition formed an unusually deep array. Emerging from behind a frontal screen of horsemen, this virtual column struck along a very narrow front just inside the Spartan right flank and punched through to initiate a rout. It seems probable that the Thebans were encouraged toward such extreme tactics in part by the enemy's sound lateral anchoring, which eliminated any practical option to exploit their superiority in cavalry at the edges of the field.

Just how dangerous such saturated ground might have proven had the Thebans risked a mounted envelopment at Tegyra may be illustrated by an action in 322 at Lamia in Thessaly.[48] The Macedonian commander there, Leonnatos, led his horsemen against Thessalian cavalry. Apparently attempting to envelop, he rode into a bordering swamp. Catching him bogged down there, the Thessalians cut Leonnatos off and shot him from the saddle, leaving his surviving comrades to flee in defeat with the body. Thus, just like all of the other varieties of terrain anchors discussed here, marshlands could form quite deadly barriers against foolhardy flank attacks.

Screening Terrain and Slope Impediments

Timoleon's use of high ground to initially screen his arrival at Crimisus was crucial in denying the Carthaginians sufficient warning time to get their entire army across the river, thus allowing the crafty Corinthian to subsequently defeat them in detail. It is important to note in this that the terrain on that occasion shielded much more than the simple approach of a distant column. Even with his infantry marching at eight men wide, Timoleon's men would have been strung out along an interval of at least 3.5km[49] (and it could easily have been twice that at only four men across). At a realistic marching pace, it would have taken no less than an hour and possibly much longer for the tail-end of such a column to catch up once the first troops had reached their general's desired back-slope position. Timoleon would then have lost more time getting his highly diverse collection of militia and mercenary contingents into order for further action. And throughout this lengthy process, the intervening upland was invaluable in hiding them from their foes across the way.

Pagondas of Thebes was a similarly aged and highly experienced general who took advantage of available terrain to screen an unexpected deployment. At Delium in 424,[50] he was thus able to sneak up on an invading Athenian army that was otherwise poised to safely retreat back home, having already crossed the Boeotian border. But the use of high ground on this occasion went beyond merely screening his arrival. It also served to disguise his strike force's true strength. By showing only the front ranks of his phalanx at the crest of the ridge, Pagondas concealed both the exceptional file depth of Theban hoplites holding its right wing and the considerable contingent of cavalry he had in reserve. And those twin deceptions went far toward luring the Athenian spearmen below into a losing uphill fight at poor odds.[51]

These sorts of ploys by veteran generals to conceal an army's arrival and/or strength are certainly striking. Nonetheless, it seems to have been much more common that hoplites openly exposed their presence and numbers to foes below on the flat. Rather than hiding behind it, these men were looking to exploit the advantages attendant with high ground toward intimidating or, if it then still proved necessary, physically defeating the enemy.

Seasoned commanders were inclined to retreat rather than attack when facing elevated opposition, with such exercises of discretion having already been described with regard to the savvy Spartan commanders Agis and Agesilaos.[52] Sometimes, though, withdrawal just wasn't practical, even for troops like those of Sparta with their high capacity to maneuver out of danger. That didn't necessarily doom them to defeat, of course, as Agesilaos demonstrated in 389 when forced to thus engage during a campaign in Acarnania.[53] His crack spearmen there overran the enemy's infantry, both heavy and light, despite having to advance up a steep incline. And other hoplites were able to capture high ground as well.[54] It's therefore obvious that holding an upslope position alone was not enough to insure success.[55] All the same, a well-experienced soldier like Agesilaos charged up a steep grade only as a last resort; and there are a number of actions that underscore just why that was so.

A good example of what could happen when an army chose to attack a foe poised above can be seen in a battle in 414 along the outskirts of Syracuse on the southern slope of Epipolae.[56] Led by a battalion of 600 picked hoplites, the Syracusan army met defeat and lost 300 spearmen in trying to dislodge Athenian hoplites well-placed atop that lofty plateau where it narrowed at Euryelus. Another battle illustrating the kind of edge higher positioning gave occurred within Athens in 403.[57] That's when Spartan-backed oligarchs ruling the city challenged a rebel force in an engagement that took place upon the eastern grade of Munychia Hill. Standing higher on that rise, a modest array of poorly equipped insurgent spearmen along with some peltasts and rock-throwers stalled the oligarchs' extremely deep-filed phalanx dead in its tracks. This formation then suffered a brutal pelting from missilemen behind and above the rebel hoplites, finally being chased from the field at a cost of 70 dead including some top leaders. Here and elsewhere, an upslope position proved to be of considerable value, whether in perpetrating a critical deception or in granting a decisive edge in combat.

Watercourses as Frontal Impediments

Crimisus River is without doubt the most successful example we have on record of employing a watercourse to reinforce a hoplite front. The tactic there helped to deliver total victory against a huge enemy host. But it is not actually the most famous phalanx action in which the victor stood on a riverbank to massacre floundering enemies below. That took place on Sicily as well, coming at the conclusion of the Athenians' fatal retreat from Syracuse in 413 as that city's forces closed on the last fleeing intruders. With one division of spearmen pursuing and another positioned ahead, maybe a thousand remaining Athenian hoplites charged into a ford on the Assinarus River.[58] These men were truly desperate; having had no access to water throughout the chase's final stages, they must have been driven as much by dehydration and irresistible thirst as by any realistic hope of breaking to freedom past the opposed array on the far bank above. Those pitiful remnants of a once mighty army thus didn't come close to a successful crossing. Speared down from the facing slope and showered by missiles coming from fore and aft, many of them failed to even attack; dropping down instead amid the horrific massacre transpiring all around to drink churned and muddy water now fouled with the blood of fallen comrades. Here, as at the Crimisus, a Sicilian phalanx used a fronting watercourse to truly devastating effect. Yet in many other actions, this same approach failed to deliver victory; rather, it at best let hoplites inflict greater damage on their enemies before making a safe retreat.

A well-described instance of this sort of lesser benefit took place at Amyklai in the winter of 370-69.[59] A coalition army under Epaminondas of Thebes had at that time entered Sparta during a period of weakness for the polis after its crippling defeat at Leuctra the previous year. But this campaign was destined to achieve very little, largely due to a brilliant defensive scheme devised by Sparta's king Agesilaos. That hoary master of war made every use he could of local topographic strong points and thereby managed to keep the invaders on the far side of the Eurotas River, whose swift winter current bounded his core home territory. Facing a contested and likely too costly crossing of that seasonally swollen stream, Epaminondas and his men had to settle for plundering on their side of its flow. Agesilaos was aware that his foes chaffed at this and set a trap that used the Eurotas to further advantage.

The Spartan monarch deliberately displayed an inadequate guard at a ford near the village of Amyklai, daring the invaders to come over at that seemingly weak point. And Epaminondas took the bait. He sent the Theban and Arcadian contingents in his van across to establish a beachhead on the far bank so that they could then screen passage of their remaining fellows. But Agesilaos lay in waiting and charged from cover with a small army as soon as those unwary hoplites reached his side of the Eurotas. Catching their enemies wet and disordered, the Spartans dealt out a good deal of damage before other elements of the opposing host finally began wading over to join the fight. With the prospect now quickly rising of facing much greater numbers, Agesilaos put his men's outstanding skill at maneuver to good use and executed a mid-combat withdrawal. His foes, somewhat battered and disorganized, could only watch him escape rearward to once again occupy daunting defensive positions. Thus, though Epaminondas had scored a tactical victory, he gained nothing worthwhile from it. His allies, as Sparta's sage king well knew, had to retire shortly thereafter for the rest of the winter. That took the Theban general out of the field as well; his ambitions badly frustrated by Agesilaos' terrain-based tactics of delay.

However, in contrast to the triumphs gained with fronting watercourses at the Crimisus and Assinarus, or even the lesser degree of Spartan success at Amyklai, a number of other armies took a sound beating trying the same tack. We've already discussed hoplites overcoming riverbed blockades on a couple of occasions during the Athenian retreat from Syracuse in 413, with Alexander the Great's heavy infantry doing the same at Issus in 333. Notably, some of those barricades came up short even though reinforced with field-works.[60] And another good example of how imperfect streams could prove as frontal barriers took place on the Greek mainland in 364. That's when a phalanx of Eleans and Achaeans charged over the Cladaus River to rout an array of spearmen from Arcadia and Argos trying to hold sway over Olympia's famous Pan-Hellenic games.[61] Yet perhaps the most telling note on the technique's limitations actually comes from Timoleon. Just three years after Crimisus, that crafty old veteran turned his watercourse-based tactics there upside down at the Damyrias River in an action that saw him decisively best a larger phalanx under the tyrant Hicetas despite its standing upslope on the stream's far bank.[62]

That hoplites could gain an edge in combat by setting up behind a watercourse seems beyond dispute. After all, rivers and streams imposed the same troublesome currents and/or treacherous footing on attackers in that position as they so often did to good effect when serving as lateral anchors. But much as noted for fronting field-works,[63] that advantage was far from insurmountable. These and similar mid-battleground barriers are best thought of as "force multipliers"; that is, they could, when properly applied, let a formation fight as if it had more manpower than was the actual case. Yet the fact is that simple manpower only occasionally proved decisive in phalanx actions. Other factors like élan, weapons skill, maneuvering ability, and combat experience frequently could and did override its effects. Therefore, like all the other types of terrain tools we've discussed, fronting riverbeds and the like were usually no more effective than the men that fought behind them.

Conclusions

A distinctive and striking figure, the Greek hoplite has for two millennia symbolized the virtues and glory of combat in classical times. And it's no different in the 21st century, with many a recent entertainment firing the popular imagination. This has created a demand for even more of such normally fictitious and frequently highly fanciful portrayals to fill our bookshelves, cinemas, and television screens. Yet, it has also inspired a good deal of rather more serious study in a quest for the truth about these impressive warriors of old. But neither time nor circumstances have been kind to this effort. Relevant archaeological finds like arms and armor are quite modest, while preserved written works by the ancients are shockingly few in number and often sadly incomplete, not to mention confusingly contradictory on occasion. Worse yet, the authors were almost universally remiss in transmitting vital information lost to us today that was common knowledge in their own time. And a good bit of the information that they do send down comes in the form of isolated anecdotes that must be used with great caution, since, critically for the diligent researcher, the plural of "anecdote" is not "data."

These unavoidable realities have shaped our attempt herein to document hoplites and their way of war in detail. We've thus had to fill many evidential gaps by going well beyond the sparse leavings from the past and integrating them with the best and most apt modern data. Important among these are analogs to a host of recent academic and operational studies that draw from a variety of disciplines spanning the full range of physical, behavioral, and medical sciences. And the emerging area of experimental archaeology provides key input as well. Exercises in reconstructed gear yield useful insights into the practical realities of fighting within a hoplite array, while laboratory and field testing of reproduced equipment reveals a great deal about its physical properties and capabilities. Of course, such a process is inherently speculative; therefore, even when bringing a wide array of sources to bear with utmost attention to balanced analyses, the results should never be taken as absolute verities. All the same, it is humbly proposed that they do represent the most secure probabilities that we can produce within the scope of our present knowledge.

Our findings fall into three general categories: Tools (weapons, armor, etc.), The Man (hoplite culture, physicality, and psychology), and The Group (how hoplites worked together and with other combatants). Tools in the form of weaponry were dominated by the hoplite spear (dory). This was a long (seven to eight foot) thrusting tool with steel head that hoplites most frequently wielded overhead as a way to both protect comrades standing behind from being struck on the back-draw and to project optimum striking-force forward into the enemy. Reasonably durable and capable of being used to ply its characteristic butt-spike (sauroter) even if broken, this device was the primary means by which hoplites inflicted damage on similarly armed foes or foreign fighters with shorter-ranged weapons of their own. Swords also saw use in hoplite combat. But these were only a secondary weapon plied in replacement for a hopelessly damaged dory. Equally characteristic of the hoplite as his spear was his large (1m or so in width), round shield or aspis (a.k.a. hoplon or Argive shield). Made of wood and usually sheathed on the front (either fully or around the outer edge) with a thin bronze coating, this was truly a marvel of engineering. The aspis' most obvious function was to ward off enemy weaponry; however, its concave design with a recessed and reinforced rim that could rest across collar and thigh also let a hoplite avoid suffocation during the deliberate press that might develop during the later stages of long battles.

Though spear and shield were by far the most fundamental and enduring elements of the hoplite's toolbox, many other pieces of primarily protective gear evolved in and out of his equipment set (panoply) over the centuries. These included a wide variety of helmets and various bits of body armor. Most notable among the latter were cuirasses, first of bronze and later of leather or stiffened linen; these were of immense value in protecting the torso and its vital organs. Less well known than these sundry bits of personal accouterment, there were several other manufactured devices that hoplites also employed to good effect. These included standing walls, temporary field works, and the earliest known examples of artillery in the form of catapults.

The bodies and minds of hoplites significantly shaped their way of war in several areas. One was in aspects of the dominant military culture in Greece. This was initially centered on local land and social issues, with most wars being modest in scale and either fought over small border tracts (eschatia) or (less commonly) to resolve internal class disputes. Fighting then evolved as it increased greatly in scope during the 5th century and into the 4th. This saw large coalitions arise to engage in near-total warfare for largely economic reasons, with mercenary spearmen becoming more common. Then (c.357), Macedonia began drawing full-time professionals from its citizenry, a practice that would spread along with that state's rising empire under Philip II, his son Alexander III, and the latter's successors. That shift toward paid military service had by the end of the 4th century almost entirely transformed the past norm of small citizen militias supporting their locally determined government by occasionally contesting disputes closely tied to the hoplites' own personal interests. Greek martial culture was now largely a matter of huge professional hosts serving the ambitions of royal despots.

Of course, their very physicality greatly affected how hoplites went about making war. These were men that prized an appearance of bodily perfection as both cultural ideal and a practical aid in combat. Exercise to enhance both athletic skill and beauty of form was the rule. In contrast, training in specific military skills was much less common save at Sparta and for a few bands of mercenaries and state-supported elites. But by the late 4th century, rising martial ambitions and painful exposure to better-trained foes led nearly all Greek states to adopt mandatory drills. Still, no matter how well conditioned or trained, hoplites were never free of the ultimate physical risk of wounds and death. And despite fairly effective medical care, phalanx battles claimed a great many lives.

Combat during the Hellenic era (500–323) thus killed an estimated 200,000 hoplites while seriously wounding about twice as many.

Beyond culture and physicality, psychology was an important factor in hoplite warfare. Its impacts included those of ingrained cultural traditions and the instilling of confidence through positive training and experiences in actual combat as a way to improve battlefield performance. And the strong fighting spirit that produced was then communally enhanced through deployments alongside relatives, friends, and even lovers. Yet hoplite morale could be delicate. We thus see it easily shaken by sudden combat reverses or in meeting events such as storms, eclipses, and earthquakes that might imply divine disfavor. Likewise, fears for family and property bedeviled those fighting on home soil such that invading armies were half again more likely to win battles when at near equal strengths. Yet, while unexpected deployments were a psychological boon for invader and defender alike, those fighting near home were better able to launch surprise attacks. These gave them not only physical advantages, but mental ones as well to the extent that they gained victory at twice the rate for their invading foes. Elsewhere with regard to psychology, there were the effects that the experience of war itself had upon hoplites' minds. Greek spearmen witnessed fearsome battlefield horrors and savage atrocities while agonizing over the endemic unfairness of war-making even as it violated their strong sense of what was right and just (themis). The harm that this did to their psyches went so far as to include episodes of psychosomatic disability and what is now known as Post Traumatic Stress Disorder.

Group behavior and routines among hoplites basically all revolved around optimizing performance within their ubiquitous combat formation, the phalanx. Through most of the history of hoplite warfare during its first four centuries, this was the Doric phalanx; so called for its early association with speakers of the Dorian Greek dialect in the Peloponnese of south-central Greece at Argos, Corinth, and Sparta. This array was wide, with ranks in the hundreds and even thousands, but shallow, sometimes having files as short as four men and rarely over sixteen with eight perhaps most common. Later, this Doric formation that exclusively used hoplites as line infantry battled the Macedonian phalanx. Philip II had created the latter in 358 as an improvement upon what he had seen of the Doric phalanx of Thebes. This new array continued to employ hoplites on its strike/offensive wing on the right; however, lighter equipped and less expensive pikemen (sarissophoroi or phalangites) now served as defensive specialists along the other wing. Whether Doric or Macedonian, phalanxes operated in much the same manner. This featured a set combat sequence, which began with advancement into contact to initiate spear fighting at close range that involved the first two ranks of hoplites on either side. In the absence of either hoplites or light-armed troops extending past to wrap around (envelop) one end of their opposition's line, such contests often became lengthy and eventually moved into closer engagement as spears broke and shorter-reaching arms came into play. This might then devolve into physical shoving with shields carried out by entire files (othismos) before one side or the other finally broke and ran under pursuit from behind.

Hoplites, though dominant, were not the only combatants that saw action in Greek battles. Others were the aforementioned pikemen, light infantry, and cavalry along with barbarian foes of various kinds including swordsmen. The Greeks developed tactical routines that allowed their spearmen to work alongside as well as fight effectively against all of these other warrior types. The invention of other techniques also let hoplites participate in naval efforts, serving as marines aboard ship, and to literally spearhead amphibious operations. Still, the overwhelming majority of their engagements took place entirely on dry land, and that was where their tactical skills best came to the fore. These featured phalanx maneuvers to prevent envelopment, redeploy for a second engagement, withdraw from a losing combat, and even feign a withdrawal and then reengage. Such complex evolutions were, however, beyond the regular militia amateur. This confined them to the exceptionally well-trained hoplite caste of Sparta, a few small units of publicly supported elites (epilektoi), and some mercenary spearmen of later years. More widespread was an ability to put terrain to good use. The most frequent routine here was anchoring one or both flanks upon a topographic feature to prevent envelopment. Many Greek generals also exploited slopes to screen deployments and/or force attackers into disadvantaged charges uphill. More rarely, savvy commanders would employ properly oriented watercourses by positioning spearmen atop the banks as a bar to enemy advance.

By combining all of the above, we hope that what has emerged from the present study is a somewhat more accurate picture of hoplites at war than has previously been available. This, of course, can never be an end product, and future investigations will undoubtedly continue to put these ancient warriors into ever better focus as new information comes to light. Our work should make clear that much of this information may come from non-traditional sources, such as psychology, swarm theory, or experimental archaeology. But, the value of these new lines of inquiry will always be in testing what could have been. The parameters will always be set by the words of the ancient Greeks themselves, and the tools they used. The goal is not to supplant the historian and the archaeologist, but to supplement their interpretation of ancient evidence with modern scientific technique.

Chapter Notes

Preface

1. Simon Hornblower (1991–2008, 2.306).

Chapter 1

1. Schooling in horsemanship and weapons handling began in early youth for aristocratic Persian males, followed by a period of mandatory military duty. Xerxes would have so served from the early to mid–490s, probably just like his father as a member of the royal bodyguard. Upon his ascension, Xerxes had assumed charge of his nation's armed forces and crushed a large-scale uprising in Egypt. This provided good preparation for invading Greece in that Egypt was similarly distant, likewise sat along a coastal route amenable to seaborne logistics, and was also defended by spear-armed heavy infantry.

2. Cyrus, having usurped his kingdom from the Medes c.550, had expanded it all the way to the Aegean; his son Cambyses next added Egypt to the realm; and Darius I had then tacked on territory along the Empire's eastern border plus in India, Thrace, Macedonia, and among the Aegean islands. Continuing this tradition of conquest would prove Xerxes worthy of a place along that line of Great Kings.

3. This reflects the highest estimate offered by Green (1970, 59) at 210,000, with a full range of other projections falling down to a mere 20,000–30,000 per Delbruck (1990, 113). All these contrast with the 3,000,000 cited by Herodotus on a contemporary monument at Thermopylae or that historian's own claim of 1,800,000 or Ctesias' estimate of 800,000, even if those include non-combatants.

4. The Persians had bested Greek hoplites six times during the Ionian Revolt (with a lone setback in a nighttime ambush). Their only loss in fixed battle against Greek spearmen had been a decade earlier at Marathon. Viewed in context of the larger pattern of general triumph against Grecian opposition, that defeat must have been seen as an anomaly due to exceptional circumstances and thus unlikely to be repeated—a case of quite understandable yet ultimately very costly cultural bias.

5. Athens was Xerxes' top target due to having aided the Ionian Revolt followed by its denial of his father's retaliatory bid at Marathon to restore the dictator Hippias as a Persian puppet.

6. The Athenians had the most diverse military in Greece, including a large number of hoplites, a substantial corps of foot-archers, horsemen (300 at this time), and the largest fleet of any polis. And their ships included over 100 specially designed for a deadly new style of maneuver warfare.

7. In addition to Marathon, the Athenians had fought Persians at Ephesus in 498.

8. Similar considerations had apparently led the Athenians to eschew use of the coastal pass west of Marathon in 490. The Persian amphibious expedition on that occasion was also easily capable of flanking such a position via the offshore. Marathon veterans like Themistocles and Aristides must have quickly condemned Tempe on the basis of that comparison alone.

9. With some 7,000 hoplites, this might actually have been the mightiest army fielded in Greece up to that time. Only the Athenians at Marathon are said to have had more men; however, it is a late tradition that places 9,000 Athenians there, which appears much exaggerated. This recognizes that more contemporary sources assign the same number of spearmen to Athens in 479 (8,000 at Plataea plus 1,100 at ten per warship at Mycale) after great economic and population expansion in the 480s had significantly boosted the number of men financially qualified as hoplites post–Marathon.

10. There was precedent for this, with the narrows below Thermopylae opposite Chalcis having been blocked with a chain in the past in order to extort fees from ships desiring passage.

11. See Herodotus (7.210–212) on the first and third attacks and Diodorus (11.6.3–11.7.4) on all three actions.

12. Diodorus (11.8.1–3); Diodorus is our sole source for this and other details on the battle's second day.

13. Leonidas was born c.540 within two years of his half-brother Cleomenes (Herodotus 5.41). He was of an age for active field duty c.520–490 in a period of peace after Sparta's last territorial conquest at Thyreatis c.545. The only attested campaigns in which he might have participated as a hoplite were two incursions into Attica under Anchimolios in 511 and Cleomenes in 510 (Herodotus 5.63.2–64.2), a surprise attack and victory at Sepeia in 494 under Cleomenes (Herodotus 6.77–78), and a small defeat of some sort against Methana dated 500–475 from archaeological finds. It is at best possible that Leonidas had led and lost what seems a very minor action at Methana, but even this must be considered far from likely.

14. See Herodotus on the Persian handicap of inferior spear-reach against Spartan arms in general (5.49.3) and at Thermopylae in particular (7.211.2). He later

noted at Plataea that the Asians "were not inferior in courage or strength, but did not have hoplite arms" (9.62.2–3); that along with the tactics associated with such weaponry is said to have sealed their doom.

15. Herodotus 7.211.3; see Chap. 4: Reengagement Maneuvers.

16. This kind of attack was called "othismos" by the Greeks and was singular to phalanx warfare.

17. The Persians had a decimal-based organization with divisions (called "myriads" by the Greeks and probably "baivaraba" in Persian, "baivarabam" singular) at the top with nominal complements of 10,000 men that then broke down into 1,000-man regiments ("hazaraba") with 100-man companies ("sataba") and 10-man sections ("dathaba")—see Sekunda (1989, 83–4). Files were normally made up of a single dathabam and thus stood ten men deep with one shield-bearer at the front. Actual or "parade" strengths would have been lower than this "paper" manpower, likely no more than 80 percent nominal for a recently mustered division and perhaps as low as 30 percent for one standing on long-term garrison duty. It is therefore likely that a baivarabam going into action at Thermopylae was aligned one regiment (with around 800 men) after another, stretching back a kilometer or so toward the western entryway. The shield-wall of each of those hazaraba would have been subject to a separate breach and rout, allowing for a new rotation of Greek spearmen to then come forward and assault the next regiment behind it in turn. All of the major assaults at Thermopylae (save for the entirely shield-equipped attack on day two) were thus actually composed of multiple sub-actions of modest duration, and it was only the serial combination of these separate combats that produced lengthy overall engagements.

18. Diodorus' unlikely story (11.9.4–10.4) of a suicide attack on the Great King's pavilion that resulted in the deaths of all the remaining Greeks is not inconsistent with this strategy; indeed, his tale might reflect a tradition that some kind of raid on the Persian camp was actually attempted with regicide in mind.

19. Leonidas' rearguard comprised those left from three contingents: "spartiates" (there were originally 300 of these full citizens from Sparta out of an apparent 1,000 spearmen sent along with the king from his own polis), Thespians (there were originally 900–1,000 hoplites from this city in northern Boeotia), and Thebans (originally 400 anti–Persian volunteers from that otherwise ambivalent polis, which eventually threw its lot in with Xerxes). Pausanius also claimed a small contingent from Mycenae stayed, but this seems most improbable. It's speculative how many of these spearmen were still operational on the third day of combat, but no more than about 1,200 would seem likely.

20. The arrangement proposed here for Xerxes' troops follows those of his first three attacks and is in line with long-standing Persian tactical doctrine. A highbred approach similar to that of the fourth assault made by the composite brigade of shield-bearers might seem more logical; however, that would have required significant reorganization of the fresh baivarabam being used. By reassigning all of its file-leaders with their shields to the forward-most ranks, the division's customary dathabam-based deployment would have been utterly disrupted to the detriment of the men's confidence; more crucial still, it would take time to accomplish (doing something similar with the composite brigade had taken most of a day) and that simply was not available. Needing to move fairly early to coordinate with the Immortals' descent, the Persians took the expedient of maintaining a standard array. Though clearly not the best way to defeat the Greeks outright, this would produce a combat sufficient in length to permit completion of the planned flanking action. It is notable here that the Persian general Mardonios with much more time at his disposal seems to have employed the idea of massing all his shield-bearers forward a year later on the Persian left wing at Plataea. Seeking an outright victory, he thereby risked a quick and utter failure (something that never happened to the Persians at Thermopylae among all their setbacks there) should the opposing hoplites break through his deep but lone shield array. And that is exactly what came to pass to put a truly disastrous finish on Xerxes' grand adventure into Greece.

21. A Greek spear (dory or doru) broken and shy a third or so of its original length no longer had a reach advantage over Persian pole-arms, while the Greek straight sword (xiphos) and down-curving saber (machaira or kopis) were not notably superior to their Persian counterpart (the straight akinakes at 20–25cm long). Note that in this final action Leonidas was not able to rotate contingents and spare his hoplites' weapons from overuse as he had earlier under otherwise similar tactical circumstances.

22. See Herodotus (7.223.1–7.226.2) for the best account of the last day's action at Thermopylae.

23. Pritchett, 1991, 169.

24. Sophocles, *Antigone*, 670.

25. Archilochus fragment 2; this is possibly a reference to his service in the Lelantine War c.710–650.

26. Hurwit, 2002, 4.

27. Snodgrass, 1964, 138 btm.

28. Snodgrass, 1964, 123.

29. Murray, 2011.

30. Roach et al., 2013.

31. Lorimer, 1947.

32. Van Wees, 2004.

33. 213821, Vatican City, Museo Gregoriano Etrusco Vaticano, 16571 Achilles painter.

34. Polybios (6.25.9) is clear on this point, saying that "the lance [dory] is so constructed ... that it may continue to be effectively used by reversing it and striking with the spike at the butt end." This allowed the stub of a broken spear still held in the hoplite's hand to serve as a short a pole-arm without resorting to an even shorter sword.

35. Matthew, 2012.

36. Hanson, 1991, 23.

37. Matthew, 2012.

38. Sancho-Bru et al., 2003.

39. Kromayer and Veith, 2008.

40. Matthew, 2012.

41. This is an often repeated anecdote among reenactors.

42. A Spherical counterweight can be seen affixed to a sauroter in the collection of the National Archaeological Museum of Athens.

43. See Chap. 3: Pikemen.

44. Diodorus 15.44.1–4; also see Nepos 11.1.

45. Hanson, 1991.

46. Bardunias, 2007, 15; Matthew 2012.

47. Van Wees, 2004, Krentz 2010.

48. See Chap. 1 and Chap. 2.

49. Luginbill 1994,.

50. Van Wees 2004.

51. Bardunias 2007, 15.

52. The spear could actually be released and then re-gripped before the shaft passes completely through the hand. See the reenactor Thegn Thrand demonstrating this: (https://www.youtube.com/watch?v=KtIPp-m69BY). With a rear weighted spear gripped close to the rear a hoplite gained little advantage by actually letting go.
53. Gabriel and Metz, 1991, 59.
54. Connolly et al., 2001.
55. Matthew, 2012.
56. DeGroote, 2016.
57. Paul Bardunias and Christian Cameron, perhaps the best authority on fighting in accurate panoply, both train point control in this manner.
58. Matthew's contention that this is not the case (2012, 23, 38) appears to be based on a mistaken appreciation of statistical data clearly showing otherwise as discussed by Ray (2014).
59. Snodgrass, 1964, 93.
60. Anderson, 1970.
61. Blyth, 1977, 25.
62. Bakhuizen, 2010, The designation of steel as "Chalcidian" may have indicated a type of steel, in the same way "Damascus" steel became a designation based on dissemination from that city.
63. Manning Imperial makes a replica of this sword type based on unpublished finds at Vergina: http://www.manningimperial.com/catalogue/arms/greek-and-roman-arms/thrusting-xiphos/664.
64. Snodgrass, 1964, 112.
65. Sekunda, 1998.
66. Xenophon, Cyropaedia, 2.3.10.
67. Cook, 1989.
68. For example: 216988, Ferrara, Museo Nazionale di Spina, T1039A.
69. Vetulonia Warrior's Tombstone, Museo Archeologico Florence.
70. Plato, Laches, 183d.
71. Xenophon *Anabasis* 3.4.15–17.
72. Herodotus' description (7.225.3) of the last stand by Leonidas' men at Thermopylae tells us that "they tried to defend themselves with their swords if they still had them, or if not, with their hands and their teeth."

Chapter 2

1. Twin Athenian victories in the west at Pylos and on adjacent Spaectaria in 425 had seen the first epiteichismos set up at the former. And a triumph at Solygeia on the east coast later that year had allowed for a similar outpost to be installed at Methana. A third such site had then become active at Scandea on Cythera early in 424 with the capture of that perioecian island just below the Laconian mainland. The last had not only facilitated attacks along Sparta's vulnerable southern coast, but also eliminated the entry point into the polis for valuable trade goods from North Africa.
2. The Spartans actually took an extraordinary counter-measure in raising a cavalry force for the first time in their history. They paired this with an equally unprecedented unit of archers in a "quick response" team meant to ward the attacks. However, neither that nor dispersing hoplites into a network of small garrisons proved effective against foes able to land by surprise in great strength. Such modest defending forces were either overwhelmed outright or so intimidated that they would not take the field (Thucydides 4.56.1).
3. Thucydides 4.76.
4. This was as large a muster of spearmen as Boeotia had to that date ever put into the field from a nominal capability of around 11,000 (1,000 men each from 11 districts).
5. Thucydides 4.93.3.
6. This Pagondas was probably the same that had been the subject of an ode by the Boeotian poet Pindar (c.518–438) and was therefore over 60 years of age at Delium (Kagan 1974, 283).
7. This was at Coronea I in 447, an engagement in which Pagondas had himself almost surely seen action as a prime-aged hoplite in his early to mid-30s.
8. Thucydides 4.92.7.
9. This was on the west side of the Paliokhani Plateau, which runs WNW-ESE in rough parallel to the nearby Euboan Channel; see Pritchett (1969, 24–34) for a detailed discussion of the area's topography.
10. This is based on manpower in 396-395, when the Boeotian League drew four of its eleven divisions from Thebes. A similar draw at Delium would have seen 2,500 or so hoplites in an approximate two-thirds contribution in proportion to the 7,000 out of 11,000 muster for the entire army. This Theban plurality among the fighting men was what had justified the Theban Pagondas being commander-in-chief.
11. Thucydides 4.93.4; Diodorus 12.70.1; the "charioteers" unit was a forerunner to the later Sacred Band.
12. Thucydides 4.96.2 and as per Pritchett's (1969, 32) modern measurements plus some allowance for erosion since 424.
13. Thucydides 4.96.4.
14. This was due to it being very difficult amid the clamorous din of close combat to tell friend from foe once intimately mixed together, especially as everyone's armor was much the same and most poleis had yet to adopt standard shield blazons. Uniform shield devices to mark a hoplite's nationality might have existed in a few poleis at this time (there is one mid–5th century poetic reference to Poseidon's trident blazons at Mantinea); however, the lambda of Sparta, Hercules' club of Thebes, sigma of Sicyon, and others are not documented prior to the early 4th century. Athens took the letter alpha for its shields then, no doubt hoping to avoid further friendly fire incidents like this most famous one at Delium (see Chap. 3: Friendly Fire, Atrocity, and Combat Trauma).
15. There were so many Thespian hoplite casualties at Delium that Thebes shortly thereafter was able to force its dominance onto their polis. This sort of selfless battlefield valor seems to have been a marked characteristic of Thespis' spearmen, who had died fighting to the end alongside Leonidas and his 300 Spartans at Thermopylae (480) and would go down heavily yet again at Nemea River (494) while battling almost alone on behalf of another lost cause.
16. Thucydides 4.96.5.
17. Thucydides 4.96.2.
18. Alcibiades related this incident, having aided his old mentor Socrates from horseback as he also fled (Plato *Symposium* 220B-222C). While Socrates would persist well into old age before being executed for supposedly teaching treason, Laches was destined to meet his end just six years after this escape at Delium, falling along with many other hoplites under his command at Mantinea I.
19. Thucydides 4.101.2.
20. The Athenians had lost a higher percentage of their hoplites at Spartolos in 429 (see Chap. 3: Light

Infantry and Horsemen), but never so great a number in one battle.

21. Such as Aeschylus (*Persians* 816–22) did in writing about Plataea (479).
22. Middle Protocorinthian aryballos from Lechaion. (Snodgrass, 1964, plate 15a).
23. Cole 1913. Note the use of thick textile armor. Examples of the taming and spear can be seen at: http://philippineamericanwar.webs.com/stallingmororesistance.htm.
24. Van Wees, 2004, 153.
25. Stamatopoulou, 2004 This chapter draws heavily from a recent examination of extant aspides and aspis fragments that is available only in Greek. We are indebted to Giannis Kadaglou for his translation and interpretation.
26. Stamatopoulou, 2004.
27. Krentz, 2010, 194.
28. http://www.gettyimages.com/detail/news-photo/police-marching-on-pro-nationalist-and-anti-rhodesian-news-photo/50708437 Xen. Hell. 2.4.25 shows that in the late 5th c Greeks could still turn to woven shields at need.
29. An example sold at auction can be seen at http://www.oriental-arms.com/photos.php?id=5634.
30. This unwanted slipping around the fore-arm had been reported as a common problem by modern re-enactors.
31. See discussion Chap.1: Hoplite Spears.
32. Christian Cameron demonstrates this in mock combat: https://www.youtube.com/watch?v=c81Oc0-jl7Q.
33. Schwartz, 2013, 163.
34. Van Wees, 2004, 180.
35. This same concept has been applied in modern times to making tank armor more effective.
36. Schwartz, 2013, 162.
37. Stamatopoulou, 2004.
38. Pliny the Elder, *Natural History* 16.209 suggests these woods for shield making.
39. This same method was used in the construction of the famously sturdy Viking ships.
40. Stamatopoulou, 2004.
41. The use of brass would have been much rarer due to its great expense, Plato noting that it was considerable as valuable as gold.
42. Stamatopoulou, 2004.
43. DeGroote, 2016.
44. Bardunias 2007, 15.
45. Recent testing by Chris Verwijmeren, Christian G. Cameron, and Giannis Kadoglou, with period-accurate arrowheads and a replica aspis have shown that Persian archers could pierce the aspis if their arrows impacted perpendicular to the shield face, but met effective resistance if hitting at an angle.
46. See armor tests in Chap.3: Armor.
47. The famed Spartan general Brasidas said after being wounded by a spear that penetrated his shield that it happened: "*When my shield betrayed me.*"—Plutarch *Sayings (of Spartans)*, Brasidas 2.
48. Blyth, 1982, 19.
49. Bardunias 2007, 15.
50. See Chap. 2: Othismos.
51. See Chap. 3: Pikemen.
52. Though this and other adoptions elsewhere of Macedonian gear might have effected only a portion of the fighting force, with hoplites continuing in service on an attack wing of the phalanx (see discussion Chap. 3: Pikemen).
53. See Chap. 3: Swordsmen.

Chapter 3

1. Far from paranoia, just such palace intrigue had brought Xerxes' own father to power.
2. Likely consisting of two regiments (hazaraba) each, these "token" musters from the Empire's many subject nationalities had been included as a demonstration of political solidarity behind the Great King.
3. Herodotus 7.89.3; the Egyptian marines' shields are described as "hollow" (concave) with a "large rim" and the spears are classified as "naval," suggesting that they were either longer than the normal infantry issue or (perhaps more likely) of a shorter variety equally suited to being thrust or thrown.
4. Herodotus 6.15.1; this describes typical Greek triremes from Chios in action off Lade in 494.
5. Manpower mandated for such vessels comes from a decree preserved on a monument at Troizen. Lighter in construction and load, these ships were optimized for maneuver, using a bronze ram on their prows to strike the opposition rather than drawing alongside for a seaborne hoplite action between marine contingents. Such triremes and their associated tactics did well at Artemisium and Salamis, but could transport much fewer troops than older models. Later designs at Athens would revert to full decks better suited to its then increasingly dominant amphibious style of warfare.
6. Each galley had 170 oarsmen. Contrary to popular cinema images, these were almost exclusively well-paid professionals or citizen draftees rather than impressed slaves (Chios alone among Greek poleis utilized slave-labor on its triremes), something equally true for Persia's naval forces.
7. Shallow-draft triremes were beached by backing against the shore and then pulling them stern-first up onto dry ground; their crewmen had more than enough muscle power for that last task. This was something done each night so hulls could dry and crews eat and sleep onshore (their narrow and very crowded ships being unsuited to such vital activities and for carrying any significant amount of provisions as cargo). Thus aligned along the strand, they could if needed provide camp facilities in support of longer term operations like extended inland raids or sieges.
8. This is really quite speculative, being based upon on-site observations by one of the present authors and the likely distribution of recorded manpower in accordance with the most common Greek and Persian tactical deployments of the period.
9. Father of later Athenian strong-man Pericles, Xanthippos was probably the chief architect of the Greek expedition's operations afloat, leaving matters largely to the Spartan king when on shore.
10. All the numbers here follow Herodotus (9.102.3) and the likely naval roster. It appears that Leotychides had spearmen from Sparta (300 bodyguards that had come aboard ships from Troizen), Aigina (400), Megara (400), Euboa (400), and Epidauros/Hermione (200). Xanthippos had hoplites from Athens (1,100), Corinth (600), Sicyon (200), and Troizen (100 epibatai from the vessels that had brought the Spartans).
11. Surviving records for such garrison units indicate strengths running from as low as 30 percent nominal up to 60 percent of authorized manpower (Sekunda and Chew 1992, 5–6), which suggests 6,000 men here might have been a maximum. At that strength, the internal organization would have had each file-forming dathabam at ten men, but cut the number of dathaba in each com-

pany (satabam) to six. Ten sataba each then formed hazaraba 600-strong with ten of those making for 6,000 in the baivarabam.

12. Perhaps this wasn't required if the Persian, Median, and Sakai marines cited by Herodotus (7.96.1) in Greece were still on hand for that task. Most marines in Xerxes' fleet were clearly native to their ships (Herodotus 7.89.1–95.2, 8.90.2), but at least a few of these imperial bowmen (maybe four as known for Athenian triremes, possibly two fore and two aft) were also present on each vessel.

13. Actually, Tigranes' education on Greek warfare must have begun prior to Thermopylae, since the Medes under his command there included veterans of Marathon. Those men would have provided him with many a first-hand account of hoplites in action during the long march into Greece.

14. This was very much the same problem that Mardonios had faced earlier that same day on his left wing at Plataea, requiring that he lead a force of sparabara against hoplites anchored along a narrow front between bounding terrain barriers. His attempted solution appears to much resemble that of Tigranes, suggesting at least the possibility that, rather than being coincidence, the similar approaches of these former comrades-in-arms might stem from past mutual planning sessions.

15. The battlefield dimensions that Mardonios faced that morning don't seem to have been much different, calling for a three-deep filing of dathaba that would have let him deploy his shield-carriers at a depth of three (or six at best if more spara were available as discussed above).

16. With 5,000–6,000 bowmen each launching an arrow every ten seconds or so, the Persian barrage would have descended at a rate of better than 30,000 missiles per minute.

17. The observation of Sparta's Dienekes at Thermopylae (Herodotus 7.226.1–2) that Persian arrows blotting out the sun would simply let him and his fellow hoplites fight in the shade was more than mere Laconic-style wit; it reflected the very real ability of sturdy aspides and body armor to stop/deflect missiles.

18. Arms and feet were particularly at risk—the only wound suffered during the initial Greek advance into Persian missile fire at Cunaxa (401) was a hoplite taking an arrow in the foot (Xenophon *Anabasis* 1.8.20). More lethal penetrations were possible at the thorax's openings for the neck and upper arms as well as along its lateral-fastenings (the Spartan Callicrates took a fatal arrow in his side that way during the opening barrage at Plataea—Herodotus 9.72.1–2).

19. The Persian "shield-wall" might have consisted of spara propped to form a barricade that was defended "hands-off" by the spearmen behind it. An ancient image of a hoplite advancing on an Asian archer in back of such a set-up offers some support for this idea; however, it appears that bowman is of the Sakae (who did not field sparabara) and has no spear. Other images that show hoplites and sparabara spear-fighting with shields held in hand seem to fit better with descriptions of mobile Persian fronts driving back the Athenian center at Marathon and pursuing Spartan false retreats at Thermopylae and Plataea. Herodotus said (9.62.1–2) that in meeting the Spartan charge at Plataea: "[the sparabara] threw down their bows" and "fought the first battle around the wicker shields." This suggests that the Persian fore-rankers stood their spara up, likely using spears as props, and fired arrows when foes were still at a distance, but then took both spear and shield in hand when it became necessary to fight close-in.

20. Herodotus 9.102.3; and very much the same sequence is even more thoroughly described at Plataea. The hoplites there apparently speared past the front "wall" of sparabara only to run into strong resistance from the other shield-bearers ranked behind. That phase of the fight "went on for a long time until they reached the point of close quarters pushing and shoving" (Herodotus 9.62.3). The othismos-driven hoplites were then finally able to force their way through and rout the unshielded Persian after-ranks; sparabara there being "hurt most by their lack of armor, for they were fighting as unarmed soldiers in a contest against well-equipped hoplites" (Herodotus 9.63.2).

21. This was acerbated by Ionians inside the camp now throwing their lot in with the mainland Greeks. It should be noted that Diodorus' account (11.34.1–36.6), likely drawn from Ephoros, gives dominant credit for the victory at Mycale to these Asian Greeks. However, Herodotus' earlier version (9.96.1–9.106.1) is much more realistic in almost all aspects and was preferred in developing the reconstruction here.

22. This is based on proportionally extending known losses recorded for the Sicyonian contingent to the rest of Xanthippos' troops and adding in a few more for the action within the camp.

23. Herodotus, who repeatedly cited the superiority of hoplite equipment over that of Persia, does not appear to have been displaying simple pro–Greek cultural bias. The Persians themselves recognized the shortcomings of their combat gear and took steps to improve it. These included: (1) introducing a small shield ("taka") for bowmen in their after-ranks, this being done sometime before 460; (2) posting their own troops equipped as hoplites at the front of battle formations, these were "kardakes"; and (3) hiring Greek and Carian mercenary hoplites in large numbers to core their infantry arrays.

24. Snodgrass, 1964, 6.
25. Snodgrass, 1964, 13.
26. Snodgrass, 1964, 13.
27. Manti, 2011.
28. This is a common complaint of reenactors wearing replica Corinthian helms. Giannis Kataglou, who has assembled one of the most accurate reproductions of archaic kit, demonstrated at the 2015 Marathon Archaeon Dromena the benefit of a properly fitted helmet in reducing this problem.
29. Thucydides sphacteria.
30. Chap. 2: The Hoplite Shield.
31. Xenophon, *On the Cavalry Commander*, 12.3.3.
32. Paddock, 1993, 365.
33. Homer, *Iliad*, 20.75.
34. Snodgrass, 1967, 73.
35. Chap. 2: Physical Attributes and Ideals.
36. Williams, 937.
37. Jarva, 1995, 51.
38. Bardunias, 2007, 11.
39. Bardunias, 2010, 48.
40. Jarva, 1995, 33. Jarva designates the tube and yoke armor as Type IV. Because his Type I–III designations are not commonly used when describing bronze cuirasses, we prefer the more descriptive tube and yoke.
41. Gleba, 2012, 51.
42. Bardunias, 2010, 48.
43. Xenophon, *Anabasis*, 3.3.20.
44. Pollux, *Onomasticon*, 7.70.

45. Xenophon, *Anabasis*, 4.1.14, Bardunias has tested leather against spear strike, and the prime factor in predicting penetration was how sharp the blade was. A "factory" edge could be stopped, but not a razor edge.
46. Alcaeus fr. V 140.
47. Herodotus, 7.63 (Assyrians), 1.135 (Persians), 2.182 (Lindos), and 3.47 (Sparta).
48. Aeneas, *Tacticus*, 29.1–4.
49. Connolly, 1997, 38.
50. Aldrete, 2013.
51. http://greekplaymasks.blogspot.com/.
52. For the stiffness achieved in stitched see Kendo head-pieces or "Men."
53. Aldrete, 2013.
54. Bardunias, 2010, 48.
55. Gleba, 2012, 47.
56. Pliny, 19.2.14.
57. Plutarch, *Alexander*, 32.5.
58. Utrecht #74D Belgian Linen, 14.5oz wt. with 80 threads per sq. in.
59. Aldrete, 2013.
60. Aelian, 2.7.
61. Rosen et al. 2007. Shear-thickening can be seen by stabbing forcefully into a dilatant like oobleck, which is a thick slurry of corn starch.
62. Premium Latigo Side Burgundy 10–12 oz. Tandy Leather # 9057–55.
63. See Chap. 2: The Hoplite Shield.
64. Jarva, 1995, 85.
65. Snodgrass, 1967, 86.
66. Diodorus, 15.44.4; these boots were known as "iphicratids" in honor of their inventor.
67. Snodgrass, 1964, 88.
68. Jarva, 1995, 107.
69. Jarva, 1995, 79.
70. Jarva, 1995, 72.

Chapter 4

1. See Chap. 4: Renewed Engagement Maneuvers and Chap. 2: Coronea II (394).
2. Parsons (1936, 87) indicates that even the partial extant remains reach up to 3m in height.
3. Xenophon, *Hellenica*, 4.4.1–6; Diodorus, 14.86.1.
4. See Lazenby (1985, 6–13) for an excellent discussion of the most likely size of the Spartan mora.
5. Xenophon, *Hellenica*, 4.4.8–9; Diodorus 14.86.3–4.
6. Xenophon, *Hellenica*, 4.4.9; the corridor's width is uncertain, but more than 1.2km seems assured given a measured spread on that order between surviving remnants at one mid-point (Parsons 1936, 86–87) plus further broadening toward Lechaion. Thus, if sensibly beyond missile range from the city-wall, Praxitas could have filed no more than two shields deep in spanning the entire interval.
7. The ability of these javelineers to effectively engage the enemy's leading rank(s) was one of the few benefits of the thin deployment of their hoplites, since such targeting was not practical from behind an array more than about four shields deep. It is also notable that their rearward posting let them guard against any attack from a small body of Boeotians present in Lechaion.
8. Xenophon uses "mercenary" ("mistophoroi") here, but all detailed references to Iphicrates' hired men elsewhere during this campaign describe them as "peltasts" ("peltastai"), and he is specifically identified as "*Iphicrates, leader of the peltasts*" (Xenophon *Hellenica*, 4.5.12). There are, in fact, no references to Athenian mercenary spearmen anywhere in our sources on the Corinthian War, thus strongly suggesting in conjunction with the more detailed identifications of peltasts elsewhere that Iphicrates' contingent on this occasion was entirely composed of javelineers, probably recruited from Thrace (Parke 1933, 50–54).
9. This was manned by the Corinthian exiles and the leftmost 500-man battalion (lochos) from Sicyon.
10. Arrays less than six shields deep seem to have had great difficulty maintaining formation integrity on the move (Goldsworthy 1996, 196–197), and even the best drilled hoplites appear to have observed a depth of four shields as the practical minimum for orderly advance.
11. Xenophon, *Hellenica*, 4.4.10.
12. Xenophon (*Hellenica*, 4.4.11–12) uses the term ὠθούμενοι (othoumenoi), a variant of the root word in othismos, to describe the pushing of the Lacedaemonians into this panicked crowd of men. He says that men were trampled, which may have been the case; however, something noted in modern crowd disasters is that often individuals reported as trampled were actually suffocated while standing in the crushing crowd of people (Fruin 2002, 5). Many of the Argives here had cast aside their aspis as they fled and had thus forfeited any protection the shield might have offered from such lethal compression.
13. Diodorus, 14.86.4.
14. And one that went beyond the main battlefield, since Xenophon also reports (*Hellenica*, 4.4.12) that: "Even the Boeotian guards at the harbor were killed, some on the walls and others while climbing up on the roofs of ship sheds."
15. Ober, (1991).
16. Munn, (1993); "Dema" coming from "To Dema" (The Link), which is the modern Greek name for the opening it blocked.
17. Thucydides, 7.5.1–3.
18. Son of Alcisthenes and not to be confused with the famed 4th century orator and foe of Macedonia's Philip II of that same name, who fought (and notoriously tossed his shield in flight) at Chaeronea.
19. Thucydides, 7.43.3–45.2; see Chap. 3: Confusion, Combat Behaviors, and Battle Trauma.
20. Possibly 3,000 rebel hoplites (some with makeshift gear) were facing 7,500 or so spearmen under Pausanius (Ray 2009, 276–277).
21. Xenophon, *Hellenica*, 2.4.31–34.
22. Diodorus 15.93.3; Plutarch Vol. II *Agesilaos*, 69: see Chap. 3: Surprise Deployments and Attacks.
23. Plutarch, *Agesilaos*, Vol. II, 69.
24. Diodorus, 15.92.2.
25. Diodorus, 15.93.4–5; Plutarch, *Agesilaos*, Vol. II 69.
26. Xenophon (*Hellenica*, 4.7.6); the expert archers from Crete serving Sparta here in 388 would have been able to outreach Argos' skirmishers atop the walls, the latter presumably being armed for the most part with shorter ranged javelins.
27. Xenophon, *Hellenica*, 1.1.33–34.
28. Xenophon, *Hellenica*, 2.4.31.
29. Olynthus II (Xenophon *Hellenica*, 5.3.3–5; Diodorus 15.21.2).
30. Olynthus I (Xenophon *Hellenica*, 5.2.40–42).

31. This likely refers to casualties among the more elite Lacedaemonian elements of Teleutias' host.
32. Herodotus, 5.63.3–5.64.2; Frontinus, 2.2.9.
33. Nepos 1.5.3–5 (*Miltiades*); this 1st century passage likely derives from Ephoros (early 4th century) and does not conflict with Herodotus' late 5th century account (6.108–115), which fails to identify the battle site.
34. Delbruck (1990, 76), which was first published in 1920.
35. Herodotus 8.28; Polyaenus 6.18.2; per Herodotus (8.27.2) this was "not many years before" the Persian invasion of 480–479.
36. The Phocians deployed 1,000 hoplites shortly thereafter in defense of Thermopylae as well as a year later in reluctant support of the Persians at Plataea (Herodotus 7.203.1, 9.17.2).
37. Xenophon *Hellenica*, 5.4.38; Munn, 1993, 53.
38. Thucydides 6.101.2; the Syracusan wooden elements here might have comprised either actual walls of some height or much easier to construct impediments of sharpened stakes atop a lower earthen feature. Quite possibly both of these methodologies saw use at appropriate points along the much more extensive Theban defense system.
39. Xenophon *Hellenica*, 5.4.41.
40. Arrian 2.10.1.
41. Arrian detailed the Persian deployment as having "*Greek mercenaries and the barbarians arrayed in a phalanx*" (2.8.8). In comparing the Asians to the mercenary spearmen, he called them "*Kardakes, who were also hoplites*" (2.8.6). This all likely reflects an eyewitness account by Alexander's officer Ptolemy.
42. And possibly less so in light of the potential for a long sarissa to perhaps span a barrier rather more effectively than a shorter spear. This might well have been a notable case where the greater reach of a pike wielded underhand could have trumped the more powerful overhand blows that a spear could deliver.
43. Thucydides, 7.78.5–79.5.
44. Thucydides, 7.80.5–6; Athens' retreat had earlier forced a crossing over the Anapus that lacked fieldworks (Thucydides 7.78.3), which likely prompted the Syracusans to add them here.
45. Plutarch, *Dion* Vol. II, 555–556.
46. Herodotus 7.176.4–5.
47. Often in the past attributed to engineers under Dionysius of Syracuse in 399 (see Marsden 1969, 48–49, citing Diodorus 14.42.1), it is now believed that these devices in the form of a "gastraphetes" (belly-bow) migrated to Syracuse after first coming into use sometime 421–401 during the sieges of nearby Cumae and Milet. Campbell (2003, 3, 5) attributes their invention to the engineer Zopyros of Taras, citing Biton of Pergamum (2nd century).
48. Plutarch, *Moralia*, 191D.
49. Polyaenus, 2.38.2, *Excerpts* 36.3; Diodorus, 16.35.2.
50. Marsden, 1969, 59.
51. Cole, 1981; Athens' Iphicrates had seized a quantity of bolts for these machines in a shipment of dedications from Syracuse heading to Delphi (Diodorus 15.47.7), strongly suggesting the presence of the weapon at that shrine as well.
52. Arrian, 1.6.8, 4.4.4; and one wonders if they found unmentioned employment at Granicus as well.
53. Polybios, 11.12.4–7.
54. Curtius, 3.8.24–11.19.

Chapter 5

1. Legendary dates for this migration range from c.1200 to 1069, but archaeological evidence suggests c.900 (Hornblower and Spawforth 1996, 495).
2. Raaflaub 1999, 129–141; though the rise of massed infantry could have stretched back as far as 1200 (Drews 1993, 209–225), its progress to the stage of phalanx warfare seems to have begun in earnest during the 8th century, with the formation reaching an advanced form by the mid-7th century.
3. Pausanius, 7.50.1; Dionysius, 4.16.2; and thus we see references to the aspis as an "Argive" shield in the ancient literature (Snodgrass, 1967, 54). Interestingly, Argos was unique in having two hill-top citadels and one was called the Aspis, though that title might have preceded invention of the true hoplite shield. As for any Argive accomplishment being more finalization than invention, it's probable that elements of the aspis came from Asia Minor, with claims of Carian invention (Herodotus, 1.171) perhaps indicative of its antilabe and porpax suspension system having originated there. If so, Chalcis on the eastern island of Euboa is the best candidate for that double grip's European gateway, being an early possessor of well-regarded hoplites and famed for skilled armor fabrication.
4. Archaeological data indicates that both Sparta and Corinth were also early to use the phalanx (Ferrill, 1985, 99–100); however, it's not possible to determine if this was in parallel with Argos or came only in response to the latter's previous success with it.
5. Tomlinson, 1972, 80 (citing Eusebius); it's possible that an even earlier battle might have been fought between Sparta and Argos in 737 (Huxley, 1962, 112, citing Solinus), but this might just be an alternate date for the same action that Eusebius set later.
6. Pausanius, 2.24.7–9; see also Strabo 8.6.11 (citing Theopompus).
7. Herodotus, 1.82; the engagement is sometimes known as the "Battle of the Champions" for having legendarily been preceded by a contest between 300 picked men from each side. This was meant to resolve the issue without a full-scale fight, but failed to do so when both parties claimed the victory. Of key note here is that the Spartans, having lost twice against a lone Argos, had been dealt a crucial defeat by Tegea in Arcadia ("Battle of the Fetters," likely sometime 590–580). Tegea was probably supported by allies that included Argos, thus in effect making for a third Spartan besting against the Argives. A major political, social, and military reform had then ensued at Sparta under Lycurgus; and it was this that within a couple of generations produced the superior army that finally beat Argos in 545.
8. Unrecorded in the literature, this battle was commemorated with captured Corinthian armor inscribed and displayed by the Argives at Olympia (Pritchett, 1979, 290–291); the surviving artifacts from this dedication include six shields, four helmets, and one set of greaves.
9. Herodotus, 6.771.
10. There was no prospect for an easy victory over the Argives. Sparta's sole triumph against them in 545 had been difficult and costly. And while the new Spartan military system responsible for that success surely inspired confidence, two other factors were stacked against it this time around. First, Argos likely held an edge in manpower. The Spartan army in this era appears to have been composed of ten lochoi of around 500

hoplites each. Citizens descended from the latest Dorian conquerors (spartiates and their derivatives of lesser status) filled five of these (the Aidolios/Edolos, Sinis, Sarinas/Arimas, Ploas, and Mesoates/Messoages contingents per literary scholia). These were each drafted from one of the polis' component districts ("obai," corresponding to the founding villages of Pitana, Mesoa, Limnai, and Konosura plus a fifth, Dyme, for all later additions). The other five lochoi were manned by non/earlier-Doric residents incorporated into the state (perioeci or "those who live around"). These less privileged Lacedaemonians served under spartiate officers, each of their units probably being paired with a spartiate counterpart to form operational bodies 1,000 strong (as per the force Cleomenes led around Argive territory after Sepeia—Herodotus 6.81). This would have pitted 5,000 or so Spartan spearmen against a likely 6,000 hoplites from Argos at Sepeia if we take Herodotus' quite improbable claim for the Argives' losses in that engagement (7.148.2) to mirror instead their total force present (Tomlinson 1972, 96). The other serious concern for Cleomenes would have been that the men from Argos had experience in phalanx combat while his Spartans did not. Sparta had not fought a major action in over 50 years, long before any of its current spearmen were of age. Conversely, nearly all the Argives must have taken part in their phalanx's recent victory over Corinth; they thus "were not afraid of open battle" (Herodotus, 6.77.2).

11. Herodotus, 6.78.2–6.80.

12. Similar advantage had been taken by the Athenian tyrant Peisistratos upon his return from exile in 546 (see Inter-poleis and Intra-polis Wars below). Cleomenes would have been well aware of this incident as he was familiar with many of its defeated democrats, having led them in ousting Peisistratos for good in 510 (Herodotus, 5.64.2).

13. See Chap. 4: Envelopment Maneuvers.

14. Plutarch *Sayings (of Spartans)*: Cleomenes son of Anaxandridas 2.

15. These included one occasion when they were again facing the Argives (in 418); see discussion in Chap. 4: Withdrawal Maneuvers.

16. Tomlinson 1972, 94.

17. See Chap. 3: Surprise Deployments and Sneak Attacks and Confusion, Combat Behaviors, and Battle Trauma.

18. Snodgrass, 1967, 70; Hanson, 2000, 217.

19. Thucydides, 1.15.1–3; he was clearly contrasting this mode of warfare with the large coalition conflict of the late 5th century Peloponnesian War that was the subject of his present work. This echoed Herodotus (5.49), who has Aristogoras claim in 499 that the Spartans fought wars over what van Wees (2004, 28) characterized as "little bits of not particularly good land and tiny boundaries."

20. In reviewing 17 known engagements between Greek states in the Lelantine War plus other conflicts c.724–501 (Montagu, 2000, 48–50; Pritchett, 1979, 290–291), it appears that 94 percent (all but Pallene in 546) likely were driven by border disputes. And looking at the period 500–451 (Ray, 2009, 293–294) suggests that 75 percent (21 of 28) of the combats then were similarly fostered, indicating that 82 percent (37 of 45) of all inter-poleis combats from the late 8th through mid–5th centuries were inspired by conflicts over land.

21. Wees 2000, 19–33.

22. Hanson 2004, 214–215.

23. Foxhall 1993, 137; this reflects the simple fact that mountain terrain covers about 75 percent of the surface of Greece to severely limit the area of easily cultivatable land (Brouwers 2013, 14).

24. Hansen 1995, 189; Foxhall 1993, 136; this can be contrasted with the 93.5ha average size of what in the United States are classified as "small" family farms (2007: *Family Farm Report*, USDA, Economic Research Service), an acreage equal to maybe 10–20 ancient Greek holdings.

25. It's estimated that 65–95 percent of all Greek citizens worked the land in most city-states (Hanson, 1995, 7).

26. Wees, 2004. 28.

27. Herodotus, 1.63.1.

28. Tomlinson, 1972, 91.

29. Diodorus, 11.68.4 (in 466), 11.76.2 (in 461), and 14.9.5 (in 404); this trend continued in the 4th century with a hoplite battle highlighting a revolt in 357 (Plutarch, *Dion* Vol. II, 555–556; see Chap. 4: Field-works).

30. Ray 2013, 34–35.

31. See Chap. 3: Tradition, Training, and Combat Experience.

32. Popular factions always included a polis' militia spearmen, who well into the 4th century usually brought their own battle gear, while wealthy tyrannical/oligarchic factions could have supplied arms to their mercenaries and allies even in the highly unlikely case that they didn't show up already equipped.

33. The wherewithal needed to own and maintain a horse at this time has been compared to that of those today able to afford a Ferrari or similar luxury vehicle.

34. Hanson, 1995, 211.

35. Thucydides, 2.13.6–8.

36. See discussion of metic numbers in Chap. 3: Cimolia I I/II; the count of these men proposed here includes age-reserves at an estimated 20 percent of the total.

37. These formed an exceptionally high percentage (nearly 55 percent) of the total male population due to Athens accepting low income citizens. Citizenship elsewhere was often restricted to the hoplite class and above; thus, those with full rights in contemporary Syracuse have been put at only about 10 percent of the male population (Asheri, 2004, 133), which was likely more the wider Grecian norm.

38. All population estimates for Athens are from Gome (1933). Note that at around one horseman for each ten hoplites, the equestrian class would have been less than 2 percent of the citizenry, while the 300 Athenian triremes on hand in 431 suggest that those providing them were below 0.2 percent of the citizen count.

39. It's known that musters at Sparta were done by year of birth from youngest men of age to oldest fit for duty as needed to fill geographic organizational units at the desired strength. Complete or near-complete age-class deployments were probably the rule, with manpower controlled by the number of units put into the field rather than sending all out below nominal strength. However, in rare cases when only younger age-classes were called up, there must have been some mechanism to ensure that an adequate cadre of more experienced men was included and not just striplings. Picked veterans likely served in such shallow musters as file or half-file leaders. It's possible that some similar kinds of age-based call-ups saw use in other poleis, but this is speculative and there must have been considerable variation in methodology from state to state.

40. The most notable exception to this was in Macedonia, where the hetairoi (companions) provided their kings with elite cavalrymen. This would seem to be a consequence of Macedonia's geographic position on the fringe of Greece and somewhat isolated from its military trends. That led to very late adoption of hoplite warfare and thus a greater reliance on horsemen as elite troops; it also was a factor in the development of a unique Macedonian style of phalanx combat that relied on these riders to work in tandem with select spearmen (the pezhetairoi or foot-companions, later called hypaspists, especially the elite royal guard or agema). Though no picked units are cited, aristocratic horsemen also persisted in neighboring Thessaly (long known for its excellent cavalry) as well as on the island of Cyprus and at Cyrene in Africa; the latter two fielding chariots perhaps as late as the early 4th century. Like Macedonia, all of these sat physically distant from military developments in the heartland of southern Greece and were anachronistic in clinging more strongly to mounted warfare traditions; though, it should be noted that the presence of broad, horse-friendly plains in their realms was a strong factor as well.

41. Pritchett, 1974, 221–224.

42. In fact, epilektoi worsted spartiates on at least three and likely four occasions. These saw the Eparitoi of Arcadia defeat a Spartan column at Cromnus (365; Xenophon *Hellenica*, 7.4.22–24) and the Theban Sacred Band come out on top at Tegyra (375) and Leuctra (371), and probably at Mantinea II (362) as well despite that engagement ending overall in a draw.

43. Allowing League states to replace their required allotment of ships and/or men and the burden of constant campaigning with a monetary contribution (phoros), the Athenians funded training and development of their own fleet (they kept 60 ships at sea for eight months of the year) while at the same time reducing those poleis' armaments and readiness. In the words of Plutarch (*Cimon* Vol. I, 652): "The allies, whose indolence maintained them, while they thus went sailing about everywhere, and incessantly bearing arms and acquiring skill, began to fear and flatter them, and found themselves after a while allies no longer, but unwittingly became tributaries and slaves."

44. Records indicate that in the year 453 alone the phoros came to 390 talents and that League funds accumulated at Athens over and above costs had reached some 5,000 talents when active hostilities against Persia ended with the Peace of Callias in 448 (McGregor 1987, 61, 70). Given an equivalency of 26kg of silver per talent, this would come to nearly $6 million for the 453 take and over $75 million for the accumulated total in 448 at today's values. These were enormous sums in an age when a year's salary for a skilled laborer was only about $1,700 in current terms.

45. Bagnall, 2004, 118.

46. Enmity arising out of this commercial competition was also definitely acerbated by hostility associated with three hoplite battles between these same states 459–458, especially with regard to an atrocious slaughter that Athens visited on Corinthian spearmen fleeing from the last of them at Cimolia II. It was yet another round of confrontation between Athens and Corinth regarding the island of Corcyra in 432 that was the proximal event leading into the Peloponnesian War.

47. Thucydides 1.19; Thucydides noted this as the "real cause" of the Peloponnesian War, since "the growth of power of Athens, and the alarm which this inspired in Sparta, made war inevitable" (1.23.5).

48. See Chap. 3: Cimolia I/II for a discussion of the First Peloponnesian War and the role Corinthian-Megaran borderland played in its Saronic War component.

49. Herodotus, 2.152.4–5; Diodorus, 1.66.12.

50. See Parke (1933) for discussions of mercenaries under the Sicilian tyrants (10–13) and in Thessaly (100–104). With regard to the latter, Yalichev (1997, 164) has noted that Jason, Thessalian tyrant of Pherae in the early 4th century, "maintained the largest mercenary army of any city-state … a private army of 6,000 mercenaries largely paid from his personal fortune." The same ruler later added to his host another 20,000 hoplites, who likely were mostly (if not all) hired men.

51. Parke, 1933, 133–142; McInerney, 1999, 208–210.

52. No less than 81 battles set hoplites against their own kind in the Peloponnesian War interval (432–404; Ray, 2009, 294–296). That's an average of better than one every 3 months over the course of 28 spring-to-fall campaigning seasons.

53. The two major exceptions to this were at Syracuse, where renewed tyranny brought about a return to dependence upon mercenary spearmen, and in Asia. The latter saw the pretender Cyrus the Younger fail in an attempt on the Persian throne using an army with some 10,000 hired hoplites. Remnants of this mercenary legion under Xenophon later aided Sparta in Asia Minor and for a while in the Corinthian War as well. Much more representative of spearmen serving for pay in this period are the Argive and Arcadian (mostly Mantinean) mercenaries in Athens' 415 invasion of Sicily (Thucydides, 6.43). These 750 men amounted to only some 15 percent of their army's hoplites. With regard to such modest deployments, Parke (1933, 17) noted: "It could not be argued that … the hired hoplite contributed much strength to either side in the Peloponnesian War." Nor is there evidence, save for the foregoing exceptions, that they did so elsewhere among the Greeks well into the 4th century.

54. Such disputes could even ensnare a polis whose association with one of the factions was rooted in distant ethnicity rather than current politics. The Ionic Athenians thus rationalized an attack on fellow democrats at Syracuse with a claim that they might join their founder Corinth and other Dorian states in the Peloponnesian League to pose a threat to Athens at some point in the future (Thucydides, 6.6.2).

55. Average pay ran to about 3 obols/day ($1.27) while on campaign for a mercenary hoplite in the mid–5th century, rising under inflationary pressures to 4 obols/day ($1.70) before the century's end and reaching 4.5 obols/day ($1.91) in the 4th (Pritchett, 1971, 14–24). That last rate compares not all that favorably to the 3 obols/day paid at the same time to unskilled slave labor (Parke, 1933, 233) and justifies Pritchett's observation (1971, 29): "That the soldier in the 4th century usually lived a hand-to-mouth existence has been recognized by all who studied the subject." It's thus easy to see why booty was so important to mercenaries, who, unlike militiamen, had no civilian job to fall back upon.

56. Just when he did this is unclear; however, it might have been as early as spring 357 in that he campaigned in Thessaly that winter, well past the normal season for an amateur force Also, Polyaenus (4.2.6) relates how Philip once lacked funds to pay the salaries owed. This must have been prior to acquisition of Crenides' highly lucrative mines in 356.

57. This likely ran to 1–2 drachmas (6–12 obols) per

day or up to more than 2.5 times the going salary for hoplites. His son Alexander would comment in 324 with regard to the pay of his Macedonians that they "earn a handsome wage" (Arrian 7.10.3), though the rate had by then probably swelled somewhat in pace with his regime's acquisition of tremendous Persian assets.

58. Pyrrhus of Epirus' army was highly Macedonian in being composed of citizen recruits (see Chap. 3: Swordsmen). The later Achaean League fielded a standing army of mercenaries and "brazen shielded" epilektoi (Polybios 5.91.4); Philopoemen would eventually retool the League's forces in the Macedonian style. The most notable exception to the use of professional phalanxes in this era would appear to be at Sparta. While the Spartans employed large numbers of mercenary skirmishers, they depended for heavy infantry upon a conscripted citizenry, which had been greatly expanded under Cleomenes III in order to boost its manpower (Griffith, 1935, 93–98).

59. We thus hear of 400 hoplites deserting their employer to join Cyrus' uprising in 401 (Xenophon, *Anabasis* 1.4.3) and 1,000 who abandoned Timoleon in 341 (Diodorus, 16.79.1). Also in this era, the citizen contingent of Syracuse walked out on Dionysius I in 392, though that episode saw his actual mercenaries remain loyal to their paymaster (Diodorus, 14.96.2; see also Caven, 1990, 183).

60. Diodorus, 16. 35.2; Polyaenus 2.38.2.

61. Diodorus, 17.93.2–95.2; Justin, 12.8.10–17; Plutarch, *Alexander* Vol. II, 188–189; Curtius 9.2.1–3.19; Arrian, 5.26.1–29.1; Strabo, 15.1.27. 32; see also Carney, 1996.

62. Diodorus, 18.34.6–36.5.

63. Diodorus, 19.39–43.8.

64. Diodorus, 20.68.4–69.3.

65. This was at Torgium on Sicily in 305, where 2,000 hoplites within a rebel force fighting the tyrant Agathocles turned against their line-mates by prearrangement with the badly outnumbered despot to give him an otherwise unlikely victory (Diodorus, 20.89.1–3); see also Freeman, 1894, 466.

66. Recorded betrayals by horsemen during battle include: Greek charioteers of Kourion at Cyprian Salamis in 497 (Herodotus, 5.110–113); Thessalian cavalry at Tanagra I in 457 (Thucydides, 1.107.2–108.1; Diodorus, 2.80.1–2); Greek colonial cavalry in the Upper Satrapies in 323 (Diodorus, 18.7.5–6); and Eumenes' cavalry at Orcynii in 320 (Diodorus, 18.40.6–8).

67. See Chap. 3: Tradition, Training, and Combat Experience.

Chapter 6

1. Thebans fought on the Spartan side against Mantinea in 385 (Plutarch, *Pelopidas*, Vol. I, 387).

2. Xenophon, *Hellenica*, 5.2.37; this saw the Theban quislings "eager to send hoplites and cavalry" against Olynthus in the Chalcidice toward buying favor with Sparta's king Agesilaos, whose brother, Teleutias, was commanding those expeditions.

3. Balfour 2010, 45; see also Hilbert (2012).

4. Thebes and other Boeotians in 379 had fought seven phalanx actions over the four decades encompassing the careers of all their hoplites (including reserves). These began with a victory (Haliartus, 395) so costly that "the Thebans thus ended the day quite crestfallen, thinking that they had suffered as many loses as they had inflicted" (Xenophon, *Hellenica*, 3.5.19). Another battle that same summer (at Naryx) against Phocis also took a discouragingly high toll (Diodorus, 14.82.7–10). They then fled the field four times (Nemea River and Coronea II, 394; Mantinean Plain, 385; and Olynthus II, 381) and were saved by allied cavalry on another occasion when they were on the verge of collapse (Olynthus I, 382).

5. See: Diodorus (15.33.4–6) and Xenophon (*Hellenica*, 5.4.42–46) on Thespiae; Plutarch (*Pelopidas* Vol. I, 394) on Tanagra III; and Diodorus (15.37.1) and Plutarch (*Pelopidas* Vol. I, 394–395) on Tegyra. In addition, though not battlefield victories per se, Theban-led armies were so intimidating that larger Spartan forces twice retreated rather than engage on unfavorable terrain in 378 (Diodorus 15.32.5–6; Polyaenus 2.1.2; Nepos 12.1.2) and 377 (Xenophon *Hellenica*, 5.4.50).

6. Plutarch *Lycurgus* Vol. I, 64.

7. See: Chap. 4: Envelopment Maneuvers.

8. This continuing respect was apparent at Malea in 368, which was known as the "Tearless Battle" for its lack of casualties among the Spartans due to their foes fleeing to avoid a fight (Xenophon, *Hellenica*, 7.1.31; see Chap. 3: Swordsmen).

9. Xenophon's account (*Hellenica*, 7.5.11–13) of an uphill victory by a tiny Spartan force appears much less probable than Diodorus' report (15.83.4) of the Spartans holding off a series of coordinated small assaults upon several naturally strong points until nightfall brought all fighting to an end.

10. See Pritchett, 1969, 37–72, for a discussion of the battle's topography. The long, north-south valley that contained both Tegea and Mantinea narrowed to perhaps around 2,400m here. The opposing phalanx likely spanned most of this at a depth of eight shields with its cavalry and light foot deployed on both wings to seal the remaining modest stretches off either flank. Covering the latter did not require the entire mounted strength of the anti–Theban coalition and an excess body of horsemen and attached hamippoi from Elis was assigned to a post in the rear to serve as an emergency reserve. This detachment would play a crucial role in the ensuing engagement (see below).

11. This consisted of 6,000 men, probably 5,000 hoplites, 500 horsemen, and 500 hamippoi javelineers—all maximums for those arms in 4th century Athenian deployments. The last had recently replaced the city's horse-archers per Xenophon (*The Cavalry Commander* 5.13; see also Spence 1993, 58–59).

12. Diodorus (15.84.2–4) is our source for these figures and also provides the orders of battle (15.85.2). He gave the Mantineans 2,000 horsemen with 3,000 for Thebes. Polyaenus (2.3.14) mentions only 1,600 Theban and allied cavalry, but this might not have been the entire mounted complement. In commenting on the resulting total of 55,000 or so combatants, Diodorus (15.86.1) claimed that "never at any other time when Greeks fought Greeks was such a magnitude of men arrayed." In fact, though, this might have been slightly less than at Nemea River in 394, which could have involved as many as 42,500 hoplites and just over 57,000 total combatants if we honor some alternative numbers from Xenophon.

13. Xenophon, *Hellenica*, 7.5.23–24.

14. Foot skirmishers for the anti–Theban alliance numbered at least 2,000, indicating perhaps 18,000 or so hoplites. Thebes' three-fold light infantry advantage (Diodorus 15.85.4) then suggests around 6,000 support-

ing some 24,000 hoplites for a significant edge of a third again more in heavy foot. At Leuctra, Epaminondas had only around 6,000 hoplites (Diodorus 15.52.3; Polyaenus 2.3.12) to face some 8,000 on the other side. The latter comes from Plutarch (*Pelopidas* Vol. II, 397) if we assume that there were some 2,000 in foot skirmishers among his reported infantry total of 10,000. It had thus been the Spartans who held a numerical advantage of a third again in heavy infantry in that earlier battle.

15. By failing to close into engagement against Epaminondas' refused right wing, Sparta's hoplite allies at Leuctra consigned it to an ultimately fatal mismatch with an overly deep Theban left. Their reluctance to fight was attributed by Pausanius (9.13.8) to hatred for the Spartans; indeed, some of them "were not even displeased" (Xenophon *Hellenica*, 6.4.15) at their hegemon's defeat. And, of course, there was an immediate benefit to their timorous stance in that they at worst suffered "but slight loss" (probably to opening missile fire) while among some "not a man of them had fallen" (Pausanius 9.13.12).

16. Epaminondas' edge in manpower might have led him to employ the entire Boeotian levy in his powerful left-wing concentration instead of just the Thebans as is probable at Leuctra. Stylianou (1998, 514) argues so based on Arrian (*Tactics* 11.2); however, is highly questionable as it would have created a very short phalanx at much higher risk for falling prey to a potentially fatal envelopment.

17. Diodorus, 15.86.1.

18. Diodorus, 15.86.2–3.

19. Diodorus (15.86.4–5) said that Epaminondas reorganized his best men into a new, close formation for a telling charge, driving the Spartans from the field while throwing his javelin and heroically pulling enemy missiles out of his own body to fling them back! Significant improbabilities here include: (a) that a formation reorganization would have been practical in the midst of combat; (b) that the Thebans fought the Spartans, who actually stood farther west (it was the Mantineans and possibly some of the other Arcadians who faced the Theban frontage); and (c) that Epaminondas was armed with a javelin rather than a hoplite spear and was exposed to intense missile fire after the phalanxes had closed.

20. Leuctra saw the Spartans fall to a final physical push under Epaminondas' plea to "give me one more step" (Polyaenus 2.3.2). A similarly long-delayed turning point came here per Diodorus (15.86.5) when Epaminondas' foes "withdrew" at last under "the sheer weight of the contingent he led." This strongly suggests it was the same sort of literal pressure that culminated in his "defeating the troops where he had concentrated his attack" (Xenophon, *Hellenica*, 7.5.24).

21. Thebes' foot skirmishers were highly skilled and not only had 200 percent greater manpower than their counterparts for Mantinea, but were also more effectively deployed (Diodorus, 15.85.4–5; see Chap. 3: Light Infantry and Horsemen).

22. It should be noted that the Athenian cavalry contributed significantly to this turn of events despite having retreated. Epaminondas had posted some Euboan horsemen and mercenary light foot in the bordering hills to prevent his foes from sending assistance from their left wing against his primary attack on their right (Xenophon, *Hellenica*, 7.5.24; Diodorus 15.85.6, 87.3). These troops were well positioned to intervene against the Eleans; however, Athens' mounted contingent had kept good order as it fell back and turned to wipe these men out, thus allowing their reserve's counterattack to proceed. This Athenian cavalry unit (a 500-rider hipparchy) appears to have been of exceptional quality and had defeated Thebes' renowned horsemen in a skirmish just a few days prior; an action that cost it several riders including Gryllus, one of the twin sons of the historian Xenophon.

23. How and by whom Epaminondas was slain is not certain (see Pausanius 8.11.5–6). Apparent dynamics of the fight suggest a Mantinean hoplite's parting strike or (rather more probably) a Spartan either maneuvered into opposition from farther down the line or simply standing in file along the unshielded (right) side of the columnar-like Theban penetration. Despite reports that this killer's name was Machaerion ("swordsman"), a spear seems most likely to have done the damage. This holds true regardless of the blow coming from Epaminondas' front (slipping past his shield to punch through his cuirass) or from the side (finding a way in at either the thorax's arm-hole or along its lateral fastening). A spear would also seem better matched to tales of Epaminondas dying only after his chest-wound was opened due to the broken haft with its spear-head being pulled out.

24. Xenophon, *Hellenica*, 7.5.25. Note that Diodorus' account (15.86.5, 87.2) disputes this aspect of the engagement, indicating at least two episodes of damaging pursuit.

25. Xenophon, *Hellenica*, 7.5.26–27.

26. Per Strabo (9.2.2), the Thebans' decline post–Epaminondas came from concentrating on military excellence to the exclusion of other virtues; yet, it would seem more apt to see their fall as coming despite such martial endeavors due to them focusing (or at least being effective) only below army command level.

27. Diodorus, 15.87.1.

28. Schwartz, 2013, 166–167; this data comes from the skeletons of around 1,000 individuals in the territory of ancient Metaponton in southern Italy (Magna Graecia). Dating from the 6th through 3rd centuries, the majority of their burials fall "well within the hoplite era." Such results are also consistent with earlier studies (by J.L. Angel and cited by Schwartz) on a smaller sample of ancient remains from Attica and elsewhere on the Greek mainland. These found a mean height of just over 162cm (5ft 5in) with a range from 148cm (4ft 11in) to 175cm (5ft 10in). And Ma (2008, 76) cites a study of 4th century Messenian burials with an average height for males within that same range at 170cm (5ft 8in).

29. See Chap. 1: Citizen Militias and Epilektoi.

30. Ma, (2008, 76) notes that a separate thigh bone and one complete skeleton recovered from the elite Sacred Band's grave at Chaeronea both belong to taller than usual men of 179cm (5ft 11in). It should be noted, however, that even such select hoplites were apparently not immune from potentially stunting episodes of childhood starvation. This is suggested by the teeth of several skulls recovered from the same site showing signs of serious systemic stress incurred during development due to either illness or severe malnutrition (Schwartz, 2009, 172). In regard to the latter, Garnsey (1988, 17) has calculated from modern data that failures of wheat crops at Athens and Larisa in Thessaly have around a 28 percent chance of occurrence annually with failures running two years in succession having about an 8 percent chance. The risk across ancient Greece was

probably somewhat similar, and we then need to add deleterious effects on food supply that could have stemmed from frequent warfare.

31. Dimensions for modern men aged 20–60 from Germany, Holland, Britain, and the USA average around 179cm (5ft 11in) and nearly 81kg (178lbs) per Schwartz (2009, 99).

32. Schwartz (2009, 99); this comes from studies on Roman remains compiled by Garnsey (1999: *Food and Society in Classical Antiquity*). But given that many of the Roman skeletons date from 79 AD (coming from Pompeii and Herculaneum) and their range for average height varies from that for Greeks only on the upper end, that difference might be entirely due to the presence of non–Mediterranean individuals in the much more cosmopolitan society of 1st century AD Rome.

33. Plutarch *Moralia* 192c-d.

34. Xenophon, *Hellenica*, 3.4.19; much the same sentiment was expressed decades later by an ambassador to the Persians who returned to Greece and reported "that he had seen in Persia numerous bakers and cooks, wine stewards and doorkeepers, but although he looked hard, he could see nowhere men of the sort that could fight with Greeks" (Xenophon, *Hellenica*, 7.1.38).

35. Xenophon, *Hellenica*, 3.4.16.

36. Plutarch, *Lycurgus* Vol. I, 73; the high value that the Spartans placed on the appearance of these athletes and others can also be seen in comments about Callicrates, a spartiate that fell to Persian arrow fire while sitting at his assigned post on the field at Plataea in 479. In relating the tragedy of this hoplite's loss, no mention is made of his skill at arms; rather, it is only noted that "he had come to the camp as the most handsome man of the Hellenes at that time, not only among the Lacedaemonians, but among all the other Hellenes, too" (Herodotus, 9.72.1).

37. Xenophon, *Constitution of the Lacedaemonians* 12.5–6: "the law requires all Lacedaemonians to practice gymnastics regularly throughout the campaign." These exercises were apparently carried out twice each day, before the morning and evening meals.

38. Van Wees, 2004, 89.

39. Salazar, 2000, 34–36.

40. The enduring nature of this admiration for bodily development is nowhere better displayed today than in "sword and sandal" films about ancient times. These seem to surge in popularity every generation; a phenomenon stretching from Italian "peplums" of the early 1960's (featuring the impressive physiques of bodybuilder/actors like Steve Reeves as in *Hercules*, *The Giant of Marathon*, etc.) into the 21st century (a recent spate of such films showing finely sculpted and digitally enhanced bodies performing entertaining but quite unrealistic renditions of battles like Marathon, Thermopylae, and Salamis).

41. Mueller and Mazur, 1996, Saxton et al., 2015.

42. Dixon and Vasey, 2012.

43. Plourde, 2008.

44. Contrast his seeming endorsement of instinct over instruction below with Xenophon's frustrated questioning elsewhere (*Memorabilia* 3.5.15) of the lack of contemporary training at Athens: "When will they [Athenians] adopt the Spartan system of training, seeing that they not only neglect to make themselves fit, but laugh at those who take the trouble to do so?"

45. Xenophon, *Cyropaedia*, 2.3.9–11.

46. Thucydides, 2.39.1.

47. Xenophon, *The Lacedaemonians*, 5.9.

48. He touted the value of "keeping your body in ... as optimal [a] condition as possible" according to his pupil Xenophon (*Memorabilia* 3.12.5).

49. "[When Epaminondas] began to interest himself in physical exercise, he aimed less at great strength than at agility; for he thought the former was necessary for athletes, but the latter would be helpful in warfare" (Nepos 15.2.4).

50. Xenophon, *Hellenica*, 6.5.23; the Thebans not only increased their own drills, but also embedded them among their allies; thus, hoplites from Phocis, all the cities of Euboa, Locris (both poleis), Acarnania, Malis, and Heraclea began to drill as well, as did the allied horsemen and peltasts of Thessaly.

51. Diodorus, 17.11.4.

52. Philostratos (*Concerning Gymnastics* 7–8); required equipment seems to always have included the shield; while for a man in the games at Plataea, which "was most notable on account of the length of the course," it seems that "the armor ... reached to the feet just as if he really had to fight."

53. Plutarch, *Moralia*, 639e.

54. Kennel, 1995.

55. Philostratos (*Concerning Gymnastics* 19); Pritchett (1974, 216) notes on this form of dancing in panoply that even when not performed fully equipped martial dancing comprised: "every variety of rhythmical, harmonious movement, or posture of the body, with ... expressive movement of the hand, being practiced to represent the manipulation of weapons."

56. Xenophon (*Anabasis* 6.1.11) said that "the Mantineans and some other Arcadians" in his mercenary contingent "arrayed in the finest arms and accoutrements they could command [and] ... danced, just as [they] do in their festival processions in honor of the Gods." Polybios (4.20.7, 12) noted that Arcadian men in early times were required to study dance from boyhood up to the age of 30, saying that even in his day they "practice military parades to the music of the flute and perfect themselves in dances and give annual performances ... all under state supervision and at the public expense."

57. McNeil, 2009.

58. This process is well depicted in the opening sequence of the film *All That Jazz* (1979).

59. Xenophon's description (*Anabasis* 1.2.15–18) of a formation-scale exercise he and the rest of his paid hoplite comrades performed for their employer Cyrus in 401 strongly suggests that mass drills were at least an occasional part of their regimen. Later, he described a fictional "mock battle" (*Cyropaedia* 2.3.17–18) that might have had some basis in an actual exercise.

60. It has been reasonably proposed (Wees 2004, 95) that this training was likely instituted after Chaeronea (338), where the undrilled and inexperienced nature of its hoplites relative to their Macedonian hypaspist foes had played a major role in Athens' defeat.

61. Aristotle, *Athenian Constitution*, 42.2–5.

62. Xenophon, *On Hunting* 1.18.

63. See Chap. 3: Tradition, Training, and Combat Experience).

64. This is well illustrated by the position of Sparta's king Cleomenes I (c.520–491): "When someone said: 'After your frequent victories over the Argives in their wars against you, why haven't you wiped them out?,' he replied: 'We wouldn't wish to wipe them out, because we want sparring-partners for our young men.'"— Plutarch, *Sayings (of Spartans): Cleomenes son of Anaxandridas*, 17.

65. Engels 1978, 151.

66. Gabriel and Metz 1991, 87; this suggests an average of 35.4 percent wounded versus 37.75 percent killed. The data comes from some highly questionable figures for defeated forces in half a dozen ancient battles, most of them involving Greeks on at least one side; however, the authors' argument that these ratios are probably more reliable than the exaggerated, raw numbers from which they stem has considerable merit.

67. These are charted in Gabriel and Metz (1991, 91–92).

68. Epaminondas' lethal wounding fits the profile here and in the Iliad as well in that a spear punctured his chest and he left the field under assistance only to die shortly from systemic shock and the loss of blood.

69. Projections offered here derive from a speculative casualty profile that was generated for a hypothetical Roman legion (Gabriel and Metz 1991, 90). Given significant similarities, this would appear reasonably applicable to Greek phalanxes as well.

70. Among these was the washing of wounds with alcohol-rich wine, an antiseptic device far ahead of its time, and cauterizing (kauteriazo) with hot metal to stop bleeding. These are both reported by the Greek physician Hippocrates (mid 5th–early 4th century). Interestingly, wine was not used as an analgesic (Salazar 2000, 63), it being thought that the wounded should eat little and only drink water. Gabriel and Metz (1991, 98) cite the Grecian practice of repeatedly cleaning wounds for several days before being closed (by suture)—a method that prevented infection and not rediscovered until the middle of World War I. They conclude (94) that "in a number of cases the military medicine of ancient armies was better at treating infection than have been most modern armies until at least the Civil War." Other ancient remedies, like honey as antibiotic or kaolin clay as a clotting agent have returned as "miracles" of modern medicine in the form of Medihoney and Quik-Clot bandages respectively.

71. Xenophon (*Constitution of the Lacedaemonians* 13.7) lists "doctors" among a Spartan king's usual field staff; and it is highly probable that a similar medical group normally accompanied non-royal commanders as well. Elsewhere, Ducrey (1985, 212) suggests that arrangements to care for combat injuries "were sometimes more, sometimes less developed"; however, Salazar (2000, 71) indicates that "in most Greek armies at war more than one or two doctors were probably available for the treatment of those wounded in battle."

72. Some physicians must always have been among a polis' near-universal draft complement, including perioeci beyond those serving in any formal staff capacity for Sparta. The Iliad suggests this as well in that the only two men specifically identified as doctors (iatroi) in the Greek army at Troy, Podalirius and Machaon (the sons of Asclepius), are both actively involved in the fighting, with the latter himself taking a wound in combat (Salazar 2000, 137–138).

73. Most medical treatment in the Iliad is done by comrades like Patroclus, who learned those skills from Achilles. Salazar notes (2000, 94) that when it came to "practical skills in treating wounds one can assume that a large number of people possessed them, mostly among those who had served in armies for a long time and among the rural population." The last would have included many (perhaps most) hoplites.

74. Manning et al, 2009.

75. "The Spartan Androcleidas, who had a crippled leg, enlisted himself among the fighting men. When some tried to bar him because he was crippled, he said: 'But what's needed to fight our foes is a man that stands his ground, not one that runs away.' Likewise the king Agesilaos, seeing a lame soldier seeking a horse, said: 'Don't you realize that war requires not men who flee, but those who stand their ground?' This last was particularly poignant in that Agesilaos himself had been lame from an early age yet had long served in Sparta's phalanxes.'"—Plutarch, *Sayings (of Spartans)*: *Androcleidas*; *Agesilaos*, 34.

76. These casualty estimates derive from projections (Ray 2009, 301–305 and 2012, 222–225) based upon literature/epigrams as well as analogs/models developed there from. Numbers/rates for non-lethal wounding come from a minimum estimate of 5-to–1 wounded-to-killed for winning armies, 1-to–1 for those losing, and a compromise 3-to–1 for both sides in the era's very few drawn engagements.

77. Xenophon, *Agesilaos*, 2.14.

78. Wellesley wrote this in the course of describing how he felt about his signature triumph over Napoleon at Waterloo in 1815.

Chapter 7

1. It was so named for being fought in and around the Saronic Gulf to the west of Attica.

2. Since Sparta maintained individual, one-on-one relationships with its allies, it tended to consider disputes between them as none of its business. Moreover, in this case, the Corinthians were far more vital to Sparta's security as the primary naval power among its allies; thus any favoritism shown in this matter would definitely have leaned Corinth's way.

3. Corinth had eight tribes (Grant 1987, 80–81) and each would have mustered a lochos of up to 600 hoplites, this being in line with the 5,000 Corinthian spearmen cited at Plataea in 479 (Herodotus 9.28.3).

4. Diodorus (11.79.3) identified these allies simply as "Peloponnesians," but they are likely the same 300 Sicyonian spearmen noted by Thucydides (1.105.3) as serving Corinth elsewhere during this period.

5. There would have been at least one attendant for each hoplite, these being shield-bearers (hypaspistai), baggage-carriers (skeuophoroi), and such (Hansen 2011, 251).

6. This reflects the force deployed by Megara in 479 to Plataea (Herodotus, 9.28.6).

7. Having previously undergone much of its eventual 5th century economic/population expansion, Athens' manpower was likely only modestly short of the 13,000 citizen hoplites of prime age fielded in 431. That was a maximum mobilization with "*the largest army of Athenians ever assembled*" and representing the polis "*in the flower of her strength*" per Thucydides (2.13.6, 2.32.2).

8. Corinth had defeated an Athenian amphibious assault in the Peloponnese at Halieis in 459 (Thucydides 1.105.1; though Diodorus [11.78.1–2] has Athens coming out on top—twice!), but that had been a purely defensive action.

9. Thucydides, 1.105.3.

10. This is indicated in the praise sent Myronides' way by comic writers of the later 5th century, who saw him as "*a representative of the good old days*" (Hornblower and Spawforth 1996, 1016); and Diodorus (11.79.3) cited him as "*a man who was admired for his valor.*"

11. The identification is not certain, but Myronides had likely served as a general at Plataea 21 years earlier. This suggests that he was probably over the 50-year age-limit for field service in 458, but might still have been below the normal full retirement age of 60, though that limitation did not apply to generals.

12. The percentage in these age groups is quite speculative, but a ratio of one reservist to four regulars looks reasonable based on projections drawn from normal mortality rates (Hodkinson 1993, 166). These also suggest a near even split between old and young. Thucydides (5.64.3) provides some contemporary support for these theoretical estimates, noting that reservists among an exceptional muster in 418 comprised "the sixth part of the Spartans, consisting of the oldest and youngest men." Amounting to nearly 17 percent of the polis' hoplites, these would add to a few of their fellows perhaps still on guard back home to also indicate an age-reserve with about 20 percent of all spearmen.

13. Thucydides, 2.13.7.

14. Smith 1919, 353.

15. Howatson, 1991, 456.

16. Thucydides, 2.31.2; this saw 3,000 metic hoplites in the field versus 13,000 citizen regulars.

17. Greater than half again, this probably gave a true physical edge as per Frederic the Great's note (1747, 314) that holding a superiority of a third or more in manpower gave an attacker a telling advantage, something probably just as true in ancient times as for the similar close-order arrays of his day.

18. Megaran hoplites had not seen action since their disastrous performance against the Persian-allied Greek cavalry at Plataea in 479 (see Chap. 4: Terrain Anchors).

19. These veterans' active careers spanned a 40-year period (498–459) and they might have seen action in half a dozen victories over Persia and its allies plus the one over Sparta at Oenoe in 460.

20. Thucydides, 1.105.3–106.2; Diodorus, 11.79.1–4; Diodorus is particularly lacking in detail here, but he does provide the name "Cimolia" for the otherwise unknown site of both battles.

21. The Corinthians were outnumbered significantly, but this fell short of being overwhelming (2-to-1 or better). They therefore probably chose to keep a couple of their most accomplished lochoi at a good depth on the right wing while thinly filing the rest of their formation. This was standard practice toward holding even at center and left until success on the right might compel a wholesale enemy withdrawal.

22. The primary post of honor was on the right of the right wing (Pritchett 1974, 190) and would have been held by the best men from the hegemon (Athens). The left wing was next in prestige, beginning at its end, and likely ceded here to Megara's regulars fighting in their homeland. The left of the right and the center in that order then received the remaining spearmen of least repute and/or priority.

23. With the Corinthians' most highly regarded hoplites (no doubt veterans of the previous year's modest victory over Athens at Halieis) assigned to their right, it would have been lochoi of less experience and secondary reputation posted to this defeated wing.

24. Both sides deployed plenty of foot skirmishers capable of giving strong chase had it been possible, with the Athenians likely having up to 300 cavalrymen as well (Spence 1993, 9); those last formed three 100-horse squadrons that were established c.477 and were surely not engaged either on the Aigina siege or in Egypt in 458. Therefore, the best explanation for this apparent lack of pursuit is that the battle had begun late in the day and concluded too close to dark for any extended further action.

25. See Xenophon (*Constitution of the Lacedaemonians* 2.1–14) and Kennell (1995) on the agoge plus Plutarch (*On Sparta*, 109–163) for the sort of anecdotes that indoctrinated Spartan youths.

26. Bowden, 1993, 33–34; see also Tyrtaeus (Stoebaeus, *Anthology*, 11, 12).

27. Euripides, *Heracles* 190–192, 162–164; written c.417, when the hoplite era was in full swing.

28. Plato, *Laches* 190E.

29. Lendon, 2005, 45; this was in the 4th century.

30. The most famous examples being two Spartans, Pantites and Aristodemos, who failed to die honorably along with Leonidas and the rest of their 300 fellow hoplites at Thermopylae in 480. The former hanged himself and the latter was called "Aristodemos the Trembler" until proving himself brave a year later by fighting to the death in the forefront at Plataea (Herodotus, 7.231–232, 9.71.2–4). It's notable in the current context that Aristodemos was also sharply criticized (and denied any posthumous prize for valor) due to having broken ranks in his eagerness to get at the enemy and thus failing to properly serve the phalanx as the Spartan paradigm for true bravery required.

31. Doric communities like Sparta seem to have been more intense on this subject than Ionian ones like Athens, or Paros where the poet Archilochus once justified shield-tossing by famously writing (fr. 5): "But I saved myself. What do I care about that shield? To hell with it! I'll get one that is just as good another time." Notably, however, Archilochus' homeland, an Ionic island in the Cyclades, was hardly a hotbed of phalanx warfare like the Sparta of his contemporary, Tyrtaeus.

32. Xenophon noted with regard to Athens that "the city does not require warlike exercises publicly"; but he still advocated that training be pursued "privately" (*Memorabilia* 3.12.5).

33. See Chap. 2: Citizen Militias and Epilektoi.

34. Kosslyn and Koenig in *Wet Mind: New Cognitive Neuroscience*, 1995: cited by Grossman and Christensen (2004, 134) with an additional note that "...giving warriors the experience of losing ... actually begins to condition a risk aversion pathway in the brain to which they may turn during similar experiences in the future—they may actually stop fighting and give up..."

35. For example, the Spartan regulars (under the age of 50) at Thermopylae in 480 had only two known opportunities to previously have seen battle. These were a defeat at Methana (dated 500–475) and a victory at Sepeia in 494. However, Methana was clearly a very minor action (known only from a dedication at Olympia: Pritchett 1979, 290) that would have had very few Spartan hoplites involved and even fewer surviving; while Sepeia had been an uncontested massacre (see Surprise Deployments and Attacks below). And a year later, having lost all but Aristodemos from Thermopylae, Sparta's elite equals/spartiates had to once again go into action at Plataea and Mycale bereft of substantial exposure to real battle.

36. Ray 2009, 298–300; Athens fought 95 significant engagements during the 5th century, winning 64 and having a single draw as noted above at Cimolia I. This was much more active and successful than the next ranking combatants at Syracuse (38 battles and 20 victories) and Sparta (29 battles and 15 victories).

37. Xenophon, *Anabasis* 3.1.9.
38. Thucydides, 3.89.1 (426), 6.95.1 (414), 3.2.24 (402?); Herodotus, 8.64 (480); and Xenophon, *Hellenica*, 4.7.4–5 (388); with regard to commanders managing to negate the effects of seeming omens, Frontinus devoted a brief section of his work on stratagems (1.12.1–12) to this challenge: "On Dispelling the Fears Inspired in Soldiers by Adverse Omens"; cited among the threats faced down: a meteor (Epaminondas of Thebes), a lunar eclipse (Syracuse's Agathocles), and a lightening strike (Chabrias of Athens).
39. Herodotus, 5.85.2.
40. Herodotus, 9.10.3.
41. Thucydides, 7.50.4; Nicias' contemporary Thucydides seems to have been firmly in the "doubter" camp when it came to divine omens affecting practical wartime necessities.
42. See Chap. 5.
43. Pausanius, 1.29.4.
44. Thucydides, 6.70.1.
45. See Chap. 4: Field-works.
46. Thucydides, 7.79.3; we do know of one Spartan commander benefiting from such storm-related signs, albeit not in the midst of battle. This was Archidamus (son of Agesilaos), who gave a speech of encouragement to his men while campaigning in Arcadia; at which point, lightning and thunder appeared (Xenophon, *Hellenica*, 7.1.31).
47. Wheeler, 1991, 146–147; Wheeler also noted in this regard that "no Spartan king survived a lost battle until Cleomenes III fled to Egypt after Sellasia (222 BC)" (151).
48. Thucydides, 4.38.1; Olpae shows the very same method at work just a year earlier. An army of Peloponnesian allies under a trio of spartiates met defeat there (Chap. 4: Withdrawal Maneuvers) and subsequent negotiations were done by Sparta's Menedaius, "who on the death of Eurylochos [the supreme commander] and Macarius [second in command] had succeeded to the sole command" (Thucydides, 3.101.1).
49. Mitchell, 1996, 97; V.D. Hanson (1995, 280–288) has been a particularly strong advocate of this view, writing about the history of hoplite warfare that "in the great majority of significant and recorded land battles, there is an undeniable pattern that defending hoplite infantry usually repelled the invaders." He bases this on examination of 16 "major pitched battles" in which 12 are said to have been won by men fighting in their homeland (p. 283). However, a broader survey of Greek hoplite battles does not appear to substantiate his conclusion (see below).
50. Ray, 2009, 285–286; evaluating 156 significant Greek engagements in the 5th century where home ground can be determined, it appears that a majority (56 percent) were won by invading forces. And that trend is stronger yet (60 percent success for invaders) when the study is restricted to only those actions where neither side had a substantial edge (plus a third or more) in heavy infantry.
51. Thucydides, 4.92.2, 5; whether these are the exact words of Pagondas as written somewhere or passed on by some kind of oral tradition, they almost certainly reflect how his contemporaries (including the experienced hoplite and general Thucydides authoring here) must have felt.
52. And should most of a community's men cut and run, its ability to impose shame or sanctions on those surviving would be negated, no matter how any abandoned allies might have felt. As widely shared acts, their escapes could hardly be condemned as individual outrages against honor.
53. As so often elsewhere, we're talking here about a contrast between the amateur militias that cored most Greek armies and better trained and motivated elites like the spartiates and various epilektoi as well as mercenaries of later eras (for whom "home soil" generally had little meaning).
54. See Holmes, 1985, 290–315; this review includes an apt quote (p. 300) from William Manchester, who served as a marine in World War II: "Men, I now know, do not fight for flag or country, or for the Marine Corps or glory or any other abstraction. They fight for one another. Any man in combat who lacks comrades who will die for him, or for whom he is unwilling to die, is not a man at all. He is truly damned."
55. That intimate couples served together in Greek armies is documented by the Sacred Band of Thebes, said to comprise pairs of lovers (Xenophon *Symposium* 8.34, which also suggests one of the two elite units at Elis might have been similarly recruited). Onasander (24.1) advised that a wise general should "station brothers in rank beside brothers, friends beside friends, and lovers beside their favorites." Sparta's Pausanius is reported to have said that "the most valiant army would be recruited of lovers and their favorites" (Xenophon *Symposium* 8.32). And Plato's character of Phaedrus (his friend in real life) is given lines to the effect that if "an army could be made up only of lovers and beloved … in battle, side by side, such troops although few in number would conquer pretty well all the world" (*Symposium* 178).
56. Diodorus, 2.80.1–2.
57. Thucydides, 1.108.1.
58. Thucydides, 1.108.2–3; Diodorus 2.83.1.
59. Thucydides, 1.113; Diodorus, 12.6; here, it was the Athenians who fell victim to a surprise mobilization.
60. Ray, 2009, 289–292; 2012, 213–217; these indicate 46 5th century surprise mobilizations before 173 substantial engagements (27 percent), with those using this tactic claiming 39 victories against only 7 defeats (85 percent rate of success); but there were a mere 7 in 187 (under 4 percent) during the 4th century, though success continued at an 86 percent pace (6 wins in 7 tries).
61. See Chap. 4: Withdrawal Maneuvers.
62. Ray, 2009, 289–292; 2012, 213–217; these indicate 33 surprise attacks in the 5th century (19 percent of all significant actions) delivering 29 victories (88 percent) and 22 in the 4th century (12 percent of all actions) for 20 victories (90 percent); thus, overall: 55 surprise attacks in 360 battles (15 percent) for 49 victories (89 percent). With regard to home soil, defenders won 18 battles against 9 defeats (67 percent rate of success) using surprise attacks in the 5th century and won 11 against 6 losses (65 percent successful) in the 4th; thus, overall: 29 victories against 15 defeats (66 percent success rate). All of this strongly disputes the popular idea that classical Greeks were so strictly bound by the concept of "honorable pitched battle" that they largely disdained the use of trickery when waging war. Further on this issue, Pritchett (1974, 156–189) provides an excellent historical review and discussion of the subjects of surprise attack and ambuscades in ancient Greek fighting, clearly showing them to have been common ploys from Homeric times onward.
63. Herodotus, 6.77–78; see Chap. 1: Sepeia (494).
64. Thucydides, 3.94.2–3 (Ellomenus); 3.107.3–4,

108.1–3 (Olpae); 3.112.1–8, 3.113.1–6 (Idomene); 4.29.1–4, 4.30.1–3, 4.31–4.38 (Spaectaria); 4.67.2–5 (Megara); 7.43.2–44.8 (Epipolae; also see Chap. 4: Barrier Walls); of particular note is the ambush at Olpae, which bears a remarkable resemblance to the tactics of Hannibal in his victory over the Romans at Trebia River in December, 218. The Carthaginian general was well-known as a keen student of Greek military history and might well have modeled his approach upon Demosthenes' feat (Polybios 3.71–74; Livy 21.54–56).

65. Xenophon, *Hellenica*, 3.4.21–24; Diodorus, 14.80.2–6; Plutarch, Vol. II *Agesilaos*, 46; Oxyrhynchus, Historian, 6.4–6.

66. See Chap. 5: Watercourses as Frontal Impediments.

67. Diodorus, 15.93.4–5; Plutarch, *Agesilaos*, Vol. II, 69; also, see Chap. 4: Barrier Walls for the Egyptian Canals action.

68. Thucydides, 7.43.7–7.44.1.

69. Polyaenus, 1.35.1–2; see also Frontinus on this trick and more in his section *"On Creating Panic in the Enemy Ranks"* (2.4.1–20), which also describes actions by Greece's Pyrrhus.

70. Thucydides, 7.44.7.

71. Herodotus, 5.85.2.

72. Thucydides, 4.96.3; see Chap. 2: Delium (424).

73. Diodorus, 20.67.2–3.

74. And as far back at least as the origins of phalanx warfare, with Homer in the late 8th century describing an example: "...three times the Trojans and famous allies whirled in panic—and twelve of their finest fighters died then and there, crushed by chariots, impaled on their own spears" (*Iliad* 18.264–266). Modern analogs also abound; for instance, it's estimated that 15–20 percent of American deaths in Vietnam came from friendly fire (Shay 1995, 125).

75. A portion of the process here seems to involve what Grossman (1995, 127) has described as a "chase instinct" in predatory animals like dogs and men, which for an otherwise forthright warrior "permits him to kill a fleeing enemy" with little psychic restraint. As a result, "it seems that soldiers inherently understand that when they turn their back they are more apt to be killed."

76. Herodotus, 6.78.2–6.80; see Chap. 1: Sepeia (494).

77. Thucydides, 1.106; added credence here comes from an Athenian reporting his own polis' bad behavior.

78. Plutarch, *Pericles* Vol. I, 224.

79. Other notable mass atrocities include Philip II's execution of 3,000 surrendered Phocian and mercenary hoplites after his victory at Crocus Plain in 353 (Diodorus 16.35.6) and Alexander the Great's seemingly dishonorable treatment of the mercenary Greek spearmen he defeated at Granicus River in 334 (Plutarch, Vol. II, *Alexander*, 151; Arrian, 1.16.6).

80. The concentration here has been on atrocious behavior toward battle survivors; however, it should be noted that there were also dishonorable acts committed against the dead bodies of fellow Greeks as well. Notable examples of this include Pericles leaving the Samians' bodies exposed after the executions noted above and Philip II's post-mortem crucifying of Phocis' Onomarchos after Crocus Plain.

81. Holmes, 1985, 205.

82. Grossman and Christensen (2004, 8–11) cite one official survey of World War II experiences that among men seeing intense combat "at the tip of the spear" about 50 percent reported wetting themselves with nearly 25 percent defecating involuntarily. And one combat vet remarked to Grossman upon hearing the latter stat: "Hell, Colonel, all that proves is that three out of four were damned liars!" The Athenian Aristophanes yields some insights on this in his play *Peace* (produced in 421), commenting on a hoplite's colorful attire that "if he ever has to fight in this cloak, he'll dye it another color, the real Cyzicene yellow [i.e. with urine]"; elsewhere saying: "And how vile this War [Ares] is to look at. No wonder we always tremble at the mention of his name and call him terrible and ferocious and the Emptier of Bowels!"

83. Grossman, 1995, 29–39; noting among several examples that S.L.A. Marshall found only 15–20 percent of soldiers had even fired their weapons during World War II combat and concluded that "the average and healthy individual ... has such an inner and usually unrealized resistance toward killing a fellow man that he will not of his own volition take life if it is possible to turn away" (*Men Against Fire*, 1978).

84. For example, improved training of U.S. recruits post–World War II raised the rate at which they used their weapons in battle from the 15–20 percent noted by Marshall to 90 percent (Grossman 1995, 35).

85. Grossman, 1995, 153–154.

86. Herodotus, 6.117.2; Epizelus remained blind for life.

87. That 2 percent lack remorse was documented for World War II by Swank and Marchand: 1946: "Combat Neuroses: Development of Combat Exhaustion" in *Archives of Neurology and Psychology* 55, 236–247 (Grossman 1995, 180); they termed mentally unrestrained lifetakers "psychopaths" (in a strictly clinical sense).

88. From a letter attributed to the philosopher Heraclitus (c.535–475), who might well have made this note based upon militia service that included fighting a battle before his native Ephesus in 498.

89. Shay, 1995, 5, 21.

90. O. Rees (Rees and Crowley, 2015, 72) citing Gorgias' *Encomium of Helen* (16–17); it is notable here that Rees' coauthor, J Crowley, argues that the ancients did not suffer from PTSD due to it being caused by factors unique to modern warfare. However, that argument is heavily disputed by the results of numerous studies that have long documented PTSD symptoms connected with a wide variety of violent experiences outside of modern combat. These include psychic trauma among victims of criminal violence (Resnick and Kilpatrick, 1994), especially rape (Kilpatrick, 2000), childhood abuse (Briere and Jordan, 2009), as well as accidents and natural disasters (Galea, Nandi, and Vlahov. 2004), with the latter events affecting not only their initial victims, but also first responders and even medical staff involved later. And indications that white non–Hispanics of middle-age and lower educational levels in the United States are experiencing an anomalous drop in life expectancy compared to their age-peers in other racial/ethnic groups and international locales due to behaviors commonly associated with PTSD (alcohol/drug abuse and suicide) as shown in a recent study (Case and Deaton, 2015) suggests that significant stresses not related to actual violence may have a somewhat similar deleterious effect if sufficiently sustained.

91. Tritle, 2000, 55–56; noting that Achilles would claim that title save for the *Iliad* being a work of fiction.

92. Tritle, 2000, 77–78.

93. Shay has documented many of their efforts to

ameliorate this problem, drawing upon what he deems the best practices as models in proposing improved procedures for addressing PTSD among modern soldiers (1994, 196–209; 2002, 208–220, 263–266).

94. Fragment, 110; Pindar (c.518–438), a citizen of Chaeronea, would have been of active duty age c.498–68 and thus highly likely to have served as a hoplite in Boeotian armies during that interval, most notably battling the Athenians to a stand-off at Plataea in 479 when he was in his prime at around 30 years old.

Chapter 8

1. See Chap. 3: Pikemen for a discussion of Macedonia's phalanx variant.
2. This opening round of fighting is known as the Archidamian War after the Spartan king, Archidamus, who was his side's prime tactician in leading its invasions into Attica.
3. Megara opposed the peace as it left control of its port at Nisaea to Athens. Corinth, perhaps Sparta's most important ally due to its naval assets and location astride the isthmus pathway into the Peloponnese, likewise opposed it since several of its valuable lost colonies were not recovered. The Thebans were fearful that Athens would now be free to rest and rearm so as to once more menace Boeotia; they thus rejected the truce on the pretext that it forced them to relinquish a captured Attic border fortification. And the Chalcidian Federation successfully lobbied the local Spartan commander at Amphipolis not to turn that city over to Athenian authority, granting it independence instead, under which it posed a continuing concern for security of Athens' nearby route for vital grain shipments out of the Black (Euxine) Sea region. The Athenians responded to these various slights by holding onto Pylos and Spaectaria rather than trading them back as Sparta had hoped. They even went so far as to return fugitive helots to Pylos that they might ravage adjacent Spartan territory (Thucydides 5.56.2).
4. See discussion of this epic rivalry in Chap. 1: Sepeia (494).
5. See Chap. 3: Cimolia I/II (458) regarding this conflict's origins.
6. Tomlinson (1972, 117) has suggested that the Spartans feared (correctly) that Argos would use the treaty's termination to attach disaffected Spartan allies and challenge for Peloponnesian hegemony. That was a major motivation behind their accepting the Peace of Nicias, since it freed resources that could now be applied toward this threat so much closer to hand.
7. Thucydides, 5.44.1–2, 5.47.1–9.
8. The only actual combat would seem to have been a minor clash of some sort in which the Spartans dusted off a foray from Mantinea in support of one of its outlying dependents that had been threatening Spartan borderlands (Tomlinson 1972, 119).
9. There were five generals present from Argos (Thucydides 5.59.5), with one of them, Thrasylus, apparently holding supreme authority.
10. Thucydides, 5.59.5–60.1.
11. Thucydides, 5.63.3–4; Agis now had ten spartiate counselors in tow that had to authorize his command.
12. This was very likely an element of Mount Alesion, whose lowermost spur extended down to about 1.5km southeast from Mantinea's outer wall.
13. See Chap. 4: Withdrawal Maneuvers.

14. Mantinea sat within a closed "polje," which is a low-lying area that effects its drainage not on the surface, but rather by streams feeding into sinkholes ("ponors" or katavothrai) that channel the flow underground to the sea. There were five such sinks around ancient Mantinea (Higgins 1996, 70–71) and stopping them up could eventually lead to inundating the city (something that did indeed happen when the Spartans used the same tactic in 385). Concern for this ploy in 418 indicates that winter and its associated rainfall had already arrived (streams would have been dry during the normal summer campaigning season). That best fits a November date; coming after expiration of Agis' four-month truce, which had likely gone into effect in July (the "middle of that summer" per Thucydides 5.57.1).
15. Pausanius, 8.11.1.
16. Pritchett (1969, 37–72) provides a thorough discussion of this oft used battleground.
17. Thucydides (5.66.2) testifies here to the Spartans' highly efficient tactical organization.
18. Thucydides, 5.67.1–68.3.
19. Pritchett, 1969, 69.
20. Thucydides, 5.68.3.
21. Cartledge (1979, 214–215); the helots included 500 or so surviving of 700 "Brasideioi" (men who had served under the Spartan commander Brasidas in the Thraceward region). These were now free but lacked citizenship rights. Brigaded with them was a force 500–1,000 strong of "Neodamodeis" or "new citizens" raised separately from the helots still at home sometime 424–421 to fulfill garrison functions.
22. There is a great deal of controversy about the size and identity of this rightmost contingent as Thucydides described it only as being "a few of the Spartans at the extremity" (5.67.1); see the discussion and notes below on Spartan manpower for the relative likelihood of this having been a full lochos.
23. Thucydides, 5.68.1, 5.71.2.
24. Thucydides, 5.64.2–3; these were clearly the polis' ready reservists, indicating that the regular field army consisted of ten lochoi averaging around 500 hoplites each for a 5,000 man total. Earlier Spartan practice had the perioeci in separate units, but each lochos here (save for that of the Sciritae and, possibly, the one posted far right) likely had a mix of classes that included perioeci. The liberated helots apparently formed a brigade that matched a pair of units to give the polis twelve lochoi sans age reserves. The roots of the Spartan army's reorganization post–403 into six morai containing two lochoi each can clearly be seen in all of this, though the actual term "mora" seemingly had not yet come into use.
25. Thucydides (5.68.2–3) presents a "calculation" designed to "estimate the numbers of Spartans present upon this occasion." This indicates that, separate from the Sciritae at 600 strong, each rank of Spartans held 448 men in a seven lochoi array standing eight shields deep. That would have been 3,584 hoplites at 512 per lochos. Beyond the implications of Thucydides' characterization of this as merely a calculation toward making an estimate, there are a couple of clues that support the idea of it being no more than a theoretical exercise that did not describe an actual deployment. The separated position of the Sciritae is not mentioned and appears irrelevant, with only the exceptional size of their unit setting it outside the multiplication as presented. Similarly, the Spartans sitting on the far right receive no mention at all, indicating that they must be included in the count of the regular lochoi without regard to

their separate placement on the field. It's clear, however, that despite being apart, these last arrayed in identical fashion to the other Spartans some distance leftward down the phalanx. That the men on the right extreme constituted an entire lochos seems most logical due to the practical advantages in confidence and effectiveness that men used to drilling and fighting as a coherent unit of long standing could bring to that assignment. All the same, the paucity of detail in our sources on this subject leaves any such proposal unavoidably speculative, with the seemingly more popular idea of this having been a smaller, specialized detachment of some kind being a viable alternative.

26. Lazenby, 1985, 155; Tegea was to send perhaps 2,400 hoplites to somewhat distant Nemea within a generation, suggesting that it might have been able to field a few more here on its own doorstep, with the lesser poleis present running the overall allied numbers up by another 1,000–1,500.

27. Thucydides' distinction between "oldest" (per the men sent home by Agis) and "older" here is informative, indicating that these Argives were not old-age reservists, but most likely a picked battalion of senior veterans under 50 and thus still eligible for active duty. Thucydides similarly describes an active-duty-aged Spartan hoplite (those otherwise being already dismissed) as "one of the older men" (5.65.2).

28. The organization of the Argive military seems to have evolved significantly since its crushing defeat at Sepeia 76 years earlier. The attested 1,000-man epilektoi unit was equivalent to (and perhaps actually consisted of) two 500-man lochoi, which likely reflects a size standard now in effect for the entire army. It has sometimes been supposed that the Argives were present in full force here, which has led to widespread speculation that Thucydides' numbers tally as few as half the Spartans that must have been present if the armies were anywhere near equivalent in size. However, this was a foreign campaign in which Argos participated to support its ally Mantinea; and a typical "allied" deployment of this type usually called for no more than a two-thirds muster. If we assume that Argos had as many as 6,000 hoplites (per Sabin's estimate [2007, 102] and as likely earlier on home ground—see Chap. 1: Sepeia [494]), then the 4,000 proposed above would have been precisely two-thirds.

29. Diodorus 12.78.4; the Mantineans had recently sent nearly 3,000 spearmen on a foreign campaign to aid Argos and might have fielded a larger force on home soil.

30. Thucydides 5.61.1, 74.3; Diodorus 12.79.1.

31. Thucydides 5.70.

32. See Chap. 4: Envelopment Maneuvers on both the natural tendency for hoplites to fade toward the right and Sparta's refinement of that into the deliberate tactic of cyclosis.

33. This would involve a variant of the well-practiced Spartan tactical evolution known as anastrophe (see Chap. 4: Withdrawal Maneuvers). It required the relocating lochoi to counter-march left and fill the developing gap at only four shields deep (per the likely 5,000m width of array for the Argive alliance troops involved in the subsequent break-thorough) while Agis' remaining Spartans extended rightward to cover the interval absented at a similarly minimal depth.

34. Perhaps scapegoats for Agis, the unit commanders involved were later convicted of cowardice.

35. If Agis had really thought to fill the pending gap with 1,000 hoplites filed four shields deep, then he was estimating it would be some 250m wide; the fact that the overlap on his right extreme eventually included Tegeans as well as Spartans (Thucydides 5.71.2) suggests that it was probably even broader than that.

36. Thucydides, 5.72.2.

37. Such disdain for pursuit was not just a reflection of the unique tactical situation here, but rather an ingrained practice, with "the Spartans fighting long and stubbornly until the rout of their enemy, but that once accomplished, pursuing for a short time and not far" (Thucydides 5.73.4). This was well summed up on this particular occasion by Sparta's Pharax, one of Agis' advisors, who noted that it was best to avoid "hazarding the issue against men who had given up all hope of life [in order] to learn what valor is when abandoned by Fortune" (Diodorus 12.79.6).

38. Thucydides, 5.73.4.

39. Thucydides, 5.74.3.

40. Keegan, 1976, 75.

41. This is parallel to the well-established norm for most Greek light infantrymen; missilemen who generally fought in open order (save for archers on occasion) throughout the history of Greek warfare.

42. Camazine, 2003.

43. Thucydides, 7.44.1.

44. Van Wees, 2004.

45. Tyrtaeus, frag. 8.

46. Rance, 2004.

47. Also, see the discussion of Persian shield-wall formations in Chap. 1: Thermopylae Day 3 (480).

48. Schwartz, 2009.

49. Dahm, 2013. Such charging out of the protection of a wall of shields to engage in heroic combat has long been suggested as a technique used in conjunction with Anglo-Saxon shield walls.

50. Tyrtaeus, 10w15, 12w19, 10w20.

51. There is no better example of what a minimally organized crowd can do than the infamous hooligan gang fights between Russian soccer mobs. A video of a clash between fans of Spartak and those of Zenit can be found here: (https://www.youtube.com/watch?v=FFpZ5YQIKgU) On the video you can see some men approach in a mass to commence hand-to-hand fighting while others throw things over the battle lines. Those at the front engage in group pushing, rout, and spontaneously rally; and all without the embedded officers and drill that has been thought a requirement for proper phalanx combat.

52. Xenophon (*Hellenica*, 7.1.31) tells us that "it is reported that the soldiers were inspired with so much strength and courage that it was a task for their leaders to restrain them as they pushed forward to the front. And when Archidamus led the advance, only a few of the enemy waited till his men came within spear-thrust."

53. Xenophon *Anabasis* 3.3.7, Long distance arching fire is possible, but direct low trajectory fire is hampered by the ranks in front. The vision needed to accurately track the distance of oncoming troops is reduced, this makes even accurate plunging fire difficult.

54. Bardunias, 2007.

55. See tests Chap. 2: Othismos.

56. Snodgrass, 1967, 51.

57. Aristotle, *The Athenian Constitution* 61 iii: "They also elect by show of hands ten Regimental Commanders [taxiarchs], one of each tribe; these lead their fellow-tribesmen and appoint company-commanders [lochagoi]."

58. Save at Sparta, whose singularly capable warriors

were uniquely said to be able to fight without regard to who it was that stood around them in their array.

59. Xenophon, *Constitution of the Lacedaemonians*, 11.6.
60. Thucydides, 5.68; in this description of the Spartans at Mantinea I, he suggests that each Spartan lochagoi could set his own unit's depth of file.
61. Xenophon, *Cyropaedia*, 2.3.21.
62. Xenophon, *Constitution of the Lacedaemonian*, 11.8 "The Lacedaemonians also carry out with perfect ease maneuvers that instructors in tactics think very difficult."
63. See Chap. 2: Coronea II (494).
64. Plutarch (*Moralia* 220a) emphasizes this in noting that a man carries a weapon for his own sake, but a shield for the sake of his entire formation's security.
65. Cawkwell, 1978.
66. Matthew, 2012.
67. Diodorus, 16.3.2l; see also Chap. 3: Pikemen.
68. See for example: 350353, Gottingen, Georg-August-Universitat, Gottingen, Georg-August-Universitat, R56 3).
69. See: Cypriot Geryon (Met #74.51.2591).
70. Pritchett, 1971, 134.
71. The thin middle of the Athenian line at Marathon may only have been four ranks deep (Herodotus 6.111.3).
72. For instance, see the likely two-deep Spartan deployment behind field-works in the Corinthian War—see Chap. 4: The Long Walls of Corinth (392).
73. See discussion regarding an attempt at this at Corcyra Cemetery (Chap. 4: Withdrawal Maneuvers; Xenophon *Hellenica*, 6.2.20–23).
74. See Chap. 2: Delium (424).
75. Xenophon, *Hellenica*, 6.4.12.
76. Xenophon, Hellenica, 4.2.13; see also Chap. 4: Envelopment Maneuvers.
77. Goldsworthym, 1997.
78. Muir, 1998, 88; In essence a bayonet charge was a test of will and resolution: whose nerve would break first. Initially the advantage probably lay with the aggressor, for he held the initiative and the momentum of his advance would carry him forward. But if the defenders' fire was sufficiently heavy to check the advance and make it falter, the initiative could quickly pass, especially if the defenders were able to exploit the moment with a counter-attack. The use of column offered advantages of speed and greater concentration of officers and NCOs to the attackers, while line maximized the firepower of the defenders, but any simple opposition between "shock" and "fire" tactics is essentially misleading. An attack relied on the fire of skirmishers and artillery to prepare its way, and might well mean resorting to musketry if the enemy appeared resolute; while defenders who relied solely on fire—not supporting it with a ready counter-attack with the bayonet—might halt the enemy's attack only to produce a prolonged firefight.
79. Perhaps an exception that proves this rule is the formation referred to a "orthioi lochoi" (Xenophon *Anabasis* 4.8.12), wherein the lochoi did not deploy down to their final depth, but instead left substantial gaps between parallel lochoi. The latter were perhaps equal to the distance each leader would have to pace out if they then had to deploy. This formation was taken-up for reasons similar to those that drove the French "columns": plowing through missile fire in order to gain a hill-top against troops that likely will not stand their ground upon contact.
80. Bardunias 2011, 64 shows why this is not an apt description.
81. Luginbill 1994, 52.

Chapter 9

1. Plutarch, *Agesilaos* Vol. II, 50; Polyaenus, 1.48.3.
2. See Xenophon (*Hellenica*, 3.5.18–21), Diodorus (14.81.1–3), and Nepos (6.3.4) on Haliartus (also Chap. 4: Withdrawal Maneuvers) and Diodorus (14.82.7–10) on Naryx.
3. See Chap. 4: The Long Walls of Corinth.
4. Frontinus, 1.4.3.
5. It's claimed that he made this march in just 30 days (Xenophon *Agesilaos* 2.1; Nepos 17.4.4).
6. See Chap. 4: Reengagement Maneuvers.
7. Xenophon, *Hellenica*, 4.3.1, 3.
8. Hamilton, 1979, 226.
9. Xenophon, *Hellenica*, 4.3.3–9.
10. Still reeling from their defeat at Nemea River, the Boeotians had failed to bar this narrow passage, apparently having only an inadequately small force ready to hand (Polyaenus 2.1.24).
11. We have an exact date for Agesilaos' arrival here as it was marked by a partial eclipse of the sun (Xenophon *Hellenica*, 4.3.10) that is known to have occurred on August 14, 394.
12. Xenophon *Hellenica*, 4.3.15; Diodorus 14.84.1; and either within or accompanying the regiment from Corinth was a 50-man volunteer group of personal bodyguards for the king (Plutarch *Agesilaos* Vol. II, 52).
13. This area had hosted a battle (Coronea I) in 447.
14. See Pritchett (1969, 85–95) for a description of the topography and its relevance to the battle.
15. See Pritchett (1969, 93), Cartledge (1987, 220), and Sabin (2007, 116); it has been proposed (Ray 2012, 25) that this number, if accurate, included perhaps some 15,000 hoplites with the remainder being cavalry (1,000 or so) and peltasts. A breakdown of the spearmen by contingent might then be: 4,500 Boeotians, 3,000 Athenians, 3,000 Argives, 1,500 Corinthians, 1,500 Euboans, and 1,500 combined from elsewhere including both Locrian poleis.
16. Xenophon, *Agesilaos* 2.9; his hoplite contingents were perhaps: 1,500 Spartans, 1,000 freed helots (neodamodeis), 2,000 Orchomenians, 4,000 Ionian conscripts and mercenaries (Diodorus 14.79.2), 2,500 Aeolians and Hellespontines, 1,000 Phocians/Malians, and 3,000 northern Greeks.
17. Xenophon, *Agesilaos* 2.9, *Hellenica*, 4.3.15; his peltasts might have numbered roughly 6,000 for a strength advantage of around +50 percent.
18. Agesilaos' battle order can be discerned via both direct and oblique references in Xenophon (*Hellenica*, 4.3.15, 17).
19. This assumes that the Theban contingent was not at exceptional depth as it had been at Nemea River. While a repeat of that behavior cannot be entirely ruled out, there is absolutely no mention of it in any of our many sources on Coronea II. That is particularly notable with regard to Xenophon's two accounts (*Hellenica*, and *Agesilaos*), since he had made pointed mention of this Theban tendency in detailing that earlier battle. It may well be that the need to deploy broadly enough to fill a gap between Lake Copais and rough or heavily vegetated ground that might help ward envelopment on the western side of the field had precluded any such overly deep filing. Alternatively, the unfortunate consequences brought about in part by the Thebans' deployment at Nemea River might either have discouraged them from overloading their files this time around or had led their present allies (nearly all of

whom having been at Nemea River as well) to forbid it lest they promptly depart and leave Thebes to fight alone.

20. Xenophon, *Hellenica*, 4.3.17.
21. Xenophon, *Hellenica*, 4.3.17.
22. Xenophon indicates (*The Lacedaemonians* 13.6) that Spartan kings usually took post on the far left of the rightmost mora in their phalanxes, presumably with any personal bodyguard present either being part of that regiment or otherwise standing with the monarch if organized separately. The next mora to the left would then sandwich him in a fairly protected spot save for any exposure to fighting at the front. At Coronea II, this procedure likely saw Agesilaos standing near the right flank of the full regiment that had marched up from Corinth and surrounded in some fashion by the 50 guards that had accompanied it. This would have required the half mora (lochos) from Orchomenos to stand next in line to his left.
23. Not only had Agesilaos' amateur allies run from the battlefield with the Orchomenians fleeing in one direction and the rest giving chase in the opposite, but it would seem that his light-armed auxiliaries (most of them, anyway) had joined the latter's wild pursuit as well.
24. This renewed engagement might have involved no more than 4,000 spearmen on each side, perhaps along a front of 500m if they were filed at a depth of eight, though the Thebons may have reformed at 16 or 25 ranks.
25. Xenophon, *Agesilaos*, 2.12.
26. Men at the very back were free to put their shoulders into those ahead and even shove their spears into the ground to use as poles in gaining greater leverage.
27. Xenophon, *Agesilaos*, 2.12, *Hellenica*, 4.3.19.
28. See Chap. 2: Physical Training.
29. Xenophon clearly indicates that "the Thebans broke through" (*Agesilaos* 2.12) on their own power and, as an eyewitness, should be taken over a bevy of later accounts that indicate the Spartans deliberately opened their ranks to let them pass (Plutarch, *Agesilaos* Vol. II, 52; Polyaenus, 2.1.4, 2.1.19, 23.2 and *Excerpts* 32.3, 45.2; Frontinus, 2.6.6)—a doubtful practicality under any circumstance.
30. Xenophon, *Hellenica*, 4.3.19.
31. Diodorus, 14.84.2.
32. Xenophon, *Agesilaos*, 2.14; see Chap. 3: Wounds and Death.
33. Xenophon, *Hellenica*, 4.3.19; see also his similar comments in *Agesilaos* 2.12.
34. Hamilton, 1979, 226.
35. Cartledge, 1987, 221–222.
36. Thucydides, 5.66.2–67.2; see Chap. 1: Mantinea I (418).
37. See Chap. 1: Coalition Wars and Mercenaries.
38. See Chap. 1: Citizen Militias and Epilektoi.
39. Xenophon, *Hellenica*, 7.4.23.
40. Xenophon, *Hellenica*, 4.8.39.
41. Maurice, *Strategikon*, 163.
42. This was a factor noted by Brasidas at Amphipolis in 422 (Thucydides 5.10.5).
43. Polyaenus, 2.1.2.
44. Thucydides, 4.91.
45. Xenophon, *Hellenica*, 6.4.13.
46. Xenophon, *Anabasis*, 1.8.16.
47. Thucydides, 5.70.
48. Lycias, 22.2.
49. Thucydides, 7.43.
50. 213821, Vatican City, Museo Gregoriano Etrusco Vaticano, 16571 Achilles painter.
51. Xenophon, *Anabasis*, 1.8.18.
52. Thucydides, 5.70.1.
53. Thucydides, 5.71.1.
54. 2015 Archaeon Dromena in Marathon.
55. Maurice, 12B.17.
56. This is very easy to do and relies on hoplites simply watching the backs of the men in front of them rather than staring past them to coordinate their deceleration. The last time you did *not* crash into the car in front of you at a red light, this is what you did.
57. Hanson, 1989, 152–159.
58. Bardunias, 2007, 13.
59. Herodotus (6.112.3) notes at Marathon (490) that this was the first time Greeks had made a running charge at an enemy. Though perhaps not entirely accurate in terms of his history, this would seem to imply a tradition at least not too long ago of stand-off fighting.
60. Sophocles, *Antigone*, 670.
61. See Chap. 1: The Hoplite Spear.
62. Euripides, *Heracles*, 190.
63. Arrian.
64. Xenophon (*Hellenica*, 4.3.19) describes this at Coronea II where Spartans and Theban met head-on and "crashing together their shields, they shoved ... fought ... killed and were killed."
65. Holiday, 1982.
66. Grundy, 1961; Hanson, 1991; Luginbill, 1994; Schwartz, 2009.
67. Van Wees, 2004; Krentz, 2010; Goldsworthy, 1997.
68. Bardunias, 2007; 2011.
69. Liddell and Scott, 1900.
70. Thucydides, 4.96.2.
71. Arrian, *Tactica*, 12.3.
72. Xenophon, *Anabasis*, 5.2.17; Plutarch, *Brutus*, 18.1; Appian, *Mithridatic Wars*, 10.17.
73. Polybios, 4.58.9.
74. Fruin, 2002.
75. Plutarch, *Aristides* 9.2.
76. Herodotus, 8.78; 9.26.
77. Schwartz, 2009.
78. Lim, 1995.
79. It should be noted here that the foremost man in line also had the job of maintaining proper contact with the sensor, and therefore could not push as freely as those added behind him.
80. Bardunias, 2007.
81. At least one of these (made by Mikko Sinkkonen) being perhaps the most accurate reconstruction ever achieved.
82. See Chap. 2: Tradition, Training, and Combat Experience.
83. This was suggested to the authors by Giannis Kadoglou.
84. Krentz, 2002, 31.
85. Krentz, 1985.
86. Plato, *Laches*, 182a.
87. Archilochus, CURFRAG.tlg–0232.6: "The shield I left because I must, poor blameless armament! beside a bush, gives joy now to some Saian, but myself I have saved. What care I for that shield? It shall go with a curse. I'll get me another e'en as good."
88. See Chap. 2: Delium (424).
89. Xenophon (*Hellenica*, 4.2.20) noted at the battle of Nemea River (494) that the immediately opposed

contingents from Thespis and Pellene carried on their own fight oblivious to what others were doing around them.
90. Pritchett, 1974, 246–275.

Chapter 10

1. See Chap. 4: *Long Walls of Corinth (392)*.
2. Looking at Xenophon's account (*Hellenica,*), Agesilaos had "left all the Amyklaians in the army back in Lechaion" (4.5.11). It is possible that they were separate from the mora there; however, details of Spartan military organization make it more likely that they were part of it. Morai appear to have held around 1,000 hoplites as per 6,000 in six at Nemea in 394 (4.2.16) and 4,000 in four at Leuctra in 371 (Diodorus 5.56.4). This is also a match in round numbers with Lazenby's calculation of nominal mora manpower at 1,120 (1989, 63–64). The 600-man parade strength cited for the Lechaion unit after the Amyklaians' departure (4.5.12) was therefore very low and unlikely due to other, "normal" attritions that could never have reached as high as +45 percent under current conditions and so very early in the summer campaigning season. Given Sparta's long-standing practice of community-based deployments, the Amyklaians certainly served together, allowing them to be concentrated by simply assigning their regiment to Lechaion. Allied garrison troops there (4.5.11) could then cover their temporary absence when the time came.
3. Parke, 1933, 52–53.
4. Xenophon, *Hellenica*, 4.4.16–17; so disdainful were the Spartans of Athens' javelinmen that they even showed contempt for some Mantineans beaten by them, "saying that their allies feared peltasts the way children fear the bogeyman."
5. Xenophon, *Hellenica*, 4.5.16.
6. Xenophon, *Hellenica*, 4.5.17; see Konecny (2014) for an excellent modern review of the battle of Lechaion and a detailed analysis (p. 22–27) of the impotence of Spartan tactics there.
7. Plutarch emphasized that their unit was "a choice regiment of full-armed Lacedaemonians" (*Agesilaos*, Vol. II, 55), thus seeking to highlight the engagement's significance despite its quite modest dimensions.
8. The Thermopylae myth had already suffered some damage from a Spartan surrender on Spaectaria in 425 (see below), but at least that incident hadn't seen spartiates running away from a fight.
9. This was most striking at Mantinea, whose hoplites had been mocked by the Spartans for fearing Iphicrates' peltasts. Agesilaos marched past there "while it was still dark, for he thought the Spartans would be mortified if they saw the Mantineans rejoicing at their misfortune" (Xenophon, *Hellenica*, 4.5.18).
10. Surveys of 4th and 5th century engagements (Ray 2009, 289–292; 2012, 213–217) indicate that less than 20 percent of them involved the use of flank barriers.
11. It seems that there normally was about one such select "combatant" attendant for every ten spearmen during the heyday of polis militias in the 5th century.
12. Xenophon, *Hellenica*, 7.5.23–25; Diodorus 15.85.2–87.3); see Chap. 2.
13. This was undoubtedly intermixed with light infantry (see discussion below on that Macedonian practice).

14. Diodorus, 16.4.6.
15. Frontinus, 2.3.2.
16. Diodorus, 16.35.4–6.
17. Herodotus, 5.110–113.2; cavalry had largely replaced chariots in most of the Greek world by the beginning of the 5th century, but they remained the basis of aristocratic mounted forces on Cyprus and in the North African Grecian province of Cyrenaica (which used four-man vehicles as at Carthage).
18. See Shipboard and Amphibious Assaults below.
19. Thucydides, 2.79.1–7.
20. The Athenians had marched into the Chalcidice with 2,000 hoplites backed by 200 horsemen and perhaps the same in foot skirmishers (certainly no more than 500, which would have been equal to a hefty quarter of their attendants). Spartolos, however, could call upon native auxiliaries (perhaps not much if any inferior in count to those with their enemy), "a few" peltasts from the surrounding coastal area of Crusis, and horsemen from elsewhere in the Chalcidice (probably Olynthus, which had around 1,000 available). A supporting force of peltasts for the latter was also surely present, Chalcidian horse being known to operate "very closely with javelin-equipped light troops" (Spence 1993, 29).
21. Thucydides, 4.31.1–38.5; see also Shepherd (2013, 68–86).
22. These lightly-armed men included 800 specialist javelineers, 800 bowmen, and a great many Athenian rowers. The latter's weaponry apparently included some slings, but most must only have had stones to be thrown by hand.
23. Diodorus 15.71.5–7.
24. Philip was lodging with the general Pammenes, a friend and disciple of Epaminondas; thus, the youth seems certain to have learned a great deal about this exploit (very likely from Epaminondas himself).
25. Frontinus (2.8.14) detailed this battle, but seems almost certainly to have misread his source and thus transposed the positions of Philip's cavalry and phalanx as proposed by Hammond (1994, 136).
26. Justin, 9.3.2.
27. Polyaenus, 4.2.13.
28. Arrian, 4.4.4–7.
29. Arrian, 3.12.1.
30. At Granicus River (334) we are told that Alexander advanced "having arrayed his phalanx in two rows" (Arrian 1.13.1). At Issus (333), "the foreign mercenaries [Greek hoplites] were stationed as a reserve force for the entire army" (Arrian 2.9.3). Issus had a restricted battleground that had an effect as well; thus, the Persians too had men in their rear: "the remaining mass of light-armed troops and hoplites, organized by tribes, was behind the [Persian] phalanx" (Arrian 2.8.8). But for Alexander, it was not solely a matter of accommodating space, but also a deliberate tactic. This is indicated in that, unlike the Persian troops who were "drawn up too deeply [for the remainder] to be of use," his fronting men were in thin files. The pike-men were just eight deep (Polybios 12.19.6) and the hoplites/hypaspists probably in files of only four.
31. It's notable on this point that Alexander himself did not employ a second phalanx in his last major battle at the Hydaspes (326) in India, where he needed all his heavy troops to match the enemy front and was actually the one with marked cavalry superiority.
32. The Persian horsemen at Granicus River "were thrust back by the Macedonian cavalry and were injured as well by the light-armed troops who were mingled

with them" (Arrian 1.16.1); the latter presumably closely dispersed among their own riders as well in order to so attack.

33. See Spence (1993, 19–23, 30–32, 58–60).
34. Xenophon, *Hellenica*, 7.5.23–24.
35. Diodorus, 15.85.4–5.
36. Xenophon, *Hellenica*, 4.6.11.
37. Sparta's need to resort to the use of outrunning hoplites as a counter to light-armed attack was due to its inherent lack of native light footmen. This stemmed from reluctance to arm the brutally subjugated helots Sparta used for support instead of the willing freeman serving as combat auxiliaries elsewhere. The Spartans would eventually follow Athens' lead by hiring mercenary peltasts to fill this role. Athenians used such mercenaries in place of their own lower class men, who served as oarsmen in the fleet.
38. Thucydides, 2.81.8; see also Diodorus, 12.47.4–5.
39. Xenophon, *Anabasis*, 3.3.15.
40. Xenophon, *Anabasis*, 3.4.17.
41. Athens had 1,600 foot archers in 431 (Thucydides 2.13.8). With 300 triremes at that time, up to 1,200 of these could have been assigned to the fleet; however, it is probable that some 100 ships were older vessels in reserve and bowmen marines on active duty might thus have numbered only 800. That would have left half the total archery contingent available to support the phalanx and other land operations. The number of bowmen previous to that is unknown, but there might have been 400 or more with the army as early as 480 in addition to any serving aboard the polis' triremes. Athens also had 200 horse-archers in the 5th to early-4th centuries (they were replaced then by hamippoi). These fought ahead of the other horsemen (Xenophon *Memorabilia* 3.3.1), fending off shorter-ranged missilemen (see Spence 1993, 56–58).
42. Herodotus, 9.21.3–22.1.
43. De Souza (2004, 103) cites a late 5th century Athenian vase showing an archer firing from behind a fronting hoplite, possibly a depiction of this very action at Plataea.
44. Thucydides, 3.97.2–98.4.
45. Thucydides, 4.125.2–3; note that here (and elsewhere where armies are likewise on the march) the formation shape must actually have been rectangular rather than truly "square."
46. Thucydides, 7.78.2.
47. Xenophon, *Anabasis*, 3.4.19.
48. Xenophon, *Hellenica*, 4.1.17–19; Gaugemela (331) saw a different response to the attack of scythed chariots, according to all of our main sources (Diodorus 17.58.4–5; Curtius 4.13.33, 15.14–17; and Arrian 3.13.5–6) the phalanx there opened up rows for the machines to pass through. This has been seriously questioned (Heckel et al. 2010) in favor of besting the charioteers in front of the phalanx, which then would have been acting more like the bulwarking element seen in earlier Macedonian victories.
49. In addition to Philip II and his mount being bested by a Thracian pikeman, we have an anecdote regarding a Persian rider "pierced by the sarissa of a Thracian peltast, after the long shaft had already passed through the belly of the horse" (Best 1969, 103; quoting Lucian, *Nekrikoi Dialogoi*, 27.3).
50. See Webber (2011, 114) on the Thracian "pike" (some 4m in length) and Iphicrates' exposure to it.
51. Diodorus, 15.44.1–4; Nepos, 11.1; see Sekunda (2014, 127–137) and Stylianou (1998, 342–346).
52. Terms applied to these soldiers suggest the use of hoplite equipment, as per "doryphoroi" (spear-carrier) in terms of the hoplite spear (dory) and "hypaspistai" and "hyperaspizantes" per the hoplite shield (aspis). That at least the latter two described traditional hoplite equipment is indicated by hypaspists employing their aspides to cover an entire body width (Arrian 1.1.9; Polyaenus 4.3.11).
53. Alexander's major contributions to infantry tactics were the concept of posting a second phalanx as a rearward redoubt in his major battles in Persia and the more aggressive use of light-armed footmen in close cooperation with cavalry on the wings of his heavy infantry arrays.
54. Compelling graphic evidence comes from the famed "Alexander Sarcophagus," celebrating either Issus in 333 (Sekunda and Chew 1992, 29–30) or Gaugemela in 331 (Heckel 2006). This clearly depicts what must be hypaspists with typical hoplite gear. And Anson (2010, 81–82) cites four other examples: soldiers with Macedonian helms and hoplite equipment painted on the "Agios Athanasios" tomb at Thessaloniki, a hoplite shield displayed on the façade of the early Hellenistic "Tomb of Judgment" in Lefkadhia, hoplite aspides on the Macedonian "shield Monument" at Beroea, and a hoplite shield with the device "AE" stamped upon a Macedonian coin dated 325–300.
55. These include a butt-spike (sauroter) for a hoplite spear dated late 4th century and stamped "MAK" to mark it as being of Macedonian state supply (Heckel and Jones 2006, 18, 20). We also have material found interred along with the remains of Philip II in Vergina (Head 1982, 106–107; see Worthington 2008, 234–241 on the security of this sometimes disputed identification). The latter includes a dory head and highly decorated hoplite aspis.
56. This defensive aspect was difficult for Doric phalanxes, and it was common for both sides in a battle to carry their own right. Theban armies of the early 4th century addressed this by holding back their weaker wing, but that approach could fail if the opposing troops advanced to initiate action anyway. The Macedonian phalanx solved this problem by providing its defensive wing with pikes that were difficult to penetrate, removing any need to depend on a lack of enemy aggression.
57. These picked riders were known as "hetairoi" (companions), and their select hoplite comrades appear to have been initially called "pezhetairoi" (foot-companions). The latter title eventually devolved onto Alexander's pikemen after his elite spearmen exchanged it for an identity as "hypaspistai" instead (Heckel, 2002, 24; Heckel and Jones 2006, 31; Bosworth, 2010, 98–99).
58. Diodorus, 16.35.1–2; see discussion of likely much superior Macedonian manpower in Ray (2012, 101).
59. Diodorus, 16.35.3–6.
60. This was at Crescent Hills; see discussion in Chap. 4: Artillery.
61. Philip twice defeated Greek phalanxes near Olynthus in 348 (Diodorus, 16.53.2) and conquered Greece with his triumph over its hoplites at Chaeronea (see Chap. 4: Chaeronea [338]).
62. Pikes in Philip II's later years and under Alexander II are likely to have been some 4.6m (15ft as per the minimum cited in Asclepiodotus 5.1) versus 3.7m (8ft) for Iphicrates' original device, though possibly ranging up to 5.5m (Heckel and Jones, 2006, 13). This would later expand to perhaps as long as 7.3m (24ft as per Polyaenus 2.29.2).

63. Ma (2008, 74–75); the pike of Iphicrates was half-again longer than a dory at some 3.7m/12ft, while the up-grade proposed here was probably 4.6m/15ft long and projected an additional point in front of the phalanx's first rank. It's notable that though sarissa remains from Chaeronea include large heads like those for Hellenistic models of great length (5.5m/18ft to 6.4m/21ft), there is no sign of the iron sleeves used to connect the shaft-segments of those later weapons (which were carried in two pieces on the march) nor of their flanged butt-spikes, but rather only smaller, simpler spikes similar to those for hoplite spears.
64. Arrian, 2.10.1–11.4; Curtius, 3.10.1–11.12; see Chap. 4: Field Works.
65. See Chap. 4: Envelopment Maneuvers regarding Leuctra (371).
66. This lack of imagination can be attributed to a dearth of generals like Pelopidas, Epaminondas, and Pammenes that had plied more creative tactics on Thebes' behalf in the past.
67. Diodorus, 18.15.1–4; Plutarch, *Phocion*, Vol. II, 261.
68. Diodorus, 18.16.4–17.5; Plutarch, *Phocion*, Vol. II, 261.
69. Diodorus, 18.12.3.
70. Plutarch, *Phocion*, Vol. II, 261.
71. Pritchett, 1974, 80–81.
72. Diodorus, 17.48.1–2; Aeschines, *Against Ctesiphon*, 165.
73. The victory of Aristonous and his garrison over Macedon's Cratevas near Amphipolis (Diodorus 19.50.7) was likely fueled by superior skirmishing on the formation flanks, turning at least the Macedonian left and perhaps achieving a double envelopment. While the defeat of Cassander's general Lyciscus at Eurymenae in 312 by Epirotes (Diodorus 19.88.5) was probably a clash of two phalanxes with pikes (see below on sarissai at Epirus), the defeat of Cassander himself at Apollonia that same year came against Greek hoplites and Illyrians. Those were "superior in number," while the Macedonian "did not have an adequate army with him" (Diodorus 19.89.2). The decisive edge in manpower would certainly have applied to skirmishers, who might well have paved the way to victory by turning the left of a short Macedonian line (Cassander probably stood/rode on the right, accounting for his escape).
74. There is a possible earlier swordsman experience reported by Thucydides (7.27.1) with regard to the Thracian peltasts of the Dii tribe that he calls "machairophoroi" or saber-carriers. However, beyond a mention of Croesus hiring Thracians with swords in 6th century Lydia (Webber 2011, 56), this is the only other known mention of Thracian swordsmen, and it's most likely that this refers only to secondary arms. Expensive swords were normally carried only by rich Thracian nobles, with common soldiers relying on cheaper, curved knives to back-up their main armament of javelins (Webber 2011, 60). Quite possibly the Dii, as very well-paid mercenaries (Thucydides 2.27.2, 29.1), were wealthy enough to universally afford machaira/saber side-arms. Certainly, Thucydides' description of their tactics (7.30.2) is consistent with traditional Thracian javelin fighting rather than sword-play (Webber 2011, 108).
75. Xenophon, *Hellenica*, 7.1.20; Diodorus, 15.70.1.
76. Diodorus, 15.70.1.
77. Xenophon, *Hellenica*, 7.1.21.
78. Xenophon, *Hellenica*, 7.1.22; note that 70 men lost at the 5–10 percent rate typical for a soundly defeated force would suggest that Sicyon had only 700–1,400 hoplites on hand and might have been outnumbered by as much as 2-to-1 in shock troops for the engagement.
79. This observation stems from two main considerations: (1) Sicyon's spearmen had much greater offensive potential with longer weapons, half the spacing width of the swordsmen, and two ranks able to strike along the front instead of one (see expanded discussion of these points regarding Pydna below); all versus only a modest disadvantage in impact energy (70.8 foot-pounds for an overhead spear thrust versus 101.3 foot-pounds for a hacking sword per Gabriel and Metz 1991, 59); and (2) the primary defensive devices, shields, also favored the hoplites in that with regard to the Celtic shield (much like that of the Iberians) "both the Greeks and Romans thought that they were inadequate protection for an unarmored man" (Head 1982, 152). The practical effect of these key advantages for the spearmen can be seen in Hannibal's recognition that his Celts were simply not up to the fighting standard of his hoplite-style African soldiers; thus, he used them as merely "a softening up force" (Wise and Hook, 1982, 17) rather than as his prime shock troops.
80. Xenophon, *Hellenica*, 7.1.31.
81. This presages the replacement of peltasts in the 3rd century with "thureophoroi" as the main form of Greek foot skirmisher (Head 1982, 47). These carried an oval center-grip shield (thureos) similar to those of the Iberians and Celts, though they were primarily missilemen rather than shock-prone swordsmen; see Chap. 2: The Hoplite Shield.
82. Pausanius, 10.20.3, 21.2–4; unfortunately for the Greeks, the parallel to 480 also included a successful skirting of the pass along the Anopaia Path, which forced them to abandon Thermopylae.
83. Pausanius, 10.23.
84. Justin, 17.2.14; these troops were contracted to provide two years of service at Macedon's expense.
85. The Epirote spearmen probably included the same picked infantry from the Chaonian tribe that is noted as being part of Pyrrhus' later army in Greece (Plutarch *Pyrrhus*, Vol. I, 543) plus a contingent from the ethnic Greeks that had been incorporated within Epirus.
86. Dionysius' battle order at Asculum (20.1) implies a Tarantine phalanx of Macedonian type with white-shielded pikemen having allied spearmen off either side. Reformed by Alexander of Epirus and modeled on Philip II's formations, it perhaps normally used mercenaries as elite shock fighters on its right wing.
87. Polybios (18.28.10) states that Pyrrhus placed his differently-armed contingents *"in alternate order in his battles with the Romans."* Dionysius describes this interspersing as being done by ethnic group at Asculum; however, having a smaller and less culturally diverse force at Heraclea, the sections there must have been based upon organizational units rather than nationality.
88. On Heraclea: Plutarch, *Pyrrhus*, Vol. I, 531–533; Zonaras, 8.3; Orosius, 4.1.8–15; and Livy, *Epitome*, 13. On Asculum: Plutarch, *Pyrrhus*, Vol. I, 536–537; Dionysius, 20.1–3; Zonaras, 8.5; Orosius, 5.1.19–23; and Livy, *Periochae*, 13.
89. Pyrrhus had brought 20 elephants to Italy and they proved most effective in frightening and driving off the Romans' horses, which were unfamiliar with the beasts' alien appearance and scent.

90. Pyrrhus lost 4,000 men at Heraclea, but killed 7,000 Romans and captured 1,800 more per Plutarch (*Pyrrhus*, Vol. I, 533) quoting Hieronymus, who was contemporary to the battle. At Asculum, his losses were 3,505 versus 6,000 for Rome according to Plutarch (*Pyrrhus*, Vol. I, 536–537) from Pyrrhus' own memoirs. It is likely that the relative losses on each side were much less disparate in the early going, mostly being confined to those portions of the front that set sword against spear (rather than pike; see discussion of this phenomenon at Pydna below); however, Roman numbers then went up unilaterally during the finishing routs and pursuits. Taking account of minor losses in subsequent campaigning and the return of his loaned Macedonians to Greece, it appears that Pyrrhus might have been short some 15 percent of his original landing force after fighting these first two battles. Though hurt less than his foes, this was a casualty rate more in line with losing than winning, leading to identification of his tactical successes as "Cadmean" (later "Pyrrhic") in being costly to victor and defeated much alike.

91. Plutarch, *Pyrrhus*, Vol. I, 540.

92. Dionysius, 20.10.1.

93. Diodorus, 17.88.2.

94. Anson (2010); perhaps up to three pike units (taxeis) taking up hoplite gear to be called "asthetairoi."

95. Plutarch's comments on these developments are ambiguous. Sparta (*Cleomenes*, Vol. II, 337) increased its manpower by "completing the number of citizens out of the best and most promising of the country people." Formerly thureophoroi, these newly enfranchised troops learned to use "a sarissa with both hands" and "carry their shields by a band." However, the rest of the army came from the existing citizen body, and these men might well have retained the traditional hoplite gear that had long distinguished their families' much prized spartiate lineage and duties. Achaea (*Philopoemen*, Vol. I, 489) reequipped its force of thureophoroi with "large [heavy] shield and long pike." This would be contradictory unless referring not only to creation of phalangites with a sarissa (and complementary pelte), but also of hoplites with a hefty aspis (and complementary dory); at least the latter using referenced body armor as well.

96. Interestingly, it was the Romans that employed elephants here in a total reversal of what Pyrrhus had done to them a century earlier at Heraclea and Asculum.

97. The spears are wielded in one hand and thus either the dory or somewhat shorter longche (for thrusting or throwing). Unfortunately, these weapons were fashioned of metal affixed to the monument, which has led to scavenging costing us the details of their design. The shields cover the entire upper body as per the traditional hoplite device, but lack the broad offset rim present on aspides of old. This would seem to have been a modification exchanging some of the earlier version's durability and comfort during othismos (perhaps now less common) in favor of saving weight to make its bearer more mobile outside the phalanx. Sekunda (2012, 18–19) documents two shield sizes, one averaging 66cm in width and the other around 74cm. But all of these date from the latest 4th to early 3rd centuries and it's therefore hard to directly relate them to the Pydna monument. However, a shield similar to the larger variety appears in the foreground on a belt from Pergamum that is perhaps from the 2nd century (Sekunda 2012, 5). The weapon shown with it appears to be plied single-handed, drawn back in an underhand grip to strike alongside the shield on the bearer's left in fending off a horseman. That grip would fit with a sarissa, but a dory could also be held low and a one-hand grip would suggest a spear of some sort rather than a true pike. A background figure that is engaging an infantryman with an unseen weapon has a shield of similar size but much more concave in appearance; thus, even should the foreground soldier be an awkwardly drawn pikeman, there would seem to have been other differently equipped fighters (spearmen?) stationed in his phalanx's front rank. A case might be made that the larger shield Sekunda describes originated as a phalangite device (for better protection against fellow sarissophoroi) and was only later adapted for spearmen, perhaps by expanding it to around 80cm width and making it more concave.

98. Livy, 44.41–42.

99. Plutarch, *Aemilius Paulus*, Vol. I, 369. Plutarch here used the word "sarissa" generically for "spear," as he does with "hasta."

100. The Paeligni cohort would have had some 500 heavy infantrymen. If these took losses at 50 percent of those claimed for their army on the day (surely a minimum interpretation of Livy's "by far the greater part") then this unit would have lost some 10 percent of its swordsmen to the Macedonians' spears. This is perhaps comparable to the damage that Pyrrhus' hoplites were able to inflict at Heraclea and Asculum.

101. Polybio, 18.30.5–11.

102. This is further underscored by the ability of both the Spartan mercenary general Xanthippus (at Bagradas River in 255) and Hannibal (at Trebia River in 218 and Cannae in 216) to defeat Roman armies using hoplite-style spearmen and cavalry.

103. An extant monument with a decree dating from the reign of Philip V honors Alexander son of Akmetos, who commanded Philip's chalkaspides (bronze shields) in 222 at Sellasia (Polybios, 2.66.5). This is decorated with the image of a Macedonian shield having an offset rim (albeit one much thinner than that of the classic hoplite aspis); so much so that it sits in recessed shadow when the edge of the device's face is well lit (Sekunda, 2012, 36–37). The chalkaspides were the pikemen that formed the main body of Philip's phalanx. However, his elite troops ("peltastai" per Polybios, using a perhaps anachronistic title) were almost surely hoplites; thus, Alexander must either have been serving with them at the time of the award or had continued to wear their gear later as a mark of distinction in his more senior command role.

104. Asclepiodotus 1.2; this tactical writer's loose use of the term "hoplite" makes Livy's note that the Macedonians deployed "hoplites" at Cynoscephalae ambiguous at best; however, Plutarch's account of the battle (*Flamininus*, Vol. I, 504–505) can be taken to indicate that a portion of the phalanx (its hoplites) had "shield touching shield" while the rest of the array (phalangites) displayed "a dense array of spears [sarissai]," with both segments being impossible for the Romans to penetrate frontally. That these different aspects (shield wall and pike hedge) represent two types of armament seems clear given that pikemen thrusting their weapons double-handed with small shields affixed to their elbow/forearms would have been physically precluded from truly locking shields edge to edge.

105. Head, 1982, 18; we can only speculate about application of the obsolete term "peltastai" (peltasts having been replaced by thureophoroi by this time) to what

were clearly heavy spearmen. The best explanation might relate it to adaptation of the larger version of the phalangite shield (still likely referred to as a "pelte") as a replacement for the hoplite aspis; that device carrying its old designation despite a new use and possibly a modestly altered design (enhanced size and concavity).

106. Polybios, 18.25.

107. A Roman monument marking the end of the 3rd Punic War (146) shows an aspis-like Punic shield and Morales (2013, 50) has suggested that hypaspists/hoplites were in use as late as 102 at Alexandria Eschate.

108. Sekunda (2006) provides an excellent review of those reforms in the 160s.

109. These appear somewhat like the larger shields described earlier for neo-hoplites; those might have been used to similar advantage (at least on occasion) when throwing a longche dual-purpose spear.

110. Herodotus, 7.89.1–95.2, 7.96.1.

111. Herodotus (8.90.2) provides an excellent example of javelineers clearing epibatai off a deck.

112. See Chap. 3: Mycale (479).

113. This highly effective operational strategy was first used by Athens' Tolmides in 457 to attack the homelands of Sparta, Sicyon, and Corinth during the First Peloponnesian War (Thucydides 1.108.5).

114. Thucydides, 4.42.1–44.5.

115. This reflects the tactic of loading and landing squadrons in the same sequence as the phalanx; triremes carrying the right wing taking the right side of the beachfront and coming ashore first, those holding the other wing landing next and to the left, and any separately embarked auxiliaries pulling onto shore last and farthest left. This mirrored what seems to have been a pattern for linear onshore camps (Xenophon *Hellenica*, 2.4.30), grounded ships in effect also forming an encampment. Such an arrangement facilitated rapid deployment of the phalanx in proper order should the landing come under attack.

116. Herodotus, 8.95; however, much more detail comes from *The Persians* by Aeschylus. The playwright fought at Salamis and likely came ashore on Psyttaleia with his fellow Athenian spearmen. The play describes how "first, came a shower of blows from stones flung with the hand; then from the drawn bowstring arrows leapt forth to slaughter." Finally, the hoplites "armed with bronze shields and spears" moved in "and cut and carved their [the Persians'] limbs like butchers until the last poor wretch lay dead."

117. Thucydides, 4.11.3–12.3; Sheperd, 2013, 43–49.

118. Thucydides, 4.10.5.

119. Diodorus (13.50.5–51.7) is the major source here; neither Plutarch (*Alcibiades*, Vol. I, 280) nor Xenophon (*Hellenica*, 1.1.18) offer much useful detail, the latter being little more than a passing reference.

120. Plutarch gives 40 ships to Alcibiades, perhaps mistaking those of both subordinates for his alone.

Chapter 11

1. Plutarch, *Marcellus*, 21.2; this is a quote from Epaminondas of Thebes.

2. Diodorus, 16.8.7; Demosthenes, *3rd Philippic* 48–49.

3. Ray, 2012, 88–92.

4. Philip had just returned from a long campaign that included unsuccessful investments at Byzantium and elsewhere in the Greek northeast, thus the prospect of having to engage in potentially even more difficult siege efforts against Athens and the like could not have been appealing.

5. Hanson, 2008, 34–35.

6. Hammond, 1994, 148.

7. Diodorus, 17.17.3–5.

8. Diodorus, 16.85.6; though the Greeks had slightly more manpower overall per Justin (9.3.9).

9. Diodorus, 16.85.5.

10. Likely these were the "laggard confederates" mentioned by Diodorus (16.85.5).

11. This was the "subordinate but unknown role" for Philip's horsemen postulated by Gaebel (2002, 157).

12. Diodorus, 16.86.2; Frontinus, 2.1.9.

13. Frontinus, 2.1.9.

14. A move encouraged in that it was inviting to go after the "soft" target of Macedonian backs straight ahead rather than turn against a seemingly much more dangerous line of pivoting mercenary spears.

15. Polyaenus, 4.2.2,7.

16. Plutarch, *Alexander* Vol. II, 145; Rahe, 1981, 85.

17. Thucydides, 5.71.1.

18. van Wees, 2004, 90; see Chap. 2: Physical Training.

19. Asclepiodotus, 10.1; Lazenby, 1989, 71.

20. Thucydides, 5.67.1, 5.68.3.

21. Thucydides, 5.71.3; see Chap. 1: Mantinea I (418).

22. Thucydides, 5.73.1; though complete victory would also require the Spartans to reform and rescue their otherwise beaten left; see Reengagement Maneuvers below.

23. Xenophon, *Hellenica*, 6.4.4–15.; Diodorus, 15.54.6–15.56.4: see Chap. 2: Othismos.

24. Stylianou (1998, 402–403) has proposed that posting of the Sacred Band in 25-man files behind only the farthest left of their fellow citizens at that same depth led to a mistaken report in Xenophon (*Hellenica*, 6.4.22) of the entire Theban contingent being 50 shields deep.

25. Hiding a unit behind the phalanx and then bringing it out for a surprise attack had already been pioneered by the exiled Spartan general Cleandridas c.433 (Polyaenus 2.10.4; Frontinus 2.3.12). See Anderson (1970, 216–219) on the possibility of similar positioning and maneuver of the Theban Sacred Band at Leuctra.

26. Xenophon, *Hellenica*, 6.4.4–15.; Diodorus, 15.54.6–15.56.4: see Chap. 2: Othismos.

27. Onasander, 21.1.

28. Ray, 2009, 301–305; 2012, 221–225: 129 envelopments in 360 engagements (36 percent).

29. In the 5th century there were 47 envelopments in 173 engagements (27 percent), which rose to 82 envelopments in 187 engagements (44 percent) in the 4th century (Ray, 2009).

30. At least 5 percent killed and especially if fatalities reached 10 percent or more.

31. Thucydides, 5.65.1–5.

32. Diodorus, 15.32.5–5; Polyaenus, 2.1.2; Nepos, 12.1.2.

33. Xenophon, *Hellenica*, 6.5.18–19.

34. Asclepiodotus, 10.1; Lazenby (1989, 65, 69).

35. Xenophon, *Hellenica*, 6.2.20–23.

36. It appears that the anastrophe maneuver in this case was designed to deepen a single wing rather than the entire phalanx as was done by Agesilaos a year later.

37. Xenophon, *Hellenica*, 3.5.18–21; Diodorus, 14.81.1–3; Nepos, 6.3.4.

38. It is notable here that Pausanius (3.5.3) offers a

different version of this engagement in which a sally from Haliartus is responsible for Lysander's death. This might be reconciled with the other accounts by adding such a foray from town in support of the Theban advance.

39. Thucydides, 5.59.5.
40. Thucydides, 5.60.3.
41. This is the fellow who famously said that "the Spartans do not ask how many the enemy are, but where they are" and was warned by his father to "either increase your strength, or reduce your self-confidence" (Plutarch Sayings [of Spartans]: Agis son of Archidamus 2; Archidamus son of Zeuxidamus 8).
42. Xenophon, *Hellenica*, 3.2.16; Diodorus 14.39.5.
43. Xenophon, *Anabasis*, 1.10.7–8.
44. Our only confirmed example of a Theban phalanx making a mid-combat withdrawal came against horsemen on the Pherae Road in 368: see Chap. 3: Missilemen: Horsemen and Light/Medium Infantry.
45. A failed withdrawal from combat not specifically identified as such would be indistinguishable from any other defeat.
46. Pausanius, 1.15.1, 2.25.1–2, 10.10.4.
47. Diodorus, 15.65.2; Polyaenus, 2.1.27; Frontinus, 1.10.3: see Ch. 5: River/Stream Impediments.
48. Thucydides, 5.73.4; Plutarch, *Lycurgus* Vol. I, 73.
49. Diodorus, 16.35.1–2.
50. Herodotus, 7.211.
51. Plato, *Laches*, 191 B–C.
52. Onasander, 21.9.
53. Surveys of 5th and 4th century battles (Ray, 2009, 293–297; 2012, 213–224) indicate that only 1.1 percent (4 out of 360) resulted in an acknowledged draw. These were at Cimolia I (458), Mazaros I (454), Laodocium (423), and Mantinea II (362).
54. In fact, some unwary commanders even abetted such folly as per Stratocles at Chaeronea.
55. Thucydides, 3.107.3–108.3.
56. Xenophon (*Constitution of the Lacedaemonians* 11.8) cites this sort of countermarch being practiced by the Spartans, though in the context of refacing for a first attack rather than reengagement.
57. Thucydides, 5.73.2–3.
58. Xenophon, *Hellenica*, 4.2.9–22; Diodorus, 14.83.1–2.
59. This last might have been a natural product, but there is at least a possibility that the Thebans were already developing slightly greater maneuvering skills, emulating Spartan cyclosis as a first step toward the much higher level of formation skills they would later display at Leuctra.
60. Xenophon, *Hellenica*, 4.3.15–21, *Agesilaos*, 2.6–14; Plutarch, *Agesilaos* Vol. II, 52; see Chap. 1: Coronea II (394).
61. Xenophon, *Hellenica*, 4.4.9–12; Diodorus, 14.86.2–4: see Chap. 4: The Long Walls of Corinth (392).
62. Something like the collapse of the Macedonian array at Pydna in 168 reflects a contested advance over rough ground rather than a disorganized pursuit exploited by maneuver. In fact, it is unlikely that phalangite pikemen ever truly "pursued," being extremely ill-equipped for that sort of work.

Chapter 12

1. Herodotus, 7.9.2.
2. Evaluating surveys of engagements in the 5th and 4th centuries (Ray 2009, 289–297; 2012, 213–221) suggests that 21 percent (74 of 360) of all significant hoplite battles during that period involved the tactical use of natural terrain features and that such use was a decisive factor in delivering victory 50 percent of the time (37 of 74).
3. Plutarch, *Timoleon* Vol. I, 327, 348–349; Nepos, 22.1.4.
4. Plutarch, *Timoleon* Vol. I, 330.
5. The timing of this invasion and the subsequent battle at Crimisus River is much disputed, with dates as late as the summer of 339 being proposed.
6. Diodorus, 16.77.2; this upside assumes that the infantry figure here tallied only hoplites, as seems to have been fairly common in such accounts; however, an alternative view that up to 2,000 of this total were light-armed suggests that there might have been as few as 10,000 Greek spearmen initially on hand.
7. Plutarch, *Timoleon* Vol. I, 345.
8. This was near the Greek colony of Egesta (Segesta), whose inhabitants (former and/or recently fled) had likely supplied Timoleon with detailed information on the area.
9. Plutarch (*Timoleon* Vol. I, 345–346) indicates the likelihood of such foreknowledge and planning, as does Timoleon telling his men regarding the Carthaginian camp that "an oracle says that whoever takes position here will be destroyed" (Polyaenus, 5.12.3).
10. Diodorus, 16.78.5.
11. Nepos (22.2.4) simply said that the Carthaginian host was "huge"; Polyaenus (5.12.15) cited 50,000 men, Plutarch (Vol. I *Timoleon*, 345) said 70,000, and Diodorus (16.77.4) 80,000.
12. The trireme was still the standard war galley at this time (Rogers 1937, 203, 212) and could carry some 150 soldiers at most, thus around 30,000 on 200 ships. Sabin (2007, 163) has proposed similar manpower using different criteria and Warmington (1960, 46) has estimated that a like-sized fleet of 200 Punic triremes carried 30,000 combatants on an invasion of Sicily in 480 (see "Himera I" below).
13. Diodorus (16.80.5) indicated 27,500 Carthaginians lost in this campaign, thus a mean of 2,750 each if these filled ten divisions. This is quite possibly a tradition related to the total force "defeated" rather than a count of actual casualties and prisoners.
14. Plutarch *Timoleon* Vol. I, 348.
15. This reflects that each of the 200 or more four-horse chariots present (Diodorus 16.80.5 indicates that many were captured in the battle's wake) had a driver and two archers, normally going into action with a small team of light infantry out-runners as well.
16. These "10,000" or so men were distinguished by their "white shields," the Greeks believing them on that basis and due to the "slowness and order of their march" to be true "Carthaginians" (Plutarch Vol. I *Timoleon*, 346). The shields were either painted or covered in leather/hides of a pale shade; these were perhaps modeled on the gear of Carian mercenaries that in days past had often served in North Africa.
17. Plutarch, *Timoleon* Vol. I, 346.
18. Diodorus, 20.10.6.
19. Plutarch suggests the Sacred Band's width (Vol. I *Timoleon*, 347) with its depth then indicted by a manpower of 2,500 (Diodorus 16.80.4) to 3,000 (Plutarch Vol. I *Timoleon*, 348).
20. Our major surviving sources, Diodorus (16.80.1–5) and Plutarch (Vol. I *Timoleon*, 345–348), differ sig-

nificantly with regard to the battle at Crimisus. The following reconstruction therefore combines elements from both accounts with logical probabilities toward best resolving those conflicts.

21. Wood, 2006, 9–10.

22. Thucydides (3.22.2) cited one of these in 428/427 at Plataea, where Peloponnesians attacking that town took off their right sandal to gain better traction on mud with one bare foot.

23. Diodorus (16.80.4–5) said that the Carthaginians lost 12,500 killed and 15,000 captured; Plutarch (Vol. I *Timoleon*, 348) claimed that 10,000 died, including 3,000 citizens (presumably the entire Sacred Band), but made no mention of prisoners.

24. See, Chap. 2: Mantinea II (362) for an excellent example of this. The anti–Theban coalition here set up across the narrowest part of the long valley hosting Mantinea and Tegea that it might block Epaminondas; and he then maneuvered to similarly bring his own left flank up against bordering high terrain as a ward against possible envelopment via Spartan cyclosis.

25. Herodotus, 7.202–225; Diodorus, 11.6.3–10.4; see Chap. 1: Thermopylae Day 3 (480).

26. Diodorus, 14.12.3–7.

27. Where the Persian pretender Cyrus the Younger would recruit him to lead Xenophon and his famous "10,000" fellow Greek mercenaries into the battle of Cunaxa in 401.

28. Diodorus, 11.20.1–5.

29. Bury, 1900, 302.

30. Diodorus is extremely exaggerated in his claims for Carthaginian manpower here, citing 300,000 men (11.20.2). A much more likely figure based on reported size of the fleet involved is only about 30,000 combatants with maybe two-thirds being heavy infantrymen (see "Crimisus River" above). Even so, this would have been vastly more than was currently on hand in Himera, which could perhaps field no more than 4,000 spearmen plus at most a tenth that each in horsemen, cavalry out-runners (javelineers called "hamippoi"), and light infantry attached to its phalanx (Ray, 2009, 88).

31. Screening their horsemen from the missiles of so many Punic foot skirmishes was not practical.

32. Diodorus, 16.35.4–5.

33. Hammond, 1994, 47.

34. This reflected both proximity to the mountainous sources of the sediment and occasional high flow rates ("flashfloods") characteristic of these arid-country watercourses, which carried away most of the fine-grained elements to leave a residual deposit of the coarsest, hard-to-transport material.

35. One of the current authors can personally attest to this, having limped through a summer field season on a badly turned ankle sustained in attempting to ford just such a babbling brook full of moss-slicked debris.

36. Missilemen on foot could match the range of opposing light infantry and far exceed that of horsemen.

37. Such "heights" not only included sheer cliffs as at Thermopylae and elsewhere, but also gentler features made hard to negotiate by heavy vegetation (in wet climes), erosional detritus littering their lower slopes (having an impact much like rocky streams), etc. However, similar to streambeds, these types of rises often required some reinforcement with light infantry to be truly secure.

38. See Chap. 4: Withdrawal Maneuvers.

39. Herodotus, 9.51.1–3, 9.59.2–9.68; Diodorus, 11.30.4–31.2; Plutarch, *Aristides* Vol. I, 448–450; Bury, 1900, 291; Burn, 1962, 518; Sheperd, 2012, 66–67.

40. The Moleis played a critical role in this, arguably the battle's turning point, since it was a large stone salvaged from its bed and hurled by a Spartan hoplite that slew the Persian leader.

41. Per Burn (1962, 533) based on modern reconstructions of the area; Herodotus (9.51.2) put the separation closer to 2,000m in estimating it at "ten stades." Either width fits the reconstruction offered here, merely affecting how deep the phalanxes would have filed in covering the front associated with each depth.

42. Herodotus, 9.21.3–9.22.1; these bowmen had 300 hoplites in support and probably numbered at least 400, being in addition to other archers deployed at four apiece on each of Athens' triremes. The spearmen probably formed a fronting screen; De Souza (2004, 103) cites an illustration of such a hoplite/archer pair on a late 5th century Athenian vase, showing them in action against a Persian horseman (something that happened near the Asopos a few days earlier).

43. Herodotus, 9.69.

44. This episode marks a rare instance of Greeks failing to employ terrain barriers against Persian (or Persian-allied) cavalry and/or vastly more numerous infantry. The tactic likely became standard as early as the battle of Ephesus (498), then seeing use against other Persian forces at Thermopylae (480), Himera I (480), Plataea (479), Mycale (479), Eion (476), and Eurymedon (c.466). Use of a mountainside to anchor one flank has even been suggested at Marathon (490; see Chap. 4: Field-works). With regard to horsemen, going unanchored was so disparaged among ancient Greeks as to inspire their axiom that anything ill-conceived was "*as foolish as fighting cavalry on the plain.*"

45. See Chap. 4: Barrier Walls and Phalanx Maneuvers for Piraeus/Halae Marsh and Chaeronea respectively; also see Chap. 2: Mantinea II (362).

46. Diodorus, 15.37.1–2; Plutarch, *Pelopidas* Vol. I, 394–396.

47. Pritchett (1982) has a good discussion of this battle's topographic setting.

48. Diodorus, 18.15.2–3; Justin, 13.5.14.

49. His 9,000 (or more) hoplites plus an equal number of their personal baggage carriers and 2,000 light infantrymen would have totaled 20,000 on foot, covering 2.5km at eight across and filed 1m apart. The cavalry would have added another 1km at four wide and a 4m file separation.

50. Thucydides, 4.91.1–4.97.5; Pritchett, 1969, 24–36; see Chap. 2: Delium (424).

51. Diodorus (19.26.5–31.5) describes an episode where a Greek commander (Antigonus in 317 at Paraetacene) used a screening upland to give the impression not that he had fewer troops as in Pagondas' case, but rather that his force was larger than its reality.

52. See Chap. 4: Withdrawal Maneuvers.

53. Xenophon, *Hellenica*, 4.6.7–11.; see Chap. 3: Light Infantry and Horsemen.

54. Albeit often with some difficulty. At Scione in 423 (Thucydides 4.129.2–131.2), Athenian spearmen dislodged a smaller hoplite force from a hill-top. It's notable, however, that they had failed days earlier in a similar attack nearby at Mende. Also, Pelopidas of Thebes led a phalanx upslope to victory in 364 at Cynoscephalae I in Thessaly (Diodorus 15.80.1; Plutarch Vol. II *Pelopidas*, 405), though doing so only after three or four earlier attempts had been repulsed.

55. Indeed, Pagondas came perilously close to losing at Delium despite having both the larger army and a favorable upslope position. He was saved only by a surprise cavalry assault against the rear of an Athenian right wing otherwise rolling uphill toward total triumph.
56. Thucydides, 6.97.2–4.
57. Xenophon, *Hellenica*, 2.4.10–19; it's notable that Xenophon probably witnessed this battle personally as a cavalryman on the losing side.
58. Thucydides, 7.84.2–5.
59. Diodorus, 15.65.2; Polyaenus, 2.1.27; Frontinus, 1.10.3.
60. See Chap. 4: Field-works for descriptions of these three engagements.
61. Xenophon *Hellenica*, 7.4.28–31; Diodorus 15.78.2–3.
62. Plutarch Vol. I *Timoleon*, 350; ironically, Hicetas had been Timoleon's ally of convenience at Crimisus.
63. See Chap. 4: Long Walls of Corinth (392).

Bibliography

Ancient Authors

Aelian (2nd century AD): "On Tactical Arrays of the Greeks," Henry Augustus, ed., *The Tactics of Aelian*, 1814, London: Cox and Baylis.

Aeschines (c.390–c.315): "Against Ctesiphon" in *The Speeches of Aeschines*, 1919, Cambridge, Loeb: Harvard University Press).

Aeschylus (525–456): "The Persians" in *Aeschylus, Prometheus Bound and Other Plays*, 1961, London, Penguin Books.

Archilochus (7th century): "Archilochus" in *Greek Iambic Poetry, from the Seventh to the Fifth Centuries BC* 1999, Cambridge, Loeb, Harvard University Press.

Aristophanes (c.445–c.375): "Peace" in *Aristophanes—The Complete Plays*, 2005, New York, New American Library.

Aristotle (384–322): "Athenian Constitution" in *Aristotle, Vol. XX (Athenian Constitution, Eugemian Ethics, Virtues and Vices)*, 1935, Cambridge, Loeb-Harvard University Press.

Arrian (c.90–c.175 AD): *The Landmark Arrian—The Campaigns of Alexander (Anabasis Alexandrou)*, 2010, New York, Pantheon Books.

Asclepiodotus (1st century): "Asclepiodotus" in *Aeneas Tacticus, Asclepiodotus, Onasander*, 1928, Cambridge, Loeb, Harvard University Press.

Ctesias (late 5th–early 4th centuries): *Ctesias' History of Persia, Tales of the Orient*, 2010, New York, Routledge.

Curtius (died 53 AD): *The History of Alexander*, 1984, London, Penguin Books.

Demosthenes (c.384–322): "The Third Philippic" in *Demosthenes, Vol. I: Olynthiacs, Philipics, Minor Public Orations*, 1930, Loeb, Harvard University Press.

Diodorus (c.80–c.20): *Diodorus Siculus, Vol. IV–X (Books XI–XX)*, 1946–1953, Cambridge, Loeb, Harvard University Press.

Dionysius (late 1st century BC–early 1st century AD): *Dionysius of Halicarnassus Roman Antiquities, Vol. II (Books III–IV), Vol. VII (Book XI, Excerpts Books XII–XX*, 1939–1950, Cambridge, Loeb, Harvard University Press.

Euripides (c.485–c.405): "Heracles" in *Euripides III: Heracles, the Trojan Women, Iphigenia Among the Taurians, Ion*, 2013, Chicago, University of Chicago Press.

Frontinus (c.35–c.104): "The Stratagems" in *Frontinus: Stratagems, Aqueducts of Rome*, 1925, Cambridge, Loeb, Harvard University Press.

Herodotus (5th century): *The Landmark Herodotus—The Histories*, 2007, New York, Pantheon Books.

Homer (8th century): *The Iliad*, 1990, London, Penguin Books.

Justin (2nd–4th centuries AD, summarizing Pompeius Trogus, late 1st century BC–early 1st century AD): *Justin, Epitome of the Philippic History of Pompeius Trogus*, 1994, Atlanta, Scholars Press.

Livy (59 BC–17 AD): *Livy, the War with Hannibal, Books XXI-XXX of the History of Rome from its Foundation*, 1965, London, Penguin Books; *Livy, Rome's Mediterranean Empire: Books 41–45 and the Periochae*, 2010, Oxford University Press.

Maurice (6th century AD): Maurice's Strategicon: Handbook of Byzantine Military Strength. G.T. Dennis, ed., 1984, Philadelphia, University of Pennsylvania Press.

Nepos (c.99–c.24): *Cornelius Nepos*, 1929, Cambridge, Loeb, Harvard University Press.

Onasander (died 59 AD): "The General" in *Aeneas Tacitus, Asclepiodotus, Onasander*, 1928, Cambridge, Loeb, Harvard University Press.

Orosius (born c.385): *Seven Books of History against the Pagans, the Apology of Paulus Orosius*, New York, Columbia University Press.

Oxyrhynchus Historian (4th century BC): *Hellenica Oxyrhynchia*: 1988, Oxford, Oxbow Books.
Pausanius (2nd century AD): Pausanius, *Description of Greece, Vol. I–IV*, 1918–1935, Cambridge, Loeb, Harvard University Press.
Philostratos (c.170–c.250 AD): "*Gymnasticus*" in *Philostratus: Heroicus, Gymnasticus, Discourse 1 and 2*, 2014, Cambridge, Loeb, Harvard University Press.
Pindar (518–c.448): *The Odes of Pindar, including Principal Fragments*, 1946, Cambridge, Loeb, Harvard University Press.
Plato (c.429–347): "*Laches*" in *Plato—Laches and Charmides*, 1973, Indianapolis, Hackett; "Symposium" in *Great Dialogues of Plato*, 1999, New York, Signet.
Pliny the Elder (1st c. AD): "*Natural History*" in 2004, Oxford, T.M. Murphy; *Pliny the Elder's Natural History: The Empire in the Encyclopedia*, Oxford University Press.
Plutarch (born before 50 AD, died after 120 AD): *Plutarch's Lives, Vol. I and II*, 2001, New York, Modern Library; *Lives*, Vol. 5, 1917, Cambridge, Loeb Harvard University Press; *The Moralia*, 2012, CreateSpace; "Sayings [of Spartans]" in *Plutarch on Sparta*, 1988, London, Penguin.
Pollux, Julius, of Naucratis (2nd century AD) 1824 Wilhelm Dindorf, Leipzig, Kuehn.
Polyaenus (died before 271): *Polyaenus, Stratagems of War, Vol. I (Books I–V) and Volume II (Books VI–VIII, Excerpts, and Leo the Emperor)*, 1994, Chicago, Ares.
Polybios (c.200–c.118): *The Histories, Vol. I–IV*, 1922–1925, Cambridge, Loeb, Harvard University Press.
Sophocles (c. 497–406 BC): Vol. I *Oedipus the King/Oedipus at Colonus/Antigone*, 1977 (trans. F. Storr), Cambridge, Harvard University Press, Loeb Classic Library.
Strabo (c.64 BC–c.25 AD): *The Geography of Strabo, Vol. IV (Books VIII–IX), Vol. VII (Books XV–XVI)*, Cambridge, Loeb, Harvard University Press.
Thucydides (c.460–c.410): *The Landmark Thucydides, A Comprehensive Guide to the Peloponnesian War*, 1996, New York, The Free Press.
Tyrtaeus (7th century): "Tyrtaeus" in *Greek Elegiac Poetry: From the Seventh to the Fifth Centuries BC*, 1999, Cambridge, Loeb, Harvard University Press.
Xenophon (c.428–c.354): *The Landmark Xenophon's Hellenika*, 2009, New York, Pantheon Books—note that due to a translation error in the above (4.5.12) see also *Xenophon, Hellenica, Vol. I (Books I–IV)*, Cambridge, Loeb, Harvard University Press; "Agesilaus," "Constitution of the Lacedaemonians," "On Hunting," "On the Cavalry Commander," in *Xenophon Vol. VII, Scripta Minora*, 1968, Cambridge, Loeb, Harvard University Press; *Anabasis*, 1922, Cambridge, Loeb (Harvard University Press); *Cyropaedia, Vol. V (Books 1–4)*, 1914, Cambridge, Loeb, Harvard University Press; "Memorabilia" and "Symposium" in *Xenophon, Vol. IV (Memorabilia, Oeconomicus, Symposium, Apology)*, 2013, Cambridge, Loeb, Harvard University Press.
Zonaras (12th century AD): *The History of Zonaras from Alexander Severus to the Death of Theodosius the Great*, 2011, New York, Routledge.

Modern Authors

Aldrete, G.S., S. Bartell, and A. Aldrete, 2013: *Reconstructing Ancient Linen Body Armor*, Baltimore, Johns Hopkins University Press.
Anderson, J.K., 1970: *Military Theory and Practice in the Age of Xenophon*, Berkeley, University of California Press.
Anderson, J.K., 1974: *Xenophon: Classical Life and Letters*, New York, Scribner's.
Anderson, J.K., 1991: "Hoplite Weapons and Offensive Arms," in V. D. Hanson ed., *Hoplites: The Classical Greek Battle Experience*, London, 25.
Anson, E.M., 2010: "The Asthetairoi: Macedonia's Hoplites," in E. Carney and D. Ogden (eds.), *Philip II and Alexander the Great: Father and Son, Lives and Afterlives*, Oxford University Press, 81–90.
Asheri, D., 2004: "Sicily, 478–431 BC," in *Ancient Greek Democracy: Readings and Sources*, E.W. Robinson, ed., Oxford, Blackwell Pub. Ltd.
Bagnall, N., 2004: *The Peloponnesian War: Athens, Sparta, and the Struggle for Greece*, New York, St. Martin's.
Balfour, D., 2010: "Boeotian Crack Troops: The Theban Sacred Band," in *Ancient Warfare*, Vol. 4, Issue 3 (June).
Bakhuizen, S.C., 2010: "Greek Steel," *World Archaeology*, 9:2, 220–234.
Bardunias, P.M., 2007 "The Aspis: Surviving Hoplite Battle," in *Ancient Warfare*, Vol. 1, Issue 3 (June).
Bardunias, P.M., 2010: "Don't Get Stuck on Glued Linen," in *Ancient Warfare*, Vol. 4, Issue 3 (June).
Bardunias, P.M., 2011: "The Mechanics of Hoplite Battle: Storm of Spears and Press of Shields," in *Ancient Warfare*, The Battle of Marathon, Special Issue.
Best, J.G.P., 1969: *Thracian Peltasts and Their Influence on Greek Warfare*, Groningen, Netherlands, Wolters-Noordhoff Groningen.

Blyth, H., 1977: *The Effectiveness of Greek Armor Against Arrows in the Persian War (490–479 BC): An Interdisciplinary Enquiry*, Ph.D. Thesis, University of Reading.
Blyth, H., 1982: "The Structure of a Hoplite Shield in the Museo Gregoriano Etrusco," *Bollettinio dei musei e gallerie pontifice*, Tipografia Poliglotta Vaticana.
Bosworth, A.B., 2010: "The Argeads and the Phalanx," in E. Carney and D. Ogden, eds., *Philip II and Alexander the Great: Father and Son, Lives and Afterlives*, Oxford University Press, 91–102.
Bowden, H., 1993: "Hoplites and Homer: Warfare, Hero Cult, and the Ideology of the Polis," in Rich, J., and G. Shipley (eds.), *War and Society in the Greek World*, New York, Routledge, 45–63.
Briere, J., and C.E. Jordan, 2009: "Childhood Maltreatment, Intervening Variables, and Adult Psychological Difficulties in Women: An Overview," in *Trauma, Violence, and Abuse*, Vol. 10, No. 4.
Brouwers, J., 2013: *Henchmen of Ares: Warriors and Warfare in Early Greece*, Rotterdam, Karwansaray BV.
Burn, A.R., 1962: *Persia and the Greeks*, London, Duckworth.
Bury, J.B. 1900: *A History of Greece to the Death of Alexander*, London, Macmillan.
Camazine, S., 2003: *Self-organization in Biological Systems*, Princeton Studies in Complexity, Princeton, Princeton University Press.
Campbell, D., 2003: *Greek and Roman Artillery 399 BC–AD 363*, Oxford, Osprey.
Carney, E., 1996: "Macedonians and Mutiny: Discipline and Indiscipline in the Army of Philip and Alexander," in *Classical Philology* 91:1, 19–44.
Cartledge, P., 1979: *Sparta and Lakonia: A Regional History 1300–362 BC*, 2nd ed., London, Routledge.
Cartledge, P., 1987: *Agesilaos and the Crisis of Sparta*, Baltimore, Johns Hopkins University Press.
Case, A., and A. Deaton, 2015: "Rising morbidity and mortality in midlife among white non–Hispanic Americans in the 21st century," in *PNAS Early Edition*.
Caven, B., 1990: *Dionysius, War-Lord of Sicily*, New Haven, Yale University Press.
Cawkwell, G.L., 1978: *Philip of Macedon*, London, Faber and Faber.
Cole, J., 1981: "The Catapult Bolts of 'IG' 22 1422" in *Phoenix* 35:3 (Autumn 1981), 216–219.
Connolly, P., 1977: *The Greek Armies*. London, Macdonald Educational.
Connolly, P., D. Sim, and C. Watson, 2001: "An Evaluation of the Effectiveness of Three Methods of Spear Grip Used in Antiquity," *Journal of Battlefield Technology*, 4, 2.
Cook, B.F., "Footwork in Ancient Greek Swordsmanship," *Metropolitan Museum Journal*, 24, 57–64.
Dahm, M., 2013: *The Shield Wall of Waldere, Medieval Warfare*, 5, 1 49–52.
Dawson, D., 1996: *The Origins of Western Warfare: Militarism and Morality in the Ancient World*, Boulder, Westview Press.
DeGroote, K.R., 2016: "'Twas when my shield turned traitor'! Establishing the Combat Effectiveness of the Greek Hoplite Shield," *Oxford Journal of Archaeology*, 35(2) 197–212.
Delbruck, H., 1990: *Warfare in Antiquity: History of the Art of War, Vol. I*, Lincoln: University of Nebraska Press (first published 1921).
De Sousa, P., W. Heckel, and L. Llewellyn-Jones, 2004: *The Greeks at War: From Athens to Alexander*, Oxford, Osprey.
Dixon, B.J., and L. Vasey, "Beards Augment Perceptions of Men's Age, Social Status, and Aggressiveness, but Not Attractiveness." *Behavioral Ecology* 23:3, 481–490.
Drews, R., 1993: *The End of the Bronze Age: Changes in Warfare and the Catastrophe ca. 1200 BC*, Princeton, Princeton University Press.
Ducrey, P., 1985: *Warfare in Ancient Greece*, New York, Schocken Books.
Engels, D.W., 1978: *Alexander the Great and the Logistics of the Macedonian Army*, Berkeley, University of California Press.
Ferrill, A., 1985: *The Origins of War from the Stone Age to Alexander the Great*, London, Thames and Hudson.
Foxhall L., 1993: "Farming and Fighting in Ancient Greece," in *War and Society in the Greek World*, J. Rich and G. Shipley (eds.), London, Routledge.
Frasier, A.D., 1943: "Myth of the Phalanx-Scrimmage," *Classical Weekly* 36, 15–16.
Freeman, E.A. (and A.J. Evens, ed.), 1894: *The History of Sicily, from the Earliest Times, Vol. IV*, New York, Clarendon Press.
Fruin, J.J., 2002: "The Causes and Prevention of Crowd Disasters," at crowdsafe.com (revised from an original presentation at *The First International Conference on Engineering for Crowd Safety*, London, March 1993).
Gabriel, R.A., and K.S. Metz, 1991: *From Sumer to Rome: The Military Capabilities of Ancient Armies*, Westport, CT, Greenwood Press.
Gaebel, R.E., 2002: *Cavalry Operations in the Ancient Greek World*, Norman, University of Oklahoma Press.
Galea, S., A. Nandi, and D. Vlahov, 2004: "The Epidemiology of Post-Traumatic Stress Disorder after Disasters," *Epidemiologic Reviews* 27:1.
Garnsey, 1988: *Famine and Food Supply in the Graeco-Roman World: Responses to Risk and Crisis*, Cambridge, Cambridge University Press.

Bibliography

Gleba, M., 2012: "Linen-clad Etruscan Warriors," in Marie-Louise Nosch ed., *Wearing the Cloak: Dressing the Soldier in Roman Times*, Oxford, Oxbow Books.
Goldsworthy, A.K., 1996: *The Roman Army at War, 100 BC–AD 200*, Oxford: Clarendon Press.
Goldsworthy, A. K., 1997: "The Othismos, Myths and Heresies: The Nature of Hoplite Battle." *War in History* 4, 1–26.
Gome, A.W., 1933: *The Population of Athens in the Fifth and Fourth Centuries BC*, Oxford, Blackwell Pub. Ltd.
Grant, M., 1987: *The Rise of the Greeks*, New York, Collier Books.
Griffith, G.T., 1935: *The Mercenaries of the Hellenistic World*, Chicago, Ares.
Grossman, D., 1995: *On Killing: The Psychological Cost of Learning to Kill in War and Society*, New York, Little, Brown.
Grossman, D., and L.W. Christensen, 2004: *On Combat: The Psychology and Physiology of Deadly Conflict in War and in Peace*, U.S.A., PPCT Research Publications.
Grundy, G.B., 1961: *Thucydides and the History of His Age*, 2nd ed., Oxford, Basil Blackwood.
Hamilton, C.D., 1979: *Sparta's Bitter Victories: Politics and Diplomacy in the Corinthian War*, Ithaca, Cornell University Press.
Hammond, N.G.L., 1994: *Philip of Macedon*, Baltimore: Johns Hopkins University Press.
Hansen, M.H., 2011: "How to Convert an Army Figure into a Population Figure," in *Greek, Roman, and Byzantine Studies* 51 (2011), 239–253.
Hanson, V.D., 1991: *Hoplites: The Classical Greek Battle Experience*, London, Routledge.
Hanson, V.D., 1995: *The Other Greeks: The Family Farm and the Agrarian Roots of Western Civilization*, New York, Free Press.
Hanson, V.D., 2008: "New Light on Ancient Battles," in *Military History Quarterly* 20:2, 28–35.
Head, D., 1982: *Armies of the Macedonian and Punic Wars 359–148 BC*, Goring-by-Sea, Wargames Research Group.
Heckel, W., 2002: *The Wars of Alexander the Great*, Oxford, Osprey.
Heckel, W., 2006: "Mazaeus, Callisthenes and the Alexander Sarcophagus," in *Historia* Band 55/4, 385–396.
Heckel, W., and R. Jones, 2006: *Macedonian Warrior, Alexander's Elite Infantryman*, Oxford, Osprey.
Heckel, W., C. Willekes, and G. Wrightson, 2010: "Scythed Chariots at Gaugamela: A Case Study," in E. Carney and D. Ogden, eds., *Philip II and Alexander the Great: Father and Son, Lives and Afterlives*, New York, Oxford University Press, 103–109.
Hilbert, C., 2012: *The Sacred Band of Thebes, and Other Stuff*, CreateSpace Independent Publishing Platform.
Holliday, A.J., 1982: "Hoplites and Heresies," *Journal of Hellenic Studies*, 102, 94–103.
Holmes, R., 1985: *Acts of War: The Behavior of Men in Battle*, New York, Free Press.
Hooker, J.T., 1980: *The Ancient Spartans*, London, J.M. Dent and Sons.
Hornblower, S., 1991–2008: *A Commentary on Thucydides*, 3 Vols., Oxford, Clarendon Press.
Hornblower, S., and A. Spawforth, 1996: *The Oxford Classical Dictionary*, 3rd ed., New York, Oxford University Press.
Howatson, M.C., ed., 1991: *The Oxford Companion to Classical Literature*, New York, Oxford University Press.
Hurwit, J.M., 2002, "Reading the Chigi," *Hesperia* 71:1, 1–22.
Huxley, G.L., 1962: *Early Sparta*, London, Faber & Faber.
Jarva, E., 1995: *Archaiologia on Archaic Greek Body Armor*, Rovaniemi, Pohjois-suomen Historiallinen Yhdistys, Societas Historica Finlandiae Septentrionalis.
Kagan, D., 1974: *The Archidamian War*, Ithaca, Cornell University Press.
Kagan, D., and G.F. Viggiano, 2013: *Men of Bronze: Hoplite Warfare in Ancient Greece*, Princeton, Princeton University Press.
Keegan, J., 1976: *The Face of Battle*, New York, Viking Press.
Kennell, N.M., 1995: *The Gymnasium of Virtue: Education and Culture in Ancient Sparta*, Chapel Hill, University of North Carolina Press.
Kilpatrick, D.G., 2000: "The Mental Health Impact of Rape," National Violence Against Women Research Center, Medical University of South Carolina.
Knight, I.J., 1994: *Warrior Chiefs of Southern Africa*, Poole, Firebird Books.
Knight, I.J., 1995: *The Anatomy of the Zulu Army: From Shaka to Cetshwayo 1818–1879*, London, Greenhill Books.
Konecny, A., 2014: "The Battle of Lechaeum, Early Summer, 390 BC," in *Iphicrates, Peltasts, and Lechaeum*, N.V. Sekunda and B. Burliga, eds., Gdansk, University of Gdansk, 7–48.
Krentz, P., 1985: "Casualties in Hoplite Battles," *Greek, Roman and Byzantine Studies* 26, 13–20.
Krentz, P., 2002: "Fighting by the Rules: The Invention of the Hoplite Agon," *Hesperia* 71, 23–29.
Krentz, P., 2010: "A Cup by Douris and the Battle of Marathon," in *New Perspectives on Ancient Warfare*, Garrett G. Fagan and Matthew Trundle, eds., Leiden, Brill, 183–204.

Kromayer, J., and G. Veith (ed. R. Gabriel), 2008: *Schlachten-Atlas zur Antiken Kriegsgeschichte, The Battle Atlas of Ancient Military History*, Kingston, Ontario, Canadian Defence Academy Press.
Lazenby, J.F., 1985: *The Spartan Army*, 2012 republication, Mechanicsburg, Stackpole Books.
Lazenby, J.F., 1989: "Hoplite Warfare," in *Warfare in the Ancient World*, J. Hackett, ed., New York, Facts on File, 54–81.
Lendon, J.E., 2005: *Soldiers and Ghosts: A History of Battle in Classical Antiquity*, New Haven, CT, Yale University Press.
Liddel, H.G., and R. Scott, 1900: *An Intermediate Greek-English Lexicon*, Clarendon Press.
Lim, L.B., 1995: "Experiments to Investigate the Level of 'Comfortable' Loads for People Against Crush Barriers," *Safety Science* 18, 329–335.
Lorimer, H.L., 1947: "The Hoplite Phalanx with Special Reference to the Poems of Archilochos and Tyrtaeus," *The Annual of the British School at Athens*, 42, 76–138.
Luginbill, R.D., 1994: "Othismos: The Importance of the Mass-Shove in Hoplite Warfare," *Phoenix* 48:1, 51–61.
Ma, J., 2008: "Chaironeia 338: Topographies of Commemoration," *Journal of Hellenic Studies* 128, 72–91.
Manning M.M., A. Hawk, J.H. Calhoun, and R.C. Andersen, 2009: "Treatment of War Wounds: A Historical Review," in *Clinical Orthopedics and Related Research*, Vol. 467, no. 8. (August), 2168–2191.
Manti, P., 2011: "Shiny Helmets: Investigation of Tinning, Manufacture and Corrosion of Greek Helmets (7th–5th c. BC), Ph.D. thesis, Cardiff University.
Marsden, E.W., 1969: *Greek and Roman Artillery: Historical Development*, New York, Oxford University Press.
Matthew, C., 2012: *A Storm of Spears: Understanding the Greek Hoplite at War*, Barnsley, Pen & Sword Military.
McGregor, M.F., 1987: *The Athenians and Their Empire*, Vancouver, University of British Columbia Press.
McInerney, J., 1999: *The Folds of Parnassus: Land and Ethnicity in Ancient Phocis*, Austin, University of Texas Press.
McNeil W.H., 2009: *Keeping Together in Time: Dance and Drill in Human History*, Cambridge, Harvard University Press.
Mitchell, S., 1996: "Hoplite Warfare in Ancient Greece," in Lloyd, A.B. ed., *Battle in Antiquity*, London, Duckworth, 87–105.
Montagu, J.D., 2000: *Battles of the Greek & Roman Worlds*, London, Greenhill Books.
Morales, J.A., 2013: "The War of the Heavenly Horses," in *Ancient Warfare* 7:1, 46–51.
Muir, R., 1998: *Tactics and the Experience of Battle in the Age of Napoleon*, New Haven, Yale University Press.
Muller, U., and A. Mazur, 1996: "Facial Dominance of West Point Cadets as a Predictor of Later Military Rank," *Social Forces* 74:3, 823–850.
Munn, M.H., 1993: *The Defense of Attica: The Dema Wall and the Boiotian War of 378–379 BC*, Berkeley, University of California Press.
Murray, S.R., W.A. Sands, and D.A. O'Rourk, 2011: "Throwing the Ancient Greek Dory: How Effective Is the Ankyle at Increasing the Distance of a Throw?" *Palamedes*, 6.
Ober, J., 1991: "Hoplites and Obstacles," in *Hoplites: The Classical Greek Battle Experience*, V.D. Hanson, ed., London, Routledge, 173–196.
O'Neill, B.E., 2005: *Insurgency & Terrorism: From Revolution to Apocalypse*, 2nd ed. (revised), Washington, D.C., Potomac.
Paddock, J.M., 1993: *The Bronze Italian Helmet: The Development of the Cassis from the Last Quarter of the Sixth Century BC to the Third Quarter of the First Century AD*, Ph. D. Thesis, University of London.
Parke, H.W., 1933: *Greek Mercenary Soldiers: From the Earliest Times to the Battle of Ipsus*, Chicago, Ares Pub. Inc.
Parsons, A.W., 1936: "The Long Walls to the Gulf," in *Corinth*, Vol. III, Part II (R. Carpenter and A. Bon: "The Defenses of Acrocorinth and the Lower Town"), Cambridge, Harvard University Press, 84–127.
Plourde, A.M., 2008: "The Origins of Prestige Goods as Honest Signals of Skill and Knowledge," *Human Nature* 19:4, 374–388.
Pritchett, W.K., 1969: *Studies in Ancient Greek Topography, Part II (Battlefields)*, University of California Press, Berkeley.
Pritchett, W.K., 1971: *The Greek State at War, Part I*, Berkeley, University of California Press.
Pritchett, W.K., 1974: *The Greek State at War, Part II*, Berkeley, University of California Press.
Pritchett, W.K., 1979: *The Greek State at War, Part III*, Berkeley, University of California Press.
Pritchett, W.K., 1982: *Studies in Ancient Greek Topography, Part IV (Passes)*, Berkeley, University of California Press.
Pritchett, W.K., 1991: *Studies in Ancient Greek Topography, Part V*, Berkeley, University of California Press.
Raaflaub, K., 1999: "Archaic and Classical Greece," in *War and Society in the Ancient and Medieval Worlds: Asia, the Mediterranean, Europe, and Mesoamerica*, K. Raaflaub and N. Rosenstein, eds., 129–162, Washington, D.C., Center for Hellenic Studies, Trustees for Harvard University.

Rahe, A., 1981: "The Annihilation of the Sacred Band at Chaeronea," in *American Journal of Archaeology*, Vol. 85, No. 1 (January): 84–87.

Rance, 2004: "The *Fulcum*, the Late Roman and Byzantine *Testudo*: The Germanization of Roman Infantry Tactics?" *Greek, Roman, and Byzantine Studies*, 44, 265–326.

Ray, F.E., 2009: *Land Battles in 5th Century BC Greece: A History and Analysis of 173 Engagements*, Jefferson, NC, McFarland.

Ray, F.E., 2012: *Greek and Macedonian Land Battles of the 4th Century BC: A History and Analysis of 187 Engagements*, Jefferson, NC, McFarland.

Ray, F.E., 2013: "Revolutionary Episodes at Syracuse in the 5th Century BCE: Some Political and Military Aspects of Ancient Greek Insurgency," *The Ancient World* 45:1, 30–43.

Ray, F.E., 2014: "Some Observations Regarding the Analysis of Artistic Data," in "Christopher Matthew's flawed analysis of the mechanics of hoplite combat: 1," Bardunias, *Hollow Lakedaimon: The Online Phitidion* (http://hollow-lakedaimon.blogspot.com).

Rees, O., and J. Crowley, 2015: "Was There Mental Trauma in Ancient Warfare? PTSD in Ancient Greece," in *Ancient Warfare* 9:4.

Resnick, H.S., and D.G. Kilpatrick, 1994: "Crime-related PTSD: Emphasis on Adult General Population Samples," *PTSD Research Quarterly* 5:3.

Roach, N.T., M. Venkadesan, M.J. Rainbow, and D.E. Lieberman, "Elastic Storage in the Shoulder and the Evolution of High-Speed Throwing in *Homo*," *Nature* 27, 483–6.

Rosen, B.A., C.H. Nam Laufer, D.P., Kalman, E.D.Wetzel, and N.J. Wagner, 2007: "Multi-threat Performance of Kaolin-Based Shear Thickening Fluid (STF)-Treated Fabrics," *Proceedings of SAMPE*, Baltimore, MD.

Salazar, C.F., 1999: *The Treatment of War Wounds in Graeco-Roman Antiquity*, Leiden, Brill Academic Publishers.

Sancho-Bru, J.L., D.J. Giurintano, A. Perez-Gonzalez, and M. Vergara, 2003: "Optimum Tool Handle Diameter for a Cylindrical Grip," *Journal of Hand Therapy* 16, 337–42.

Saxton, K.T, L.L. Mackey, K. McCarty, and N. Neave, 2015: "A Lover or a Fighter? Opposing Sexual Selection Pressures on Men's Vocal Pitch and Facial Hair," *Behavioral Ecology*, arv 178.

Schwartz, A., 2009: *Reinstating the Hoplite: Arms, Armour and Phalanx Fighting in Archaic and Classical Greece*, Historia Einzelschriften 207, Stuttgart, Franz Steiner Verlag.

Schwartz, A., 2013: "Large Weapons, Small Greeks: The Practical Limitations of Hoplite Weapons and Equipment," in D. Kagan and G.F. Viggiano, eds., *Men of Bronze: Hoplite Warfare in Ancient Greece*, 157–175, Princeton, Princeton University Press.

Sekunda, N., 1998: *The Spartan Army*, Oxford, Osprey.

Sekunda, N., 2006: *Hellenistic Infantry Reform in the 160's BC*, University of Gdansk.

Sekunda, N., 2012: *Macedonian Armies After Alexander 323–168 BC*, Oxford, Osprey.

Sekunda, N., 2014: "The Composition of the Lakedaimonian Mora at Lechaeum," in N.V. Sekunda and B. Burliga, eds., *Iphicrates, Peltasts, and Lechaeum*, Gdansk, University of Gdansk, 49–65.

Sekunda, N., and S. Chew, 1992: *The Persian Army 560–330 BC*, Oxford, Osprey.

Shay, J., 1994: *Achilles in Vietnam: Combat Trauma and the Undoing of Character*, New York, Simon & Schuster.

Shay, J., 2002: *Odysseus in America, Combat Trauma and the Trials of Homecoming*, New York, Scribner.

Shepherd, W., 2012: *Plataea 479 BC: The Most Glorious Victory Ever Seen*, Oxford, Osprey.

Shepherd, W., 2013: *Pylos and Sphacteria 425 BC: Sparta's Island of Disaster*, Oxford, Osprey.

Smith, G., 1919: "Athenian Casualty Lists," *Classical Philology* 14:4 (October), 351–364.

Snodgrass, A.M., 1964: *Early Greek Armor and Weapons*, Edinburgh, Edinburgh University Press.

Snodgrass, A.M., 1967: *Arms and Armor of the Greeks*, Ithaca, Cornell University Press.

Spence, I.G., 1993: *The Cavalry of Classical Greece: A Social and Military History with Particular Reference to Athens*, Oxford, Clarendon Press.

Stamatopoulou, V., 2004: "Hoplon: The Argolic Shield and Its Technology," Ph.D. Thesis, Aristotle University of Thessaloniki.

Stylianou, J., 1998: *A Historical Commentary on Diodorus Siculus Book 15*, New York, Oxford University Press.

Talbert, R.J.A. (trans.), 1988: *Plutarch on Sparta*, London, Penguin.

Tomlinson, R.A., 1972: *Argos and the Argolid: From the End of the Bronze Age to the Roman Occupation*, Ithaca, Cornell University Press.

Tritle, J.A., 2000: *From Melos to My Lai: War and Survival*, London, Routledge.

Van Wees, H., 2004: *Greek Warfare: Myths and Realities*, London: Duckworth.

Vernant, J.P., 1991: "Between Shame and Glory: The Identity of the Young Spartan Warrior," in Zeitlin, F.I., ed., *Mortals and Immortals: Collected Essays*, Princeton, Princeton University Press, 220–243.

Webber, C., 2011: *The Gods of Battle: The Thracians at War 1500 BC–AD 150*, Barnsley, Pen & Sword Military.

Wheeler, E.L., 1991: "The General as Hoplite," in Hanson, V.D., ed., *Hoplites: The Classical Greek Battle Experience*, London, Routledge, 121–170.
Williams, A., 2003: *The Knight and the Blast Furnace—A History of the Metallurgy of Armour in the Middle Ages and Early Modern Period*. Leiden, Brill.
Wise, T., and R. Hook, 1982: *Armies of the Carthaginian Wars 265–146 BC*, Oxford, Osprey.
Wood, C.E., 2006: *Mud: A Military History*, Washington, D.C., Potomac.
Worthington, I., 2008: *Philip II of Macedonia*, New Haven, Yale University Press.
Yalichev, S., 1997: *Mercenaries of the Ancient World*, London, Constable & Co. Ltd.

Index

abatis 56
Acarnania 147, 162, 186, 204
Achaea 75, 162, 187, 216
Achilles 14, 47, 129, 194, 205, 208, 212
Acraean Bald Rock (413) 57–58, 95
Aegitium (426) 148
Aemilius Paulus 155, 216
Agathocles 71, 202, 207
agathos (good man) 91
agema 163, 201
Agesilaos 79, 94, 99, 117, 123–126, 140, 142, 169, 174, 186–187, 198, 202, 205, 207–208, 211–213, 217–218
Agis 108–109, 152, 166, 168, 170, 173, 186, 209–210
agoge 74, 91, 206
Aidolios/Edolos 200
Aigaleos Ridge 52
Aigina 88–89, 94, 100, 196, 206
akinakes (sword) 194
akontion (javelin) 13-Dec
Alcibiades 158–159, 195, 217
Alesion, Mount 209
Alexander (of Epirus) 153–154-215
Alexander III (the Great) 45, 57, 60, 70–71. 84, 103, 143, 145–146, 149, 151, 153, 155, 163, 187, 190
Alexander Sarcophogus 214
Alexander son of Akmetos 216
Alexandria Eschate 145, 217
alpha 195
Amasis (king of Egypt) 44, 45
amphibious 140, 157
Amphipolis 123, 152
amphora 14, 56
Amyklai 99, 140, 171, 187
anastrophe 169
Anatolian helmets 40
Anchimolios 193
andreia (manly virtue) 91
ankyle 12, 13
Anopaia Path 8, 11, 59, 181, 215
Antigonus 153, 219
antilabe 30, 32, 33
Apollo 25, 140
Apollonia 152, 215

apron (for shield) 34
Arcadia 76, 82, 141, 153, 187, 199, 201, 207
Archidamian War 106–197, 144
Archidamus (son of Agesilaos) 59, 207, 210
Archidamus (son of Zeuxidamus) 209, 218
Archilochus 206
Ares 160, 208
arete (courage) 91
argilos armor 45
Argive shield (aspis) 29, 112
Argos 106–109, 124, 168, 171, 187, 191, 198, 199–200, 209–210
Aristides 184, 193
Aristodemos (of Argos) 29
Aristodemos (of Sparta) 206
Aristonous 215
Artayntes 37
aryballos 29
Asculum (279) 154, 156, 215–216
ash (wood) 15
Asopos River 184
aspis, aspides 29, 32, 34, 35, 112, 117, 118, 134, 156, 166
Assinarus River (413) 186
Athens 106, 109, 113, 123, 140, 144, 147, 153, 157, 158, 161–162, 165, 171, 173–174, 186, 193–196, 199–201, 203–204, 209, 213–214, 217, 219
Attic helmet 41
Attica 12, 37, 54, 56, 60, 65, 94, 152, 193, 203, 205, 209

baivarabam, baivaraba 10, 37, 194, 197
Battle of the Champions (545) 199
Battle of the Fetters (590–580) 199
battleaxes 23
belly-bows 59
Beneventum (275) 154
bodyguards 10, 68, 196, 211
Boeotia 12, 24–25, 36–37, 66, 74–76, 78, 96–98, 123, 126, 145, 161, 169, 173–174, 184, 194–195, 209
Boeotian War 57, 74–75

Bomarzo shield 30
Brasidas 148
Brasidoi 107
brass (copper-zince alloy) 33
bronze (copper-tin alloy) 33
Byzantium 181–182, 217

Cacyparis River (413) 38
Callias 140–141
Callicrates 197, 204
Cambyses 193
Cannae (216) 216
Carthage 100, 156, 176, 179, 213
Cassander 215
catalogos 66
Celts 35, 152–153, 177, 215
Cephesus River 123, 160
Chaeronea (338) 81, 85, 92, 150–151, 160–163, 167–169, 171–172, 174, 198, 203–204, 209, 214–215-218–219
Chalcidian Federation 209
Chalcidian helmet 41
Chalcidian steel 21
Chalcidice 144, 202, 213
Chalcis 64, 193, 199
chalkaspides 216
Chaonian (Epirote tribe) 215
charioteers and footmen (Thebes) 26, 67, 195
chariots 144, 149, 177, 182, 201, 208, 213–214, 218
chase instinct 208
Chigi vase 12, 46, 119
Chios 196
chokepoint 7, 8
Cimolia I/II (458) 87, 89–92, 97, 101, 201, 206, 218
circumvallation 52
Cladaus River 187
Clearchus 103, 182
Cleomenes I 56, 60, 62–63, 99, 193, 200, 204
Cleomenes III 38, 202, 207
Cleonai 62, 107–108
Coapais, Lake 123–124, 184, 211
Corcyra 65, 162, 169, 201, 211
Corhagus 152
Corinth 11, 29, 48–52, 54–55, 57–58, 60, 62, 68, 85, 88–90, 94,

229

Index

101, 106, 123, 126, 148, 162, 174, 176–177, 191, 196, 199, 200–201, 206, 209, 211–212, 217
Corinth, Long Walls (392) 48–51, 54–55, 60, 174
Corinthian helmet 39–41, 43, 197
Corinthian War 48, 74, 123, 126, 140, 173–174, 198, 201, 211
cornel (wood) 15
Coronea 26
Coronea I (447) 98, 195, 211
Coronea II (394) 48, 77, 85, 117, 123–126, 142, 174, 202, 211–212
Crenides 201
Cresent Hills (354) 150, 214
Cretan helmet 41
Crimisus River (341) 95, 175–179, 186, 218
Crocus Plain (353) 148, 150, 183, 208
Cromnus (365) 201
Cunaxa (401) 129, 144–148, 170, 197, 219
Cyclades 37, 206
cyclosis 63, 76, 166–167, 173, 210, 218–219
Cynoscephalae (197) 156, 216
Cynoscephalae (364) 78, 219
Cyprus 30, 144, 201, 213
Cyrenaica 213
Cyrene 201
Cyrus, the Great 5, 193
Cyrus, the Younger 103, 114, 123–124, 201–202, 204, 219
Cythera 195
Cyzicus 158–159

Damyrias River 187
dance 83
Darius I 5, 193
Darius III 57
Dascyleium (395) 149
dathabam, dathaba 39, 194, 196–197
Datis 56
Decelea 54
dekadarch 114, 116
Delian League 67, 87
Delium (424) 24–29, 96, 100, 120, 139, 185, 220
Delos (Cyclades) 37
Delphi 59, 68, 153, 171, 199
Dema Wall 52, 57
demes 126
Demetrius 153
Demosthenes (general) 24–25, 53, 99–100, 103, 144–145, 148, 158, 208
Demosthenes (orator) 92
Dercyllidas 123, 170
Dienekes 197
Dion 58
Dionysius I 199, 202
Dionysius II 58, 176
Dobruja Plain (339) 145
Dorian spear 29
Dorians 61
Doric phalanx 73, 102, 105, 145, 191

Doris 97
doru/dory 14
dorudepranon (pole-sickle) 23
double envelopment 53, 89, 167, 215
Drabescus (c.465) 95
drachmas 201
drepanon (sickles) 23
dunasteia 74
Dyme 200

earthquake 94, 100
eclipse 94, 207, 211
Egypt 37, 44, 54, 68, 70, 88, 97, 149, 193, 206–207
Egyptian Canals (460) 99, 208
Egyptian marines 36, 37, 196
Eion (476) 219
elephants 154–155, 215–216
Elis 67, 75, 77, 106, 202, 207
Ellomenus (426) 99, 207
enchiridion 22–23, 137
enomotarchs 113–114
enomotia 113–114, 117, 120, 126
Epaminondas 73–74, 81, 84–85, 99, 145, 166–167, 187, 203–206, 207, 213, 215, 217, 219
Eparitoi (Arcadia) 67, 201
Ephesus (498) 193, 208, 219
epibatai 37, 159, 196, 217
Epidauros 106, 176
epilektoi 61, 66–68, 83, 93, 102, 107–109, 126, 192, 201–203, 206–207, 218
Epipolae (413) 53, 99–100, 208
Epirus 153, 215
Epitadas 95
epiteichismos, epiteichismoi 24–25, 195
Epizelus 102, 208
epomides 42, 43, 80
Eretria 64
eschatia, eschatiai 64, 88, 190
Euboa 7, 64, 162, 196, 199, 204
Euboan Channel 7, 11, 25, 181, 195
Eumenes 71, 202
Eurotas River 187
Eurybiades 94
Euryelus (414) 186
Eurylochos 207
Eurymedon (c.466) 87, 219
Eusebius 199
Euxine Sea (Black Sea) 145, 209

five companies (Argos) 108
flutes/pipes (Spartan) 122, 128
fog of battle 100
foot race 81
force multipliers 188
The Four Hundred (Elis) 67

Gabene/Gabiene 71
Galatians/Gauls 153
garrison 37–38, 52, 58, 74, 88, 140, 182, 194–196, 209, 213, 215
Gaugemela (331) 146, 214
gesso 33

Gorgias 102, 208
Gorgidas 74, 78
graben 180
Granicus River (334) 146, 199, 208, 213
Gryllus 203
guilloche pattern 30, 32

Halae Marsh (403) 53, 55, 184, 219
Haliartus 26, 123, 169
Haliartus (395) 123, 169–170, 202, 211, 218
hamippoi 25, 77, 184, 202, 214, 219
Hannibal (Barca) 208, 215–216
Harmodios blow 23
hazarabam, hazaraba 38, 194, 196–197
hegemon 75, 88, 107, 123, 206
Helicon, Mount 123–125
Hellenic 36, 85, 170, 187, 191
Hellenistic 13, 70, 118, 153–157, 214–215
Hellespont 158
helots (helotoi) 34, 63, 107–109, 124, 209, 211, 214
Heraclea 154
Heraclea (280) 154, 170, 204, 215–216
Heraclitus 208
Herculaneum 204
Hercules 81, 92, 195, 204
Hermione 196
hetairoi (horse companions) 201, 214
Hicetas 176, 187, 220
Himera 180, 182
Himera I (480) 180, 182–183, 218–219
Hippagretas 95
hippeus (Sparta) 67
Hippias 193
Hippocrates (general) 25–28
Hippocrates (physician) 205
home soil 75, 91, 94, 97, 107, 191, 207, 210
Homer 14, 84, 208
hopla 5, 44
hoplomachoi 136, 139
horst 180
Hydaspes River (326) 155, 213
hypaspists 57, 71, 85, 149, 151–152, 154–156, 162, 164–168, 201, 213–214, 217
hyperaspizantes 214
hyperetes 66
Hysiae (c.669) 62

iatroi (doctors) 85, 205
Iberian 152
ice pick (overhand method) 19
Illiad of Homer 84, 205, 208
Illyrian helmet 41
Immortals 8, 11, 59, 80, 181, 194
India 155, 193, 213
Ionia 37, 68, 123, 182
Ionian Revolt 144, 193

Index

Ionians 37–38, 124, 197
Iphicrates 16, 35, 47, 49–50, 141, 149–150, 198–199, 213–215
iphicratids 198
The Island (Plataea) 184
Issus (333) 45, 57, 60, 150, 156, 187, 213–214
Italo-Corinthian helmet 41
Ithamitres 37

Jason of Pheae 201
javelin 23, 143, 145, 157, 158

kaolin clay 45, 46
kardakes 197, 199
kegelhelm 40
Kleroi/Cleri (410) 158
knemides (greaves) 46
Konosura 200
Kourion 202
kranos 39

Lacedaemonia 54, 75–77, 82, 124, 171
Laches 28, 92, 172, 195
lamda 195
Lamia (322) 151, 185
Laodocium (423) 218
Larisa 203
leather 24, 33–36, 42–47, 124
Lechaion (390) 140–142, 144–145, 147, 198, 213
Lelantine Plain (c.710(64
Leonidas 7–11, 38–39. 58–59, 142, 172, 181, 193–195, 206
Leonnatos 185
Leontini 102, 176
Leotychides 37–40, 196
Leuctra (371) 75–77, 81, 95, 137, 166, 187, 201, 203, 213, 215, 217–218
Liby-Phoenician 177
Libyan 177
lightening 95, 178, 207
Lilybaeum 79
Limnai 200
linen 24, 33–36, 42–46, 124
lochagos 113–114
lochos 107, 109, 113–114, 116, 123, 166, 198, 205, 209–210, 212
Locris 123, 204
longche (spear) 13, 216–217
lophos (hill) 106
lover 97
Lucian 214
Lyceum 54
Lyciscus 215
Lycurgus 75, 81, 199
Lyncus Plain (358) 143
Lysander 169–170

Macarius 207
Macedonia (Macedon) 34–35, 59, 65, 70, 195, 123, 145, 148–149, 153, 171, 190, 193, 201
Macedonian phalanx 105, 118, 145, 149, 151, 155, 191, 214
Macedonian shield 216

machaira/kopis (saber) 22
Machanidas 60
Machaon 205
Magna Graecia 203
Malis 204
Mantinea 106, 168–169, 171, 195, 202–203, 209–210, 213
Mantinea I (418) 105–109, 166, 173, 211
Mantinea II (362) 143, 146–147, 201, 218–219
Mantinea Plain (385) 126, 202
Marathon (490) 56, 60, 93, 162, 147, 167–168, 193, 197, 204, 211–212, 219
Mardonios 36–38, 175, 184, 194, 197
Mardontes (Persian general) 38, 40
marines 23–24, 36–37, 140, 148, 157, 159, 192, 196–197, 214
Marrucini cohort 155
Mayweather, Floyd, Jr. 78
Mazaros I (454) 218
Medes 38, 193, 197
Megalopolis (331) 95
Megara 88, 90, 99, 162, 184, 196, 205, 208–209
Megarid 88–89
Melea (Tearless Battle) 153
Mende (423) 219
Menedaius 207
menis 102
mercenaries 44, 49–50, 58, 65, 67–70, 103, 105, 124–126, 147, 150–153, 162, 164–165, 168, 176–177, 182, 190, 199–202, 207, 211–215, 218–219
Mesoa 200
Mesoates/Messoages 200
Metaponton 203
meteor 207
Methana 195
Methana (500–475) 193, 206
metics (metakoi) 25, 66, 89–90
Micion 152
Middle Gate (Thermopylae) 7–9, 11, 58–59, 181
Mindarus 158–159
mistophoroi 198
mitre (bely-plate) 42
mock combat 18, 41, 82, 131, 196, 204
Moleis 184, 219
mora 49–50, 113, 123, 140, 142, 198, 209, 211, 213
mud 53, 176, 178–179, 219
Munychia Hill (403) 186
muscle cuirass 42
Mycale (479) 36–40, 157, 193, 197, 206, 219
Mycenae 194
Myronides 88–91, 97–100, 205–206

Nauplia 54, 62
Nemea River (494) 48, 123, 126, 173, 195, 202, 211–212
Neodamodeis 34, 209, 211

neo-hoplite 156, 217
Nicias 94, 106, 207
North Africa 65, 71, 88, 195, 218

oarsmen/rowers 37–39, 152, 159, 196, 213–214
obai 200
oblique order 32, 76
oblique stance 18
obols 201
Oenoe (461) 171, 183, 206
Oenophyta (457) 98, 100
Oeroe 184
oligarchy 53, 69, 74
Olpae (426) 99, 178, 207–208
Olympia 29, 32, 34, 187, 199, 206
Olympia (mother of Alexander) 153
Olympic Games 166
Olynthus I (381) 55, 126, 198, 202
Olynthus II (382) 126, 198, 202
The One Thousand (Argos) 67
Onomarchos 59–60, 150, 171, 182–183, 208
Orchomenos 123–124, 212
Orcynii (320) 220
Orneai 197–108
Ortygia (357) 58
othismos 17, 29, 49, 59, 90, 112, 121–122, 125, 127, 132–134, 136–138, 164, 167, 179, 191, 194, 196–198, 210, 216

Paeligni cohort 155, 216
Pagondas 25–26, 28, 96, 120, 185, 195, 207, 219–220
Paliokhani Plateau 195
palisade 37–38, 40, 57–58
Pallene (546) 65, 200
Pammenes 78, 213, 215
panoplia (panoply) 2, 5, 15, 19, 24, 36, 81, 111–112, 133–134, 137, 139, 190, 195, 204
Pantites 206
Paraetacene (317) 219
parataxeis 113, 126
Parnes, Mount 28, 52
Parthenon 68
Pasimachus 50
patris (patriotism) 91
Patroclus 205
Pausanius (Spartan general) 53, 94–95, 183–184, 198–199, 207
Peace of Callias 201
Peace of Nicias 209
Peisistratos 65, 200
Pelopidas 74–75, 78, 215, 219
Peloponnese 11, 24, 29, 41, 48, 52, 61–62, 68, 74–75, 78, 152, 169, 173, 191, 205, 209
Peloponnesian War, First 68, 78, 171, 201, 217
Peloponnesian War, Great 24, 53, 66, 68, 74, 103, 105–106, 123, 200–201
peltas summetrous shield 35
peltastai (spearmen) 143, 156, 198, 216–217

Index

pelte 143, 216
pempadarch 114, 116
pentekosteres 113
pentekostyes 113
Pericles 81, 101, 196, 208
perioeci 107, 177, 200, 205, 209
perizoma 42
Perseus 155–156
pezhetairoi (foot-companions) 201, 214
Phaedrus 207
phalangite/pikeman 57, 70, 105, 140, 149–150, 155=156, 162, 164, 167, 191, 214–218
Phaleron 56
Pharax 210
Pharnabazus 170
Pherae 171, 183, 201
Pherae Road (368) 145, 218
Philip II 59, 70–71, 81, 85, 105, 143, 145–146, 149–150, 153–154, 160–165, 167, 171–173, 183, 190–191, 198, 201, 208, 214–215, 217
Philip V 216
Phlius 184
Phocian Wall 58
Phocion 152
Phoenicia 37, 157
phoros 201
phyle 126
Phyrgia 42, 149
pilos helmet 41–42, 137
Pindar 163, 195, 209
Piraeus 53–54, 184
Piraeus/Halae Marsh (403) 53–54, 184, 219
Pitana 200
Plataea (479) 94, 122, 147, 172, 183–184, 193–194, 196–197, 199, 204–206, 209, 214, 219
Ploas 200
Podalirius 205
polemarch 113
polis, poleis 7
polje 209
Pompeii 204
ponors (katavothrai) 209
poplar (wood) 20, 32
porpax 30–34, 155
Porus (403) 181
Poseidon 94, 195
Praxitas 48–52, 55, 57, 199
promachoi 67, 107, 113, 125
Psammetichos 68
psiloi, gymnesioi 67, 88, 143, 152
Psyttaleia (480) 158, 217
pteryges 39, 42
Ptolemaic Egypt 70
PTSD (post traumatic stress disorder) 102–103
Punic War 217
Pydna (168) 72, 155–157, 215–216, 218
Pylos (425) 158, 195
Pyrrhus of Epirus 153–154, 156, 202, 208, 215=216

reserve 77, 89, 143, 145, 156, 158, 185, 202, 213–214
reservists 89, 90, 108, 206, 209–210
Rhamnus (322) 152
Rhodes 147
rightward drift 90, 166, 173
Rome 153–154, 204, 216

Sacred Band (Carthage) 177–178, 219
Sacred Band (Thebes) 67, 74–76, 120, 126, 161, 165, 167, 195, 201, 207, 217
Sakae 197
Salamis 12
Salamis (480) 12, 36–37, 94. 158, 196, 204, 217
Salamis, Cyprian (498) 144, 202
salpinx 128
Samos 37, 101
Sarinas/Arimas 200
sarissa, sarissai 35, 118, 145, 149–152, 155–156, 199, 214–216
Saronic War 88, 201
satabam, sataba 144, 197
satrap 36, 170
satrapy 37, 202
sauroter (butt-spike) 9, 11, 14–16, 20, 22, 125, 137, 164, 190, 194, 214–215
Scandea 195
Scione (423) 219
Sciritae 102, 108–109, 166, 209
scutum (Roman shield) 31–32
Segesta/Egesta 218
Seleucid Asia 70
Sellasia (222) 207, 216
Selymbria 181–182
Sepeia (494) 61–63, 65, 98, 101, 193, 200, 206–210
shock combat 5–6, 8–9, 36, 39, 51, 54, 57, 70–71, 84, 105, 147–152, 156–158, 162, 167, 173, 177, 215
Sicily 6, 59, 65, 68–69, 176, 178, 180, 182, 186, 201–202, 218
Sicyon 34, 48, 50, 86, 140, 152–153, 195–196, 198, 215, 217
siege-wall 52
sigma 195
Sinis 200
Siphae 24–25
The Six Hundred (Syracuse) 67
skirmishers 26, 55, 67, 69, 108, 124, 143–144, 146–148, 151–153, 162, 164, 177, 181–182, 198, 202–203, 206, 213, 215
slingers 54, 145–147
Socrates 28–29, 81, 92, 139, 172, 195
Solinus 199
Solygeia (425) 144, 157, 195
spara 9, 11, 39–40, 199
sparabara 9, 11, 36, 38–39, 158, 197
Sparta 22, 24–25, 34, 37, 44, 48, 61–62, 67–68, 73–75, 79, 81–83, 87–88, 92–93, 98, 101, 103, 105–109, 114, 123, 126, 140–143, 151–152, 166–167, 170–171, 181–183, 186–187, 190–192, 194–196, 198–202, 205–206, 209, 211, 214, 216–217
spartiates (equals, hominoi) 11, 68, 74, 79, 83, 92, 93, 166, 194, 200–201, 206–207, 213
Spartolos (429) 142, 144, 147, 195, 213
Sphacteria (425) 95, 99, 144–145, 147, 195, 208–209, 213
storm 95, 177–178, 182
stratiotai 71, 73, 82, 107, 168
Stratocles 165, 218
Styphon 95
swordsmen 132, 140, 152–153, 156, 159 191, 208, 215–216
syllogon 66
Syracuse 52–53, 57–58, 65, 67–69, 94–95, 99, 148, 152–153, 176, 182, 186–187, 199–202, 206

taka 197
Tanagra 25, 98
Tanagra I (457) 97–98, 202
Tanagra III (376) 75, 202
Tarentum 153–154
taxiarch 113–114, 116
taxis 113–114, 121, 138–139, 141
Tearless Battle (368) 153, 202
Tegea 106, 108–109, 199, 202, 210, 219
Tegyra (375) 75, 77–78, 184–185, 201–202
telamon (shield strap) 32
Telecleides 176
Teleutias 55, 199, 202
Tempe Pass 7, 193
Thebes 34, 137, 49, 57, 67, 73–75, 77–79, 81, 83, 96, 120, 123, 125–126, 145–146, 152, 161, 166, 169, 171, 185, 187, 191, 195, 202–203, 207, 212, 215, 217, 219
themis 102, 194
Themistocles 193
Theopompus 199
Theramenes 158–159
Thermopylae 5–12, 38, 58, 92, 95–96, 123, 142, 153, 172, 181
Thermopylae (480) 5–12, 38–39, 58–59, 92, 95–96, 142, 172, 181–183, 193–195, 197, 198, 204, 206, 213, 219
Thespiae 202
Thespiae (378) 76
Thessaly 7, 56, 59, 68, 70–71, 74, 123, 145–146, 150–151, 165, 171, 185, 201, 203–204, 219
theurophoroi 35, 215–216
thorax (cuirass) 39, 42, 44, 47
Thracians 25, 215
Thrasybulus 158–159
Thrasylus 209
The Three Hundred (Elis) 67
thunder 95, 164, 178
thureos shield 35
Thyreatis 62–64, 193

Index

Timoleon 175–180, 185, 187, 202, 218, 220
Timophanes 176
Tirgranes (Persian general) 38–40. 197
Tiryns 62
Tisaphernes 170
Tolmides 217
Torgium (305) 202
Trebia River (218) 208, 216
Triballi 145
trident 195
trireme 76, 216
Troizen 196

trophy 78, 86, 90, 109, 126, 139
Troy 157, 205
truss (for shield) 33
Tyche 48
type J spearhead 13

Upper Satrapies (323) 202

velocitas 81
Veranius 172
Vergina 15, 195, 214

watchword 128
Waterloo (1815 A.D.) 109, 205

Wellesley, Arthur 86, 205
willow (wood) 32

Xanthippos 38–39, 196
Xerxes 5–12, 36, 38, 58, 67, 193–194, 196–197
xiphos (sword) 21
xyston (cavalry lance) 150

zeugitae (hoplite class, Athens) 89
Zeuxidamus 218